DESIGN NOW

Industry or Art?

The German Architecture Museum, Frankfurt, on the occasion of the exhibition "Design heute"

DESIGN NOW

Industry or Art?

Edited and with commentaries
by Volker Fischer

With essays by
Volker Albus, Jochen Gros and Matteo Thun

Prestel

First published in German in conjunction with the exhibition
"Design heute. Masstäbe: Formgebung zwischen Industrie und Kunststück"
shown at the German Architecture Museum
Frankfurt am Main (1988)

Translation from the German by Hans Brill

Cover illustration: Matteo Thun, table lamps "Stillight", 1986
Frontispiece: The German Architecture Museum, Frankfurt,
on the occasion of the exhibition "Design heute".

Published by
Prestel-Verlag, Mandlstrasse 26, D-8000 Munich 40, Federal Republic of Germany
Tel. (89) 38 17 09 0, Telefax (89) 38 17 09 35

Distributed in continental Europe and Japan by Prestel-Verlag,
Verlegerdienst München GmbH & Co KG,
Gutenbergstrasse 1, D-8031 Gilching, Federal Republic of Germany
Tel. (81 05) 21 10, Telefax (81 05) 55 20

Distributed in the USA and Canada by te Neues Publishing Company, 15 East 76th Street,
New York, NY 10021, USA
Tel. (212) 288 0265, Telefax (212) 570 2373

Distributed in the United Kingdom, Ireland and all other countries
by Thames & Hudson Limited, 30 – 34 Bloomsbury Street, London WC1B 3QP, England
Tel. (1) 636 5488, Telefax (1) 636 4799

Design: Dietmar Rautner
Typesetting: Fotosatz Max Vornehm, Munich
Colour separations: Karl Dörfel Repro GmbH, Munich, and
Reinhold Kölbl Repro GmbH, Munich
Printing and binding: Passavia Druckerei GmbH, Passau

Printed in Germany

ISBN 3-7913-0854-8 (German edition)
ISBN 3-7913-0922-6

Contents

DESIGN NOW

There is no question that the nineteen-eighties have seen big changes in concepts of and attitudes to design. Creations that break with the conventions of classical design – in the seventies appreciated and bought only by a few specialists, collectors and museums – today feature prominently in exhibitions and in the media, and are the centre of interest in museums and galleries.

Who would have dreamt a few years ago that Sotheby's would be holding regular auctions of international avant-garde design of the last twenty years, from Ettore Sottsass to Gaetano Pesce?[1] Exhibitions of and publications on contemporary design are burgeoning not only in Italy, as hitherto, but throughout the western industrialised world; shops and boutiques in towns and cities everywhere are jumping on the bandwagon. West Germany, France, Spain, Italy, Great Britain, the United States and Japan each have a dozen or more galleries specialising in avant-garde design. "Design" has become a word to conjure with, it impresses people, not just the hardy regulars you meet at the ever more frequent – and ever more esoteric – congresses, symposia and product presentations. The up-and-coming manufacturer smartens up his mediocre wares with the label "designed by . . .", regardless of whether he is pushing kitschy imitations of Baroque fireplaces, High-Tech fit-it-yourself iron staircases or a new system of garden fencing; we even have designer matches, pencils, pasta. Politicians nowadays allocate substantial grants and subsidies to design research, design prizes, and even new design institutions. The top echelons of industry have suddenly discovered an enthusiasm for product design of which there was little evidence before. In London it has been possible to establish a design museum with the help and support of industry, the first and so far only independent museum in Western Europe to be specifically devoted to the genre.

At the same time, the established designs of the twentieth century, those products that possess a distinctive image associated with a particular designer – Mies, Breuer, Le Corbusier or Eileen Gray, for example, in the field of interior design –, have now achieved the unassailable status of "modern" classics. They appeal to a well-defined, highly sophisticated segment of the market. In one of the best locations in New York (one can imagine the sort of rents asked) there is a tiny one-room gallery, opened a few years ago, that specialises in design classics of the twentieth century. The products are exhibited in the form of small models: the aura of the original is evidently now enough to clinch a sale.

Large and small groups of young designers make their mark almost overnight, at least in the media if not in the business. In Germany, for instance, press and television have embraced the phenomenon of "new German design" with an almost erotic passion: the objects are presented in lavish pictures, often in the trendy settings that the *Zeitgeist* demands. The 1987 Documenta – the most important international exhibition of contemporary art – was the first to show design, thus keeping up with the trend; there was, however, a distinct bias in favour of purely subjective, artistic designs. Once again designers were marketed as supposedly free avant-garde artists with all the freedom of action that that implies; afterwards, of course, came the smug remarks about "socially irrelevant *l'art pour l'art* attitudes". It is probably inherent in the system that the mass media – and we can today include the exhibition carousel under this heading – should behave like voyeurs. A trend is often only really established when attention is called to it through media coverage after the event, though of course it cannot be created artificially without there having been something there in the first place.

Leaving aside the special case of individualistic avant-garde design-as-art, what is the situation regarding the acceptance and the ramifications of new developments in design in, for example, the Federal Republic of Germany? Contrary to popular opinion, it is obvious from the current state of the business that design is rapidly, perhaps too rapidly, gaining in relevance. Fifteen or twenty years ago someone like Philip Rosenthal was not taken seriously when he suggested that design, particularly avant-garde design, could be one of *the* decisive parameters in management policy. Then, and for a long time afterwards, the Germans were looking enviously across the Alps and praising to high heaven Italien firms such as Cassina, Zanotta, B & B Italia, Arflex, Driade, Artemide, Busnelli, Brunati, Alessi, and Poltrona Frau; these were not just firms like the German ones, they were cultural institutions in their own right, they sponsored cultural events, their bosses – or rather patriarchs – gave the impression of being cultural attachés rather than managers interested in profit.

In the meantime, however, word about "corporate identity" has reached the executive floor, and there have been dramatic changes in Germany, too. Firms ranging from conservative to middle-of-the-road are looking to avant-garde design. Manufacturers who previously mass-produced neutral consumer goods with the emphasis on ergonomic quality, aiming to satisfy some unspecified cross-section of demand, now attack separate target markets. There has been such a differentiation of consumer groups that products aimed at a general market alone no longer guarantee a healthy balance-sheet. Marketing strategists have to take more and more account of the younger generation of consumers who attach a greater importance to individual concepts, and it is becoming increasingly obvious that standard ranges need to be supplemented, if not replaced, by "postindustrial" products that smack of "culture". In Western Europe and North America, the number of households

with money to spare has grown enormously over the past twenty years or so; this new-found wealth does not just disappear into the savings account, but is being used more and more to buy prestige goods, articles that bear witness to a person's "life-style", as Bazon Brock has called it. The sociologist Erich Fromm, comparing the late sixties with the present day, speaks of a cultural transition in which "what you are" is no longer so important as "what you have", the big-spending strata of society now define themselves not so much through opinions and convictions as through outfits and accessories, life-style attributes.[2] The names alone of recent target market collections are indicative of the expectations of the new consumer groups: "Ambiente", "La Galleria", "Art Deco", "Fifties", "Vienna Collection", "Anthologie Quartett" all have an exclusive, cultural ring about them. And if we look at the "table-top" collections of Alessi in Italy or of Swid Powell in the United States, and consider the image of Philippe Starck in France or of the Castiglionis in Italy, it becomes clear that the "what you have" philosophy is consolidating itself in all the postindustrial nations. The International Design Yearbook (1988) lists more such collections than ever before. It is a buyer's market, which makes it a com-

mercially interesting proposition to have your products styled by famous designers and architects: objects with designer labels fetch higher prices, the manufacturers earn more money and at the same time cultivate their image. However, the possibilities for the avant-garde to play a role within industrial production depend a lot on the structure of the market itself and the policy of the big manufacturers towards avant-garde currents. In this respect, however, other countries are still a long way behind Italy: there, avant-garde groups are given financial backing by big companies – Memphis by Artemide, Alchimia by Zanotta; and Alessi have their own avant-garde department, Officina Alessi. In Germany, the establishment of financially guaranteed islands of experimentation within the broad economic structure of large companies is only beginning slowly. Thus, Vitra – a classical-conservative company well known for their furniture by Charles Eames – have made quite an impact with the "Vitra Edition" consisting of eight chairs by contemporary designers; Franz Schneider in Brakel (FSB), hardware manufacturers hitherto of negligible interest for the design scene, caused a worldwide furore with a few door-handle models by top international designers; and firms that merely distribute avant-garde design in

Fig. 1– 3   Details of three of the installations in the exhibition held at the German Architecture Museum in Frankfurt am Main, 1988

the Federal Republic, such as Quartett or Teunen & Teunen, are not only registering a continuous growth but have recently started manufacturing themselves.

"Design Now", as these few examples must suffice to show, has become popular both in theory and in practice, à la mode even. There is an euphoric craving for fine "art which is also useful"[3], fuelled by commercial interests, by the media, and by the ideologists. It is only too easy to forget that first came changes in the theoretical principles of design, without which all these manifestations would hardly be plausible. Nor does it help us to understand the situation when museums and the media promptly, perhaps over-hastily, give their seal of approval to art-objects of the most subjective character, primarily hand-made creations in the craftsman tradition, which are consequently of little relevance for industrial design. This bias of interest – perhaps a typically European problem – could mean that we lose sight of the philosophical and perceptual premises that underlie "Design Now" and of the historical and more than ephemerally important developments in the field over the last fifteen years. The cult of novelty in design is largely dependent on the aura of internationally established star designers, whose personality often becomes more important than their work. The "image" oscillates between product and personality, it attracts attention, so that in the end there will be only forty or fifty designers left from the whole profession who dominate the scene.

In the light of the developments sketched above it seems to me useful to identify the main currents in contemporary design and to discuss them with reference to a well-founded selection of examples. The key questions we shall have to ask ourselves are easily established. What, today, are the leading stylistic concepts that make up the kaleidoscope of contemporary design? How is it that certain designers, such as Dieter Rams and Stefan Wewerka in Germany, have an impact on style and form that goes far beyond individual objects and ultimately represents a continuum of attitudes that could very well be called a "philosophy"? Are there today "external" influences, which substantially modify the basis of design? Will technological advances, as in the field of miniaturisation and microelectronics, perhaps change the face and the core of design more decisively than any stylistic trend, no matter how distinctive? Are outsiders encroaching on the preserves of the designer, are architects and engineers perhaps better at the job? Have not hitherto marginal areas of design, for instance those of "no name" products or of "personal design", come to dominate the whole spectrum? A chapter has been devoted to this boom in "peripheral" design, which I have called the "new culture of the banal".[4]

All these questions – when we consider that the ubiquity of design threatens to blunt our understanding of the concept and of its relationship to objects, without which we could not say that an artefact were "designed" – make it advisable to return again to the quest for yardsticks. A "yardstick", a tool for the measurement of quantities, can also be a standard against which quality is measured: both in the literal and in the figurative sense, yardsticks today play a complex role in the field of design.

As a result of the publicity that new designs are immediately accorded in the media, the strands of historical development tend to become obscured. Thus, it would be not a bad idea to present a few historical examples from the treasure-trove of industrial design. Before looking at the contemporary scene, we shall therefore review the two genres, chairs and lamps, that have undoubtedly produced a greater variety of forms than any other. These surveys are intended to give an indication of the technical and stylistic innovations that have taken place in the twentieth century alone, and to relate them to the overall design context of their time. The selection of the fifty examples in each genre becomes more difficult and more subjective the closer one gets to the present. The first place to look for yardsticks, then, is in the historical evolution, here we will often find models that have lost nothing of their validity over the years and are well worth looking at again.[5]

Standards are set not only by the intrinsic quality of a specific design but even more by the extent to which it defines and leaves an impression on man's environment. This effect will be greater when individual designed objects are more closely related to each other in the sense of a comprehensive family of products and a product strategy. The whole will then be more than the sum of the parts: it will be an all-embracing attitude, a philosophy. We have deliberately chosen to illustrate such "worldviews" through the biography and œuvre of three German designers; the approach in their design strategies and the constraints imposed on each by production techniques are paradigmatic of international developments.

Dieter Rams has an international reputation: his Functionalist designs have made his name a byword for good design in the "classic modern" manner. Since the fifties he has been responsible for the distinctive image of Braun electrical appliances, such as radios, clocks, kitchen equipment, shavers and, formerly, optical equipment, and he has also placed his stamp on the Vitsoe furniture ranges. Braun design has been instrumental in promulgating the image of typically German "functional" design in Western Europe, the USA and Japan. Many Rams models have made design history, first and foremost the famous "SK4" radio-gramophone of 1956, the so-called "Snow-White's Coffin"; the white box seemed positively revolutionary at the time with the stark simplicity of its lines and the strictly rational layout of the controls. Rams's maxims are: simple instead of complicated, unpretentious instead of pretentious, durable instead of fashionable, functional instead of emotional, intelligent instead of interesting. For Rams and his disciples, however, it follows that "simple and sober" is also *morally* better than "complicated and full of frills"; thus, even the tritest imitators of Rams's ideas were – more or less automatically – able to claim ethical legitimation. Similar mechanisms were at work in the Functionalism of postwar German architecture. Not without justification, many objections have been raised to such an unbending automatism: they have resulted in today's broad spectrum of new product vocabularies and styles, which have left Functionalism far behind but are still reacting to and thus orientated on it, albeit *ex negativo*. The stylistic attitudes presented here – Alchimia/Memphis, Post-Modernism, Minimalism, Archetypes, High-Tech, Trans-High-Tech – can only be grasped and understood as attitudes in relation to Modernism and Functionalism and the history of their reception. But it must not be forgotten that Rams's ergonomic and functional design always incorporates an ethos, there is more to it than his apologists often realise, and it is quite capable of recognising and formulating the symbolic associations of an object.

Stefan Wewerka is the second of our designers to be introduced in his biographical setting. He is more of a "baroque" personality than Rams, but like him he has an urge to flood the whole world with his designs, or at least to identify and to shape down to the last detail the particular world of his client. Both men, in their own way, are fervid believers in the synaesthetic effect. Where Rams proceeds in a logical and straightforward way, Wewerka works with a different, though equally convincing sort of logic to distort and fragment the familiar. Inasmuch as he cannot leave anything as it is, but destroys and transmogrifies it, only to put it together again immediately in a new way, he rethinks the obvious and enriches our conventional repertoire of ideas about the characteristics of objects – whether jewellery, architecture, furniture, sculpture, isolated facades, books, or films – with new interpretations, new ways of seeing them. These are much more than simple additions to the genre in question, they broaden its ontological spectrum.

Holger Scheel, from Stuttgart, is a material fetishist in the best sense of the word. His chairs, tables and, most recently, drinking glasses celebrate the sensuousness of materials and the formal characteristics that proceed therefrom. Besides stark geometrical furniture which emphasises its own structural logic, he designs voluptuously upholstered chairs reminiscent of Novecento or Art Deco forms. In the wealth of its associations, the stressing of historical and cultural connections, and the often humorous paraphrasing of virtually archetypal forms, Scheel's furniture is Post-Modern, although at the same

Fig. 4   Studio 65 (Archizoom),
"Cactus" coatstand
Re-issued by Gufram, 1986

Fig. 5   Studio 65 (Archizoom),
"Capitello" chair
Re-issued by Gufram, 1986

Fig. 6   Cover of the book *High-Tech*
by Joan Kron and Suzanne Slesin, 1978

time it has a more controlled elegance that betrays a greater awareness of form than most Post-Modern designs. The work of Rams, Wewerka and Scheel also illustrates the influence of manufacturing and marketing considerations on the present-day German design scene. While Rams's products are adapted during the design process to the requirements of a rationalised production line, so much so that they bear little evidence of intrinsic creativity, Werwerka's furniture for Tecta is manufactured in modest runs, more like multiples of art-objects than industrial production; moreover, Wewerka has carried out at least as many private commissions to furnish individual apartments as he has designed furniture models. Holger Scheel's work, until recently, consisted entirely of one-off designs made by hand and of limited gallery editions; that is the price, he says, "when one keeps the compromises to a minimum."

Along with these designers and their philosophies, the stylistic approaches already mentioned cover, I think, just about the whole field of contemporary design. Interestingly enough, these new tendencies all began to take shape in the nineteen-seventies, when the dominant role of Functionalism was being seriously challenged. The Venturi school had become established and was, together with the last flickerings of the Pop Art movement, beginning to influence design. Post-Modernism made its entrance with pluralist, multi-coded objects in an ironical vein of historicism and symbolism, bidding farewell to the plastic era of the sixties with what else but plastic objects: the "Cactus" coatstand and the "Capitello" chair by the Italian Archizoom group (Fig. 4, 5). High-Tech was waiting in the wings, and became firmly established with the publication of the famous *High-Tech* book by Joan Kron and Suzanne Slesin in 1978 (Fig. 6). Trans-High-Tech was soon to follow. Ungers and Rossi did not jump on the Post-Modernism bandwagon: instead of following in the train of Pop Art and the culture of the banal and seeking to unmask and satirise superficial appearances, they thought in ontological categories. Ungers's morphological method, practised since the early sixties in architectural projects, can like Rossi's "archetype" approach be compared in its reductionist aesthetic to Minimalism. It is only recently that Minimalist aesthetics have become established in various fields such as painting (Neo-Geo), fashion (Issey Miyake, Giorgio Armani), and design (Philippe Starck, Shiro Kuramata, Zeus), but its roots lie in the iconographic pruning that took place in art movements of the seventies, such as Land Art and Concept Art, and in the "magical" reductionism of art-forms like the "Individual Mythologies" and the "Archaeology of Memory". Alchimia and, in its wake, Memphis mark another important watershed in object design, reacting against both Functionalism and Italian "Bel Design" with an agglomerative aesthetic that with childish ingenuousness takes apart the constituent elements of an object and then reassembles them in new ways.

The discipline of design has been infiltrated by methodologies from other professions. One reason for

Figs. 7 – 12   Mobilair
(Rolf Pendias), "Skyline"
cupboard series

Fig. 7   "Seagram Building"
Fig. 8   "AT & T Building"
Fig. 9   "Transamerican Building"
Fig. 10   "RCA Building"
Fig. 11   "Chrysler Building"
Fig. 12   "Pan Am Building"

this, as has already been mentioned, is the rapidly dwindling respect for demarcation lines between the disciplines, particularly apparent over the last ten to fifteen years. It may well be that nearly all historically important designs have been created by architects, but until recently this only affected the *crème de la crème* of designs. Today, however, the poaching of design commissions is not so much the exception as the rule. Post-Modernism has contributed greatly to this tendancy because its philosophy rejects on principle hierarchies of importance between large- and small-scale objects, i. e. between architectural and design projects. In addition, there is what might be called the "Memphis syndrome", which makes of the design process an ostensibly simple, almost dilettantish pastime for all. Both these factors, and especially the former, explain why architects have been turning increasingly to the design of small objects, above all those that go to make up the cultivated table. In Italy this is known as "Micro-Architecture", in America they speak of "table landscapes" or "table-top" objects. These labels show that the design process for objects of this sort is understood as comparable in principle to architectural design, though of course on quite a different scale. Not only do we find little houses and other miniature buildings on our dinner and coffee tables: the whole logistic of these artefacts is architectonic, because the parts that go to make up a coffee-pot, tray, lamp, étagère or what-have-you are conceived as distinct elements and combined additively, as in building. Thus, the architectonic parameter "statics" is also symbolically represented. Not surprisingly, these "diner's paradises" are usually presented in exhibitions and catalogues as townscapes on the table top. The fantasy of being able to walk inside these examples of mini-architecture sparks the viewer's imagination, there is a poetry of alienation about them, a juggling of "yardsticks", not without irony.

Furniture, too, is increasingly being designed as imitation architecture, in almost all the styles we shall consider. Architecture, in fact, is being used more and more as a medium for the marketing of products and services, because it gives the impression of being intrinsically respectable on account of its size, solidity, construction and appearance. As Volker Albus notes in his contribution to this catalogue, skyscrapers are the favourites for this purpose because no other type of building is so universally seen as representing power, wealth and superiority.

Perhaps the most momentous impulses for contemporary product design, however, come from advances in technology, especially in connection with the growing possibilities of miniaturisation. The field of lighting is a good example: when a whole room can be lit to daylight standards by means of a wire strung across it with fingernail-size naked halogen bulbs, then one can no longer talk in conventional terms of lighting fixtures and the design of lamp housing. Here, High-Tech is a truely technological phenomenon. In architecture and design, on the other hand, High-Tech is a stylistic concept which refers more to the applicative use of the relevant materials to create a specific visual impact. Objects are getting smaller and smaller across the board, a technology of miniaturisation is on the march and, as Jochen Gros documents in his article, a new

enthusiasm for stylistic experimentation seeks to keep up with the trend. This process of miniaturisation has been most far-reaching in computers and audio, phonographic and optical equipment, where it is achieved with the aid of electronic chips and microprocessors, i. e. static components of control circuits. Now, though, miniaturisation has moved into the sphere of mechanics: American research institutes have succeeded in reducing gear-wheels, connecting-rods, and axles – moving mechanical parts – to dimensions of the order of 100 micrometers, no thicker than a human hair; the components are chemically etched in silicone wafers. With these techniques it

Fig. 13   Peter Maly, facade cupboards, sketch, 1987

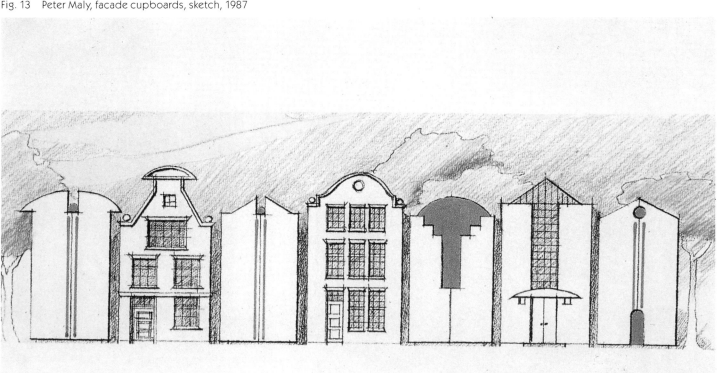

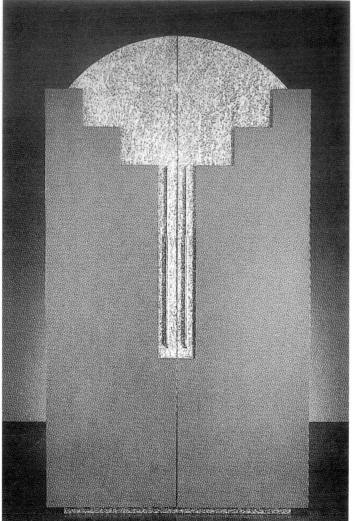

Fig. 14   Peter Maly, "Minos" facade cupboard, sketch, 1987

becomes possible to imagine appliances that could, for example, be introduced into the blood stream for surgical purposes.

Even without utopian scenarios, it is evident that such developments open up vast new possibilities. At a recent conference on computer hardware the superiority of fifth over fourth generation computers was compared to the possibility of building a Rolls Royce for five pence – and in the size of a 5p coin. Such developments in manufacturing technology will obviously affect design at least as much as stylistic influences or exemplars. One can foresee that the yardstick as a tool of measurement will have outlived its usefulness when, as has been forecast, the entire collection of the Library of Congress in Washington with its millions of volumes will be stored in a ten-centimeter cube from which everything will be retrievable, volume for volume, page for page and letter for letter. At this point, design will be neither necessary nor meaningful, will not exist any more. To present such a perspective, with its horizons and limits and its international alternatives, does not however mean that we prophesy an early end to design.

The reverse is true: when technical parts become so small that they are no longer visible to the naked eye, the casing, which encloses the works, and in Functionalist theory should externally reflect the internal structures as clearly as possible, will be available for the purposes of design. What are we to do with the new freedom brought by technology? That is the challenge for the designer today.

But not only the miniaturisation of technical components provides greater scope for design, miniaturisation in production technology also offers exciting new possibilities. Nowadays, a technique such as CAM (computer-aided manufacturing) can alter the look of a design so as to produce short-run series within an overall mass-production programme, using one and the same machine and without any appreciable increase in cost. This will ultimately affect marketing policies, for the customer might now start manufacturing himself. If in 1970 production runs of machine-made goods were only cost-effective in quantities of five thousand upwards, the current break-even figure is in the neighbourhood of fifty. Thus, there is the prospect that restaurants, museums, boutiques, and other shops will be manufacturing and selling their own distinctive in-house products as sole suppliers. The idea of "corporate identity" would become more tangible: industrially produced designs, from carpeting to chairs, could have company logos incorporated without appreciable extra cost, thanks to this new technique. The role of the designer will assume a new aspect: where in the traditional quantity manufacturing system his responsibilities ended when the machines began to roll, and the finished product bore little trace of the personal touch, the age of the designer-cum-manufacturer is now dawning. Advanced technology gives the contemporary designer an enormous advantage over the traditional craftsman: he can realise his ideas not just in one-off artefacts, but in series. "Art-object" and "industrial design" no longer constitute a strict dichotomy.

These new developments in production processes also mean that we have to reassess the implications of the concept "avant-garde". In the past, the word was generally used to describe what did not fit in with the officially sanctioned values of society, and thus almost always had an "anti-industrial" connotation. This is not invalidated by the fact that various design movements, from Arts and Crafts and Viennese *Jugendstil* (Art Nouveau) to the Bauhaus and the Ulm School, have tried either to develop their axioms from the realities of industrial production or conversely to exert an influence on industry through their design principles. But the situation was never, I believe, comparable to that of today, where we find avant-garde within the established structures of production. In the field of computers, for example, we can see how avant-garde designs and ideas, which would have been dismissed as bizarre and ridiculous in the conventional world of industry, can very quickly come to dominate the "official" structures of major firms: Silicon Valley and the hackers have brought about big changes at IBM, Siemens and Nixdorf. And I find that a studio like "Frog Design" in Germany, which works for various industries in different parts of the world, could well be classed as part of the avant-garde scene. If it is true that, at least in design, the avant-garde is changing its position, the consequences could be both positive and negative: if critical detachment suffers, there will undoubtedly be new opportunities to put ideas into practice and thus to exert an influence. The thesis that industrial design today has avant-garde qualities is therefore one of the major themes of the exhibition and the catalogue, in view of the media exposure given to one-off designer artefacts, this would seem to be a useful approach.

With the aid of various yardsticks we have attempted to give some sort of structure to what Matteo Thun has called a "semantic chaos". The contradictions and the connections between the Modern Movement and Post-Modernism are everywhere evident both in questions of style and in the production context: that is what makes design now such a fascinating object of study.

Notes

1   The sky seems to be the limit for some design enthusiasts. When Gaetano Pesce's "Sansone" table was auctioned at Sotheby's it fetched several times the retail price, although it is still available in the shops. Because of the manufacturing process, each example of this table differs slightly from the others, but it is hard to see how this could justify such an inflated price.

2   Bazon Brock, Hans U. Reck, IDZ Berlin (eds.): Stilwandel als Kulturtechnik, Kampfprinzip, Lebensform oder Systemstrategie in Werbung, Design, Architektur, Mode (Berlin 1986); Outfit. Kleidung, Accessoires, Duftwässer (Spiegel-Dokumentation, Hamburg 1986).

3   "Kunst, die sich nützlich macht" was the title of an important exhibition (Munich 1985) that presented the largest collection of twentieth-century design in West Germany, the Neue Sammlung in Munich. An indicator of official attitudes towards design in the Federal Republic is the fact that the collection does not have exhibition space of its own, let alone its own museum.

4   Volker Fischer: "Zeitgeist zum Anfassen, zur Kulturalisierung des Banalen", in Jahrbuch für Architektur 1987/88", pp. 184–196 (Wiesbaden 1987); English version: "Post-Modernism and consumer design", in The Post-Modern Object (Art and Design 3: 3/4, 1987, pp. 67–72).

5   A reference book on lines similar to those suggested here was published as a special edition by a West German magazine, and has since become something of a bible for furniture shops, interior designers, and even antique dealers; interestingly enough, it has even been translated into Italian. Möbel, die Geschichte machen. Moderne Klassiker (Hamburg 1986).

The purpose of this exhibition is to find and present yardsticks for the assessment of contemporary design; by way of historical introduction we have compiled two short anthologies to show the evolution of chairs and lamps in the twentieth century. We could write a fairly comprehensive history of design by discussing these two genres alone, for they are so rich in variety that they particularly well illustrate the essential characteristics of the various periods and styles. The exemplars we have chosen will help to provide a historical orientation: they reflect changing "lifestyles", attitudes to functionality, and technical innovations, and often possess symbolic qualities. The most outstanding examples have come to be acknowledged as "classics" which outlive the age that produced them.

Each of these objects has its place in the history of design, though the significance it has for us today may be quite different from the impact it originally made. Many seem as modern as the day they first appeared on the scene, regardless of the changed social context. Others have acquired the aura of museum-pieces, all the more so as they have been taken out of their original context; this is true, for example, of objects from the Viennese school and from the Bauhaus. Anyone who owns one of these "modern classics" or is interested in these things will have felt the magnetism of this aura. What was going on at the time in art, architecture, interior design, technology, ideas of space and how people use it – an idea of all this can be gleaned from the study of these exemplars.

A comparison of the two anthologies presented here will show that the first decade of the century already produced several milestones in chair design, while modern ideas about the functional use of light were first applied in lamp design around 1920, rapidly establishing themselves in the years that followed.

The Austrian architect Adolf Loos had already uttered his famous dictum "Ornament is a crime" before the turn of the century, in reaction against the highly decorative facades and interiors of late nineteenth-century Austrian and German architecture. The chairs from the first decade of the twentieth century, however, show that the call for more abstraction had failed to find any immediate response. What links the designs of Charles Rennie Mackintosh, Josef Hoffmann, the Thonet brothers, and Frank Lloyd Wright is not only that they were often conceived architectonically as part of a comprehensive interior design, but also that they use ornament itself as a structural element. The ornamental construction determines both the appearance and the aesthetics of the design.

The same applies to the decade 1910–1920. One of the leading movements in architecture and painting at the time, the Dutch De Stijl group, produced chair and lamp

EXEMPLARS

designs on almost identical principles: plane surfaces set off in primary colours create with their marked angularity a space-defining, three-dimensional framework. Walter Gropius, who created one of the first masterpieces of modern architecture with the Fagus shoe-last factory in Alfeld an der Leine, designed on the same succinct, cuboid lines. Frank Lloyd Wright's "Midway" chair is also based on the cube model, though it is here fragmented in a way that looks forward to the geometrical vein of thirties Art Deco.

The decade from 1920 to 1930 is today seen as *the* classic period of interior design. It is the epoch of Le Corbusier's "modern classics" designed for his villas of the twenties, and of Mies van der Rohe's furniture for private residences and for the German pavilion at the World Fair in Barcelona. With the Barcelona chair, if not before, the new "laboratory" style had become validated for prestige furniture, reflecting the traditional values of bourgeois society. Tubular steel was now being used extensively, chromium plating gave it the necessary aesthetic touch for the domestic interior (the Dutchman Mart Stam had initially constructed cantilever chairs from gas piping). Many later designs were based on this principle: opening up a whole new range of possibilities, tubular steel, or flat steel as in the "Brno" chair, now supplanted the less practical wooden bars, which had to be shaped by heat procedures. Furniture of this period has in common a strong spatial presence, it helps to give definition to the environment it stands in.

Between 1930 and 1940, the Modern Movement in its various manifestations such as the Bauhaus or De Stijl and the influence of Russian Constructivism were brutally cut short by the emergence of Fascist systems in much of Europe, whose cultural arbiters preached a return to folksy nationalistic styles. Elsewhere new technologies were being developed: in Scandinavia, for example, Alvar Aalto experimented with shaped birchwood, and Paul Wegener also shared the renewed interest in organic materials as being alone appropriate for man. Alvar Aalto was the first, in the mid-thirties, to construct out of bent wood a cantilever chair without back legs. At the beginning of the decade there were already in France and Italy forerunners of what became known in the seventies as High-Tech: René Herbst's nickel-plated tubular steel chair strung with rubber springs or, somewhat later, Hans Coray's "Spartana" chair of perforated sheet steel, which inspired many similar designs in later years. Eileen Gray, who had worked closely with Le Corbusier in the twenties, created asymmetrical tubular steel chairs and other furniture with a strong spatial presence, which provided a suitable framework for the sophisticated elegance of Parisian Art Deco. Jean Prouvé, whose prefabricated architecture aroused great interest in the thirties, experimented with

furniture made of sheet steel bent to give it rigidity; the technical sophistication of his designs has been influential up to the present day, the so-called Porsche chair being one of the most recent models in this vein.

The decade of 1940–1950 is notable for the debut of one of the most important designers of the twentieth century, Charles Eames. During the war he had experimented with laminated wood technology for artificial limbs, and he subsequently designed moulded plywood chairs of great structural elegance. The three-dimensional shaping of plywood and, above all, new methods of joining rubber, wood and metal had a lasting impact on furniture design the world over. In Central Europe little was produced in the way of memorable designs in this decade of the war and its aftermath.

Far from the European turmoil, on his estate Taliesin in the Arizona desert, Frank Lloyd Wright was designing furniture, on the principle of the fragmented cube, developing ideas that for example Czech furniture designers had experimented with twenty years before. The form-language of Wright's furniture is however modernistic and prophetic of future trends.

In Germany and her former allies, the experiences of the lost war and the collapse of the systems of values promoted by the overthrown regimes led in the fifties, especially in the early years of the decade, to a profound mistrust of ideas associated with the past. It was time for a new start; things historical, even quotations or mere hints of past ages, were highly suspect because something of the discredited value systems was bound to cling to them. Thus began the age of the amoebiform or kidney-shaped tables and the "bull's-eye" architecture, which may have been modelled on nature but certainly not on any of the previous works of man. Bertoia designed chairs of wire rods, Saarinen a tulip-shaped armchair on a flared base, Egon Eiermann a chalice-shaped chair of wickerwork. Gino Sarfatti's chandelier, on the other hand, looks like an early anticipation of High-Tech. The flat "Diskus" wall-lamp and streamlined "Pendulum" lamp by Arne Jacobsen, and Poul Henningsen's pendent with spreading scales like a pine cone, are some of the forms inspired by nature. In 1956 Charles Eames designed his famous "Lounge Chair", which remains today the most classical of chairs for television-viewing and relaxation.

The determination to make a clean break with the past, rejecting all decorative elements and other stylistic paraphernalia, marked the beginning of the movement which as Functionalism was to have consequences in the sixties and seventies that were not always positive. The chairs of Dieter Rams are paradigmatic for this attitude, although they are of a far higher quality than most other Functionalist furniture; Rams does not allow the constraints of the production line to overrule aesthetic considerations.

Alongside Functionalism, the influence of art movements such as Pop Art began to make itself felt in sixties design.

The bean-bag seat by Gatti, Paolini and Teodoro and the plastic furniture by Archizoom, such as the chair in the form of an Ionic capital and the coat-stand modelled on a cactus, are such borrowings from the world of art; they display that touch of irony that was to become such an important feature of design in the late seventies and the eighties. The swaging process now made it possible to fashion plastic chairs from a single casting; Verner Panton and others had not been able to fully master the technical problems involved, and Helmut Bätzner produced the first successful design of this type, the so-called "Bofinger" chair of 1966, on which many later models were based. Since the beginning of the sixties, the Castiglioni brothers in Italy had been experimenting with the adaptation of lighting techniques from the world of technology for domestic use, the technical features are prominent in their designs, which have an aesthetic of their own that underlines the novelty of the approach.

In contrast to the sixties, the new decade is marked by undermining of the general confidence and optimism that had accompanied the years of rebuilding and the consolidation of the "economic miracle"; it was now beginning to be recognised that there were limits to growth and to natural resources. The reaction in the world of design was a new emphasis on individuality: each object was to be seen for itself alone, and not as a constituent of some all-embracing whole. Ingenious construction details are no longer the focus of attention and tend to be concealed, as in the Archizoom group's "Aeo" chair. Similarly, the "Wink" chair by the Japanese Toshiyuki Kita hides its internal mechanics; with its hinged ears it has a humorous quality, like a Mickey Mouse paraphrase. In 1974 Rodney Kinsman created his "Omkstack" chair, the most successful High-Tech chair of all time, which can be used equally well indoors or outdoors. The seventies as a whole were characterised by a fragmentation of wholes into virtually independently functioning subsystems, each with its own framework of attitudes, and the field of design was no exception.

In the eighties, the most important thing to happen to furniture was the blossoming of the Memphis style, an Italian approach that developed out of the work of the Alchimia group of the latter half of the preceding decade. Here was a new product language with a vocabulary of primary shapes in combination, a liberal sprinkling of wit and irony, and a strong symbolic message. The furniture of Mario Botta and Matteo Thun reflects a contrasting standpoint, with a growing use of High-Tech principles on a higher aesthetic or ornamentalised plane. The "Costés" chair by the French designer Philippe Starck and the designs of the Milanese Zeus group are examples of a new Minimalism hovering between elegance and austerity. The chairs of the Cologne architect Stefan Wewerka, on the other hand, are distinguished by an asymmetry which requires the sitter to adopt unconventional postures. In the field of lighting for domestic interiors, low-voltage and halogen systems were developed which allowed the use of miniaturised light sources of previously unheard-of intensity and diffusion. The historical examples presented here have deliberately been restricted to fifty of each genre. They are intended to increase our awareness of the cultural significance of a designed object and of the changes that have taken place in attitudes over the years.

The more we understand of these attitudes and the more examples we study in the various genres, the better will be the criteria at our disposal for the assessment of new tendencies in design. In this respect, the two anthologies are not intended to be exhaustive historical reviews, but rather didactic aids to a better appreciation of present-day design.

EXEMPLARS

1 *Thonet Brothers:* "Modell 209" chair, **1900**
With their chairs of bent wood and functionalist and reductive designs, the Thonets pioneered the "modern" approach from the mid-nineteenth century onwards. Many of their products, particularly their chairs, achieved six-figure sales. The "Modell 209" has become the epitome of the Viennese chair, all over the world.

2 *Charles Rennie Mackintosh:* "Hill House 1" chair, **1902**
Mackintosh was the leader of the "Glasgow school". The "Hill House" chair demonstrates the treatment of the constructive elements as ornamentation, and typifies the severe elegance that is also characteristic of the architecture and object designs of the Viennese school as represented by Josef Hoffmann and Otto Wagner.

3 *Josef Hoffmann:* "Purkersdorf" armchair, **1903**
This chair of slatted wood, originally designed for the Purkersdorf sanatorium, exemplifies the architectonic approach to furniture. Despite its cubic shape, it gives a light and airy impression. For the surface of the seat Hoffmann uses the webbing which until then was generally only used for the underpart. The black-and-white-square pattern of the seat, like that of the loose cushion, creates a graphic effect, such as was to become so characteristic of Op Art more than half a century later.

4 *Charles Rennie Mackintosh:* "Willow 1" chair, **1904**

This chair is an extreme variant of the ontological approach to design. The graphic patterning of the high back creates a "room within a room" with its perspectival design, almost like a dividing screen. Like the "Hill House" chair, the "Willow" has been back in production since 1973.

5 *Frank Lloyd Wright:* "Robie" chair, **1908**

As with the Glasgow school or the Viennese school, for Frank Lloyd Wright ornament is never added on to the design, it is always an inherent constructive element. This chair, with a high back that is both solid and transparent, was an integral part of the interior design for the Robie house. Grouped as a series around a table, these chairs also create a "room within a room". The extreme reduction of decoration makes this design one of the starting points of the Modern Movement. With the re-issue of this model, authorised by the Frank Lloyd Wright Foundation in 1986, a choice of red, blue or grey is available for the upholstered seat.

6 *Josef Hoffmann:* "Fledermaus" chair, **1909**

This chair was originally designed for the Cabaret Fledermaus in Vienna. Like the Thonet chairs, it is made of steam-bent beech staves. A characteristic feature are the spherical braces, which are important for the statics of the object. The fabric is in a design typical of Viennese *Jugendstil* around the turn of the century.

7 *Walter Gropius:* "D 51" chair, **1911**

Gropius designed this chair for the Fagus works, one of the key starting-points for modern industrial architecture. The chair is also architectural in design and almost archetypal in its reduction. The arms bend and continue round to the back, which is smaller than usual, the dominant characteristic is thus that of a spatial framework. Nevertheless, the chair has an imposing and "prestigious" appearance.

4

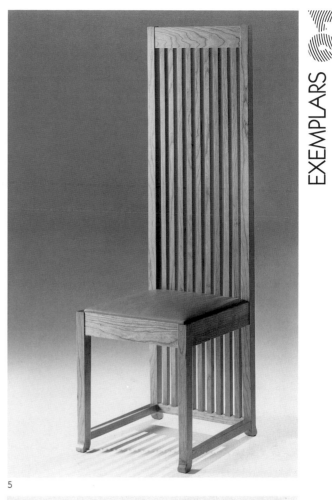

5

6

7

8

9

8 *Frank Lloyd Wright:* "Midway 1" chair, **1914**

Wright designed this chair for the Midway Gardens Entertainment Center in Chicago, which was demolished in 1929; he designed similar chairs for the Imperial Hotel in Tokyo. The hexagonal form of the back and the oblique rear legs create a Constructivist variant of the cuboid Art Deco of Czech designers.

9 *Gerrit T. Rietveld:* "Rood en Blauw" [Red and Blue] chair, **1918**

Rietveld conceived and designed this chair as a spatial object, not as a functional seat. It consists of two boards and a number of battens and is distinguished by its severe geometry, which impresses itself on the spatial surrounds. In its use of primary colours and its geometric shape this chair is a three-dimensional variant of the De Stijl maxims which Piet Mondrian was following in painting and Theo van Doesburg in architecture.

10 *Marcel Breuer:* "Wassily" armchair, **1925**

This armchair was the first ever to be made of tubular steel. The version on sale today, for all its structural complexity, appears natural and unproblematic. Breuer wanted to create a piece of furniture in which a single length of tubing was bent to form a cubic contour. The traditional padded seat, back and arms are replaced by stretched fabric or leather. Seat and back give slightly when one sits down.

11 *Le Corbusier, Pierre Jeanneret, Charlotte Perriand:* "LC 1" armchair, **1925 – 28**

This delicate chair was modelled on the safari chair. The chromium-plated frame is mitre-welded, and the backrest is mounted to allow compensatory movement. For all its slender proportions, the chair looks very distinguished.

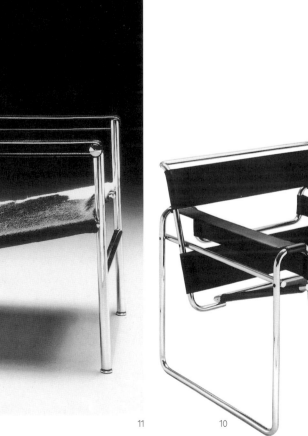

11

10

12 *Le Corbusier, Pierre Jeanneret, Charlotte Perriand:* "LC 2" armchair, **1925 – 28**

The full name of the chair is "LC 2 Fauteuil grand confort", and originally the padding of the leather cushions was much softer and more resilient. The modern version is severly cuboid, although it is also extremely comfortable. The body is enveloped and supported by the small seat, into which one sinks, and the solid-looking arms. The steel tubing frames the upholstered elements and emphasises the cube concept.

13 *Eileen Gray:* "Non-conformist" armchair, **1926**

The form of this design is programmatic. The asymmetry creates a sculptural effect of an object in space. The "Non-Conformist" might have been designed yesterday; its "historical" classicism is counterbalanced by a "trendy" eccentricity.

14 *Mart Stam:* "S 32" chair, **1927**

With the "S 33", designed one year before this chair, Mart Stam created the first "free-swinging" tubular steel chair without rear legs. For the "S 32" he was granted copyright protection by the West German supreme court in 1962; this is a very rare distinction for a designer, far more significant than the registering of a patent or a design. The "S 32" was originally made for the Weissenhofsiedlung in Stuttgart, an avant-garde housing project. The seat and back of wickerwork over bent wood frames contrasts with the single length of tubular steel – an integration of machine aesthetics and the domestic environment.

15 *Le Corbusier, Pierre Jeanneret, Charlotte Perriand:* "LC 7" swivel chair with armrests, **1929**

This chair is really a spartan swivel stool, rendered comfortable by the soft roll of the back. Today it is also available in various colours, such as Le Corbusier used for his box-type furniture.

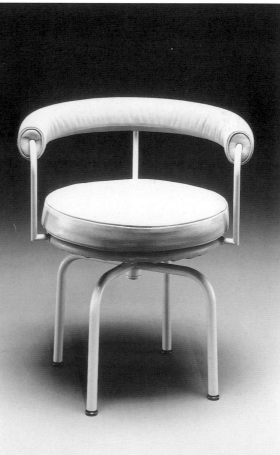

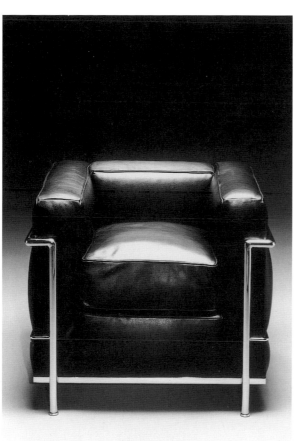

12

13

14

15

16

17

18

19

16 *Ludwig Mies van der Rohe:* "Barcelona" easy-chair, **1929**

Mies was greatly influenced in this design by Schinkel's cast iron chair of a hundred years before. This is particularly evident in the elegant sweep of the chromium-plated sprung steel legs. The chair was designed for the German pavilion at the 1929 World Fair in Barcelona. Although it looks unpretentious, it is a very sophisticated chair, the work of highly skilled craftsmen; it is so heavy that it is very difficult to move once it has been placed in a room.

17 *Ludwig Mies van der Rohe:* "Brno" armchair, **1929**

Designed for one of his most famous buildings, the Tugendhat house in Brno, this chair also looks like an application to design of Mies's ideas on architecture. The nobility of the chromium-plated sprung steel frame is counteracted by the severe angle of the combined seat and back, which seems as if suspended.

18 *René Herbst:* Nickel-plated chair, **1930**

This chair uses rubber springs for the seat and back, each of which has steel anchors that hook into the frame of nickel-plated steel tubing. The arrangement recalls the elastic straps used to secure packages on a bicycle. This use of technical devices makes the chair a forerunner of the High Tech style.

19 *Jean Prouvé:* "D 80" high-backed armchair, **1930**

Prouvé was more an engineer than a designer. From 1925 onwards he experimented with folded sheet metal, electrical spot welding, and stainless steel. The "D 80" is more a "sitting machine" than a conventional chair. The whole body of the seat can be tipped back by virtue of the guidetracks on the inner surface of the baseplates. The formal idiom is industrial and dynamic.

20 *Giuseppe Terragni:* "Follia" chair, **1934**

This epitomises the combinatory, additive approach that was only to come into vogue several decades later. Two chromium-plated sprung steel bars, attached to an archetypal stool of plain, block-like design, support the small rectangular backrest. This is a deliberate break with the harmony-conscious, integrative approach to design.

21 *Gerrit T. Rietveld:* "Zig-Zag" chair, **1934**

This chair is more like a symbolic object or semiabstract sculpture than a functional and ergonomic seat. Like the "Rood en Blauw" chair, it reveals Rietveld's reductionist approach to design. The several planes are joined with traditional mortise-and-tenon joints.

22 *Alvar Aalto:* "69" chair, **1933 – 35**

This chair is representative of the wide spectrum of Scandinavian furniture, which, particularly in the period between 1930 and 1960, was characterised by the use of shaped elements of laminated wood. The chair has solid wooden legs, but incisions at the bends make them as formable as the laminated wood itself. Aalto's many designs for furniture have made Scandinavian work famous throughout the world, as have the designs of Hans J. Wegner and Ole Wanscher. This is a reductionist aesthetic that takes due account of its material, in a sensitive combination of elegance and simplicity.

23 *Hans Coray:* "Spartana" chair, **1938**

This chair is both aesthetically and technically an early anticipation of the High Tech idea. It is made of an extremely light aluminium alloy, unknown before. This material does not absorb heat and is stainless, so the chair can be used in the open air as well. The profiled legs recall the ideas of Jean Prouvé.

20

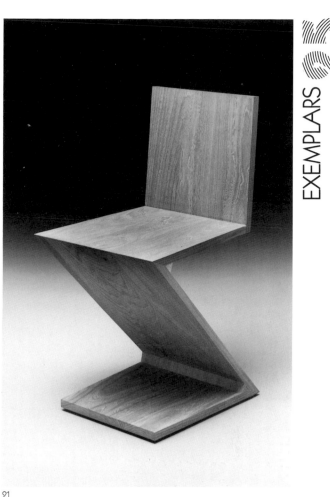

21

22

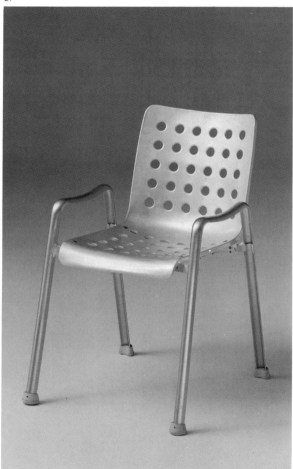

23

24

25

26

27

24 *Charles Eames:* "Plywood" chair, 1946
Eames was the first to experiment with three-dimensionally moulded plywood shells, a technique he developed while working on artificial legs during the war. The seat of this chair is flexibly mounted on a metal frame. The combination of wood and metal with rubber connectors was only evolved after long series of experiments, and the principle influenced many subsequent designs.

25 *Frank Lloyd Wright:* "Taliesin" armchair, **1949**
Wright's formal vocabulary, which was still very close to the geometric ornamentation of the Viennese and Glasgow schools in his work of the early years of the century, now appears to have changed completely. This is a fragmented cube, like an Art Deco sculpture, it stands alone, and is no longer integrated in an overall ornamental scheme for a room.

26 *Charles Eames:* "Dax" armchair, **1949/51**
The "Dax" chair can be seen as a further development of the plywood chair, using a new material. Originally it was intended to be made of coated metal, but fibreglass was used in the end, mainly on grounds of cost. Starting from an "universal" basic form, Eames developed a number of variants of this seat body.

27 *Harry Bertoia:* "420" chair, **1952**
Bertoia himself has called this chair a sculpture, consisting of air rather than solid material. The "420" is one of a series of chairs with many variants, all make use of wire grating, and some are fully upholstered. Looking back, we can see in these chairs one of the main aesthetic concepts of the fifties.

28 *Arne Jacobsen:* "3107" chair, **1955**

Both the seat body in shaped laminated wood and the attachment to the metal frame follow the earlier models of Charles Eames. Since this chair can be stacked, is light and yet aesthetically "rounded", it became one of the most frequently used chairs for lecture rooms and conference halls. It was also nicknamed the "Christine Keeler" chair after a photograph of her sitting back to front on one became world famous – for she was responsible for the downfall of a British cabinet minister.

29 *Eero Saarinen:* "151" chair, **1956**

Saarinen was the first to use the single leg with flared base for the chair. Its elegant shape also earned the chair the name "Tulip". The seat of shaped plastic is attached to the cast aluminium base with a swivel joint. This design also spawned a whole family of chairs, with matching tables.

30 *Achille and Piergiacomo Castiglioni:* "Sella" telephone stool, **1957**

Again and again, the Castiglionis have achieved startling effects with their ingenious use of elements borrowed from other fields. In this stool design, which is more reminiscent of a shooting-stick, a bicycle saddle serves as seat. The large hemispherical base enables the user to change his posture while sitting.

31 *Achille and Piergiacomo Castiglioni:* "Mezzadro" stool, **1957**

Here too, the seat comes from a totally different world: this time from a tractor. Although this is a one-legged stool it is a very stable seat, as the weight is broadly distributed over three points. Like the bicycle seat, it has often been copied.

28

29

30

31

32

33

34

35

32 *Gio Ponti:* "Superleggera" chair, **1957**

A chair that defies stylistic classification, it can
be identified as a prod-
uct of the fifties, though
relatively independent of
the characteristic vocab-
ulary of the decade. It is
so light that is could
almost be balanced on
one finger, it is fragile yet
comfortable. Ergonomi-
cally sound, the design is
convincing in its simplicity.

33 *Charles Eames:*
"EA 105" aluminium chair,
1958

The chairs of Charles
Eames's aluminium group
are still those for which
the term "high-tech" is
most appropriate – not
as a stylistic categorisa-
tion but as an indication
of the production tech-
nique and the mastery of
it. This chair and its fel-
lows have been sold all
over the world, and they
are now available not
only with imitation
leather or fabric uphol-
stery but also with an
extremely fine synthetic
netting; this reinforces
the "technical" effect.

34 *Dieter Rams:*
"602" easy-chair, **1960**

For Rams, whose work has
become the epitome of
the classical functionalist
approach in postwar
design, aesthetic reti-
cence is a supreme prin-
ciple: simple is better
than complicated, soft is
better than loud,
restrained better than
striking. The "602" chair
was designed by Rams for
both private and public
use, for the domestic living environment and the
world of work.

35 *Verner Panton:*
"Panton" chair, **1960**
There was a very similar predecessor to this chair, made of wire netting and newspaper, as early as 1952. Panton's version is made of slightly springy plastic, moulded in one piece. This design was almost paradigmatic in ushering in the forward-looking, optimistic elan of the sixties. Such a shape is only possible with this particular material and modern production techniques.

36 *Dieter Rams:*
"620" armchair, **1962**
Here Rams has placed large, inviting cushions in a framework of polyester panels of a markedly cubic contour. Although the chair is very much heavier, and thus more formal, than the "602", it is also mobile, and can be adapted to changing requirements. The facing-plates and side panels can be detached and replaced individually. A variation on a swivel base is available, and this form of the "620", with its footstool, is a functionalist variant of the lounge chair, extremely comfortable for reading or watching television.

37 *Helmut Bätzner:*
"BA 1171" chair ("Bofinger chair"), **1966**
The stackable "Bofinger" chair, so-called after its first manufacturer, was the first chair to be made from a single piece of plastic by deep drawing. It is taken straight from the polyester mould, needing no subsequent finishing.

38 *Gian Carlo Piretti:*
"Plia" folding chair, **1968**
The technical innovation of this chair is the joint consisting of three metal disks, which enables the chair to be folded to no more than five centimetres thickness. The elegant transparency achieved with the see-through plastic surfaces of the seat and back and the chromium-plated or painted metal frame make this, too, a typical product of the sixties.

36

37

38

39

40

39 *Pierro Gatti, Cesare Paolini, Franco Teodoro:* "Sacco" easy-chair, **1968**

This sack for sitting on is a chair without a frame, with ideological undertones. It is an object which gives physical form to the anti-establishment feelings of the late sixties. The leather sack is filled with a multitude of little balls, which arrange themselves around the contours of the body and support it by collecting at the points of pressure.

40 *Archizoom (Paolo Deganello):* "Aeo" chair, **1973**

This chair is supplied as a compact kit for self-assembly. "Aeo" is derived from "alfa e omega", the first and last letters of the Greek alphabet. The tubular frame has a cover of fabric or leather, which gives the chair a fresh, spontaneous look through the absence of a well-defined form; it is more like a T-shirt than an armchair cover.

41 *Rodney Kinsman:* "Omkstack" chair, **1974**

Kinsman is one of today's leading High Tech interior designers. The "Omkstack" chair recalls Hans Coray's "Spartana" chair of almost forty years earlier, but it is painted. It can be stacked, and is one of the most frequently used outdoor chairs.

42 *Stefan Wewerka:* "B1" chair, **1977–79**

This three-legged chair is more like a sculpture than an ergonomic item of furniture. It was initially made from two chairs that had been sawn in half. The asymmetrical shape permits a wide variety of postures when sitting, and its impact is thus dynamic rather than static. The curved back creates an intriguing contrast to the slender legs, and the arm broadens out to serve as a writing-rest.

41

42

43 *Toshiyuki Kita:* "Wink" easy-chair, **1980**

The "Wink" paraphrases the concept of a car seat: the back can be adjusted by turning the wheel at its base, and the inclination of the seat is also reminiscent of the automobile world. So this is really a High Tech design. However, the use of various luridly coloured covers, which can be pulled over the actual upholstery like a T-shirt, also recalls Pop Art. The wings, which are independently adjustable, look like big ears and have earned the chair the nickname "Mickey Mouse".

44 *Stefan Wewerka:* "B 5" chair ("Einschwinger" chair), **1982**

A piece of tubular steel, 3.2 m long, was after a long series of experiments bent into eight equal segments to create a cantilever chair – extremely gracile, but permitting the sitter a wide variety of postures. Jean Prouvé paid the "-Uniflex" a fine compliment when he said it was the last word in free-swingers.

43 44

45 *George J. Sowden:* "Palace" chair, **1983**

The "Palace", a chair from the third Memphis collection, is made of wood painted in different colours; it is thus exemplary for the additive aesthetic of this stylistic trend. The aesthetic idiom of the Memphis designers, who argued that an object should no longer be conceived integratively but as built up of individual parts, became one of the dominant vocabularies of the eighties.

46 *Michele de Lucchi:* "First" chair, **1983**

This creation is also a typical example of the Memphis aesthetic and features an additional anthropomorphic element: the upper frame with the two balls on which to rest the arms and the circular backrest create in conjunction with the legs the abstraction of a figure.

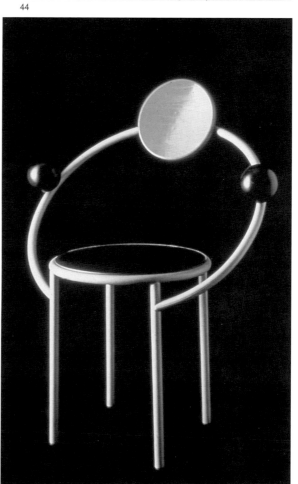

45 46

47

49   50

47   *Philippe Starck:*
"Costés" chair, **1985**

The "Costés" chair is the
best-known example of
the new reductive,
minimalist approach to
form. Designed for a café
in Paris, it soon created a
sensation all over the
world. The rounded shell
echoes the style of the
fifties, but the chair also
stands for a formal con-
cept that reacts against
the anecdotal frills of the
Memphis and Post-Mod-
ern movements.

48   *Mario Botta:*
"Seconda" chair, **1982**

The slender frame of
galvanised steel has an
extremely hard seat of
perforated sheet steel,
but in contrast a backrest
of soft polyurethane
foam. This modern-look-
ing model is one of a
series of chairs and
tables.

49   *Mario Botta:*
"Quinta" chair, **1985**

Even more than the "Sec-
onda" chair, the "Quinta"
is striking for its unusual
shape. The dynamic
sweep of the supporting
frame is almost aggres-
sive, and the perforated
seat and back suggest the
tension of a permanently
vibrating surface; they do
in fact give slightly when
sat upon, and are more
comfortable than their
appearance would
suggest.

50   *Philippe Starck:*
"Miss Wirt" chair, **1987**

This chair by the leading
French designer of the
day is really only a small
stool with a screen
placed behind it as high
as a seated human figure.
The conjunction of the
two elements creates a
novel variant of the chair
concept. But an idea like
this, which seems so
obvious and simple, is
the result of years of
experience in design: it is
the simplicity that is unexpected and surprising.

48

51 *Anonymous:* "Opal" hanging lamp, **1920**

Opal glass balls were already being used before the turn of the century as a simple and effective form of electric lamp. It is not known who designed this model, but architects like Adolf Loos, Josef Hoffmann and Peter Behrens used such lights in their interior designs. This was the first lamp to dispense with the customary historicist ornamentation.

52 *Gerrit T. Rietveld:* Hanging Lamp for Dr. Hartog, **1920**

The spatial geometry of this structure reflects the layout of the room with its furniture, and thus acknowledges a debt to the contemporary aesthetics of the Dutch De Stijl group in architecture and painting, as exemplified in the work of Mondrian and van Doesburg.

53 *Anonymous:* De Stijl lamp, **c. 1923**

The relationship of surfaces and volumes in this lamp is influenced by developments in De Stijl painting. To use a naked bulb without a shade as the source of light was quite unusual at the time.

54 *Wilhelm Wagenfeld:* Bauhaus lamp, **1924**

This lamp was made at the Bauhaus for Moholy-Nagy. Here too the functions are clearly evident, the cable between the base and the shade being shown. The opal glass shade, greater than a hemisphere, displays an elegant classicism. The modern product is a copy of the original Bauhaus lamp, and the design is now regarded as one of the crucial steps in the evolution of the Bauhaus style.

51

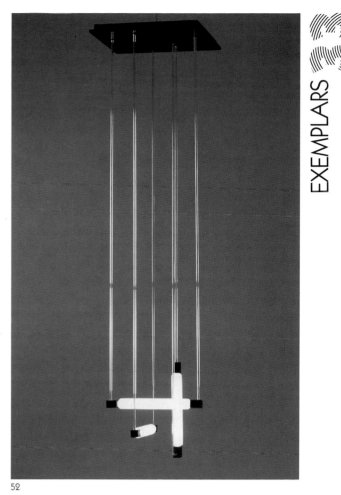

52

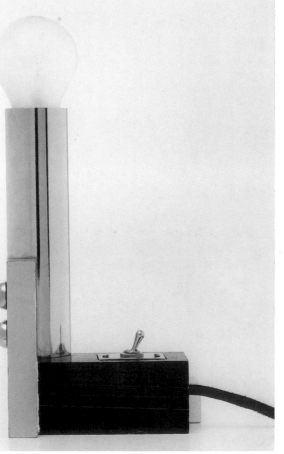

53

54

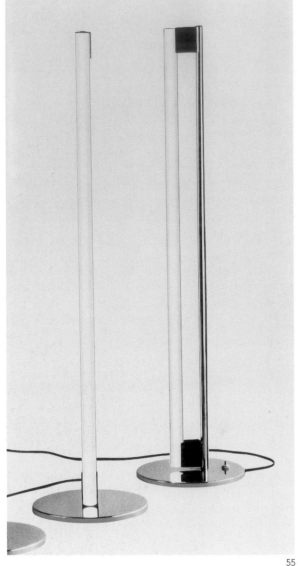

55

56

55 *Eileen Gray:* "Tube Light", **1927**

Eileen Gray uses fluorescent tubes here for the first time in a standard-lamp, an elegant creation in keeping with the chic Art Deco interiors of contemporary high society. In its reductive but modernist elegance, the chromium-plated steel stand is altogether characteristic of Eileen Gray's style as a designer.

57 *Gio Ponti:* "0024" hanging light, **1931**

In this hanging lamp the shade also functions as diffusor: the horizontal glass disks grouped around the glass cylinder create the technoid effect of a soft ball of light.

58 *Jac Jacobsen:* "Luxo L 1", **1937**

Experiments with similar lamps were being done in Britain in the early thirties. The jointed arm, with coil springs that enabled it to be angled as desired, was already patented in England in 1934. Jacobsen acquired the patent for the whole of Scandinavia and gradually built up a monopoly for desk lamps, which today covers the rest of Europe and the United States as well. It is estimated that more than 25 million of these lamps have now been sold. The design has served as model for literally hundreds of imitations, and it has become the archetype of the desk lamp.

59 *Pietro Chiesa:* Table lamp, **1939**

This table lamp of brass and crystal glass architecturally defines the spaces it occupies. The opal glass shade can be tilted to adjust the direction of the beam.

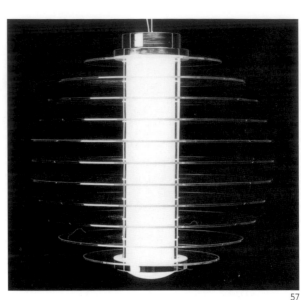

57

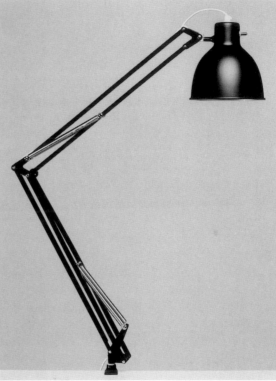

58

56 *Christian Dell:* "15-1192-21-20" wall light, **1930**

This concertina lamp was one of the first to be mass-produced as an office fitting, and its aesthetics clearly owe much to the Bauhaus. The open reflector on its concertina bracket offered a hitherto unknown flexibility in workplace lighting.

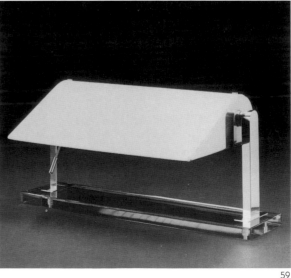

59

60 *Isamu Noguchi:* "Akari" hanging light, **1952**
The shell is still made of paper and bamboo as originally, although there are now many cheaper versions with a wire frame. The irregular bamboo lattice and the milky translucency of the rice paper shade create an oriental effect, recalling not only Chinese lanterns but the moon itself. This was also the declared aim of the designer. The name of the lamp is the Japanese word for "illumination".

61 *Max Ingrand:* "Fontana" table lamp, **1954**
This lamp has the traditional vase shape, but here the base emits light as well. Under the shade two qualities of light can be selected, creating in effect three lamps in one.

62 *Arne Jacobsen:* "AJ Diskus" wall lamp, **1956**
This very shallow glass case is extremely difficult to make. It consists of two layers of glass, which create the opalescent effect. Particularly in serial arrangement, the lamps create the impression of circles of light floating against the wall.

63 *Poul Henningsen:* "PH Cone" hanging lamp, **1958**
This lamp is composed of a scale-like arrangement of laminae. It emits a cascade of light like a firework. The natural form of the pine cone was clearly the inspiration here.

64 *Gino Sarfatti:* "2097/30" chandelier, **1958**
With this chandelier Sarfatti succeeded in creating the first High Tech version of a genre otherwise dominated by classical forms. The sockets of the naked bulbs and the wires are in full view, but the arrangement does not exclude traditionalist associations.

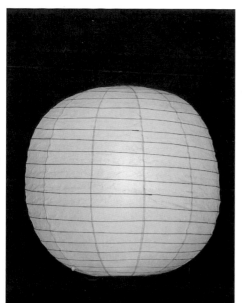

60

61

62

63

64

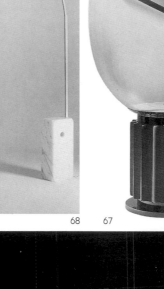

65

68   67

65 *Arne Jacobsen:* "AJ Pendulum" hanging lamp, **1960**

This light consists of two metal shades, one fitted into the other. While the outer reflector diffuses the light evenly over the room, the inner one directs the light from the silvered bulb downwards: two methods of light transmission in one lamp.

66 *Achille and Piergiacomo Castiglioni:* "Toio" standard-lamp, **1962**

The Castiglionis used a reflector from a car headlight for the first time here to light an interior. The structure of the stand, which conceals neither wires nor transformer, and the reflector itself assign this lamp to the High Tech field. It was the first low-voltage lamp to go into series production.

67 *Achille and Piergiacomo Castiglioni:* "Taccia" table lamp, **1962**

The base of this lamp recalls a fluted column, an allusion to the classical tradition. But the metal reflector with its clear glass diffuser resembles the dish of a radio telescope. The dialectical contrast of quite different fields of reference within one design object is characteristic of the work of the Castiglionis.

68 *Achille and Piergiacomo Castiglioni:* "Arco" standard-lamp, **1962**

The vast sweep of the elegant steel shaft, which has a maximum radius of two metres, enables this lamp to illuminate a dinner table for six or eight persons without getting in the way. The heavy marble base is necessary as counterweight to the wide arc. The reflector is also adjustable, giving the lamp even greater flexibility.

69 *Robert Haussmann:* "C 300" light-structure, **1964/65**

This system creates spatial structures like those of a molecular lattice. The chromium-plated bars and globe-type bulbs can be combined in various ways: the resulting effect is more or less static and constructivist.

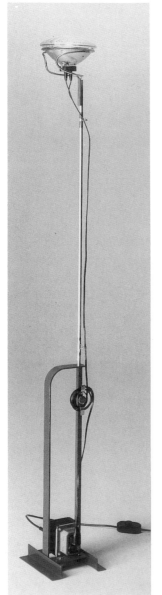

66

69

70 *Enzo Mari, Anna Fasolis:* "Polluce" standard-lamp, **1965**

This lamp is like a street-lamp brought indoors. The shaft is of telescopic construction, so that the height is adjustable.

71 *Gino Sarfatti:* "600 P" table lamp, **1966**

This reading-lamp stands firm even on a sloping surface, since the base consists of an imitation leather sack filled with ballast pellets, and thus adapts itself to the angle of inclination. The naked bulb has a reflector-plate and so provides a bright beam of light over a limited area. The lamp has affinities to the Pop Art movement, like Pietro Gatti's sack-chair (pl. 9).

72 *Joe Colombo:* "Colombo 281" table lamp, **1966**

This table lamp exploits the properties of acrylic glass for directional light transmittance. The light comes from the base and is directed through the transparent C-shape of the lamp: only the cut edge actually emits light.

73 *Tito Agnoli:* "Agnoli 387" standard-lamp, **1967**

This is one of the first, now classic, standard-lamps with a formally independent source of light, consisting of a bulb and holder. This reduced form had a major influence in subsequent years, inspiring numerous similar designs. Here the base is a stone block – the archaic is thus combined with a spartan technology.

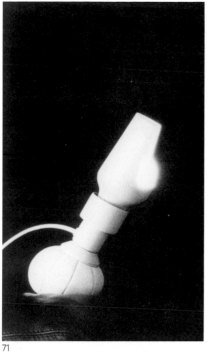

71

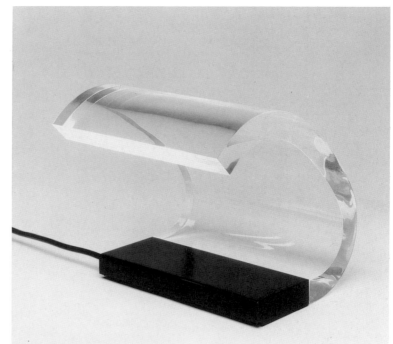

72

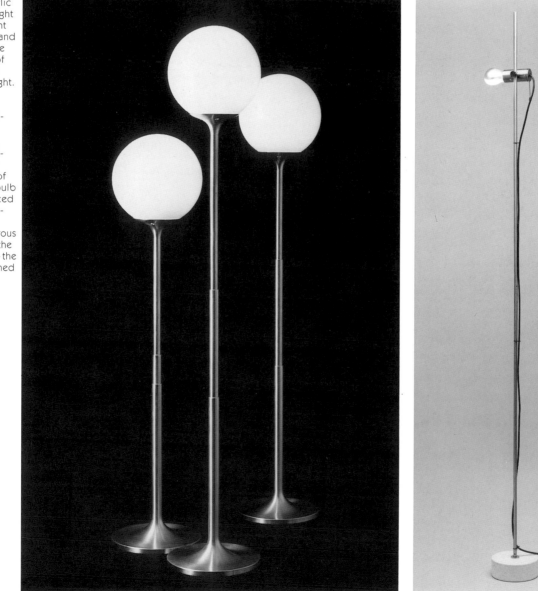

70

73

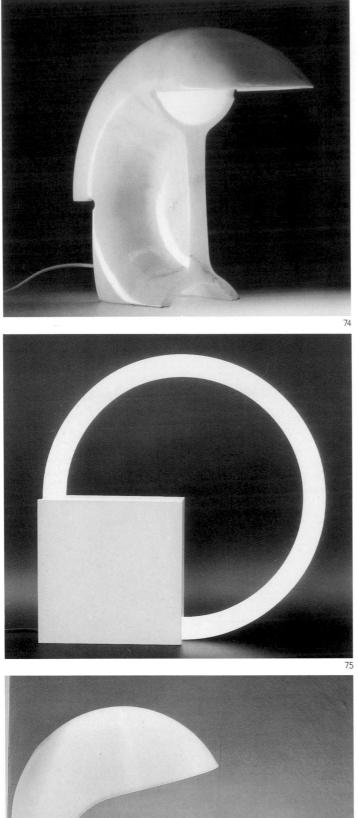

74

75

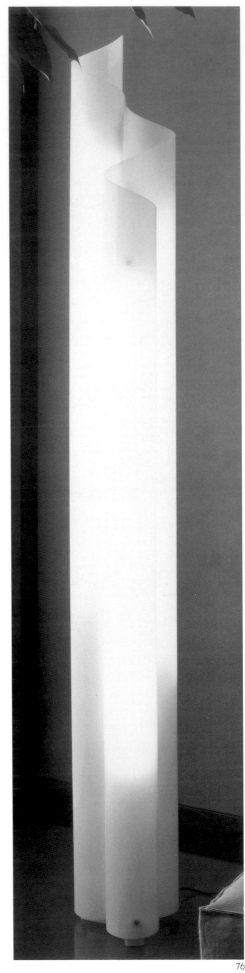

74 *Tobia Scarpa:*
"Biaggio" table lamp,
1968

Scarpa, one of the lead-
ing designers in Italy, has
often experimented with
the lucid quality of thin
slabs of marble, like
his famous father, the
architect Carlo Scarpa.
This lamp can only be
made by hand and the
technique is extremely
laborious. The heavy mar-
ble base becomes prog-
ressively thinner to culmi-
nate in the translucent,
rounded shade. The
effect is suggestive of a
mediaeval cathedral win-
dow.

75 *Aldo van den
Nieuwelaar:* "TC 6" wall
or table lamp, **1969**

This lamp is an example
of the reductionist aes-
thetic which has been
rapidly gaining ground
in the Netherlands over
the last twenty years. The
formal tension between
circle and square not
only recalls the De Stijl
aesthetics and the Bau-
haus maxims of the twen-
ties, it is also akin to the
"spartan" tendencies in
contemporary art, as in
the American "Hard
Edge" painting and
sculpture or ABC art.

76 *Vico Magistretti:*
"Chimera" standard-
lamp, **1969**

Magistretti has attempted
here to reproduce the
flowing characteristics of
material in a static object,
using curved opal-white
metal acrylate. This transfer strategy endows the
lamp with poetic qual-
ities.

77 *Elio Martinelli:*
"Foglia" table lamp, **1969**

This deep-drawn plastic
shape looks as if it had
been cut out of an egg. In
retrospect, we can see
that it symbolises one of
the dominant stylistic
strategies of the sixties.
The softline aesthetic,
which was often a natural
consequence of the
deep drawing technique,
was characteristic of the
decade and appears in
many designs for plastic
chairs as well (pl. 35, 37),
it is also to be seen in the
casings of radios and
record-players.

77

76

78 *Marco Albini, Franca Helg, Antonio Piva: "AS41Z" ceiling light with swivel arm,* **1970**

The striking feature of this pendant is its mobility. The articulated structure enables the lamp to be moved horizontally over a wide radius, so that it can be positioned above a table, for example.

79 *Pio Manzù, Achille Castiglioni: "Parentesi" standard-lamp,* **1970**

Here a steel rope is attached to the ceiling, and anchored in a heavy metal disc so that it is taut. The reflector lamp is fastened to a clamping-tube through which the rope runs, thus the lamp can be rotated and moved up or down. As the name suggests, the designers are here alluding to the aesthetic of the casual and inconsequential, the "parenthetical observation".

80 *Livio Castiglioni, Gianfranco Frattini: "Boalum" multipurpose light,* **1970**

This creation was inspired by the hose of a vacuum cleaner. The technical realisation presented many problems; the many small bulbs inside are joined together like Christmas-tree lights with snap connections. The "Boalum" can be hung on the wall, draped over a table or arranged on the floor, and several lengths can be joined together. The seemingly aleatory configurations possible give it a sculptural aura.

81 *Isao Hosoe: "Hebi" table lamp,* **1970**

This lamp is also made from flexible tubing, as used in electrical installations. The tube can be bent into any position, and the reflector can be rotated. The lamp is relatively inexpensive, costing under £ 40, and the price has not been raised since it was first marketed.

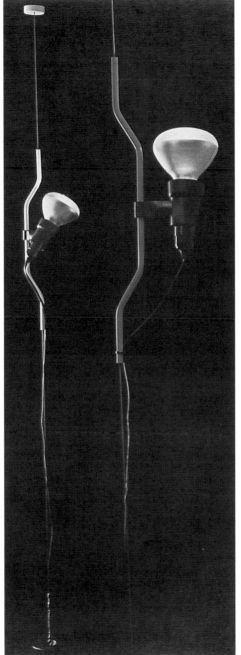

79

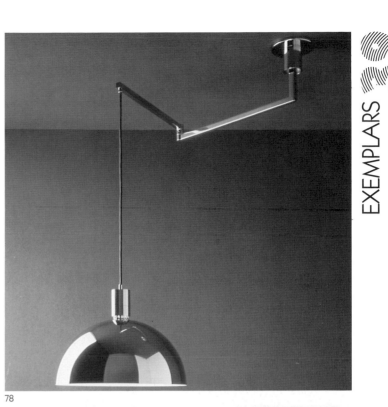

78

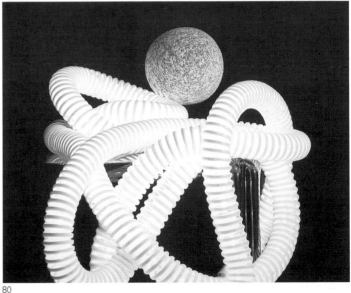

80

81

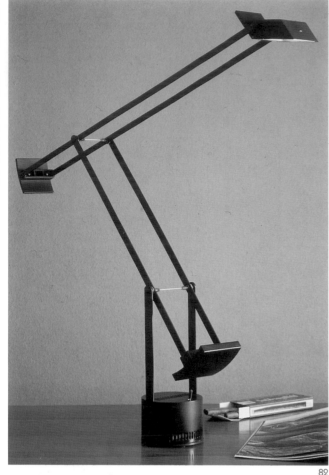

82

82 *Richard Sapper:* "Tizio" table lamp, **1970**
After lengthy experimentation, Sapper succeeded in creating the first low-voltage lamp in which the current is supplied not via a cable but via sliding contacts. The various parts of the lamp are so balanced that they do not need springs. The sculptural image of the "Tizio" recalls the pumping machinery on oilfields, and is thus High Tech in style. It is available in a table and a standard-lamp version.

83 *Verner Panton:* "Panthella" table or standard-lamp, **1971**
The hemispherical shade of opal acrylic glass is mounted on a stand with a flared base, a feature also seen in television sets and chairs of the fifties and sixties (pl. 29). The lamp is a typical example of the final phase of Pop Art and "softline" culture.

84 *Achille Castiglioni:* "Noce 1" wall or ceiling light, **1972**
Here again Castiglioni has transferred an element from the primary production sphere into the living-room: this time the building-site lamp. This transfer process is characteristic of the High Tech style in interior design as a whole; the "upgrading" of banal objects is also a technique employed in Pop Art.

83

85 *Örni Halloween:* "Macumba 177" hanging light, **1974**
The small reflector with its halogen bulb casts its light into an aluminium sieve; this lets some of the light through, but also distributes it all over the room, even creating a pattern of light on the ceiling. The effect recalls the old oil-lamps.

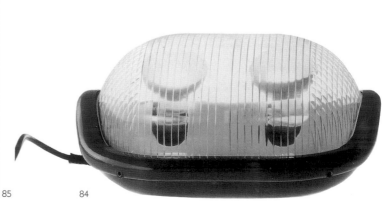

85   84

86 *Tobia Scarpa:*
"Papillona" standard-lamp, **1976**
The aggressive triangular shapes of this lamp create an archaic effect, like an Egyptian stele. The base, the split shaft and the lamp proper are designed to illustrate the flow of the current: it is accumulated in the base, conducted upwards in the core of the shaft, and transformed into light at the top. The shade is of metallised glass, and extensive tests were needed to develop it, because the temperature here rises to several hundred degrees Celsius.

87 *Kazuhide Takahama:*
"Kazuki 3" standard-lamp, **1976**
White fabric stretched over fine wire frames creates lamps that suggest extremely abstracted figures or faces. Reminiscent of the sculptures of a Cycladic culture, they are available in various sizes, so that they can be grouped like a family: this intensifies the anthropomorphic effect.

88 *Marcello Cuneo:*
"Calla" standard-lamp, **1976**
A slender metal shaft bears a lamp that looks like paper casually rolled up to form a bag. The synthetic fabric employed creates a poetic, milky light. The association with the white blossoms of the arum *(calla)* is obvious. The technical design of the lamp is so simple that it can be sold in kit form.

89 *Vico Magistretti:*
"Atollo 233" table lamp, **1976/77**
This lamp is another example of the sculptural approach to lighting. The cylindrical base tapers to a point, on which the hemispherical shade appears to be delicately poised. The stark illumination of the conical tip enhances the optical illusion of a floating object.

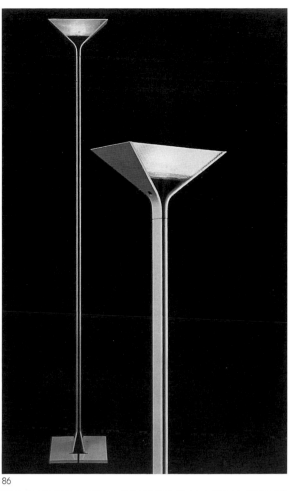

86

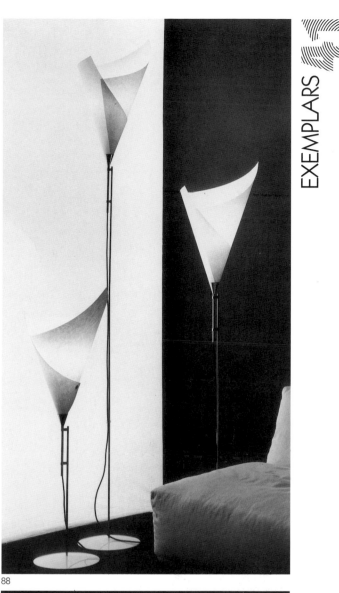

88

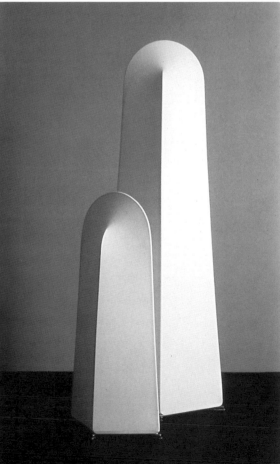

87

89

90

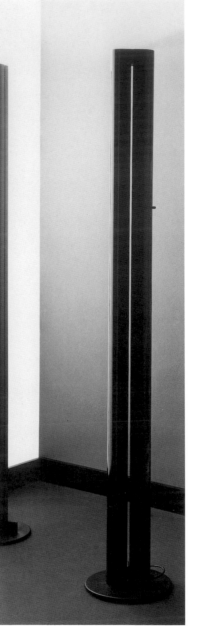

91   94

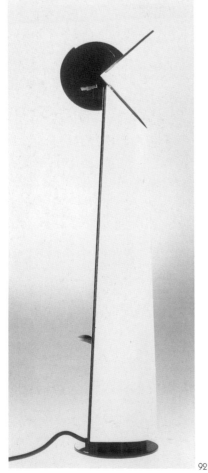

92   93

90 *Achille Castiglioni:* "Frisbi" hanging light, **1978**

The highly polished chromium-plated metal shade reflects the light onto a diffuser-disk, suspended as if floating by fine steel wires, which protects the eyes from glare. The lamp embodies the frozen dynamics of a frisbee in flight.

91 *Gianfranco Frattini:* "Megaron" standard lamp, **1979**

The glossy-finished shaft of moulded aluminium, with a contrasting steel base covered in black rubber, reveals a long, vertical, extremely thin slit of light. The lamp also casts a diffuse light upwards, so that here again two different lighting techniques are combined and contrasted in one object.

92 *Achille Castiglioni:* "Gibigiana" table lamp, **1980/81**

This lamp, which is made in two different heights, focusses the light by a mirror technique; this also enables the beam of light to be projected at different angles. In terms of gestalt psychology, the object also has zoomorphic qualities.

94 *Ettore Sottsass:* "Callimaco" standard-lamp, **1982**

Sottsass is the leading figure in a new, "additive" design aesthetic, in which form, function and texture are no longer seen as logically interdependent, as in Functionalism, but often treated disparately in the same object. This lamp of metal painted in various colours looks like a dumb-bell stood on end: the conical reflector is echoed by a similar, somewhat larger cone which serves as the base. A handle is attached in the middle of the shaft, a deliberate borrowing from the prosaic world of industrial fittings. The design thus combines various "cultural" strata.

93 *Martine Bedin:* "Super" table or floor lamp, **1981**

This lamp featured in the first Memphis collection; it looks like a child's toy, and is suggestive of a hedgehog or a pull-along duck. The holders for the bare bulbs are painted in rainbow colours, creating a playful, happy and optimistic mood.

95 *Ron Arad:* "Aerial Light" remote-control-lamp, **1982**

Ron Arad, head designer of the London avant-garde group One Off, which is currently leading the field in Trans High Tech design, here pokes fun at the computer mania of the High Tech generation. The arm of the "Aerial Light", which ends in a small halogen lamp, can be extended and turned with the aid of an infrared remote-control device. The object is less important as a source of light than for the surprise-effect provoked by its technology.

96 *Livio and Piero Castiglioni:* "Scintilla" lighting system, **1982/83**

The Castiglionis were the first to start experimenting with tiny halogen lamps in the mid-seventies. The cone-shaped bulbs of this system are fixed on current-carrying wires hung from wall to wall. Also available are separate elements that can be attached directly to the ceiling, permitting the construction of light-cascades or chandelier formations. Originally commissioned for and tested in commercial distribution centres, the system is increasingly being adopted in the domestic environment.

97 *F. A. Porsche:* "Kandido" table lamp, **1982/83**

This lamp is based on an ingenious principle: three telescopic rods, to the end of which the lamp proper is attached, are mounted on a heavy triangular base. The design permits not only height adjustment but also virtually unlimited variations of radius and angle. This is another low-voltage light with high luminous power in relation to the size of the light-source.

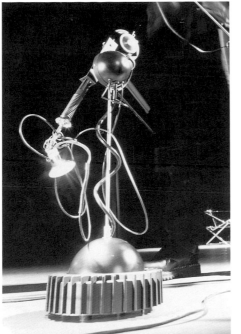

95

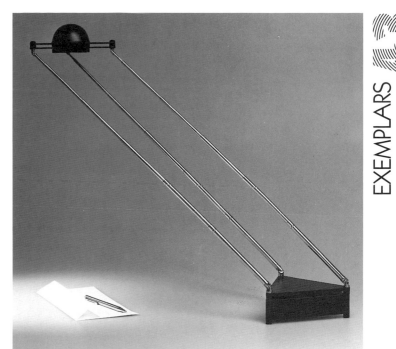

97

96

98

98 *Ingo Maurer & Team:* "YaYaHo" low-voltage lighting system, **1984**
Maurer's system builds on the discoveries made by the Castiglionis, but it has a more poetic effect. The tiny light elements – halogen bulbs or multimirror reflectors – are mounted on current-carrying cables, which look as if they had been thrown casually over the support wires. High Tech today can be handled naturally and with consummate ease.

99 *Matteo Thun, Andrea Lera:* "Chicago Tribune" standard-lamp, **1986**
This lamp is an example of the Microarchitecture approach, which is becoming increasingly established in design: small objects are treated on the same principles as large objects or architecture itself. The skyscraper association is greatly intensified in that the cylindrical body of the lamp, made of sheet metal, contains rows of perforations precisely drilled by laser technique, giving the impression of storey upon storey of illuminated windows.

100 *Mario Bellini:* "Eclipse" spotlight, **1987**
This range of spots using low-voltage halogen bulbs consists of a basic body, lamp attachments and accessories. It is an example of the advanced possibilities in dramatically defined lighting available today. Colour and ultraviolet filters, lenses, honeycomb louvres and antiglare attachments make these lights highly professional pieces of equipment, more a product of the technician's drawing-board than of purely aesthetic design considerations; they are almost as complex as a camera.

99

100

In industrial and even more so in interior design today, it is not hard to make out a number of distinct currents or attitudes that present features characteristic enough to justify their being seen as so many "styles", in the classical sense of the word – a sense that cannot, for example, be applied to the miscellany of one-off "art-works" or "emotive collages"[1] that are the fruits of the "Anything goes" philosophy. The stylistic approaches that make up the world of design can also be observed in other visual fields such as architecture, painting, fashion and advertising, and thus we shall see that the traditional idea of style as something that transcends categorical boundaries provides a useful orientation when we attempt to describe the contemporary design scene.

Concepts of Form in Present-Day Design

Most designed objects not only possess a distinctive identity of their own, they also present certain features shared by a number of other objects, all of which reflect a particular approach to be challenge of design. We can today identify six major currents of thought, Alchimia/Memphis, Post-Modernism, Archetypes, Minimalism, High-Tech and Trans-High-Tech, each with its own very specific stylistic vocabulary. Design based on Functionalist, predominantly ergonomic criteria can be seen as a counterbalance to these tendencies, a still valid approach that has however lost much of its erstwhile significance; it is adequately and paradigmatically represented here by the work of Dieter Rams and his associates. Functionalism, it must be remembered, has been an important stimulus for these more recent developments, if only in the sense of provoking a more or less negative reaction and a quest for alternatives. There are of course other new directions which might be discussed, such as the ecological school, the "Retro" style, and the revival of Constructivist and De Stijl attitudes in design. However, there are various reasons for not devoting greater space to these trends. Eco design, like Eco architecture, has in my opinion produced few examples of high formal quality that convincingly demonstrate environmentalist theories; the recycling of used materials might however be an interesting avenue for exploration, as suggested by Jochen Gros's aesthetically, i. e. formally, satisfying tyre sofa (Fig. 1). Style-Retro is a nostalgia for the form-languages of the past, above all of the thirties, but increasingly for that of the fifties as well: when it is not just a case of almost literal plagiarism in a new, contemporary dress, it has a lot to do with Post-Modernism, and is thus illustrated under that rubric. The revival of constructivism and De Stijl in the sense of an ongoing creative development has been more evident to date in jewellery and in architecture (Coop-Himmelblau, Frank Gehry, Rem Koolhaas, Zaha Hadid, Peter Wilson) than in interior design (some rather pedantic variants of the Mondrian and Doesburg idiom can be seen in Danilo Sivestin's desks and cup-

boards for Rosenthal). It remains to be seen whether recent forays in this direction by the New York Masque team (Fig. 2) or Monika Wall from Stuttgart (Fig. 3) will help to establish a stylistic continuum in the field of design.

Stylistic criteria, though of course not the be-all-and-end-all in a study of cultural phenomena, are particularly useful in the articulation of an exhibition, because only thus can the links between different objects and different designers be directly visualised. I believe that the six styles presented here, plus Functionalism as number seven, give a good idea of the spectrum of contemporary design. For it is only since about 1970 that the process of disintegration and reassessment of the old concept of "good form" has been fully operative. Previously, reactions against Functionalism had hardly got beyond the stage of avant-garde experiments, which were designated as "art" and as such confined largely to the gallery and museum scene.

The projection of the optimistic idea of "good form" into the technological utopia led around 1970 to the formulation of the High-Tech approach in architecture and design.[2] Starting from the transfer to the private sphere of technical materials and processes and ideas from the world of work – perforated metal, nuts and bolts, aluminium sheeting, glass, highly polished surfaces – the stylistic vocabulary of a new, distinctive design language was soon created. Fifteen years later this technology-based optimism had become very down-in-the-mouth: in the face of environmental pollution and the overexploitation of natural resources it seemed obsolete, indeed impertinent. A new style was evolved to reflex the situation: it used the vocabulary of High-Tech, but treated it as relics of a civilisation in ruins, decayed, almost magical source material – this was Trans-High-Tech.

If these two approaches represent the projection of Functionalism and the abrupt end of this projection, Alchimia/Memphis and Post-Modernism, on the other hand, are protests against Functionalism and stand for a fundamentally different attitude. They emphasise the more than incidental function of symbolic associations, poetic and narrative elements, and historical references. Both styles had their roots in the early sixties when Functionalism was in full swing, and hence incorporated from the start a subversive element. Today they are major currents in design, as in architecture, offering attractive alternatives to the ergonomic one-sidedness of Functionalism; the image of Functionalism itself is now beginning to change under these influences.

Two other new directions are becoming increasingly important in the wake of Functionalism and High-Tech on the one hand and Memphis and Post-Modernism on the other, particularly in reaction against the uninspired work of epigons of these movements. Minimalism, which is associated with names like Zeus, Philippe Starck, and Shiro Kuramata, reveals an obvious irritation at the "tittle-tattle" or plain solipsism of Memphis and Post-Modern designs. It is an austere philosophy which reduces chair and table legs to spidery thinness and fragility, has a predilection for matt black or semimatt surfaces, and makes seats – at least optically – ascetic and uncomfortable with such devices as knobbly rubber upholstery. It has a pronounced aversion to being too obvious, saying too much, symbolising too much. Minimalism protests against the flood of visual stimuli in which individual messages are lost, not only in advertising but also in architecture and furniture design from Historicism to Memphis and Post-Modernism. The Archetype movement militates against this flood of images in another way; it seeks to reduce objects to their fundamental, invariable essence, much like structuralism, which by bringing together and correlating all the historical variations of a myth endeavours to discover the (almost invariably lost) original version. This is a strategy that aims to strip an object of all historical accretions and non-intrinsic constituents. In architecture it usually bears the label Rationalism and is linked with the names of Oswald Mathias Ungers and Aldo Rossi, and more recently the Krier brothers, Giorgio Grassi, and the Ticino school. Ungers and Rossi have also designed ranges of furniture and tableware in accordance with their architectonic credo. This current of design is likely to become more important as a stylistically consequential counterbalance to Functionalism and Modernism on the one hand and to Memphis and Post-Modernism on the other. Like Minimalism, Archetypal design stands for a new rigourousness in dealing with objects: symbolic qualities are by all means acceptable – within reason – but anecdotal and overly individualistic gestures are shunned.

In my opinion, the six stylistic directions presented here make up a kaleidoscope that will give us a fairly comprehensive idea of the relevant attitudes in design over the last fifteen years. It has not been a procession of successive styles: all these movements exist concurrently in their own right. In drawing attention to the various currents we have tried to remain impartial, our goal being to provide clear stylistic guidelines for the assessment of concepts of form.

Fig. 1   Jochen Gros, tyre sofa, 1975

Fig. 2   Masque, neoconstructivist furniture, 1987
Fig. 3   Monika Wall, spiral bookcases, 1985

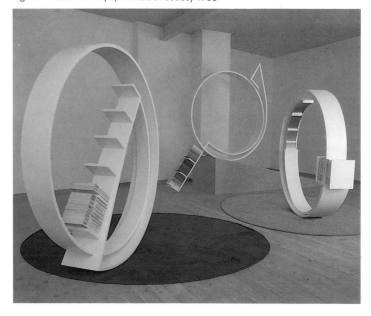

The concept of High Tech became established in design largely through the book of the same name by Joan Kron and Susan Slesin,[1] first published in 1978, which also defined its parameters. In architectural circles, "High Tech" stood for an amalgam of "high style" and "technology", and the term was used to describe buildings made of or using prefabricated parts; Kron and Slesin were thus able to trace a pedigree for the style including Charles Eames's famous house of 1949 and the 1930s architecture of Jean Prouvé and Pierre Chareau.

HIGH TECH

In design, High Tech stands above all for a process of transfer of technical elements from the primary sphere of industry to the private world of the home. In their new environment, such seemingly incongruous elements enjoy an aesthetic upgrading, their functionality is seen in a new light. For instance, metal-section shelving for the storage of spare parts in car factories is designed, marketed and bought not on aesthetic, but on strictly utilitarian, functional and ergonomic considerations. If the same shelves are transferred to a domestic setting, the process of transfer will itself give them aesthetic qualities, which are then expressed through judgements of taste: How simple, how strong, how beautiful! Susan Sontag has described a similiar process with regard to kitsch and its acceptance by intellectuals. Something can be so bad in aesthetic terms that somehow it is in fact good, it is "camp".[2] The transfer from the public and technical to the private sphere produces changes in the object's network of relationships; for the designer it opens up new possibilities, creates new aesthetic references, and changes the criteria of suitability of materials. Through this process, and through the application of these insights to a wide variety of objects – from vases to cupboards, from canteen equipment for the domestic kitchen to office furniture systems for home use – a new style has been created.

The High Tech style gives aesthetic value to the structural and the constructive, and is created through the domestication of elements that are otherwise used only in industry. "These everyday industrial materials have no history other than that of their economic and practical significance, and this gives them a character of aesthetic minimalism. The formal language of High Tech tries to find its expression without cultural and in a way, without humanistic references. The technical or, if you like, aesthetic aspects of industrial materials become an independent and highly precise language of style, and that is what makes this philosophy of form fascinating, perhaps even tragic: for it may degenerate into parody. The static dignity of High Tech architecture is reduced in many design objects to a mere symbolism of technology – an image, a fiction, a game."[3]

Some fifty internationally important examples of this industrial High Tech style in architecture have been built since the thirties. The most important so far are the Centre Georges Pompidou by Piano and Rogers (1977), the Hong Kong and Shanghai Bank by Foster (1985), and Lloyds of London by Rogers (1986).[4] In interior design, on the other hand, there are innumerable examples, of which only a very limited selection, chosen for outstanding design qualities, is shown here. It should not be forgotten that High Tech has become a "mass market" style with wide variations in quality. As is the case with antiques, exemplars can now be found in the department stores.

In Germany, the Munich architect Andreas Weber has designed "container systems", chests of drawers and tables of stainless steel and aluminium, with visible fittings and corner pieces, sunken handle recesses and mirror-coated interior storage surfaces (pl. 106 –109); they might have come from canteens, intensive care units, laboratories, or jumbo-jets. These pieces of furniture have hardly any forerunners apart from the cabin trunks, which in terms of form, though not of aesthetics, themselves continue the tradition of historical models – in this case, the English teak style of the colonial era. The chairs and tables of Rodney Kinsman and Haigh Space Ltd. are, in contrast, contemporary variations of steel tubing sections and perforated sheet metal that can look back on a long tradition (pl. 101, 102). Hollow aluminium sections were first used for chair legs by Hans Coray, whose "Landi" chair created a sensation in 1938 and has been in production, unchanged, for fifty years (cf. pl. 23); perforated sheet aluminium was also first used here for the moulded seat. René Herbst's "Sedia" has been available for even longer; it has a frame of nickel-plated steel tubing with elastic luggage straps attached as seat and back supports (cf. pl. 18). Kinsman, certainly one of the most influential of contemporary High Tech designers, developed the tubular steel and perforated metal chair "Omkstack" in 1971 (pl. 101); it has since become the best-selling garden chair of the postwar period. For his "Tractor" chair (pl. 105) he used a tractor seat on a one-legged support, thus paraphrasing the Castiglioni brothers' 1957 "Mezzadro" stool (pl. 31).

The *object trouvé* air of these objects is a common characteristic of High Tech, seen in the wide range of materials and objects from the industrial world which have found their way into the domestic environment since the mid-seventies; they include perforated metal sheets, aluminium struts, rubber studs, brushed steel, reinforcement matting and mass-produced prefabricated parts from production lines generally. Nevertheless, alongside their ergonomic features these objects now embody aesthetic considerations: Kinsman's perforated metal sheets have in fact been designed, not just cut out with plate shears. The elegant tubular steel chairs of his "Tokyo" series (pl. 103, 104) express this additional aesthetic value, and show a close affinity to the aristocratic minimalism of a Philippe Starck (pl. 224 – 227).

Another, more innovatory line of thought is currently being pursued by the Milanese architect and designer Matteo Thun (pl. 110 –115). The perforation patterns of his container cupboards and skyscraper lamps are not simply punched but precision-cut by laser. The patterns of holes thus create open structures which, like the pattern decorations in the Memphis style of the Italian firm Abet Laminati (pl. 182), are individual rather than industrial resolutions of form.

Thun has designed cupboards and, with Andrea Lera, lamps using these computer-perforated sheets. On the cupboards the patterns have a purely decorative effect, and sometimes seem to have been painted on, but in the lamps they are strongly iconographic, suggesting skyscrapers through the illumination from within and through the shape of the object. These lamps in the guise of miniature buildings illustrate a category of contemporary product design that can be designated "Microarchitecture" (see below).

The architect Mario Botta from Ticino, Switzerland, uses another High Tech principle for his tables and chairs. Punched metal sheets, flat-bar steel profiles, rods, and aluminium frames help to create images alien to our ideas about familiar categories of objects. Botta's work is related both to architectural constructivism and minimalist sculpture. His "Prima" chair (pl. 120) has a paper-thin clip-on seat of springy sheet steel and a backrest formed by two cylindrical polyurethane blocks, which also give slightly under pressure. The "Seconda" (1982) is the matching version with arms (pl. 121). Both these chairs, and even more the "Quinta" (pl. 126), give visible expression on the one hand to transparency and lightness through their extreme exploitation of specific material qualities and on the other hand to sculptural and architectonic allusions reminiscent of De Stijl furniture of seventy years earlier, with its wooden components in primary colours (pl. 9, cf. pl. 124, 125). The "Tesi" table (pl. 122) reinforces this impression of transparency created through material: the triangular contour of the base of close-meshed perforated steel creates visual interference patterns reminiscent of a moiré effect.

The work-station and table systems by Bruce Burdick and Norman Foster, though also intended for the private customer, are the products of a highly developed systematology. Foster's office furniture system (pl. 127, 128), introduced at the 1987 Milan Furniture Fair, undermines all conventional ideas of work-station design. These tables, which Foster first developed for his own office, extend into the third dimension with vertically stepped echelons of integrated shelving. They are in the best meaning of the word 'customised'. The work surfaces themselves can be adjusted in size, height and inclination through a system of variable planes and mountings. The technological sophistication of the system – chrome steel and glass with visible fastenings – determines both its aesthetic affirmation and the roots thereof in particular associations: who is not reminded here of the optimal use of space and ergonomics in the interior planning of aircraft, ships and vehicles? Foster himself likens his system to the spatial organisation of interiors in the field of transport. Storage and production areas, surfaces for mechanical and verbal communication, can be flexibly combined and rearranged. The product name "Nomos" is Greek for "norm", an abstract word denoting a way of behaving or functioning rather than a class of objects. What it signifies is the mode in which concepts might be realised or processes carried out, not the concepts or processes themselves. Furthermore, the system is as applicable to private environments as it is to public or business offices. The qualities of "surface" and all its many possibilities are explored and objectified. Foster himself says: "'Nomos' provides surfaces for meals and meetings, for conversation and drawing, for projection and presiding, for working in teams and singly, with keyboard and terminals or with pencil and paper, with intelligence and memory".[5]

In addition to conquering the vertical dimension, which helps to achieve optimal use of valuable floor space, particularly in commercial installations, the system takes into account the changing infrastructure of rooms. The installation of cables in buildings and the reequipment of work places with up-to-date lighting, telephones, and power supplies, as well as with micro and mainframe computers and other communications equipment, is becoming ever more important and is being carried out at an ever increasing pace. "Nomos" is designed with this in mind and provides suitable structures, horizontally and vertically adjustable, that can easily be added to according to need. The system consists of precision-made components whose multiplicity of possible combinations is, as yet, unequalled by any other system – not even by Bruce Burdick's "Tech-Group", which might offer the most obvious comparison. In "Tech-Group" (pl. 123) shelves, filing cabinets, machine stands, glass conference tables, surfaces for electronic equipment, sorting elements, lamp mountings and desks are all threaded in a line on an aluminium bar. In symbolic terms it reflects and upgrades the linearity of production-line flow. The associations of the "Nomos" system on the other hand are more democratic because of its extension into three dimensions. "Nomos", in its detailing, also avoids the impression that "Tech-Group" gives of the "educated bourgeois", with its recourse to the chrome and glass elegance of "classics of modern design". What the two systems have in common, however, is that they facilitate the logical adaptation of office organisation to the particular working methods, speeds and circumstances of individuals and noticeably increase the efficiency and effectiveness of the work processes. For the user, the threat posed by such systems also represents a challenge: how to use these ingenious offerings of High Tech, which manifestly have the power to optimise the basic office processes, in ways that are both creative and individual? In this respect the "Nomos" system is like a computer: its democratic potential only unfolds when it is seen for what it is, a thing of no intrinsic value that is only there to serve and taken for granted as a foil to its master. It is only then that the symbolic language that echoes working conditions and production processes in the domestic and communicative spheres – a basic feature of High Tech – begins to make sense.

One of the currently important areas in which the progress of advanced technological development comes directly to the notice of nonspecialists is that of lamps and lighting. Particularly in the interior design of public buildings and offices, specifications for lighting systems are often as technical and complicated as the most modern audio and video systems. Light has become a sort of fourth dimension, especially in architecture: it helps to create the desired aesthetic effect.[6]

A world-class contender in this field is the German firm Erco. For the boardroom of Norman Foster's Hong Kong and Shanghai Bank, for instance, they developed computer-controlled oval light kennels, which can produce practically any kind of illumination via integrative and additive processes, and which also incorporate the audio systems. Lighting engineers nowadays are highly paid specialists who juggle expertly with wall-washers and down-lighters, halogen and low voltage technology, angles of scatter and impact, heat coefficients and variable colour filters (cf. pl. 100). In domestic lighting, High Tech exploits the latest advances to present possibilities of extreme miniaturisation. Thanks to halogen technology a tiny bulb can if necessary act as a complete lamp itself and illuminate a whole room; lamp casings in the traditional sense are no longer necessary. Such a transcendent use of High Tech, which in Italy is associated with the Castiglioni brothers and in Germany with Ingo Maurer,[7] no longer needs, as it were, to flex its muscles and is more representative, it seems to me, of the Trans High Tech philosophy (see below).

Urs Gramelsbacher's "Corda di Arco" lamp (pl. 116), is exactly on the borderline between the two styles because its symbolism and iconography will do for either. A man-sized metal bow is held in tension by a pair of silver-plated copper wires in lieu of a bowstring, the arrow is replaced by a halogen bulb which can be adjusted for height, and the visible transformer constitutes a stable base. Hans Dinnebier of Düsseldorf, in his "Clip" model, has also used height-adjustable reflector lamps, which can be safely moved while switched on (pl. 117). The "Clip" design has been developed into a complete track lighting system. A more conformist style of classic High Tech is exemplified by the "Basis" and "Lift" lamps of the Serien-Raumleuchten company (Manfred Wolf and Jean-Marc da Costa). While the former (pl. 118) emits its halogen light indirectly via a reflector, the latter (pl. 119) is designed as a direct light source with infinitely variable height adjustment. Both are characterised by the emphasis on the interlinking of the various elements, the additive architectonic structure. They give the impression of being miniature versions of much larger formal relationships: another pointer to the link between the High Tech vocabulary and the fields of microarchitecture and miniaturisation.

101

102

103

104

105

106

107

108

109

110

111

112

114   Matteo Thun
and Andrea Lera
"WWF Tower" standard-
lamp, 1985

115   Matteo Thun
and Andrea Lera
"Joseph" standard-
lamp, 1985

116
Urs Gramelsbacher
"Corda d'Arco" stan-
dard-lamp, 1983

117   Hans Dinnebier
"Clip" standard-lamp,
1980

118
Jean-Marc da Costa
"Basis" standard-lamp,
1984

119
Jean-Marc da Costa
"Lift" hanging lamp,
1983

114

115

116

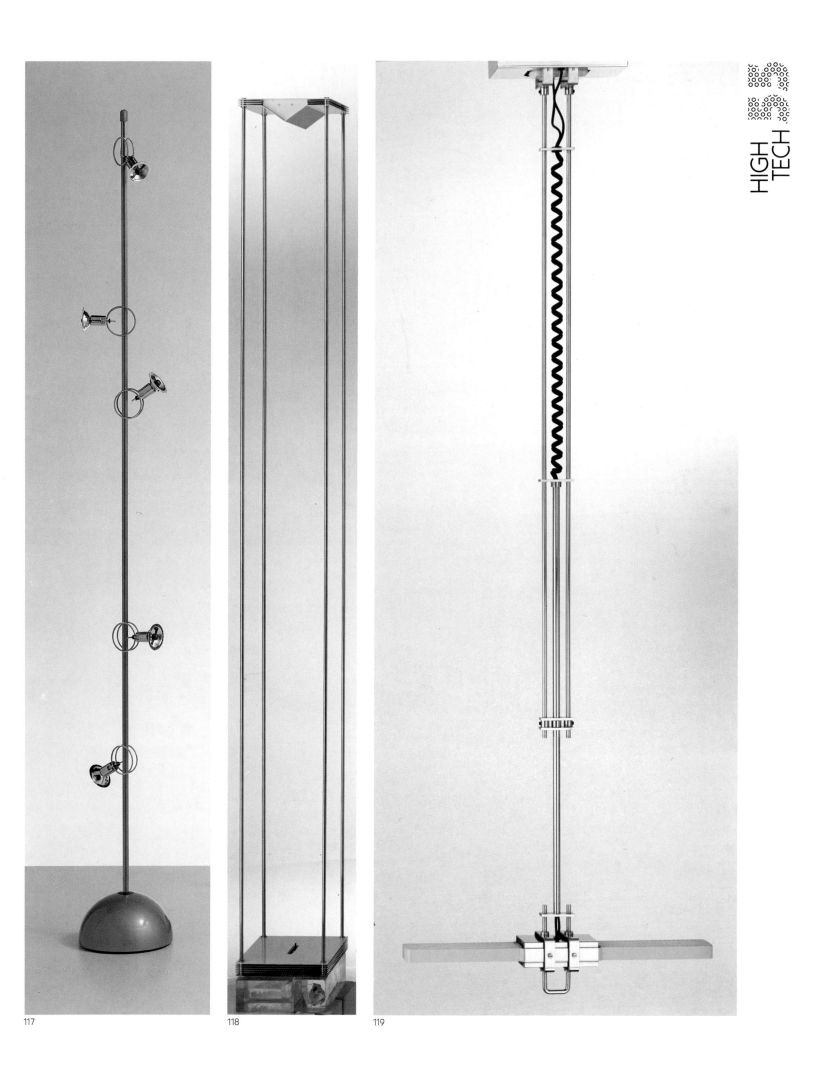

117

118

119

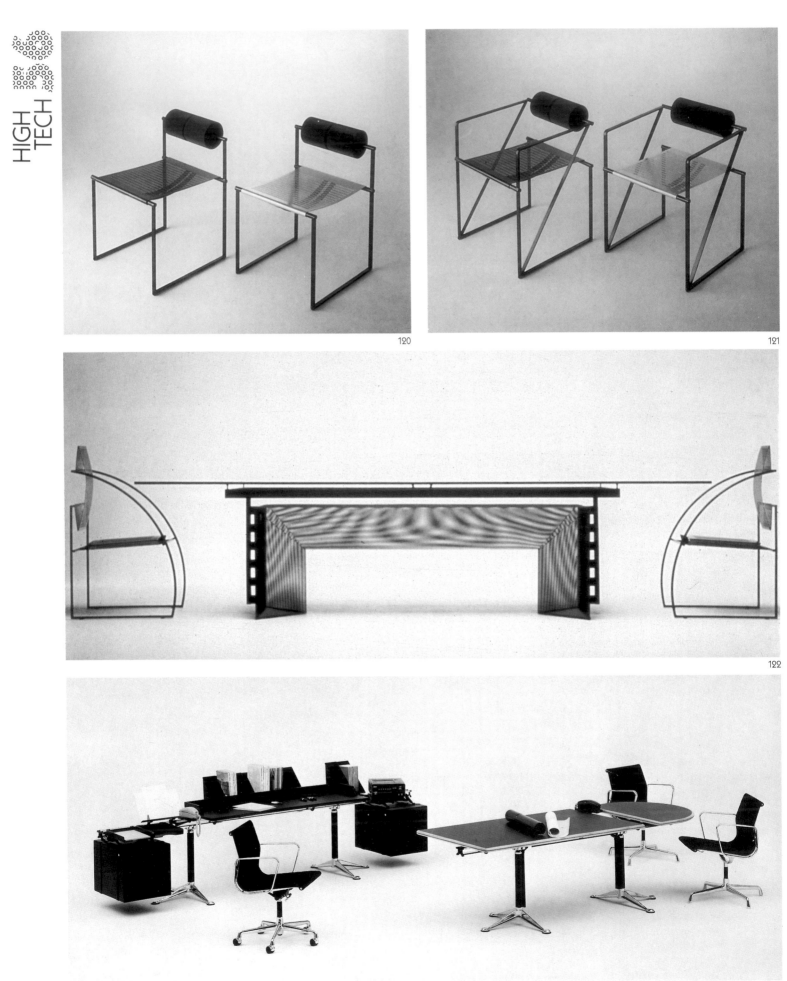

120

121

122

123

120 Mario Botta
"Prima" chair, 1982

121 Mario Botta
"Seconda" chair, 1982

122 Mario Botta
"Tesi" table, 1986

123 Bruce Burdick
"Burdick-Tech Group"
office workplace
system, 1982

124 Mario Botta
"Quarta" chair, 1985

125 Mario Botta
"Latonda" chair, 1987

126 Mario Botta
"Quinta" chair, 1985

124

125

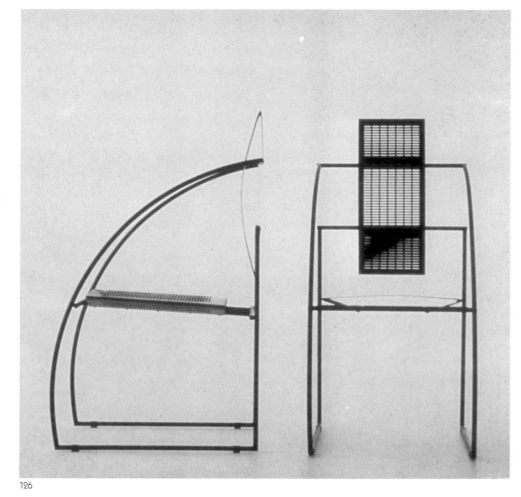

126

127

128

One of the basic maxims of Modernism used to be that if science and technology made something feasible, it should then automatically be done. This idea, hitherto not seriously challenged, was first questioned in the realm of aesthetics around 1980. It is certainly more than a coincidence that the questioning, which began in architecture, consisted in new ways of using the formal vocabulary of High Tech, the very style that had been responsible for the greatest advances within the parameters of Modernism. The materials of High Tech, such as glass, steel, aluminium and perforated metal, and some of its techniques, are also used in Trans High Tech, but at the same time are transformed and alienated, as if seen from a distant future – a future apparently so advanced that it has left behind the limitations imposed by technology. In such a level of civilisation, the creed of technology is merely a nostalgic memory, and the artefacts of the old era are seen as quaint archaeological finds. Technology is now no more than a fetish or a totem, an animistic idea, not least because the real "high technology" is becoming ever more abstract and incomprehensible. The time shift which becomes apparent in technological artefacts has, in itself, a poetic quality.[1] Such objects are, like overgrown ruins, increasingly seen as part of "Nature". (This stage of civilisation is anticipated for instance in the science-fiction visions of the film designer H. R. Giger.)

In this respect the Düsseldorf design team Kunstflug "aerobatic" have created a particularly impressive series of objects they call "Tree-Lamps" (pl. 129). Oak tree-trunks, man-high, unplaned but with the bark removed, have been painted in gaudy colours and fitted with fluorescent tubes or rings.

Besides their associations with the dark German forests, and perhaps allusions to the current plight of the tree, they also manage to transport age-old German sentiment into the era of punk and neon culture. These "light-trees" amalgamate two widely separated stages of civilisation: the Stone Age and the age of technology, the dug-out and Erco. The Belgian Gerard Kuijpers archaises the furniture design he develops in creative feedback with his wife, the sculptress Désirée Verstraete, in another way (pl. 130 – 133). His steel, glass and stone components look as if they are frozen together or bolted on, and even when there are formal dynamics in the design they give the impression of being paralysed. The table, chair and telephone stand have granite surfaces and blocks which successfully combine sculptural qualities with practicality. Edges or particular surfaces of the otherwise polished stone are usually left rough to give the pieces an air of being incomplete, or chance finds. The influence of Land Art projects of the early seventies, such as those of Richard Long, is evident, as are references to prehistoric artefacts such as the menhirs

TRANS
HIGH TECH

of Stonehenge. The mythic and archaic is crossed with elements of industrial civilisation, the natural linked with the constructed, the machinemade with the handmade. Such a design strategy is motivated by a curiosity like that of a structuralist ethnographer. The Italian designer Gaetano Pesce works in an analogous manner. His chair for Vitra-Edition (pl. 134) gives the impression of a prehistoric, almost ethnological, object. The seat and backrest combination is formed from a single piece, black and with its surface deliberately left rough, like a freshly stripped and not yet cleaned hide: it suggests an animistic disguise or mask. The shell is asymmetrically supported by eight metal legs as thin and stick-like as insect legs, with suckers for feet. The chair as totem: the achievements of industrial society are still exploited, but as if their real sense had been lost or obscured. The object becomes a distorting mirror of civilisation and our attitude to the past: an almost pathetic, and yet highly expressive, chair-mask. At the 1987 Milan Furniture Fair Pesce's designs for Cassina were the talking-point of the show. They included a table with a polished version of the steel lattice used for reinforced concrete as support for an irregular-shaped cast slab (pl. 135), an animistic bureau, and an easy-chair series with backrests that can be individually "draped" round the sitter like a shawl (pl. 136).

Advanced technology in the guise of quasi-archaeological artefacts is also produced by the London group One Off, whose leading designer is Ron Arad. His most famous work is the "Concrete Sound System" (pl. 137), a modern hi-fi installation built into blocks of reinforced concrete from demolition sites. The system comments with morbid sarcasm on the High Tech fetish of compatibility, including as it does synthesizer, tape-recorder and television in the same concrete look. In a similar vein, One Off have transformed old Rover car seats with curved anchoring-frames into new chairs with a martial air, punk variants, so to speak, of Mendini's species of Re Design (pl. 139). Here, as in High Tech, there is a process of transfer from the realm of primary production to the domestic sphere. But in contrast to the High Tech treatment, the technical and technological ambience is neither celebrated nor even accepted, it is held at arm's length as though it had decayed, was rusted and obsolete, a leftover from another era, something that has gone out of fashion. In Ron Arad's designs as well, the elements of industrial society and High technology are used as if they were archaeological souvenirs of a vanished age.

The mood of such objects is inevitably ambivalent, since they draw their poetic qualities from intimations of catastrophe, from the presumed end of the world or from whatever ruins are left afterwards.

The dominant aesthetic concern is the exaggeration of terror, an escalation which, to be sure, also dominates the decor of trendy boutiques, with-it zeitgeist hairdressers and cool "warehouse" clubs. Other One Off objects, the screens, the tables, the recent chairs, the shredder, and even the remote-controlled "Aerial Light" lamp (pl. 138, 140, 142–144) also dance on the dormant volcano of allegedly non-risk technological progress. The achievements of various phases of the technological revolution continue to be used notwithstanding, but rather as totems whose original purpose has been forgotten. One Off, as well, have done a chair for Vitra-Edition. This "Well-Tempered Chair" by Ron Arad (pl. 141) toys blasphemously with middle-class ideas of furniture by parodying a conventional shape. Large metal sheets, which give the impression of being razor-sharp, are looped and riveted to create the likeness of a well-stuffed armchair in the classic tradition. It is as if the sterotyped image of an armchair recalled from memory had suddenly materialised. Visually, it both evokes and negates the comfort which it in fact genuinely offers. Shiro Kuramata has created a more minimalist variation for the same collection with his "How High the Moon" chair (pl. 145). This is made of extremely thin flat-welded rhomboid steel mesh, as normally used for the internal reinforcement of plastered surfaces. It plays on associations of expansive opulence and bourgeois satiety, which the form evokes but the substance fails to confirm.

In many of the above designs one can sense allusions to risk and injury, and these become more obvious in the following examples. The Cologne group Pentagon have taken a plane bookcase of rusty Cor-Ten steel in tall rectangular format and with the help of a steel cable metamorphosed it into a highly tensed bow-and-arrow object, which can still however be used as a bookcase (pl. 147). Conventional expectations of formal, material and functional properties have been overturned. In the same vein, the Frankfurt architect Marie-Theres Deutsch designed a writing desk, which she executed in collaboration with the sculptor Klaus Bollinger (pl. 146). This table is on the borderline of the genus, more a piece of engineering that tests extreme possibilities of design, construction and perception. Much as with Pentagon, visual stimulation is provided by the clever manipulation of statics. A concrete tabletop weighing 120 kg rests on two delicate-looking legs of pre-stressed spring steel, which are irregularly angled and only arrive at their ultimate shape under the weight of the tabletop. The construction is held together with tension cables, locking screws and shaft plates, which balance the opposing forces. The mechanics permit infinitely variable adjustment of the height and inclination of the work surface. As in such High Tech examples as Norman Foster's "Nomos" and Bruce Burdick's "Tech-Group", all the structural elements are openly displayed, but whereas in the former the apotheosis of technology is celebrated in a "homage to construction", here they are seen in all their labile fragility. There are metaphors of catastrophe in both

the design and the choice of materials of this object. There is a conscious juxtaposition of the crumbling with the clinical, an evocation of taboos and phobias of injury, risk and angst. The expressive mode of this table links it with the designs of One Off, Pentagon and Kuijpers, with the architecture of Frank Gehry, SITE, Richter & Gerngross and Coop Himmelblau, and the painting of Ben Willikens, Hannsjörg Voth and Lambert Maria Wintersperger. By a sarcastic use of its vocubulary the technological euphoria of High Tech is unmasked for what it is, a superficial utilitarian optimism which fails to correspond to the real experiences of everyday existence. The table symbolises the coldness of modern life, disillusion with the dogma that the progress of democray is necessarily linked with the development of technology, and disgust with a society that in this respect is more intoxicated by promises than by their fulfilment. There is also the brutality of our cities, so often expressed in bare concrete, which is epitomised by this table. When it is measured against our conventional understanding of furniture our expectations are at once both sharpened and blunted. Touch confirms that it has a material reality which one can hold onto, while one's understanding denies that it is what it seems to be and the resulting uncertainty gives rise to a mounting sense of fear. Another feature that plays an important role in the philosophy behind this design is what we might call "process symbolisation". The truthful representation of technical necessities and constraints, which Carlo Scarpa or Jean Prouvé for instance turned into a highly sophisticated aesthetic of technological elegance, is taken up again here, but only in a tentative, disillusioned way; it is not carried to its logical conclusion. Technological criteria and machine aesthetics are expressed as work in progress, as if under construction or as if the objects were semifinished goods. The table, though finished, gives the impression of being incomplete, and as a result the viewer's imagination is led into the exciting adventures of the design and construction processes. The object thus represents the visual, objectified realisation of a calculation in statics. In this respect it is a product of Magrittean logic.

Besides the use of metaphors of technological catastrophe – the pessimistic extension of High Tech thinking – another possibility of Trans High Tech is the minimalisation of technology and materials aesthetically and/or in actual construction. The Frankfurt design duo Gin-Bande have produced an extraordinary example of this with their "Tabula Rasa" pull-out furniture (pl. 148), first shown as a prototype at the 1987 Milan Furniture Fair. This seating and table combination is designed to be just big enough for three people or, if required, for thirty. It is an extendable table which with its attached benches emerges from a modest size box; it works on the basis of an optically simple, but technically complex, concertina mechanism. This is the table as archetype of community and communal life, as centrepiece of many events from tête-à-tête to christening party; it is appropriate for both private and public gatherings, according to the number of places pulled out. The spartan ingenuity of this design need not shrink from comparison with the work of Shiro Kuramata or Philippe Starck.

A leading feature of technical progress for some time now has been the general tendency towards miniaturisation. In the field of lamps and lighting this has been facilitated by the development of the halogen lamp and low-voltage systems. Halogen lamps, formerly used only by professional photographers and for slide projectors and car headlights, combine powerful light emission with long life. A quartz bulb no thicker than a pencil acts practically as a pinpoint source of light. The filament continually renews itself through a cyclical process. This means that for domestic lighting lamps can be much smaller without any loss of power. The most important designers in this area are the Castiglioni brothers, who have worked for Flos, Artemide and Fontana Arte. Their most technically advanced series, "Scintilla", was developed in 1978 and has been in production since 1983. Power wires are stretched from wall to wall and tiny reflector lamps of up to five-hundred watts, powerful enough to illuminate a large room, are mounted on these; they can be moved as needed. Similar solutions have also been sought in Germany. In 1984 Belux presented Hannes Wettstein's "Metro" system, which had better safety features than its Italian forerunner, however, on ground of cost, it was not generally marketed by the manufacturer. At the same time, Ingo Maurer and the Design M company developed the "YaYaHo" system (pl. 150). Typically for Maurer-designed lighting it playfully blurs the distinctions between technical necessity and artistic exaggeration. Rods with miniaturised spherical bulbs like little moons, or lengths of flex balanced by counterweights and fitted with tiny but powerful multimirror lamps, are laid across the bare, wall-to-wall supply wires. The illumination is enhanced and concentrated through the multifacet reflectors within the lamps. The colour and shape of the components is more poetic than "techno-cool", and more inspired by Asia than by Europe. The use of highly developed technology in a casual, off-the-cuff manner, coupled with light sources which are ironic and reminiscent in form, is also the distinguishing mark of Murer's "BaKa-Rú" system (pl. 149) and his "Ilios" standard-lamp (pl. 151). Till Leeser's "Viola" lamp (pl. 152) is also comparable: the relatively small light source is again a 300 W halogen bulb. Leeser adds irony to the poetry of Maurer's designs: the two thin wire stalks that support the lamp housing look casual and fragile, almost indistinguishable from the trailing power cable. This optical illusion shows that the logic of statics need not be apparent to the eye. What can be sensed here is the same attitude to technology as that which permeates Daniel Weil's electronic gadgets (pl. 578, 579). High Tech thinking is characterised by euphoria about innovative technologies and the increasingly vertiginous spiral of progress, but these lamps, like Weil's designs, express misgivings and do not even pay lip service. In Trans High Tech the vocabulary of progress is used sceptically, its validity is questioned, so that this stylistic strategy is one of the most topical of contemporary design directions. Its importance is bound to increase, if only because in the design of everyday objects it aesthetically prefigures the changes brought about by the third technological revolution and thus represents a first attempt to make them accessible to the senses.

129

130

131

129 Kunstflug
(Heiko Bartels,
Harald Hullmann)
"Baumleuchte" I and II
standard-lamps, 1981

130 Gerard Kuijpers,
Désirée Verstraete
"Zigzag" chair, 1984

131 Gerard Kuijpers,
Désirée Verstraete
Telephone stand, 1984

132 Gerard Kuijpers,
Désirée Verstraete
Lounge table, 1983

133 Gerard Kuijpers,
Désirée Verstraete
Japanese étagère, 1984

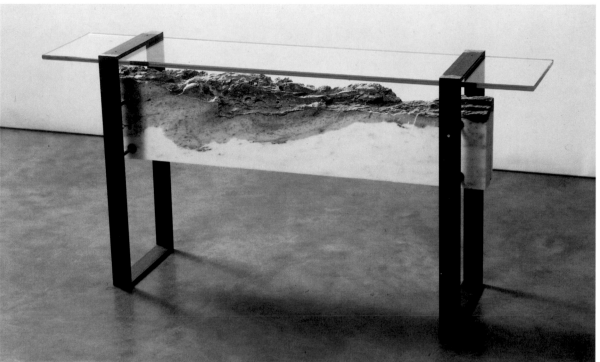

132

133

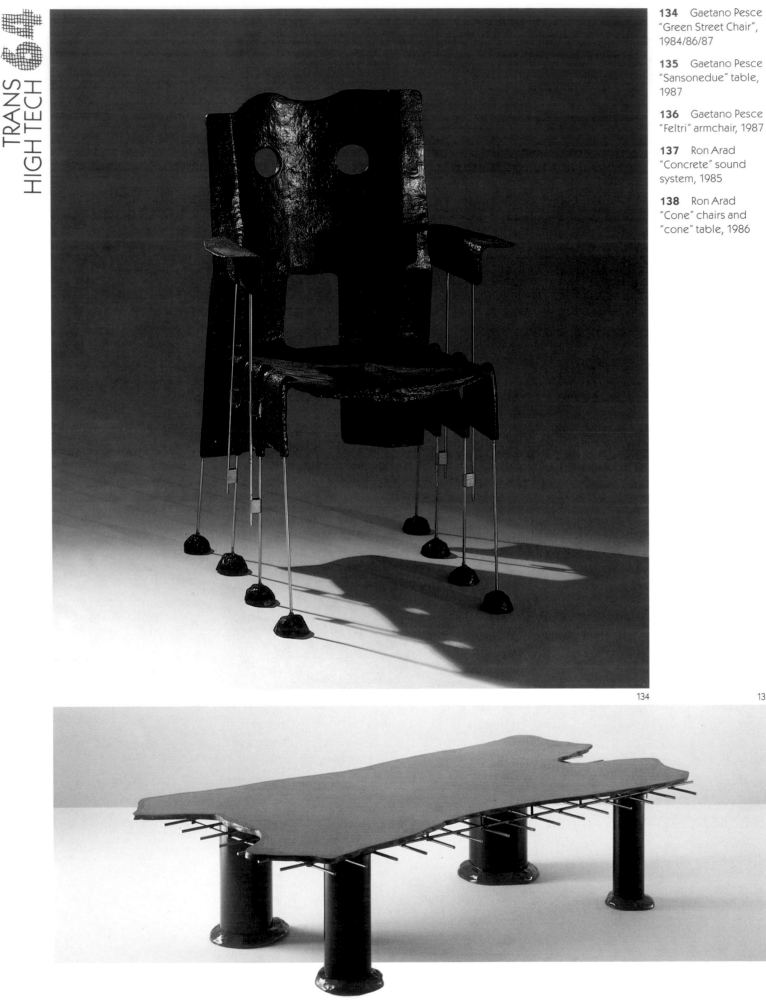

134   135

135

136

137

138

139

140

139 Ron Arad
"Rover" chair, 1985

140 Ron Arad
"Horns" armchair,
1986/87

141 Ron Arad
"Well-tempered" chair,
1986/87

142 Ron Arad
"Aerial Light" remote-
control lamp, 1982

141

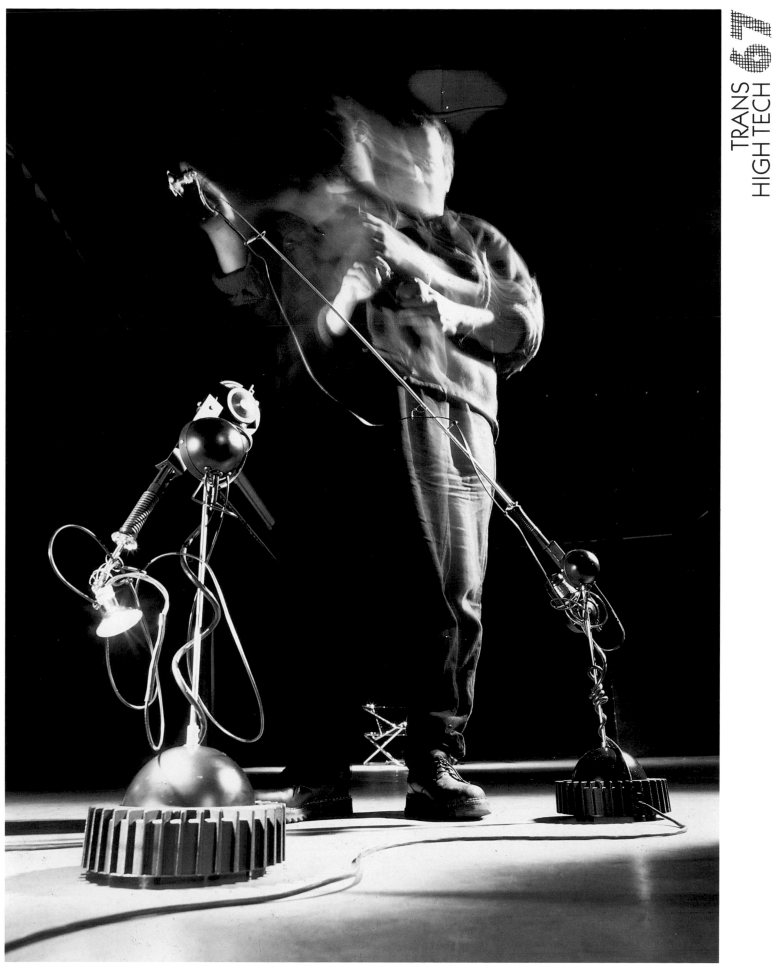

143 Ron Arad
Paper-shredder, 1986
(one-off)

144 Ron Arad
"Deep" screen, 1987

145 Shiro Kuramata
"How High the Moon"
armchair, 1986/87

146
Marie-Therese Deutsch
and Klaus Bollinger
Desk, 1986

147 Wolfgang
Laubersheimer for
Pentagon
Braced shelving, 1985

143

144

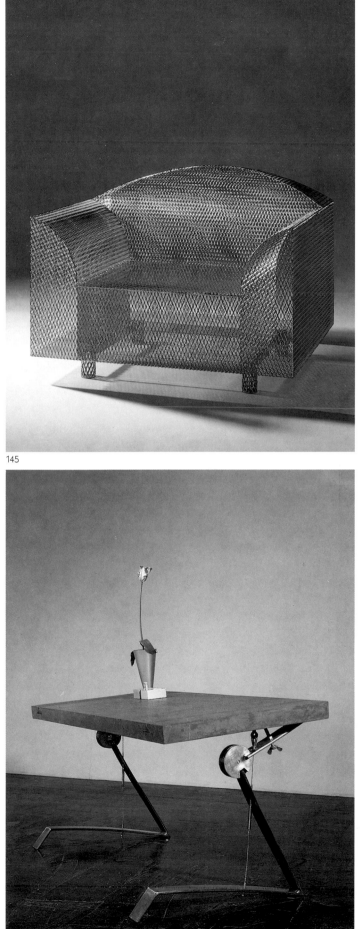

145

146

147

148 a, b, c
Gin-Bande
"Tabula Rasa" pull-out
table-and-bench com-
bination, 1987

149
Ingo Maurer & Team
"BaKa-Rú" low-voltage
halogen lighting
system, 1985/86

150
Ingo Maurer & Team
"YaYaHo" low-voltage
halogen lighting sys-
tem, 1984

149

150

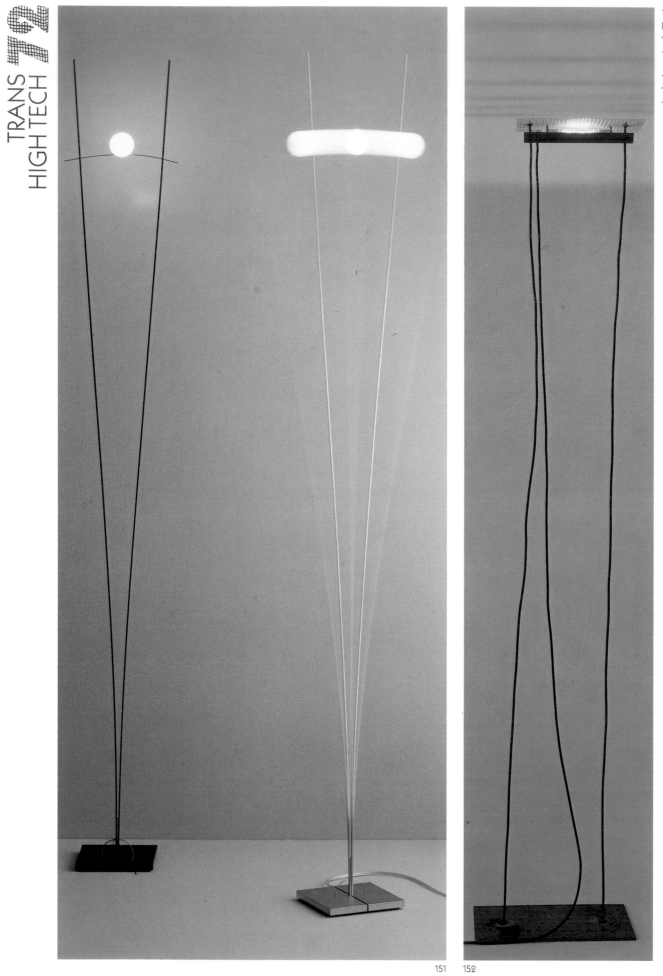

151 Ingo Maurer,
Franz Ringelhan
"Ilios" standard-lamp,
1983

152 Till Leeser
"Viola" standard-lamp,
1985

151   152

The "Radical Design" movement began in Italy back in the mid-sixties. It was opposed to the classic Italian post-war style of "Bel Disegno" then prevailing, which was associated with such designers as Gio Ponti, Marco Albini, Vico Magistretti, Mario Bellini, the Castiglionis, Joe Colombo, Marco Zanuso, Afra and Tobia Scarpa, Gae Aulenti, Gianfranco Frattini, etc. The Radical Design groups such as Superstudio, Archizoom, ZZiggurat and Studio 45, and later also their manufacturing association, Global Tools, projected the popular aesthetic of Pop Art onto the design scene. If misgivings about a consumer society that inflated both production and consumption to self-destructive levels could logically be expressed at all in the design of products, then only in those which rebel against unthinking production and consumption. Certainly the most far-reaching protest against the dogmas of functionalism and "good taste" in design sprouted from ground prepared by Radical Design and began with the foundation of Studio Alchimia in Milan in 1978/9 by Adriana and Alessandro Guerriero and Bruno and Giorgio Gregori. Alchimia achieved worldwide renown through its association with Alessandro Mendini and Ettore Sottsass. More than one hundred designers, including non-Italians, have worked in and for the studio. The chief publicist for the group was and is Mendini, who from 1960 onwards was editor of *Casabella* and *Modo* and then publisher of *Domus*. Sottsass left Alchimia in 1981 when Memphis was founded. Designers such as Andrea Eranzi, Michele de Lucchi, Paola Navone, Aldo Cibic, Matteo Thun, Massimo Morozzi, and Ugo la Pietra, who have had a decisive influence on the image of Italian avant-garde design, were themselves moulded by the formal language and theoretical framework of Alchimia. The name proclaims the group's programmatic intention of turning dross into gold, the unceasing quest of mediaeval alchimists. It is interesting to note that while Sottsass and Mendine were formulating their theory of "banal design" the architects Venturi and Moore were each developing an aesthetic of the banal and ugly inextricably interlaced with aspects of Pop Art and with the vogue of kitsch. Robert Venturi turned to popular culture with his dicta "Mainstreet is almost all right" and "Less is a bore", as did Charles Moore with his "art of creating a significant public space". Expressions of popular culture are welcomed because they are seen as organic growths, ratified by their historical reality; they are authentic and original, and hence have genuine aesthetic value. The moving force behind this theory is the recognition that aesthetic values associated with the "lower classes" could have a potentially important corrective role in the formulation of a progressive avantgarde aesthetic. Mendini for instance, in the 1978 Alchimia catalogue *Elogio del Banale* ("in praise of the commonplace"), argues: "Kitsch is the Trojan horse of the

masses." Through minor but critical alterations, ordinary objects and appliances from the everyday world of the consumer were to be transmuted into the material of aesthetic reflection: this was the basis of Mendini's "Re-Design". Objects in common use, such as department store lamps, electric irons, hats and shoes (pl. 157, 158), on the one hand, and examples of classic design such as Knoll, Miller, Olivetti, and Braun products, on the other, are resprayed and encrusted with spiky projections and coloured patches. The revamped surfaces are thus alchemically "transmuted". Existing pieces of furniture, such as fifties chests-of-drawers, antique wing chairs, kidney-shaped tables or box-type furniture, whatever comes to hand, are draped in a stylish new decor, sometimes Surrealist, sometimes Impressionist, Cubist, Art Deco, "fifties style" or Pop (pl. 155, 156, 159, 160). Such total ornamentation does not change the structural realities of the object: appearance is altered while real form remains untouched, the recourse to features of historical repertoires and styles has an "ennobling" effect. Mendini's "Kandinsky" sofa (pl. 153) and his "Proust" chair (pl. 154) have become classics of "neo-modern" design.

For Alchimia, the key factor of contemporary cultural experience is that people tend to see only "splinters" and "fragments" of style, and this has a dis-associative effect. The insight that these fragments must be recombined in new and satisfactory ways was first adumbrated in paintings and drawings (pl. 164 –168). It is an aesthetic of collage, the combination of diverse elements, values and fragmentary experiences of modern life to make a new aesthetic statement of a new object. It tolerates clashes of materials as imperturbably as it contrasts the sublime with the ridiculous, the highly aesthetic with the stylistically impoverished (pl. 161). When the pictorial language of a Miró, Pollock, Léger or Kandinsky is transposed onto a piece of furniture, its very materiality, the concreteness conferred on it by years of use and habits of perception, is questioned. Unlike Postmodernism, this pictorial language is not mere embellishment with quotations but a revestment in a new expressive cloak. "With the help of the modern, the modern is itself glossed."[1] Currently, such methods are being used by architects such as Rem Koolhaas and his Office for Metropolitan Architecture, Peter Wilson, and Zaha Hadid, and to some extent by painters such as the Neo-Fauves.

When cheap objects are "re-designed" it is only logical to use cheap materials. Ettore Sottsass uses synthetic laminates and pulpwood with "banal" decorations, and prefabricated parts such as fittings and handles from public authority furniture or public transport. Sottsass propagates a non-culture which is unspecific in social and hierarchical terms, and thus belongs to no one and, at the same time, to

ALCHIMIA/ MEMPHIS

everyone (pl. 178, 181). He celebrates the iconography of the commonplace, which in his case is also fed by his experience of and affinity with the unabashed banality of design in the cultures of many non-European peoples. Mendini, on the other hand, has withdrawn, perhaps somewhat narcissistically, from the design business and now only paints. His paintings are nevertheless powerful abstractions of the effervescent symbolic language of Alchimia (pl. 162, 163).

The underlying mental disposition of the Alchimia group has been both its strength and its weakness. The celebration of design as a synaesthetic and subversive game favours individual expressive experiment rather more than, for example, commercial reliability. It treats design as a metaphor for ideas, concepts, ideologies, and even utopias. But why should design, as a language of objects, not be direct, unmediated communication, a semantic vehicle? Do we have to go on believing that objects have something to do with morality? Is it really true, as the Bauhaus, the Ulm school and assorted functionalists have tried to make us believe, that reduction to the bare essentials is morally better? Should we let our freedom to create product languages be enchained by a moralistic teleology based on wishful thinking? Do we really believe that with "better" design a new and better model of mankind will automatically appear on the horizon?

The rejection of this rationalistic moralising, a rejection implicit in all the sixties and seventies movements of Radical Design up to and including Alchimia led in 1981 to the foundation in Milan of a new group, Memphis, which presented itself and was immediately marketed as the "New International Style". The name "Memphis" alludes both to the ancient Egyptian capital and to Elvis Presley's burial place in Tennessee, and thus neatly sums up the historical and the Pop Art constituents of the design programme, which amounts to an ironic rehash of the most varied ingredients. The international mix of designers that initially assembled round Sottsass and Mendini (although the latter are now seeking to distance themselves from Memphis) have on the whole learnt a lot from the formal and stylistic experience of Alchimia. Collages of the most contrasting materials, garish flecked and serrated patterns, softly blurred neon colours, gaudy Pop colours and, in the most recent collections, milky Postmodern colours, small dog's-tooth checks and large zebra stripes, a mix of Hollywood flair and fifties style, of Pop and ironically historicising classicism, are all stirred in with "crazy" ideas for new uses. The recipe produces playful and carefree heterogeneous interiors. It is remarkable that Japanese, American, Austrian, Italian, German and Spanish designers all work in the same product language, even if, as one founding member recalls, the outwardly homogeneous look, especially of the first collection, was only achieved after hundreds of drawings had been sent back again and again for modification.[2] This is one of the reasons why, compared with Alchimia's protest designs, Memphis appears as an

altogether smoother, less irritating amalgam. On the other hand, the product language and design strategy – the "spontaneous mutations", in Memphis language – are more direct. They simultaneously accept and create what Matteo Thun has called "semantic chaos", and hence are welcomed by those who are fed up with functionalism. The Bauhaus dogma, later propagated by the Ulm school, of the mutual affinity of design, materials and purpose is undermined, often carried to absurd extremes. For the Memphis movement and its precursors, formal creativity – not only in interiors but also in product design, from lamps and electric irons to coffee-makers and toasters – is conceivable only in primary colours, basic geometric shapes and construction, techniques that, optically at least, appear to be wilfully naive (pl. 169, 175, 185–187). Their approach has become important in commercial product design because its charging of household objects with semantic-symbolic significance meets a need felt by a good many consumers.

This visual promise of simplicity – though the ideological and technical bases of Memphis designs are in fact far from simple – has since the early eighties spawned a multitude of imitators who all consider themselves to be "designers". Dilettantes obsessed with the "total" objet d'art, with the renaissance of the craftsman, though they themselves have had little or no training, bodge together chairs and lamps, sofas and beds which, as long as they are eccentric and brightly coloured, are "Memphis" style. The accompanying media circus is usually more interested in the anti-bourgeois atmosphere of this design environment than in the designs per se. Hence the important and far-reaching changes introduced by Memphis in the concept of design have increasingly faded into the background. In psychological terms, this urge to simplify is not far removed from regressive behaviour, but it serves to humanise the objects of a High Tech, computerised society. Memphis designs are often reminiscent of animals, anthropomorphic figures and robots (pl. 169–171, 176); they are thus endowed with a presence and personality that lifts them above the usual ergonomic, functional and anonymous object. The form and colour of these objects, with their childish "building-block" mentality of construction layer upon layer, piece by piece, are impertinently optimistic and American, in the tradition of Hollywood and Las Vegas (pl. 175, 179). Here form follows expression and only barely remembers the function. Frequently the form seems to militate against the function, as with the "shark" table (pl. 174), the "robot" bookcase (pl. 169), and the "duck" lamp (pl. 170). Patterns are created which deliberately avoid quoting from the annals for form and style and are in no way variants of these; instead, like Alchimia, they are either transmutations of everyday objects or derivations from the visual vocabularies of the military world, transport, marketing or advertising (pl. 177, 182). In the most recent collections there has been a trend towards a certain historicism in design and decor; Ettore Sottsass has been veering towards the visual language of Michael Graves, and in this respect Memphis is drawing closer to Post-Modernism. But it remains true, all the same, that for Memphis material qualities are subordinated to the treatment of surfaces, and neither patterns, decors, colours, nor individual forms are permitted to give clues as to the nature of the materials used (pl. 172, 173, 184). Thus the three classic elements of design, form, function and material, which have always been defined through their mutual dependence, here become independent. This is a truly Copernican revolution compared with the principles of functional design.

The elements of Memphis design strategy discussed above have also found their way into the collections of otherwise more conservative manufacturers, from Arflex and Artemide, Belux (pl. 178, 179, 181) and Bieffeplast via

Cassina and Driade to Röthlisberger, Vitra (pl. 183), and Zanotta. If in 1981/82 it was still something of a sensation when the Paris fashion designer Karl Lagerfeld furnished his entire apartment with Memphis pieces, Ettore Sottsass's commission to style the boutiques of the international Esprit chain on Memphis lines has not caused many eyebrows to be raised. Acceptance of this design language is so widespread that a new special series of the Volkswagen Golf is called "Memphis", although it has nothing to do with the style; not even the upholstery justifies the appellation, despite the fact that the development of patterns and decorations has been one of the consistently strong points of the Memphis designers (pl. 182). There is even a range of pots and pans for which the makers, Silit, found the name irresistible. The style has also infiltrated college design classes (pl. 188–191).

153
Alessandro Mendini
"Kandinsky" sofa, 1978

154

155

155

154
Alessandro Mendini
"Proust" armchair, 1979
"Bau-Haus" collection

155
Alessandro Mendini
Redesign of the Thonet
"214" chair of 1859,
1973

156
Alessandro Mendini
Redesign of the Breuer
"Wassily" armchair of
1925, 1973

157
Alessandro Mendini
Shoes from the "Robot
Sentimentale" series,
"Set for the Gentleman"
project, 1983

158
Alessandro Mendini
Helmet from the "Robot
Sentimentale" series,
"Set for the Gentleman"
project, 1983

Alessandro Mendini, redesign su sedia Breuer, 1978

156

157

158

159
Alessandro Mendini
Redesign of a chest-of-
drawers from the 50s,
1980/81

160
Alessandro Mendini
Redesign of a chest-of-
drawers from the 50s,
1980/81

161
Alessandro Mendini
Cupboard, 1981

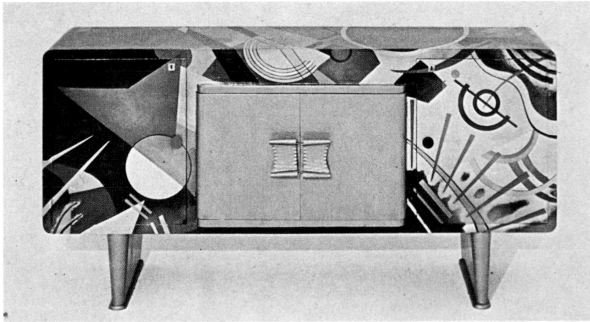

159

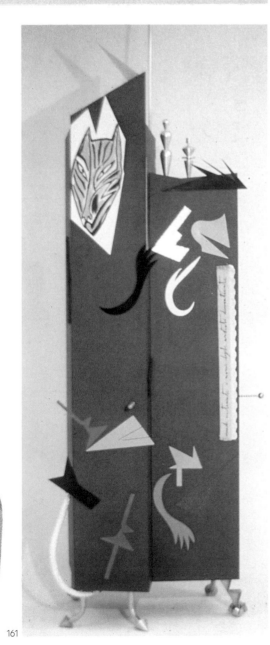

160

161

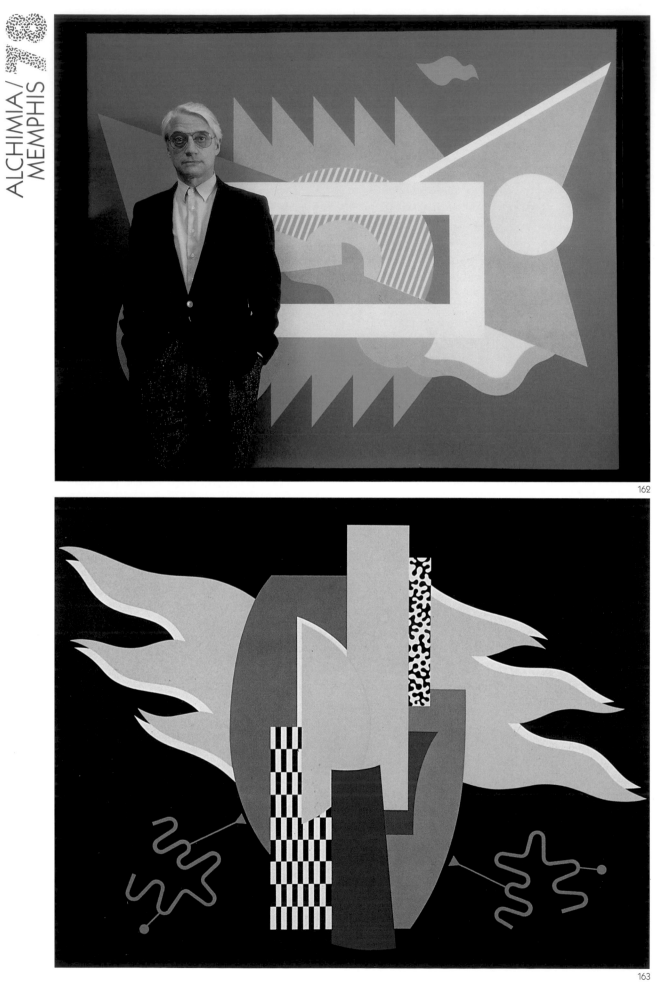

162
Alessandro Mendini
Untitled, 1987

163
Alessandro Mendini
Untitled, 1986

164 Bruno Gregori
"Fabric Pattern", 1984

165 Bruno Gregori
Design for a new
kitchen, 1986

166 Giorgio Gregori
Design for an alphabet,
1986

167
Alessandro Guerriero
"Tiger" design for a
carpet pattern, 1986

162

163

164

165

166

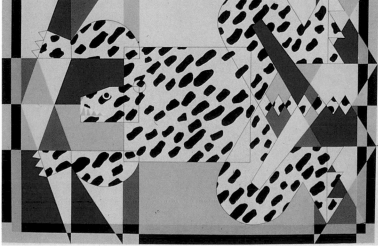

167

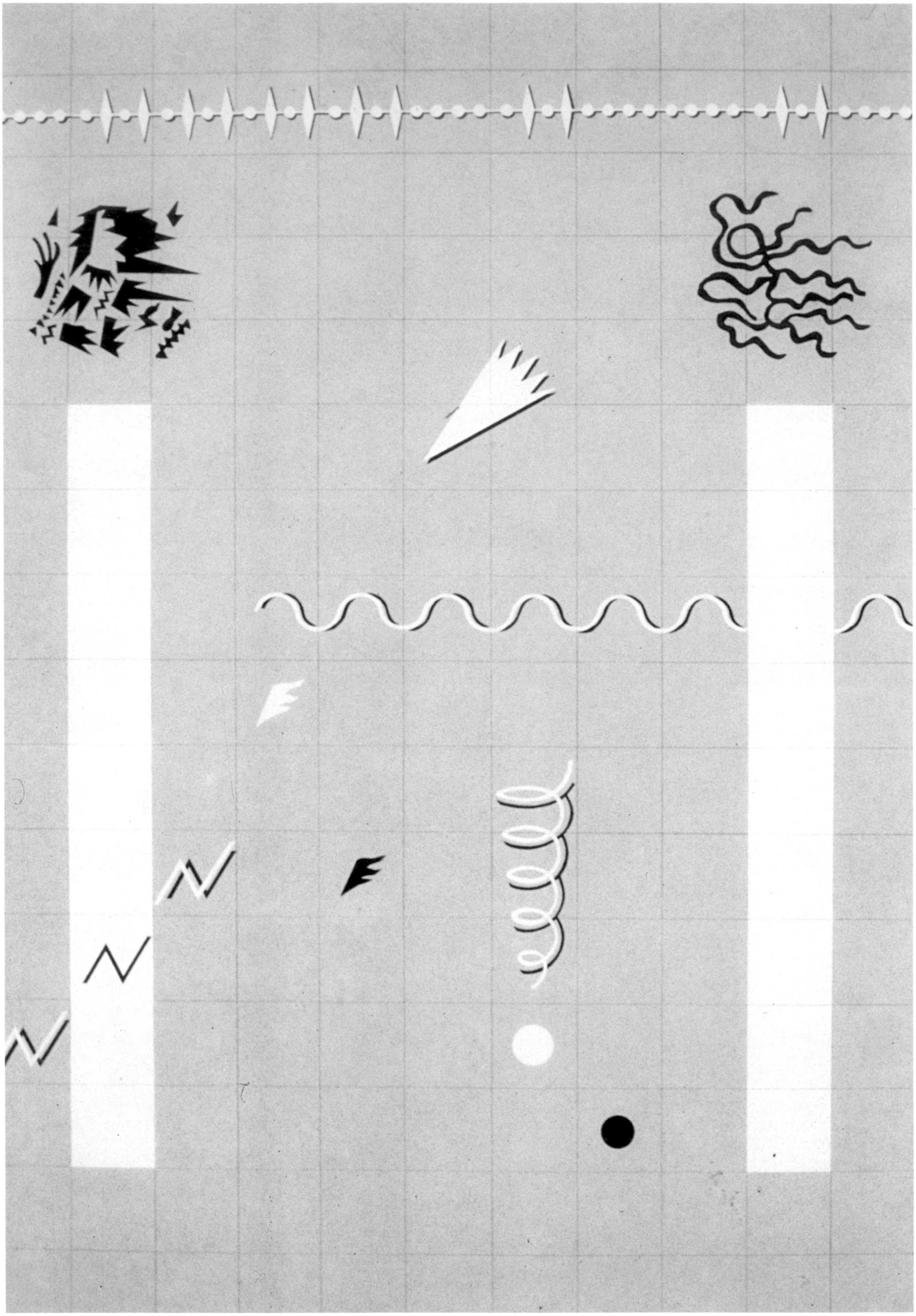

168 Carla Ceccariglia
Design for tiles for
Appiani, 1982

169 Ettore Sottsass
"Carlton" bookcase,
1981

170

171

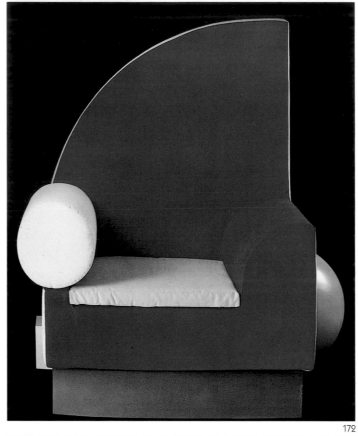

172

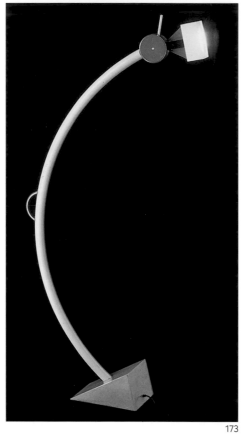

173

174

170 Ettore Sottsass "Tahiti" table-lamp, 1981

171 Martine Bedin "Super" standard-lamp, 1981

172 Peter Shire "Bel Air" armchair, 1982

173 Ettore Sottsass "Treetops" standard-lamp, 1981

174 Peter Shire "Brazil" table, 1981

175 George J. Sowden "Palace" chair, 1983

176 Michele de Lucchi "First" chair, 1983

177 George J. Sowden, fabric by Nathalie de Pasquier "Oberoi" armchair, 1981

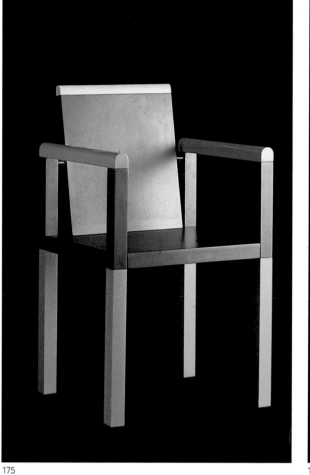

175

176

177

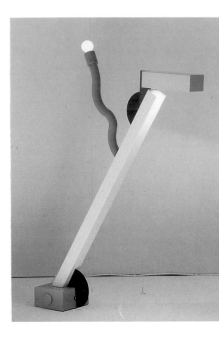

178

179

180

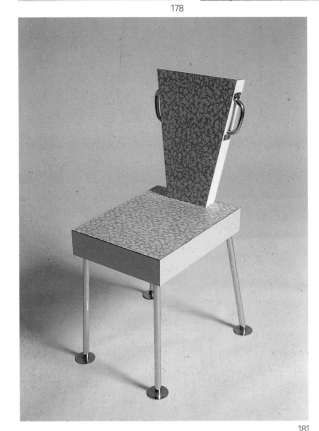

181

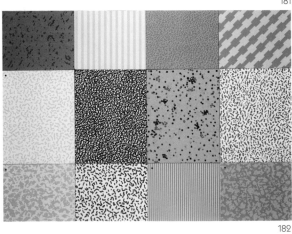

182   183

178   Ettore Sottsass
"Le Strutture Tremano"
table, 1979

179
Michele de Lucchi
"Sinerpica" lamp, 1979

180   Ettore Sottsass
"Quisisana" ceiling
light, 1979

181   Ettore Sottsass
"Seggiolina da Pranzo"
chair, 1980

182   Collage of laminate patterns

183   Ettore Sottsass
"Teodora" chair, 1986/
87

184   Ettore Sottsass
"Cargo" multifunctional
unit, 1981

185
Michele De Lucchi
Hair-dryer (prototype),
1979

186
Michele de Lucchi
Iron (prototype), 1979

187
Michele de Lucchi
Vacuum cleaner
(prototype), 1979

184

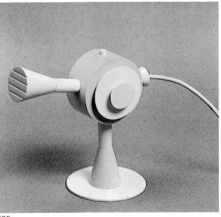

185

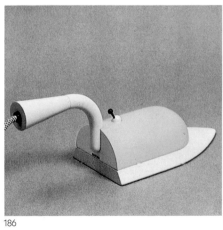

186

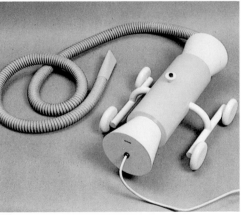

187

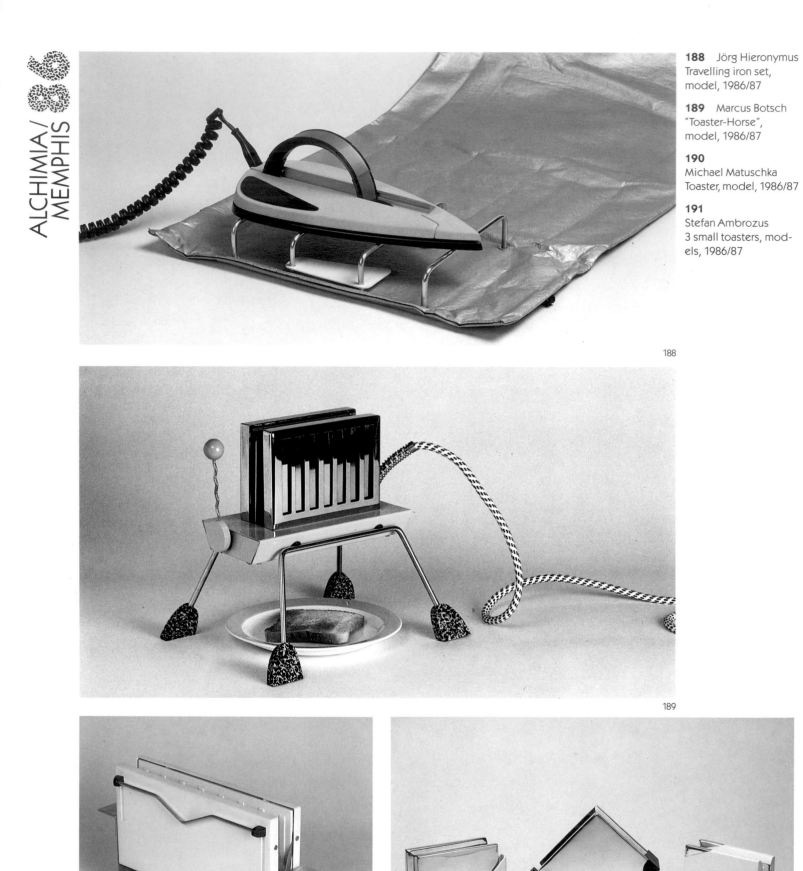

188 Jörg Hieronymus
Travelling iron set,
model, 1986/87

189 Marcus Botsch
"Toaster-Horse",
model, 1986/87

190
Michael Matuschka
Toaster, model, 1986/87

191
Stefan Ambrozus
3 small toasters, models, 1986/87

188

189

190

191

Post-Modernism in architecture is already a quarter of a century old. It has been accepted not only in the realm of theory, but to a far-reaching extent also in architectural practice.

Probably only defenders of rigid functionalism and nostalgic Bauhaus apologists still refuse to accept the inevitable. Today, the cause for concern seems to be that the achievements and insights of Venturi, Moore, Stirling, Hollein, Tigerman and Isozaki will be reduced to simplistic, reach-me-down formulae. At three or four removes they may degenerate into a new form of kitsch, easy on the eye, tailor-made for the suburban bungalow, with oriels and columnettes adorning facades across the land! Post-Modernism is basically characterised by the rediscovery of ornament, colour, symbolic connections and the treasure-trove of the history of form. In interior design, Post-Modernism is largely the creation of the same pioneers who had already formulated it in architecture. But interior design is only one of the areas in which such convictions and design strategies have become accepted. The Post-Modern look is becoming increasingly popular in product design, as exemplified in the field of "table culture" and "living environments".

Robert Venturi's furniture (pl. 192–195), designed in 1983/4 for Knoll International, appears – at least on first impression – to be simpler and more appealing than his buildings. In his theory of architecture, the high purity of the Modern Movement should be contaminated with elements of the ordinary and the everyday, the world of consumption, the subculture, and historical bricabrac. Accordingly, his chairs and tables are contemporary paraphrases of historical furniture styles. More specifically, these paraphrases are based on the hybrid, bastardised versions of period furniture that fill the pages of American mail order catalogues. In Venturi's designs Chippendale, Gothic Revival, Empire, Sheraton, Biedermeier, Hepplewhite, Queen Anne, Art Deco and Art Nouveau features appear in stencil-like starkness and constitute ironic formal substrata, their ornamental severity helping to regain an otherwise lost dignity, an almost classical air which the commercial reproductions never had or could hope to have. Besides the single-colour model, which looks as if it had been fashioned with a fretsaw, there are three others that have been artistically enhanced by screen printing, the Chippendale version, for instance, has an all-over flower pattern in subdued colours overlaid with Jasper-Johns-type stripes at odd angles (pl. 192). The same decoration is used by Venturi for a set of china (pl. 476). This "Grandmother" pattern is a particularly significant demonstration of Venturi's skill in combining the most contrasting cultural attitudes, stylistic strata and frames of mind.

POST-MODERNISM

Michael Graves, in a series of chairs and upholstered furniture for Sawaya & Moroni (pl. 196–198, 200), has similarly revived the formal vocabulary of past times in the main elements, whose bulky silhouettes still retain the character of cardboard cut-outs. Graves's use of classic historical sources is however less specific, and hence his designs are essentially contemporary, the forms of the backrests and legs are historically inspired but in no way are they exact quotations. Much the same can be said of his "Ingrid" standard-lamp (pl. 203). Form and surface characteristics of the furniture collection owe something to the lascivious elegance of Art Deco, and have affinities both to Philippe Starck's minimalism and to Hans Hollein's strong sense of form. The latter's "Marilyn" sofa (pl. 199) is a good example of what has been called the "Retro" style: with its medley of the stylistic vocabularies of the thirties and fifties, its maplewood veneer frame and its satin upholstery, it possesses a vibrant, even exaggerated sophistication, and might almost be the three-dimensional equivalent of a picture by Tamara de Lempicka or the blow-up of an Art Deco brooch.

Charles Jenck's "Sun Chair" (pl. 201) is a blend of mock-Egyptian elements and ornamental Art Deco with a veneer. The underlying concept is akin to that of the "Sternensessel" ("Star Chair", p. 202) of the Frankfurt architects Norbert Berghof, Michael Landes and Wolfgang Rang: furniture should be a stimulus for fantasy, memories, dreams, longings, poetry and fairy-tales. The symbolic references become even clearer in the "Frankfurt Skyscraper-Cupboard" (pl. 204–206, 208), which is a piece of microarchitecture modelled on a city skyline. It is made of stained bird's-eye maple, as is the "Vertiko" cupboard, with its columned canopy for "something very special" (pl. 207). It is a clear demonstration of the renewed interest in beautiful materials, fine workmanship and sophisticated forms, in the traditional craftsmanship of specialised cabinetmakers that is a feature of Post-Modern interior design generally (pl. 209, 210). But are not these forms and designs eclectic or even nostalgic in their recourse to historical precedents? This would no doubt be true if it were not for the ironic glosses on and reinterpretations of earlier styles that, as in Venturi's designs, establish the contemporary note. The lateral projections at the top of "Vertiko", for instance, are atavistic features located where its historical forerunners, from the Renaissance to Neoclassicism, would have had scrolls or volutes to support a slat of greater dimensions. Here there is nothing to support, the top of the cupboard is formally integrated with the outline concept. The canopy, with its halogen stars, is incongruously dimensioned: it is smaller than one would expect and hardly looks like an integral part of the cupboard – it is as if a fruit-dish or some such object had been placed on the top. The wood employed is almost too exclusive for words, so that one might well call it ironically a new "antique". If good middle-class furniture is the ideal, this attitude of noblesse oblige is almost scandalous. In its whole philosophy is it not representative of the yuppies, the spoilt children of democracy, who now seek to become aristocratic lords of the manor? Yet a wholesale appropriation of feudal values and obsolete artistic symbolism is thwarted by the partial alteration of the traditional form. Post-Modern furniture is charged with poetic and literary associations, wit, irony and deeper meaning, it takes an often mischievous delight in dallying with history. Thus, despite all its elegance and luxurious facade, it is anything but superficial or conservative. Stanley Tigerman's "Tête-à-Tête" two-person sofa (pl. 212), an artfully ergonomic contribution to the battle of the sexes in the form of a Pop-influenced lollipop blow up, shows this even more clearly. Similar examples include the door model by SITE, with a multilaminate fist-hole edged in delicate colours (pl. 215), Frank Gehry's armchairs of meticulously glued corrugated cardboard (pl. 211), or even Matteo Thun's "Rainer" sofa, covered in a rash of flowery decoration like grandad's wing chair, but owing its design strategy to the subversive ideology of Memphis (pl. 213). Finally, there is Dakota Jackson of New York, who designs for large-scale production. His "New Classic" series attempts a synthesis between Modernism and Post-Modernism. The pieces look like classics by Le Corbusier or Mies van der Rohe, though they have renounced Adolf Loos's dictum "ornament is crime" (pl. 214, 216, 217). They make numerous references to history but are not historicist. Their avant-garde potential and their provocative rhetoric are the result of an intelligent mixture and a precarious balance of various semantic contexts. They allude to the modern classicism of the twenties, the elegant and wanton linearity of Art Deco, the colour symbolism of Pop Art and the soft, milky palette of the Post-Modern colour sense of a Michael Graves or a Charles Moore.

Post-Modernism, in design too, is the most implacable opponent of the quest for abstract purity. What Post-Modernism shares with all the other new directions outlined here is the insight that nowadays aesthetic vocabularies have to emerge from and relate to a pluralist society with its complex network of influences, values and imperatives; only then can a new richness of form be created. What sets the movement apart is its appropriation of diverse cultural strata, which enhance each other when they are fused together. The vocabulary of everyday life and the vocabulary of the past, seen through the images of memory and filtered through contemporary experience, combine to create the treasure-trove of Post-Modernism.

192

193

194

192 Robert Venturi "Chippendale" chair, 1984

193 Robert Venturi "Queen Anne" chair, 1984

194 Robert Venturi "Art Deco" chair, 1984

195 Robert Venturi "Sheraton" chair, 1984

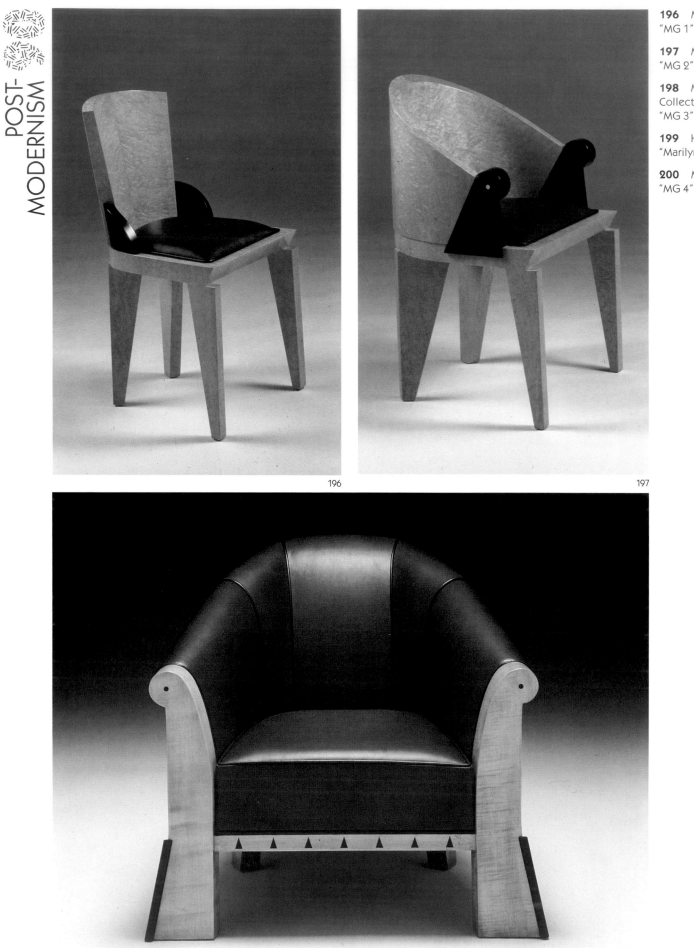

196

197

198

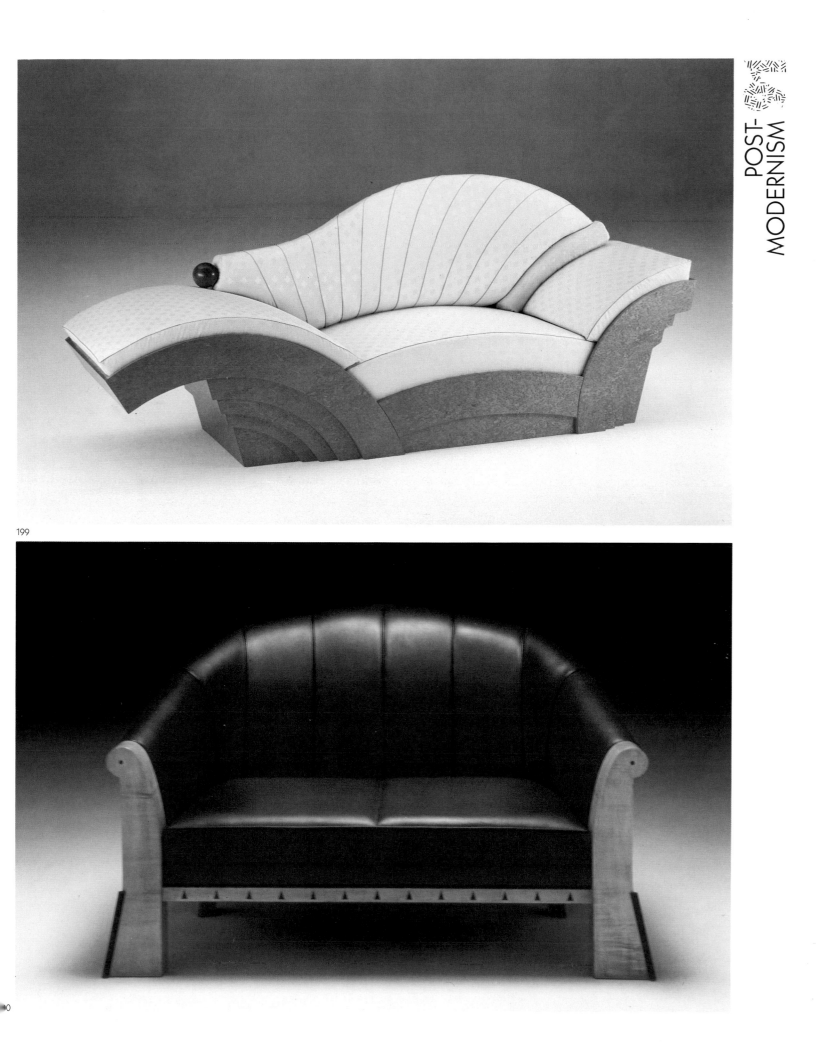

199

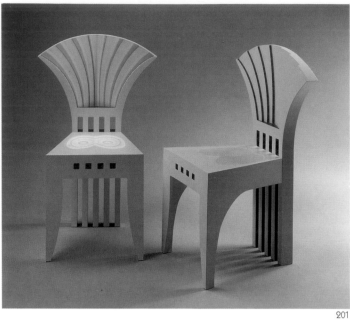

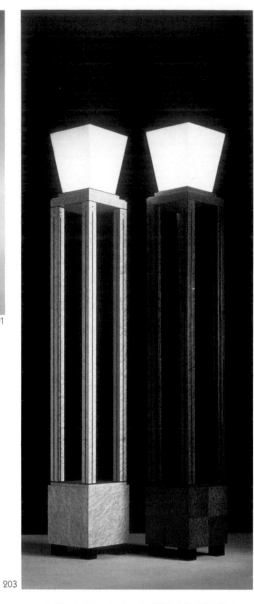

201 Charles Jencks
"Sun Chair", 1985

202 Norbert Berghof,
Michael A. Landes,
Wolfgang Rang
"F 3" chair ("Sternen-
sessel"), 1985/86

203 Michael Graves
"Ingrid" standard-
lamp, 1987

204–206
Norbert Berghof,
Michael A. Landes,
Wolfgang Rang
"F 1" bureau, 1985/86

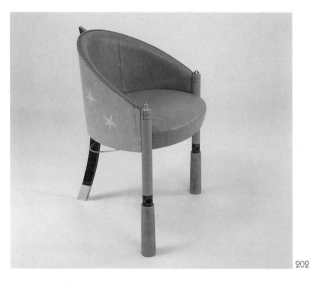

201

202   203

204

205

206

207 Norbert Berghof,
Michael A. Landes,
Wolfgang Rang
"F 2" ("Vertiko")
Frankfurt cupboard,
1986

208 a, b
Norbert Berghof,
Michael A. Landes,
Wolfgang Rang
"F 1" bureau, 1987
(one–off)

209

210

209/210
Norbert Berghof,
Michael A. Landes,
Wolfgang Rang
"F 5" chair and "F 7"
table, 1985/86

211 Frank Gehry
"Little Beaver" armchair,
1980

212 a, b
Stanley Tigerman
"Tête-à-Tête" double
easy-chair, 1983

211

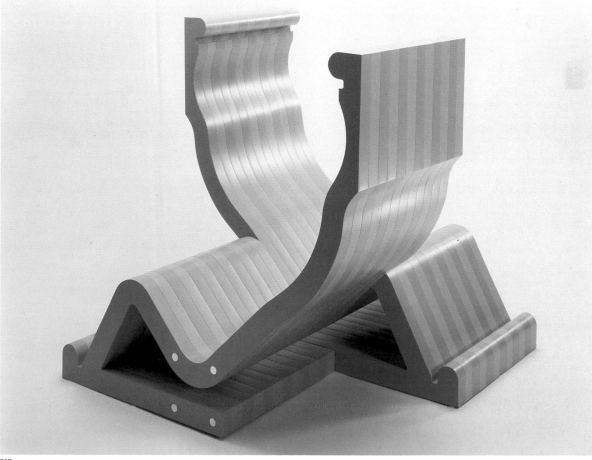

212

213

21

213 Matteo Thun
"Rainer" sofa, 1983

214 Dakota Jackson
Console, 1983

215 a, b SITE
(James Wines and
Alison Sky)
Door, 1983

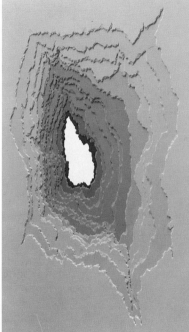

215

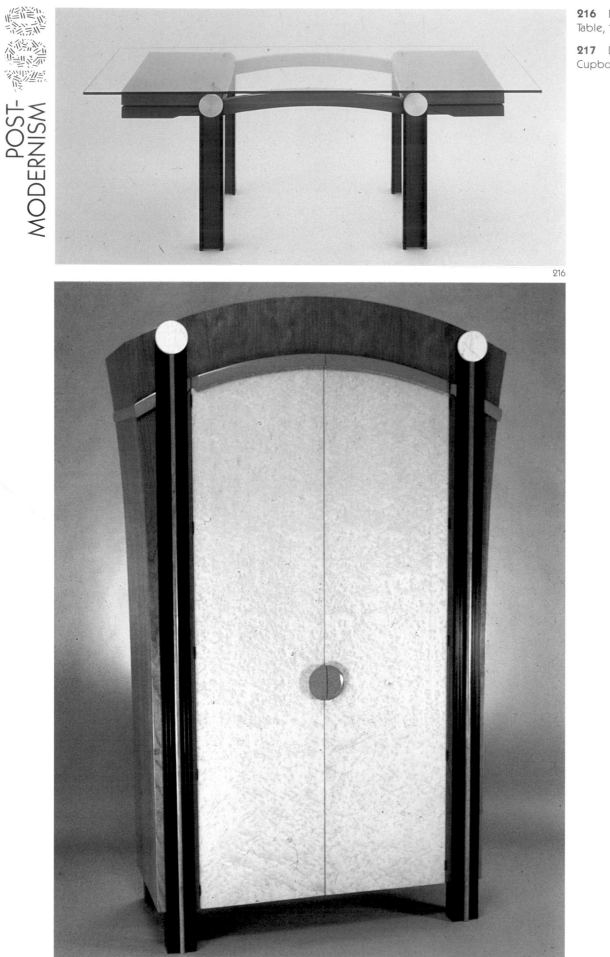

216 Dakota Jackson
Table, 1983

217 Dakota Jackson
Cupboard, 1984

216

217

Minimalist designs are characterised by an extreme aesthetic reductivism. This can best be understood as a reaction against the stylistic languages of Alchimia and Memphis on the one hand and Post-Modernism on the other, with their strong symbolic content often heavily charged with historical allusion. Minimalism is cryptic, with a Calvinist rigour, and its main visual characteristic is the total renunciation of colour. The surfaces of the structural elements are normally either dull black or dull metallic, occasionally silver or gold. The upholstery seldom panders to the anatomy, lacks stuffing, and favours hard surfaces such as rubber knubs. The Zeus group was founded in Milan in 1984, with an international policy not unlike the inaugural strategy of Memphis, but an ideology quite distinct. Like Memphis, Zeus practises design of every sort, not only furniture but also fashion, textiles, graphics and product design. Its guiding light, Maurizio Peregalli, deliberately located the workshops and sales outlet in the traditional crafts quarter of Milan. His production studio, Noto, first became well known for fitting out the shops of the exclusive fashion designer Giorgio Armani. The seating designed for this commission, two armchairs, one with a triangular and one with a quadrilateral seat, two bar stools and an ordinary chair, consciously avoids any element of decoration. It has an elegant modesty which gives visual expression to the desire to go to the very limits of ergonomic friendliness. Not inappropriately, one of the Zeus chairs of maplewood veneer boasts the same "Savonarola" (pl. 231, cf. 230, 232). The square-section metal frame is sprayed grey-black, and the arms are sheathed with very thin rubber as a minimum concession to the user's comfort. The seat, consisting of a rubber knub mat, looks more puritanical than it really is. The Zeus lamps and clothes-stands similarly give the impression of Calvinistic abstraction verging on symbolism (pl. 235, 236).

This approach to design, whose graphic reductivism echoes Far Eastern aesthetics, is also demonstrated by the Japanese designer Shiro Kuramata. A trained architect, he is one of the most important of contemporary designers. His reductive formal language is graphic to the point of rigidity, it expresses a morality of "Less is more", and has an almost immaterial quality. In addition to designs for various Memphis collections, he has furnished the Issey Miyake boutiques in Paris and New York in a manner that complements the clothes. For Capellini he has designed emblematic wave-form cupboards which cite the elegant S curve of High Gothic madonnas in a highly ironic manner; for Kuramata they function as "hidden places of private surprise".[1] They are also reminiscent of Oriental symbolism and the elegance of the terse line of a wave in a Hokusai woodcut. His chair models "Sing Sing Sing" and "Apple Honey" are made of matt finish chromiumplated steel

MINI-MALISM

tubing, as reticent as the Zeus pieces, but more dynamic in form (pl. 233, 234). The self-assured open parabolas of the legs, arms and backrests ironically demonstrate a fascination with the stylistic vocabulary of the fifties, and also with the elegant linearity of classical Japanese painting. Minimalism celebrates geometry as expressive medium and at the same time as aesthetic calculation. Such a combination of abstraction and expression, which deliberately renounces individual artistic gestures, best suits the cool attitudes of career-minded yuppies, for whom aesthetic engagement is a component of "lifestyle", and hardly involves existential connotations. Only attitudes like these can explain the success of the French designer Philippe Starck's objects for interiors. He has been one of the stars of the international design scene ever since he "did" the Café Costés in Paris. The name of his "Ubik" series, which includes the "Costés" chair and its sister, the "Pratfall", comes from the title of one of his favourite science fiction novels, by the American Philipp K. Dick. Almost all the names of the pieces in the series are taken from characters in the book. The elegantly curved wooden shells of the chairs evoke memories of the pretentious form-language of Art Deco, boiled down however to its basic visual skeleton and calculated statics. The elementary character of the metal parts creates a sense of formal tension by subtly contradicting the elegance of the curved wooden back and armrests (pl. 219 a). The "Costés" chair has been remarkably successful in America, Europe and Japan and promises to become one of the design archetypes of the eighties (cf. pl. 47). Most of Philippe Starck's designs are simultaneously marketed in these very different cultures, and thus also represent the concept of the world as global village; the trendy set, be they called "yuppies" or "ultras" or whatever, act and react similarly all over the world. The international fame of these designs so impressed President Mitterand that he invited Stark to furnish both the Élysée palace and his own apartment (pl. 219 b).

The "Von Vogelsang" chair (pl. 225) has a tubular steel frame supporting a concave seat of sheet steel. The rear legs terminate at the level of the seat, this enhances the springiness of the backrest and, more significantly, determines the aesthetic appearance of the whole thing, suggesting a negation of the conventional idea of a chair. The "Sarapis" stool (pl. 224) of square-section steel with a flat seat of steel mesh is given formal and ergonomic sophistication by the spring steel arc that supports the curved rod of the backrest. A stylistic echo is provided by the footrests, curved bars of circular section, but chromium-plated. Two different worlds, two formal concepts meet here. "Mickville" (pl. 223) is a small table which at first impression looks much like Achille Castiglioni's occasional furniture, but it shows its distinctiveness through two crucial features: firstly, the tabletop folds back on its three-legged frame, secondly, the lifting ring is of flat steel. The novelty in the use of material and form may be minimal, but it creates the gripping ambivalence of the design. The "Tippy Jackson" table (pl. 220) is also a folding table, its interest lies in the graphic simplification and structural sophistication of its system of support. A central swivel-joint, not connected to the tabletop, articulates three arc legs, each of slightly differing radius so that they can be folded, and carrying a vertical prop that supports the tabletop. This mechanism strengthens the impression of graphic simplification when the table is folded: it then looks like a minimalist painting by Sol LeWitt. The "Titos Apostos" table uses a similar principle (pl. 221). In contrast to the "Ubik" series, which was designed for the Italian Driade company, Starck's work for the French firm XO, for whom he is art director, often displays zoomorphic traits. The "Dole Melipone" table (pl. 222) and the "Pat Conley No. 1", "Mister Bliss" and "Dr. Sonderbar" chairs (pl. 226 – 228) are distinguished by an impetuous power that is kept

in bounds by formal succinctness. The chairs have the aura of predators lying in wait. The chairs and tables of the "Lang" series (pl. 218, 229), for all their elegance, are equally aggressive. The single supporting chair-leg of steel and the table-legs are reminiscent of shark fins, or of fifties streamlining.

The reductivist renunciation of visual opulence does not necessarily involve any loss of symbolic power, it proclaims the toughness of life in the big city and flourishes on it. There are comparable examples of new rigour in architecture, for instance in the work of Max Dudler, Kollhoff & Ovaska, and Brenner & Tonon.

A neo-modern style, without illusions and nostalgic reminiscences, it appropriately reflects and represents an important facet of present-day life – the Zeitgeist. It is no coincidence that Zeus or Starck furniture reminds one of the archetypal mythical notations and cyphers of contemporary painters such as A. R. Penck. Curious though it may seem, from here, from the ultimate reductivism, the myth is not far removed.

218   Philippe Starck "J" armchair, 1986

219 a   Philippe Starck "Pratfall" armchair, 1982

219 b   Elysée Palace, Paris: François Mitterand's conference room with "Pratfall" chairs

218

219

220

221

220 a, b
Philippe Starck
"Tippy Jackson" table,
1982

221 a, b
Philippe Starck
"Titos Apostos" table,
1985

222 Philippe Starck
"Dole Melipone" table,
1981

223 Philippe Starck
"Mickville" table, 1983

222

223

224

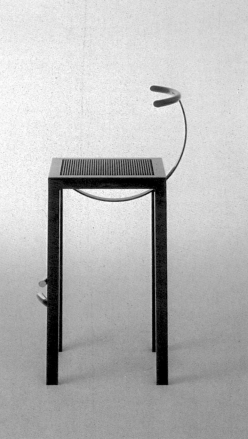

225

224 a, b
Philippe Starck
"Sarapis" stool, 1985

225   Philippe Starck
"Von Vogelsang" chair,
1984

226   Philippe Starck
"Pat Conley No. 1"
armchair, 1983

227

228

227 Philippe Starck "Dr. Sonderbar" chair, 1983

228 Philippe Starck "Mister Bliss" kneeling-stool, 1982

229 Philippe Starck "M" table, 1986

230 Zeus (Maurizio Peregalli) "Poltroncina" chair, 1982

231 Zeus (Maurizio Peregalli) "Savonarola" chair, 1984

232 Abdenego and Anna Anselmi "Sardegna" chair, 1984

233 Shiro Kuramata "Apple Honey" chair, 1986

234 Shiro Kuramata "Sing Sing Sing" armchair, 1986

229

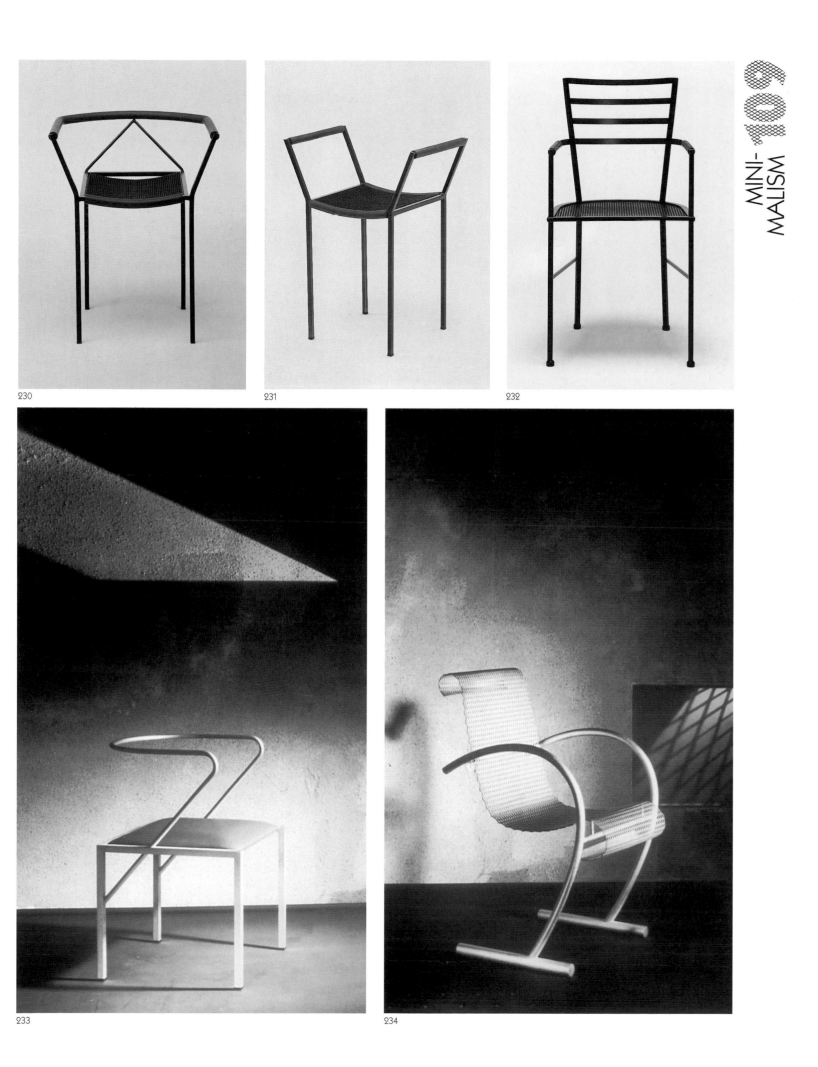

230

231

232

233

234

236

235

235 Zeus
(Roberto Marcatti)
"Arcade" standard-
lamp, 1985

236 Zeus
(Vincenzo Javicoli and
Maria Luisa Rossi)
"Batista" clothes-rack,
1986

ARCHE-TYPES

The variety of objects created by designers to satisfy basic human needs and assist people in their activities has become so vast that one can speak of a cornucopia of choices. Sitting, sleeping, eating, and drinking can nowadays be carried out in, at and with more exciting shapes than probably ever before. No-one who goes shopping for a chair with no set idea of what he wants can escape the impression that there are more varieties of chair than posteriors to place on them. A similar state of affairs exists with beds, tables, lamps, cupboards, cutlery, plates, cups, and glasses. The variety of options available becomes several times greater when one includes all those products fashioned after historical styles. Individual products have ever shorter lives, for objective reasons and with subjective consequences. The consumer society demands and facilitates an ever faster turnover of goods on economic grounds, and design becomes – willingly or reluctantly – its accomplice. In fact, design often plays a crucial role because it can alter the appearance of objects without changing their nature. "This craze [for continually bringing out new models] would naturally be inconceivable without the inherent threat of boredom within an over-consuming capitalist society, where throw-away products with built-in obsolescence encourage the rapid change of fashions; [this is] only possible in wealthy societies which can afford to experience the psychopathology of surfeit."[1] In contrast and indeed in opposition to the kaleidoscope of short-lived styles a longing seems to have arisen for the essence, essentials and longevity of objects, for an aesthetic of forms whose validity is unaffected by the passing of time.[2]

One direction in contemporary interior and product design, allied to similar concepts in architecture, tries to define the basic "primary" form of an object, instead of just producing yet another chair, table, chest or bed according to "arbitrary" criteria. The design is arrived at through analytical research based either on the intrinsic form of the object itself or on the methodical study of particular functions performed with its aid. Stefan Wewerka (q. v.), for instance, studies functions such as "communication at the table" or "sitting as an anthropological constant" and thereby arrives at new formulations of objects. However, in the context of this chapter, the designs of two architects have been more important in setting a style. Oswald Mathias Ungers and Aldo Rossi are leading representatives of European Rationalism whose works have entered architectural history. Referring to his buildings, Ungers speaks of a "thematisation" of architecture, by which he means the attempt to trace the not always obvious interweavings of the social, historical and environmental contexts and then to develop the plan accordingly. Aldo Rossi is more interested in the archetypal images of particular forms and types of buildings; he is concerned with what could, in a sense, be called the anthropological constants and perceptual images of these forms and types, which are firmly rooted in the human conceptual system, beyond all individual and historical variations. As a result, his reductive designs often have a pronounced ascetic air. Convictions of this sort are expressed by Ungers and Rossi in their designs for furniture, and for smaller objects (pl. 252 – 257, 437). The process through which these designs are created is similar to the strategies of structuralist researchers: by eliminating the subjective variations that encrust a theme they seek to uncover the invariable essence of an object. Aldo Rossi's "Cabina dell'Elba" cupboard (pl. 237), despite its Post-Modern colourfulness, is at first reminiscent of a simple hut or sentry-box or, more precisely, a beach hut. It is a form of minimal architecture, not part of the hierarchy of elevated architectural styles, a homely development without artistic or stylistic pretensions. Timber-faced beach huts on these lines are also a leitmotif of Rossi's architectural designs. In all his work, historical concepts are objectified and at the same time transcended by being reduced to their essence. This cupboard, like his other pieces of furniture (chairs, chests-of-drawers, cabinets, pl. 238 – 241), is assembled from basic geometric shapes and produces an overall image which is both historicist and nonhistoricist: the designs are of today and their colours are those of contemporary fashion, but on the other hand they could equally well be from the thirties or an earlier period. They are particularly closely related to the shapes of traditional rural culture, except that they have been "upgraded" by the use of high-quality materials and rigorous proportions. This gives Rossi's objects an aura of classical historicism. They seem, somehow, to be swimming against the current of history, almost as if time had rubbed off on them. They are typical rather than individual pieces, of an almost elemental purity.

Ungers also intends his furniture designs to represent the archetypal validity of certain forms and functions. His furniture programme for the German Architecture Museum in Frankfurt (pl. 242 – 245), developed in conjunction with the Rosenthal company, is notable for its system of dimensions derived from the module of the museum's architecture. One of its main characteristics is the reductivist emphasis on graphic black-and-white contrasts. The basic elements in black beech are counterpoised by the absolutely flat, white leather squares of the seat upholstery and the white surfaces of the tables. The dominant theme is the elementary shape of the square, which gives abundant opportunity for variation, but also important is the scope for arranging the furniture in various schemes within the architectonic space. The series includes bench elements, corner seats, tables, and desks. The chairs, in particular, are not functional from an ergonomic standpoint — they have been described as "bea utifully uncomfortable". They have a rigorous rationality which sets them clearly apart from the self-indulgent and solipsistic "artworks" of contemporary German design. Unger's creations are aesthetic objects deriving from fundamental philosophical convictions; as with Aldo Rossi, the type is emphasised rather than the individual appearance. When the furniture is arranged in groups or rows, its architectonic qualities produce a positively monumental effect, a small-scale version of the spatial structures and ideas of the Architecture Museum itself. Together with the building, the furniture constitutes a *Gesamtkunstwerk*, a "total work of art" that, as Ungers himself claims, stands in the tradition of Frank Lloyd Wright, Mies van der Rohe and Le Corbusier: the symbiosis of architecture and interior design.

More recent designs by Ungers are also indebted to architectonic influences. The "Candelabrum" standard-lamp (pl. 247) with its cubic capital and the "Cabinet Tower" hifi cabinet (pl. 246), designed for the 27th Triennale, give the effect of being small buildings inside a large building. They draw attention to the "interior/exterior" dichotomy; what we see is not always what we expect ("inversion", as it is known in architectural theory); they again demonstrate Unger's predilection for variations on the square. Another recent design is for an eight-part seat programme (pl. 248 – 251), which is reminiscent of the almost immaterial and weightless "Quaderna" table series of the Sixties by the Florentine group Adolfo Natalini and Superstudio. The cubic grid structures which, in various combinations, form the seating surface are however framed by wooden shells in the Ungers version. It also contrasts with the aesthetics of the twenties, when rectilinear leather-covered elements were held in shape by metal tubing, then a new discovery (pl. 12): Ungers expresses his concept through planes and solids set in architectonic opposition. In this series he uses for the first time rounded forms, semicircles and quarter-circles, and oblique angles. The geometric discipline characteristic of these weighty chairs, which in the drawings at least seems almost incongruous in objects of this size, is seen even more clearly in the designs for a new tea and coffee set. The various items (coffee-pot, tea-pot, sugar-bowl, milk-jug, ashtray and tray) are conceived as microarchitecture and result from the summation of basic geometric forms, like Aldo Rossi's espresso coffee-pots (pl. 437, 463). The six pieces of Unger's set are all based on a single scale of proportions, as can be seen from the synoptic diagram (pl. 252).

Knobs, bases, handles and spouts are sharply differentiated in form from the bodies of the objects, in marked contrast to the ideology of functional design; the additive aesthetic creates in fact an aura of coolness and severity. A different application of the same principle can be seen in the "Tea and Coffee Piazzas" of the Alessi company (pl. 435 – 445).

Ungers created his model of the ideal chair as a one-off for himself about fifteen years ago. The stark, cubic throne of natural wood stands in his house in Cologne. When you sit down a door closes in front of you. This is microarchitecture as a sort of second skin. The idea of the body, of man, being enclosed inevitably casts a spotlight on the rituals of leisure, and thus stimulates the re-examination of traditional attitudes. Under this aspect, Ungers is a classicist searching for the eternal rules of life in society. He wants to offer guidance; for some, the path he indicates may seem to be all too straight and narrow, but his designs nevertheless convey a dignity that is more than transient. The creations of Ungers and of Rossi are not subject to the dictate of what is modern or not, they follow a logic which is only at first glance paradoxical, they are both contemporary and timeless.

237 Aldo Rossi
"AR 1" cupboard
("Cabina di Elba"),
1982

238

239

240

238 Aldo Rossi
"AR 2" chair, 1983

239 Aldo Rossi
"AR 3" chest-of-draw-
ers, 1983

240 Aldo Rossi
"AR 6" kitchen cup-
board, 1983

241 Aldo Rossi
"AR 4" tallboy, 1983

242–245 O. M.
Ungers
Chair, table and desk
programme for the Ger-
man Architecture
Museum in Frankfurt,
1982/83

242 Office

243 Exhibition area

244 Exhibition area

245 Lecture room

246 a–d O. M.
Ungers
"Cabinet Tower", 1986
(prototype)

242

243

244

245

247

247 a, b O. M.
Ungers
"Candelabrum" stan-
dard-lamp, 1986

248 O. M. Ungers
Easy-chair No. 1 b,
1987

249 O. M. Ungers
Easy-chair No. 1, 1987

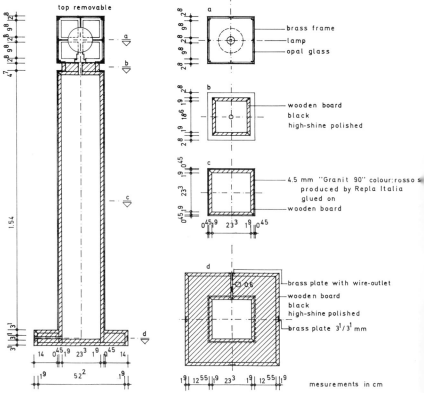

top removable

a
b
c
d

1.54

7

52²

a
brass frame
lamp
opal glass

b
wooden board
black
high-shine polished

c
4.5 mm "Granit 90" colour: rosso s
produced by Repla Italia
glued on
wooden board

d
⌀ 0.6
brass plate with wire-outlet
wooden board
black
high-shine polished
brass plate 3¹/3¹ mm

mesurements in cm

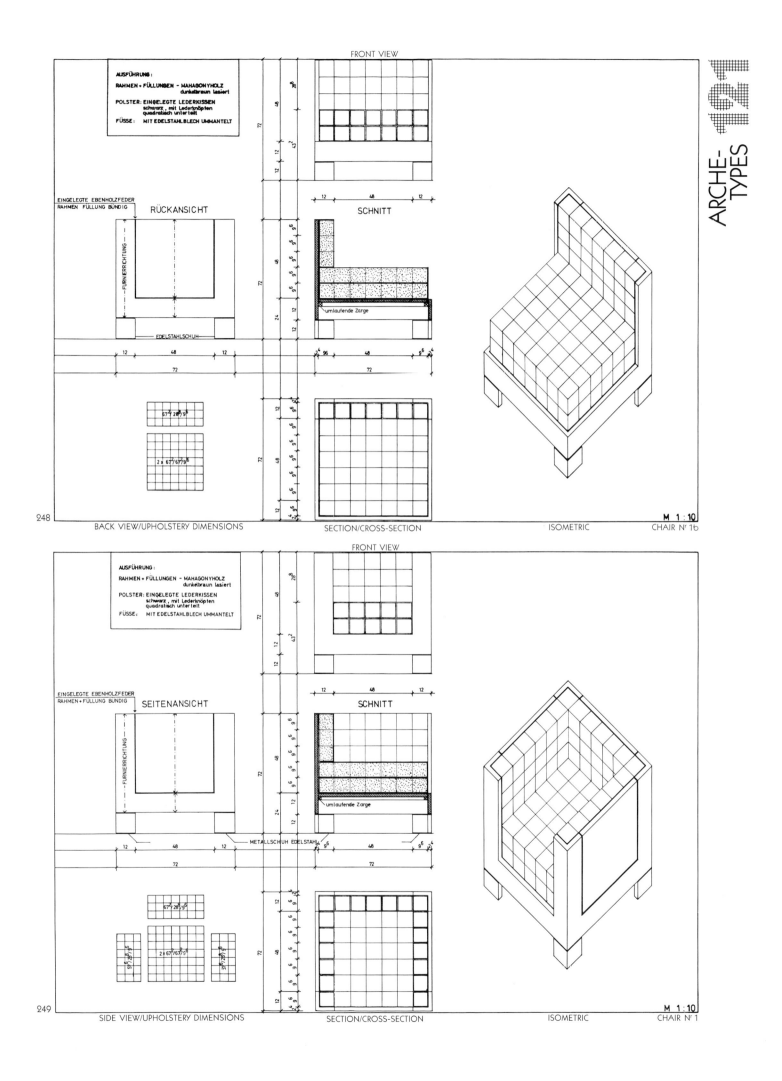

FRONT VIEW

AUSFÜHRUNG :

RAHMEN + FÜLLUNGEN - MAHAGONYHOLZ
dunkelbraun lasiert

POLSTER: EINGELEGTE LEDERKISSEN
schwarz , mit Lederknöpfen
quadratisch unterteilt

FÜSSE :   MIT EDELSTAHLBLECH UMMANTELT

EINGELEGTE EBENHOLZFEDER
RAHMEN FÜLLUNG BÜNDIG

RÜCKANSICHT

SCHNITT

FURNIERRICHTUNG

umlaufende Zarge

EDELSTAHLSCHUH

248   BACK VIEW/UPHOLSTERY DIMENSIONS   SECTION/CROSS-SECTION   ISOMETRIC   **M 1:10**

CHAIR N° 16

FRONT VIEW

AUSFÜHRUNG :

RAHMEN + FÜLLUNGEN - MAHAGONYHOLZ
dunkelbraun lasiert

POLSTER: EINGELEGTE LEDERKISSEN
schwarz , mit Lederknöpfen
quadratisch unterteilt

FÜSSE: MIT EDELSTAHLBLECH UMMANTELT

EINGELEGTE EBENHOLZFEDER
RAHMEN + FÜLLUNG BÜNDIG

SEITENANSICHT

SCHNITT

FURNIERRICHTUNG

umlaufende Zarge

METALLSCHUH EDELSTAHL

249   SIDE VIEW/UPHOLSTERY DIMENSIONS   SECTION/CROSS-SECTION   ISOMETRIC   **M 1:10**

CHAIR N° 1

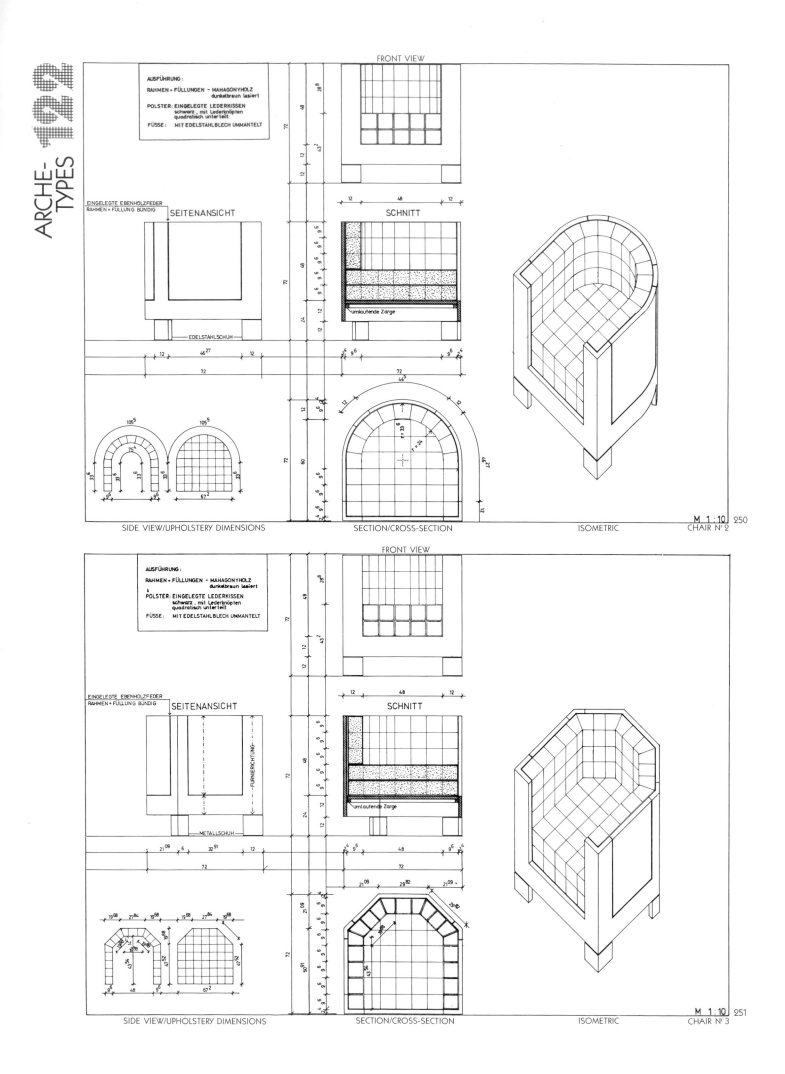

182

AUSFÜHRUNG:

RAHMEN + FÜLLUNGEN - MAHAGONYHOLZ
dunkelbraun lasiert

POLSTER: EINGELEGTE LEDERKISSEN
schwarz , mit Lederknöpfen
quadratisch unterteilt

FÜSSE: MIT EDELSTAHLBLECH UMMANTELT

FRONT VIEW

EINGELEGTE EBENHOLZFEDER
RAHMEN + FÜLLUNG BÜNDIG

SEITENANSICHT

SCHNITT

umlaufende Zarge

EDELSTAHLSCHUH

SIDE VIEW/UPHOLSTERY DIMENSIONS

SECTION/CROSS-SECTION

ISOMETRIC

M 1:10 250

CHAIR Nº 2

AUSFÜHRUNG:

RAHMEN + FÜLLUNGEN - MAHAGONYHOLZ
dunkelbraun lasiert

POLSTER: EINGELEGTE LEDERKISSEN
schwarz , mit Lederknöpfen
quadratisch unterteilt

FÜSSE: MIT EDELSTAHLBLECH UMMANTELT

FRONT VIEW

EINGELEGTE EBENHOLZFEDER
RAHMEN + FÜLLUNG BÜNDIG

SEITENANSICHT

SCHNITT

FURNIERRICHTUNG

umlaufende Zarge

METALLSCHUH

SIDE VIEW/UPHOLSTERY DIMENSIONS

SECTION/CROSS-SECTION

ISOMETRIC

M 1:10 251

CHAIR Nº 3

250 O. M. Ungers
Easy-chair No. 3, 1987

251 O. M. Ungers
Easy-chair No. 2, 1987

252 a, b, c O. M.
Ungers
"Neue Klassik" tea and
coffee service, 1987/88
a: Proportional diagram
of all items
b: Coffee-pot
c: Arrangement on tray

253 O. M. Ungers
Coffee-pot from the
"Neue Klassik" service,
1987/88

254 O. M. Ungers
Teapot from the "Neue
Klassik" service, 1987/
88

255 O. M. Ungers
Sugar-bowl from the
"Neue Klassik" service,
1987/88

256 O. M. Ungers
Milk-jug from the "Neue
Klassik" service, 1987/
88

257 O. M. Ungers
Tray from the "Neue
Klassik" service, 1987/
88

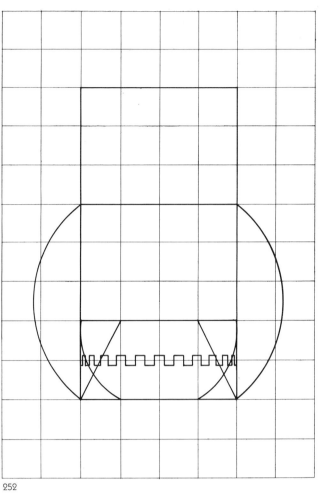

252

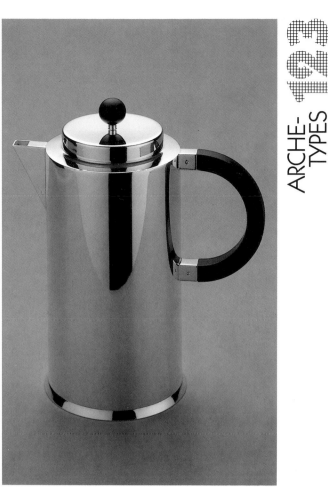

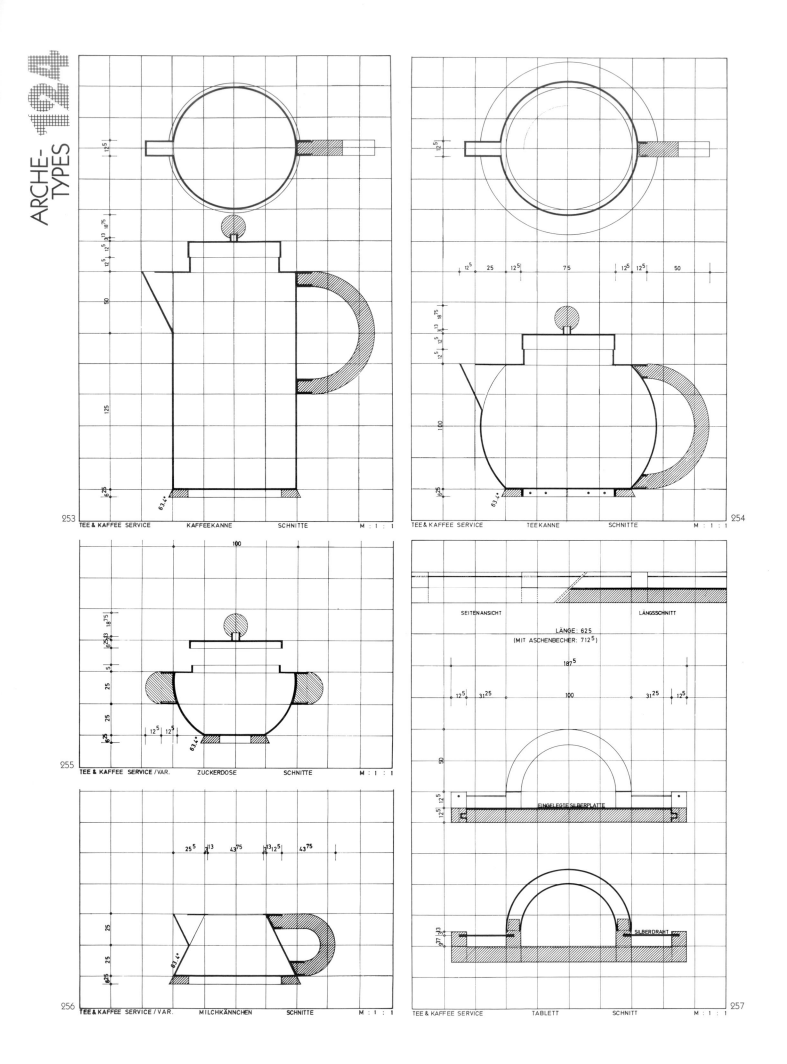

253 TEE & KAFFEE SERVICE   KAFFEEKANNE   SCHNITTE   M : 1 : 1

254 TEE & KAFFEE SERVICE   TEEKANNE   SCHNITTE   M : 1 : 1

255 TEE & KAFFEE SERVICE / VAR.   ZUCKERDOSE   SCHNITTE   M : 1 : 1

256 TEE & KAFFEE SERVICE / VAR.   MILCHKÄNNCHEN   SCHNITTE   M : 1 : 1

257 TEE & KAFFEE SERVICE   TABLETT   SCHNITT   M : 1 : 1

SEITENANSICHT

LÄNGSSCHNITT

LÄNGE: 625
(MIT ASCHENBECHER: 712⁵)

EINGELEGTE SILBERPLATTE

SILBERDRAHT

As a key exponent of Functionalist design Dieter Rams is a hero for the proponents of the philosophy and a bogeyman for its critics. He is a trained architect and interior designer; since 1956 he has been designing electrical appliances for the Braun company and since 1957 furniture ranges for Otto Zapf, who in 1959 joined with Niels Wiese Vitsoe in founding the firm now known under the latter's name. These manufacturers appreciated the importance of quality design as a major element in their commercial strategy even before Rams joined them, so the ground was already prepared for his ideas. Braun's policies of product design had been established in 1953 as a result

DIETER RAMS &

of a survey analysing attitudes to style in the domestic sphere: this analysis indicated the readiness of the market in postwar West Germany to accept functional design of the type associated with the Bauhaus and Ulm schools. Erwin and Artur, the sons of the founder, Max Braun, from whom they had taken over management of the firm in 1951, acted on these findings and were ably assisted by Fritz Eisler, who joined the company in 1953 as head of the design department. Similarly, in Vitsoe and Zapf Rams from the outset found support for his concept of design, whose starting-point was human beings and their everyday needs. It was a belief that society could be improved through the development and mass production of goods for a "better life", based on designs that were functional in the best sense of the word. These designs were usually created in team-work, the product language developed through the analysis, appreciation and extension of the ideas of Hans Gugelot, Wilhelm Wagenfeld and Herbert Hirche, ideas that played a decisive role at the Hochschule für Gestaltung (College of Design) in Ulm.

The Ulm designers saw themselves as the spiritual heirs of the Bauhaus: the ultimate aim of all design at the college was to bring order to the seeming chaos of industrially produced objects, so that their functions and uses would be readily understood by the layman. This was and still is the primary aim of Functionalism, its most important design strategy; it is also the strategy of Dieter Rams. "Good design is the least possible design. Our only real option is to return to simplicity. To leave out everything that is unimportant, and thus to emphasise what is important, is for me one of the crucial principles of design: simplification in every respect." The statement reveals both the fascination and the problems of this classic Functionalist approach. The "simplicity" of which Rams speaks is here justified on moral grounds, in the Bauhaus and Ulm tradition. What is "unimportant" is decided by the designer alone or by the design team, not by the user for whom the object is after all intended; this traditional philosophy sounds somewhat arrogant in the light of more recent attitudes.

Rams has designed about five hundred products in the thirty years or so that he has been working for Braun and Vitsoe. They have grown into a stylistic continuum which, subjectively and objectively, is probably unique in the world of product ranges and corporate images. Rams and his colleagues know that however demanding the objective criteria of an industrial design there is always room for the personal touch.[1] However, a recognisable personal style in the design of a technical product is only permissible for Rams when it improves the functional qualities of the object, and not when, as so often, it merely enhances the aesthetics; the first duty of design is to organise and define an object in such a way as to optimise its usefulness.

Exhibitions and publications the world over have paid homage to the work of Dieter Rams and his team, acknowledging its creative quality and the unity of its stylistic continuum. An informative monograph on Rams was published in 1980 on the occasion of an exhibition at the International Design Centre, Berlin.[2] The book, like the exhibition, was designed on the classical principles of the Modern Movement: it is a small, black, almost square book containing series of black-and-white photographs of the products with captions in classical Bauhaus sans-serif typography and hardly any sketches or drawings. More recent publications, however, reveal a change in attitude to these allegedly "timeless" designs. The scene-and-style magazine *instant*, which has been appearing in Frankfurt and Wiesbaden for the past few years in the opulent format of Andy Warhol's *Interview*, published a Rams special issue in which the sequences of Rams objects were enlivened by double-page spreads featuring mannequins. This sort of presentation treats Rams's designs as part of the world of "camp", raising them almost to the status of cult objects.

It is not surprising that there are now exchange marts for collectors to swap and complete their collections of old Braun products, and a fan magazine to further this cause.[3] Rams's designs paradigmatically reflect, or are supposed to reflect, the very essence of Modernism, a concept of timeless validity. Could it be that Modernism will itself end up as an antique? Is it getting dusty?

The designer himself would prefer to remain modestly in the background, but he has nevertheless probably influenced the visual awareness of the postwar generation to a greater degree than anyone else. Numerous honours have come his way. In 1987, for example, the exhibition "German Design" was opened at the Science Museum in London in the presence of the Duke of Edinburgh; to coincide with this the German Foreign Office produced a film about Rams, which was distributed to Goethe Institutes (the German cultural centres) world-wide; the government thus helps to promote Functionalist designs as part of the national heritage. Rams is also one of the few German designers to have been made an honorary fellow of the Royal Society of Arts.

The continuity of his design strategy means that Rams sees his creations as evolving within the context of a long-term programme. He seeks to foster the idea of product "families", wherein several items are related to one another, and the set is completed over a period of years. In this respect he did not just anticipate the "system" concept of the hifi and computer industries, he was one of the prime movers. Thus, the ultimate goal of "compatibility" characterises both Braun radios, shavers, clocks and kitchen appliances and Vitsoe chairs and cupboards. It is certainly no coincidence that in the course of time the Braun product range has become more clearly defined, rationalised, and concentrated. Optical apparatus, for instance, such as slide projectors, flash attachments and cameras, is no longer manufactured; and the entire hifi sector was transferred in 1981 to the a/d/s (Analog and Digital Systems) company. The Braun design studio however remains responsible for the design of all new audio equipment for Braun and a/d/s.

It is striking, as a glance at Dieter Rams's work will show, how many of his ideas anticipate what other designers and manufacturers, not only in Germany, have since taken up. Krups, Rowenta, Siemens, Phillips, Wega and Telefunken have all profited from the product idiom evolved for Braun. Of course, even Rams's designs are influenced by the period in which they originate, the *Zeitgeist* of a particular decade. For instance, Rams products of the fifties and sixties – gramophone/radio combinations, radiogrammes, short-wave receivers and portables – feature wooden elements in the casing, like other products of the era: the loudspeakers have fabric coverings, the portables have the typical plastic straps of the period (pl. 264). But even just the names were already an indication of a different mentality: the Braun radios of the fifties were not christened "Granada" or "Caprice" in the prevailing fashion, they were simply and unpretentiously called "Exporter 2", "TP 1", "T 4", "T 41" or "atelier 1/2/3". The arrangement of the controls is precise but reticent, the effect is of a carefully balanced compromise between aesthetics and logic, or rather, the aesthetics result from an inner logic. In the late fifties, there were still a lot of prewar wireless sets, or later variations of the same type, in use in Germany and other European countries, except perhaps Scandinavia. The painter Richard Hamilton, one of the founders of Pop Art, recalls: "In 1958, while visiting the College of Design in Ulm, I first saw the work of Dieter Rams. The envy I felt when in nearly all the student's rooms I entered I found the extraordinarily elegant Braun radio/record-player became a lasting memory, which I took back with me to London. This 'Phonosuper' (pl. 261) was the ubiquitous symbol of the aims of the school – a futuristic example of very well made, user-friendly design. The fact that it was actually in production filled the students with confidence in the 'brave new world' that they were learning to create."[4]

The "CE 11" tuner of 1959 and its successor in the Studio 2 range (pl. 263) have visible securing screws on the front fascia, and the tuning knobs are larger than necessary; in this respect they represent more than pure ergonomic necessity, they are symbols of turning and touching. They articulate the fascia graphically in a way that is reminiscent of the Concrete Art of the period (such as the paintings of Lohse, Albers, Vasarely, and Geiger). The function of the object is always shown "truthfully", without disguise or ornament, embellishment or frills. The design is structured by the functional components – it seems the natural solution – and not by elements which have nothing to do with function. The "Phonosuper SK 4" (pl. 261), a compact radio/record-player, was a pioneer of this approach and also one of its early successes. Designed by Rams in association with Hans Gugelot in 1956, it has an integral loudspeaker and a horizontal control panel. Originally, the hinged cover was to have been of metal, but then transparent plastic was chosen because of vibration; this gave the unit its nickname "Snow-White's Coffin", and made it one of the most publicised technical objects ever.

Rams's designs were often ahead of their time, or at least ahead of mainstream developments. With conventional fifties objects "one thought of an idyllic, wholesome world, but in the case of the "SK 1" [designed in 1954 by Dr. Eicheler and Artur Braun] there was no 'painted face' to mask the technical features. It had no round or oval shapes, no 'magic eye' loudspeaker-covering of fabric and golden thread, no braiding, no ornamental mouldings, no walnut, no ivory-coloured toggle switches. Instead there were rectangular, stark-edged forms, light-coloured wood, light-coloured plastic, glass and perspex, with grilles, holes and slits. The practical functions of the equipment were no longer concealed, it was as if the living-room had become an operations room. The colours were mainly light and unassuming, unusual too in their combination – white, pale grey and grey: the lightweight materials used throughout contributed to the general aura of the design, and combined with the sleekness of the contours to suggest the self-confidence of a fresh start. Forms were beginning to free themselves, the search for a new identity rejected not only the traditionalism of German oak but also the new German trend towards soft, mellifluent contours – the kidney-shaped table, the 'fried egg' look."[5]

Such a description would be equally apt for the products of the sixties, for in that decade too petty bourgeois values and reactionary narrow-mindedness were far more typical of the Federal Republic of Germany than democratic tolerance and cosmopolitanism. "Softline" was now the watchword, as in the "D 40" slide projector (pl. 268). The "T 1000" (pl. 267) became the epitome of portable radios: its aerials were longer, and projected optimistically upward, as if to proclaim the self-assuredness of the resurgent nation. Because of its almost unlimited reception range, above all in the short-wave bands, it was the first radio to be termed a "world-wide" receiver, but it was also the last portable made by Braun, because Hong Kong and Japan were now beginning to capture this market. Other impressive products of the decade include the "FS 80" television of 1964 (pl. 275), which already anticipated such widely adopted features as the screen curving out from the casing and the splayed foot pedestal. There was also the "CSV 250" amplifier of 1966 (pl. 274), and the "T 2/TFG 2" table lighter of 1968 (pl. 278), a perfect example of Rams's economy of form: it is heavy, prestigious, and plain. Not only is the body of the object a cylinder, but the only other formal component, the push-button, gives the impression of having been carved out of this same monolithic block – an additional formal element is thus dispensed with. When the push-button is pressed it clicks home with the satisfying clunk of a Rolls-Royce door to trigger the flame, which appears on the upper surface like a magic pearl.

The first product of the next decade, the "TG 1000/1020" tape recorder of 1970 (pl. 280, 281), represents a new trend in body design with a change of colour from white or light grey to matt black (pl. 282, 283, 286, 290, 291). The functional clarity which distinguishes the casings and control panels of Braun products was becoming ever more perfect. The first large-scale retrospective exhibition of Braun design, "Form – nicht konform" (Form – Not Conformist), was held at the Darmstadt Institute for New Technical Form in 1976, after twenty years of continuous development of the company's design policy. Previously there had been an exhibition at the Louvre in 1963, participation in the third "Documenta" in Kassel in the same year, and in the thirteenth Triennale in Milan in 1964. There had also been a travelling exhibition which started in Tokyo in 1965.

One of the favourite themes of Rams's design policy has been the possibilities of combination and compatibility. Thanks to hifi technology and other advances in manufacturing techniques, what had been disparate pieces of equipment could now be designed as modules of a series. The softline aesthetic, a consequence of the thermoplastic moulding technique, prevailed until the mid-seventies: a typical feature is the lectern-like inclination of the display panel on the "Cockpit" radio/record-player (pl. 283, cf. pl. 286, 290). This is however something of a hindrance for the stacking of compatible units, and the flat slab contour now began to dominate the field; loudspeakers were also becoming more and more compact. The "RS 1" integrated audio system of 1977 (pl. 291) was designed together with Peter Hartwein, who from about 1980 onward assumed overall responsibility for the audio range. It exemplifies the sharpness of outline and frontal deployment of controls characteristic of seventies audio systems. These features were anticipated as early as 1962 in the "Audio" system, whose units could be combined horizontally or vertically, wall-hung or free-standing. The household equipment produced by Braun, such as coffee-makers, mixers, fan heaters, can-openers (pl. 288), hotplates, lemon-squeezers (pl. 287), toasters, and table grills, comprises as wide a range as the audio equipment. The various

items of this range are seldom designed by Rams himself in detail, although he has to give his imprimatur. The underlying philosophy is always instantly recognisable, as for instance in the "Aromaster" coffee-maker of 1987 (pl. 292) or the "Vario 6000" lightweight electric iron of 1987 (pl. 293): "The basic idea of the functional approach has always been to rise above all 'styles' and let the design be determined primarily by the practical realities of use."[6] Sometimes, however, – and why not, indeed? – the details of the designs seem positively exuberant, charged with associations, verging on the Post-Modern. The most recent coffee-maker of the "Aromaster" series, the "KF 40" of 1987, gives the impression of a compact fluted column. This results from the water reservoir being designed as a cylinder, into which a second cylindrical shape (consisting of the coffee-pot, filter and hotplate) is half inserted, creating in plan two overlapping circles (pl. 292 c). Moreover, the filter-holder swings out on an unexpected axis, while alongside the fluted body the handle of the pot looks like that of a petrol-pump (pl. 292 d). Although the designer, Hartwig Kahlcke, describes the handle in typical terms of Braun philosophy, his reasoning is Post-Modern: "Formally, the handle of the glass coffee-pot derives from the circle, which is the basic structural element of the machine. Although it may not at first sight look it, this shape – together with the inner divider which improves the grip – is also optimal from the haptic and ergonomic viewpoint."[7] Mateo Thun might have put it the same way. And talking of ergonomics, we should mention that the fluted cylinder contains a cable-tidy into which the flex disappears.

On the other hand, Dieter Rams himself was principally responsible for the look of the Braun clocks and pocket calculators, certainly between 1970 and 1980 (pl. 286, cf. pl. 294 – 299), he was adviser and co-ordinator for the electric shavers. The dominant colour in these groups of products is now also matt black. A modern electric shaver is a very complex affair (pl. 300, 302 – 305); there is hardly any room here for creativity or spontaneity, although Rams has explained that the idea for the soft plastic studs on the casing, to provide a secure grip, was borrowed from ski-boot soles. To keep pace with changing fashions, a beard-trimmer has also been developed (pl. 301).

Electric shavers are one of Braun's oldest lines. They were developed before the war, and in 1950 Braun launched the "S 50", the first electric razor with a flexible, tissue-paper-thin cutting foil, an oscillating block and armature. The triumphal march of Braun shavers really began in 1962 with the "Sixtant" designed by Müller and Gugelot (pl. 270), with its state-of-the-art cutting mechanism. The matt black model remained in production for eight years practically unaltered, and continued to be marketed with technical modifications, but under the same name, until 1979; only then was it superseded by the "Micron" range. Such durable products, which do not need to be replaced so often, are very rare in a world where consumer goods have increasingly shorter lives.

The changing concepts of design have not passed Braun by without making their mark. This is evident from some unexpected combinations of equipment as well as from some surprising innovations, not just on the technical side. Recently, Braun combined a hair-dryer with a travelling iron (pl. 306); the "Voice Control" alarm-clock can be turned off by verbal command (pl. 295, 296). Poetic and imaginative features have forced their way into these examples of a Functionalism which is allegedly so rational. The predilection for matt black in the clocks, calculators, shavers, lighters and audio equipment is sometimes enlivened by coloured control knobs and buttons, which provide a psychological trigger function. As Rams has said: "It must be made much more obvious that a product also has 'psychological' functions. It must explain itself and be easily understandable by virtue of its design and graphic structure, and it must fit in with the individual environment of the user."[8] The latest models in the "Atelier" range are available in a "crystal grey" finish, no doubt as a sop to the yuppies, for whom a free-standing matt black tower would be too sombre and a white one too optimistic (pl. 307, cf. pl. 308, 309). Is this a return to the "fiery mouse-grey" of the Ulm school?

With pocket calculators, exhaustive trials have helped to optimise the ergonomics of operation, starting from the fundamental question of whether the keys should be convex or concave. Keeping pace with advances in the miniaturisation of internal workings, Braun now markets a solar-powered model the size of a cheque card and just as thin, like its cheap rivals from Hong Kong and Japan (pl. 299). There is a small but crucial difference: the Braun calculator costs twenty times as much. However, there are many who are prepared to pay the higher price in order to possess a Braun product: not only is it much better technically, but you are buying "design" and not just a gadget that functions perfectly.

Dieter Rams's designs for the furniture-makers Wiese Vitsoe are, like those for Braun, part of a long-term concept. According to Niels Wiese Vitsoe, he and Otto Zapf founded the company expressly to manufacture Rams-designed furniture, and they gave him a free hand from the start. Rams has formulated some of his principles of interior design: "My furniture should not be symbols of prestige or status. I want to make things that are unobtrusive, furniture that leaves room and does not dominate its surroundings. It should fit well and appropriately into whatever the user has chosen for his own individual surroundings. Actually, it should be 'visible' as little as possible."[9] These are the same principles as underly the designs for Braun. Rams also applies his concept of functions to furniture: "The furniture I design is usable furniture. It must, in the first place, fulfil a function. Function, especially in regard to furniture, I understand in the broadest sense of the word – including its psychological dimensions. For me, design is not just the fashioning of an external form, much less a component added in the final stages. Design

is for people. It must be ergonomically correct, that is, it must be attuned to man's abilities, scale of dimensions, senses, and power of comprehension. Since my work is concerned with utility, I have tried over the years to improve my understanding of the multiple processes that constitute use: how a cupboard, a shelf, a chair is used, for instance, how furniture should admit of being moved around, how various items can harmonise with and complement each other. I try to systematise my designs so that they will enhance utility. This system must be as simple, logical and transparent as possible, so that anyone can understand it."[10]

In some thirty years Rams has designed thirteen programmes for Vitsoe, which however constitute a coherent product family in ergonomic, technological, visual and aesthetic terms. He began with the "570" range of tables and the "571/572" wall-cupboard assembly system (pl. 310); both designs date from 1957 and are still in production. Visually, at least, they have hardly changed, although some technical features like nuts, bolts and braces have been improved. In 1960 followed a shelving system ((pl. 312), a cloakroom concept (pl. 313), and the "601/602" two-legged chairs on runners (pl. 34, 311). These, along with the "620" armchair, can be seen in museum collections, and have won many design prizes. The "620" model (pl. 36, 314) was given copyright protection by the West German supreme court in 1973, an almost unique distinction for a furniture design, the only other case to date being the "free-swinging" chair by Mart Stam (now manufactured by Thonet) (pl. 14). The court's judgement of the Rams armchair held: "The design of this chair is a personal, intellectual creation of high aesthetic content."[11] A solid wooden frame with a sprung core and side and rear panels moulded in fibreglass-reinforced polyester support the seat and back cushions. The concept is flexible, and the basic armchair in its high- or low-back version can be adapted to form rows or sofas, or be combined with a footstool (pl. 314 b); a swivel base is optional. With the aid of quarter-circle side-tables the chairs can be arranged to form a rounded square. Although the aesthetics of the moulded polyester panels clearly point to the sixties origin of this design, the chair has an almost timeless validity; in retrospect, it is one of the "theme images" of the interior design of its decade.

Subsequent programmes included reclining chairs and shallower armchairs, roll-fronted desks, a cupboard system with slat-built sliding doors adaptable to virtually any wall surface (pl. 315); and tables (pl. 316, 318). A range of chairs designed in 1986 in association with Jürgen Greubel (pl. 317) is intended for both public and private environments. Overall, Rams has consistently worked to create a coherent range of tables, chairs, beds, armchairs, cupboards – the archetypal furniture of mankind. "I have had the good fortune to find in Niels Wiese Vitsoe a manufacturer with whom I have been able to work continuously since the establishment of the firm in 1959. Company and designs have developed together... There are probably not more than a dozen firms worldwide who have an attitude to their products that I could go along with."[12] Rams's work as a whole illustrates his unwavering loyalty to forms once discovered. Modifications are made only after painstaking attention to points of detail. These modifications are often so discreet that a product may look practically unchanged for years, as in the case of the Braun "Sixtant" and the "570" table programme. On the occasion of the exhibition of his work in Berlin, a critic wrote: "[Rams takes] a sceptical attitude to all speculative thinking... He obviously realises that before all the possibilities of the present have been exhausted the next step may not be taken. He would presumably not approve of the discussion of ideas that go beyond what is feasible. It would probably be a fair assumption to say that the driving force that makes his pragmatic work so successful derives from his silence on speculative matters... Rams's utopia, as far as the visible work is concerned, is no more than an exact description of contemporary reality. By making this description as precise as possible, he paves the way for future developments."[13]

Abstinence from utopian thinking is for Rams both a strength and a weakness. He has often produced designs which were not viable for technical or economic reasons. Presumably, Rams has never considered making an issue of it with the management; he is after all one of the few designers in Germany at least to have worked their way into the boardroom. Nor has he ever been tempted to produce "counter-designs" for rival firms. He has never thought of himself as an "artist" or an autonomous creative agent, but always as part of a complex set of interwoven relationships within the strategy of a company. He has often been criticised for this "conformist" attitude by successive generations of students and critics, as the reaction against Functionalism gathered momentum. But it is the one attitude that allows a designer to play a decisive role in the creation of a company's corporate identity in the long run. The patience and steadfastness with which Rams goes about making subtle improvements to existing forms is

perhaps his most impressive characteristic. Such almost self-effacing pertinacity lacks the pathos of showy and strident novelty: products designed by Dieter Rams just wait quietly to be used. The aim of design, as Erwin Braun once put it, can be compared with the virtues of an English butler, a model of courteous, almost imperceptible attentiveness. The discreetness of the products is their ergonomic and aesthetic forte. But in order for us to have a vivid picture in our minds of the world of goods which surrounds us, there must be not only unpretentiousness and reticence, but also their opposites. Only an awareness of the multiplicity of the various tendencies and points of view in design can enable us to make a conscious choice of styles. Although Functionalists like Dieter Rams have always denied it, Functionalism has become one style among many others. It is rightly to be seen as an important component of the total palette of expressive possibilities, but to regard it as the one and only way to meet all human needs for form and design smacks of arrogance and presumption, of cultural monopoly. Referring no doubt to Memphis and its aftermath, Rams once said: "[All Braun designers have] an aversion to products which make themselves too important... Utility objects are there to be used, and should not get ideas above their station. They should recede into the background when not in use and give man room to create his own individual, self-determined and vital environment. They are neither work of art nor cult object, neither status symbol nor background decoration."[14] Such verdicts are especially problematic in the light of more recent schools of thought. Is it not important for the vitality of an environment that people should surround themselves with objects of daily use? What actually is the objection to a chair or a lamp being also a status symbol or a work of art?

In the face of such a categoric denial of the cultic power of household objects, it is a rather ironic symptom of changing attitudes that it should be the early Braun products that have become cult objects for collectors. They are now a part of the cultural heritage – status symbols and works of art, in fact.

258 Re-Design HFG Ulm – Braun Produktgestaltung "Exporter 2" radio, 1955

259 Braun Produktgestaltung (Dieter Rams) "LO2" loudspeaker, 1958

260 Braun Produktgestaltung (Dieter Rams) "atelier 1/2/3" radio, 1957 and "L 2" loudspeaker, 1958

261 Braun Produktgestaltung (Hans Gugelot, Dieter Rams) "SK 4" radio and record-player ("Phonosuper"), 1956

264 Braun Produktgestaltung (Dieter Rams) "TP 1 Phonokombination" with "T 4" pocket receiver, 1959

262 Braun Produktgestaltung (Dieter Rams) "EF 2" flash attachment, 1958

263 Braun Produktgestaltung (Dieter Rams) "CE 11" radio, 1959 (later stereo version)

265 Braun Produktgestaltung (Dieter Rams) "T 41" pocket receiver, 1959

266 Braun Produktgestaltung (Dieter Rams) "H 1/H 2" fan heater, 1959

258

259

260

262

261

263

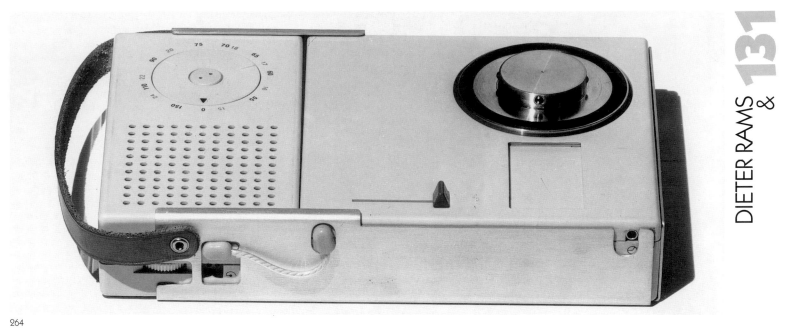

264

265

266

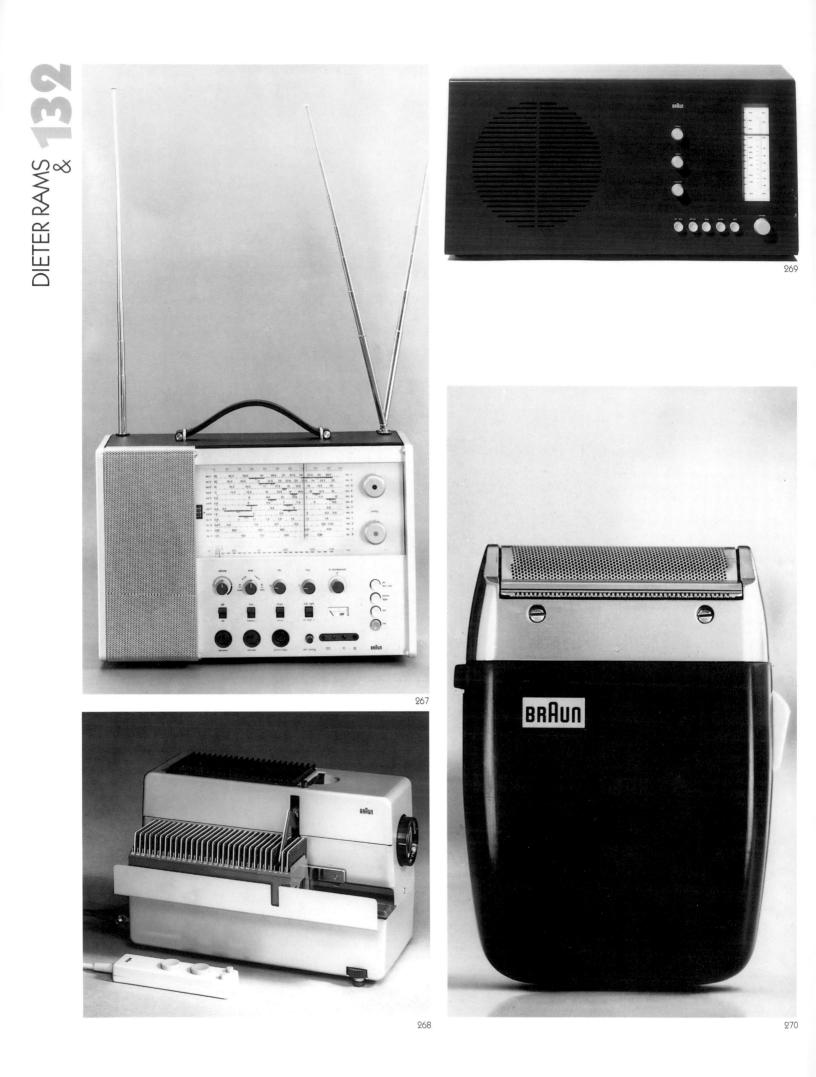

267

268

269

270

267 Braun Produkt-
gestaltung
(Dieter Rams)
"T 1000" short-wave
receiver, 1962

268 Braun Produkt-
gestaltung
(Dieter Rams)
Remote-control slide
projector, 1961

269 Braun Produkt-
gestaltung
(Dieter Rams)
"RT 20" radio ("Tisch-
super"), 1961

270 Braun Produkt-
gestaltung
(Alfred Müller,
Hans Gugelot)
"Sixtant" mains shaver,
1962

271 Braun Produkt-
gestaltung
(Dieter Rams)
"TG 60" tape-recorder,
1963

272 Braun Produkt-
gestaltung
(Dieter Rams)
"TS 45" control unit,
1965

273 Braun Produkt-
gestaltung
(Dieter Rams)
"CE 500" tuner, 1966

274 Braun Produkt-
gestaltung
(Dieter Rams)
"CSV 250" amplifier,
1966

271

272

273

274

275

276

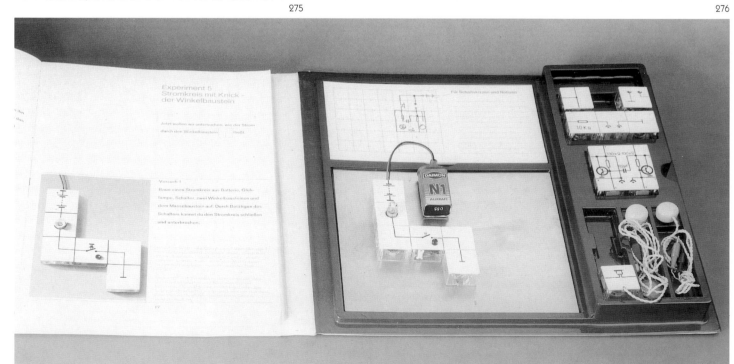

277

275 Braun Produkt-
gestaltung
(Dieter Rams)
"FS 80" television set,
1964

276 Braun Produkt-
gestaltung
(Dieter Rams)
"FS 1000" television set,
1967

277 Braun Produkt-
gestaltung
(Dieter Rams,
Jürgen Greubel)
"Lectron" experimental
and learning system,
1967

278 Braun Produkt-
gestaltung
(Dieter Rams)
"T 2/TFG 2" table lighter,
1968

279 Braun Produkt-
gestaltung
(Dieter Rams)
"KMM 2" coffee-grin-
der, 1969

280 Braun Produkt-
gestaltung
(Dieter Rams)
"TG 1000" tape-record-
er, 1970

278

279

280

281

282

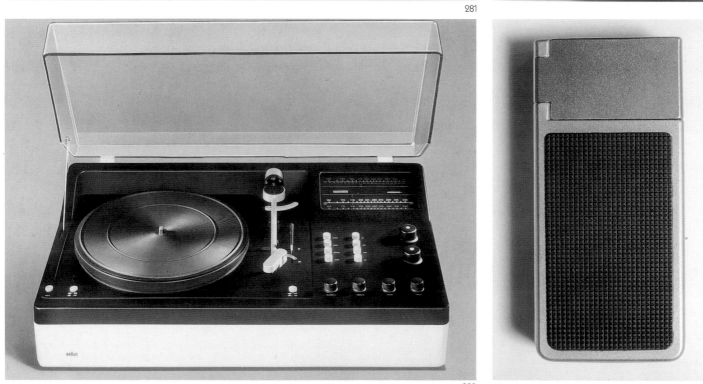

283

284

285

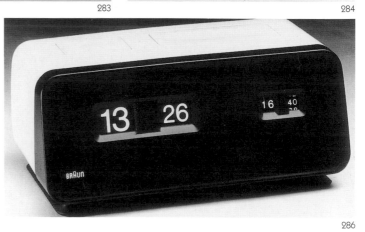

286

281 Braun Produkt-gestaltung (Dieter Rams) "TG 1020" tape-recorder, 1970

282 Braun Produkt-gestaltung (Dieter Rams) "F 111" flash attachment ("hobby"), 1970

283 Braun Produkt-gestaltung (Dieter Rams) "Cockpit 250/260" record-player with radio, 1970

284 Braun Produkt-gestaltung (Dieter Rams) "Mactron F 1 Linear" lighter, 1971

285 Braun Produkt-gestaltung (Dieter Rams) "HLD 4" hair-dryer, 1970

286 Braun Produkt-gestaltung (Dieter Rams) "Phase 1" alarm-clock, 1971

287 Braun Pro-duktgestaltung (Dieter Rams, Jürgen Greubel) "MPZ 2" lemon-squeezer, 1972

288 Braun Produkt-gestaltung (Dieter Rams, Jürgen Greubel) "DS 1" tin-opener, 1972

289 Braun Produkt-gestaltung (Dieter Rams, Florian Seiffert, Robert Oberheim, Peter Hartwein) "Sixtant 8008" mains shaver, 1973

290 Braun Produkt-gestaltung (Dieter Rams) "Regie 308" radio, 1973

291 Braun Pro-duktgestaltung (Dieter Rams, Peter Hartwein) "RS 1" studio system, 1977

287

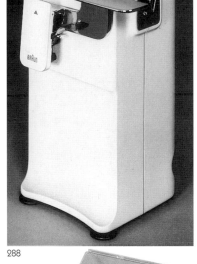

288

289

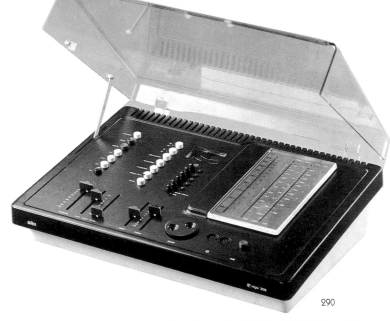

290

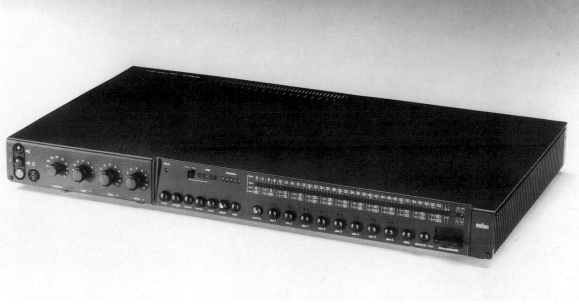

291

292 a–d
Braun Produktgestaltung (Hartwig Kahlcke) "Aromaster 10 KF 40" coffee-maker, 1987

292 e Braun Produktgestaltung (Hartwig Kahlcke) "Aromaster 10-plus KF 45" coffee-maker, 1987

293 Braun Produktgestaltung (Ludwig Littmann) "Vario 6000" lightweight iron, 1987

294

295

296

297

294 Braun Produkt-gestaltung (Dietrich Lubs) "quartz ABW 30" bat-tery wall-clock, 1983

295 Braun Produkt-gestaltung (Dietrich Lubs) "voice control AB 312 vsl" battery alarm-clock, 1985

296 Braun Produkt-gestaltung (Dietrich Lubs) "voice control AB 45 vsl" battery alarm-clock, 1984

297 Braun Produkt-gestaltung (Dietrich Lubs) "quartz AB 46–24 h" mains and battery alarm-clock, 1985

298 Braun Produkt-gestaltung (Dieter Rams, Dietrich Lubs) "control ET 55" pocket calculator, 1981

299 Braun Produkt-gestaltung (Dietrich Lubs) "Solar card ST 1" cheque-card pocket calculator, 1987

298

299

300

301

302

303

300 a, 302–305
Braun Produktgestaltung (Roland Ullmann)
"micron vario 3" electric shaver, 1987

300 b Braun Produktgestaltung
Design studies for the "micron vario 3" electric shaver, 1987

301 Braun Produktgestaltung (Roland Ullmann)
"exact universal" beard-trimmer, 1986

306 Braun Produktgestaltung (Robert Oberheim)
"Silencio travel-combi PI 1200", 1987

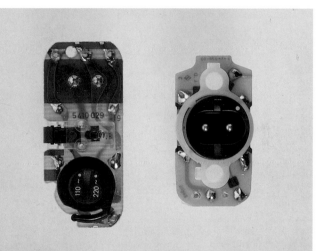

304

305

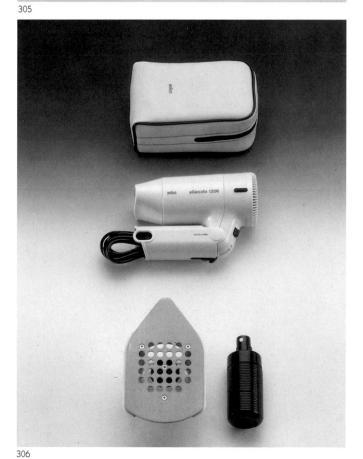

306

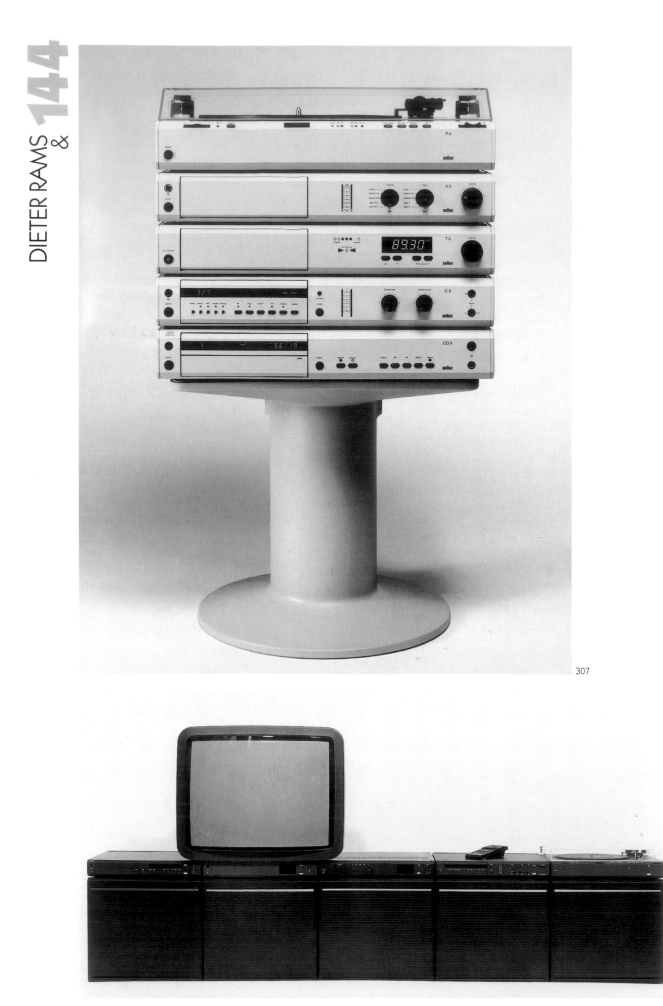

307 Braun Produkt-
gestaltung
(Peter Hartwein,
Dieter Rams)
"Atelier" hi-fi stack (on
disc pedestal), 1987

308, 309 Braun Pro-
duktgestaltung
(Peter Hartwein,
Dieter Rams)
"Atelier" TV stack, 1987
308: horizontal arrange-
ment on cabinets
309: vertical arrange-
ment on cabinet

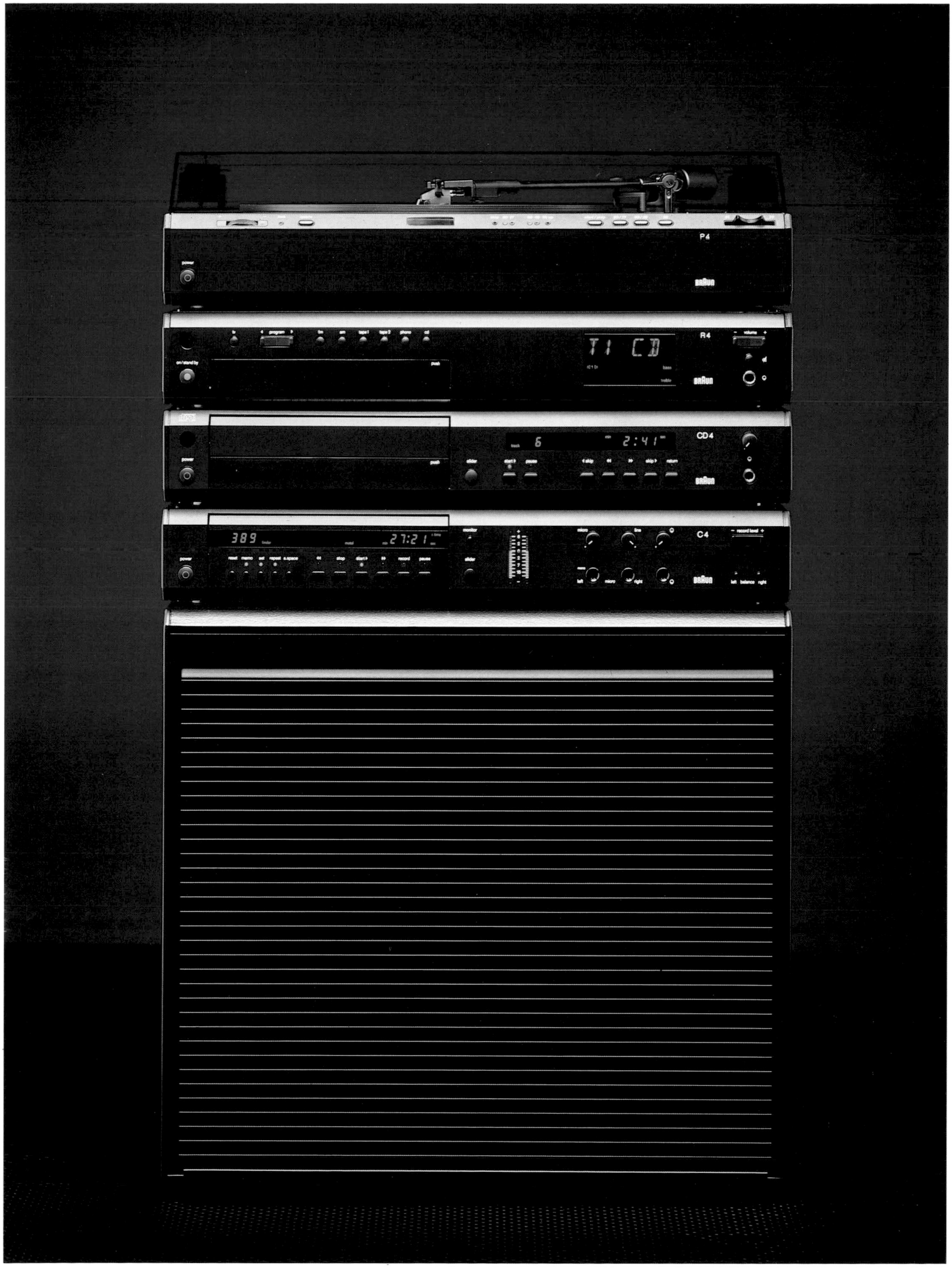

9

310

311

312

310 Dieter Rams "570" table prog-ramme, 1957

311 Dieter Rams "601/602" easy-chair, 1960

312 Dieter Rams "606" shelving system, 1960 (originally wall shelving, from 1970, on free-standing, from 1973 on space structur ing programme and "710" auxiliary units, 1971

313 Dieter Rams "610" cloakroom prog-ramme, 1961

314 a, b Dieter Rams "620" armchair range, 1962

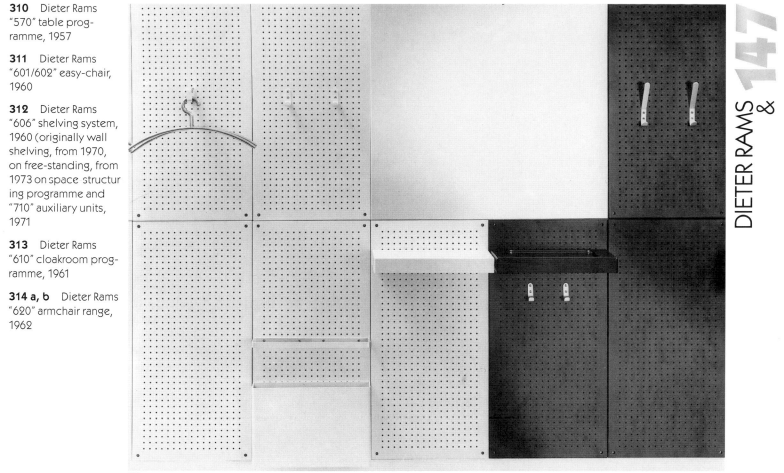

313

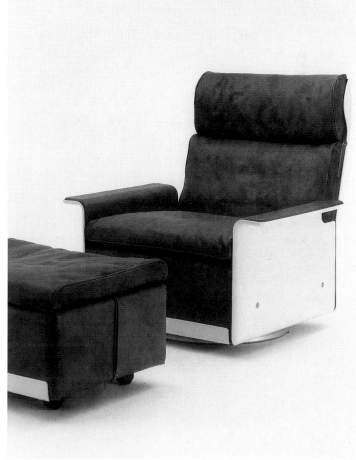

314

315 Dieter Rams "690" sliding-door system, 1969

316 Dieter Rams "rundoval 860" table, 1986

317 Dieter Rams, Jürgen Greubel "862" chair range, 1986

318 Dieter Rams, Jürgen Greubel "850" conference-table range, 1985 (model)

315

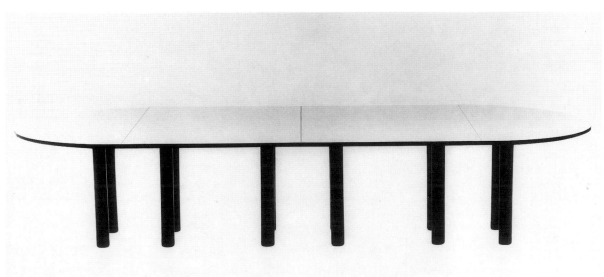

316

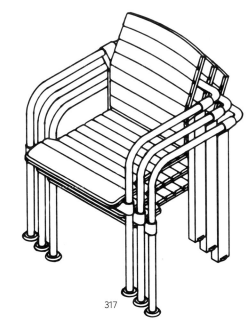

317

318

Wewerka is an artist, interested and at home in all media. Trained as an architect, he has designed buildings, though few projects were realised; his early competition designs have nevertheless been very influential in the postwar architecture debate. He has also done many drawings of architectural subjects, transformed them through photography, and turned them into collages with the aid of various artistic techniques. He has written books, designed furniture and fashions, painted pictures and stage sets, made films and dabbled in Action Art. He has no compunction about making himself his own theme, in fact, he relishes it, often venturing into the realm of satire and travesty.

STEFAN WEWERKA

He is full of contradictions: he can be obstinate to the point of obduracy, and at the same time surreal and dadaist, ironic and clownish.

He is always moving on, and distrusts the idea of settling down in any one place. He has three residences but is most at home on trains – rather be nowhere than somewhere. A film about Wewerka and his work, made by Lothar Spree in collaboration with the artist,[1] shows his predilection for cramped train compartments and, in sharp dialectical contrast, the boundlessness and immateriality of the landscapes that rush past the window. This might help us to understand what goes on inside Wewerka's head: a few of the fleeting, often distorted impressions that impinge from the outside world are analysed and reworked over and over again, familiar concepts are demolished and reconstructed. This process, which often transcends the boundaries of traditional categories, does not just produce another subjective variation on a theme, it uncovers something more of the essence thereof.

Although Wewerka was active as an architect in the fifties, he first became known in the sixties and seventies as an artist who manipulated objects. It was above all his weird versions of chairs that caught the public eye and found their way into the museums. Wewerka sawed apart, unscrewed, deformed and dismantled, and then put the parts together again, but without a seat, with one leg or with three – chairs from the hall of mirrors or the crazy-house. He sees his method as a sort of subversion of conventional perceptual images, whether through art, architecture, ordinary household furniture, fashion, film or other aesthetic genres. In 1961 he propped a half-chair up against a bare wall, as if it had been overlooked when the wall was built (pl. 319). In 1965 he had a soft rubber chair lolling on the floor, unable to hold itself up (pl. 322); in the sketches he calls it an "eraser" (pl. 321, 323). In 1966 one of his chairs looked as if the corner of a wall or maybe a pillar encroached into the seat, creating the effect of a useless console or a grossly exaggerated architectonic detail (pl. 320). Traditional preconceptions are irritated and undermined by such objects. This type of artistic activity belongs to the broad

field of the Object Art of the sixties, but it also relates to certain "blow-up" techniques of Pop Art and to the "transmaterialisations" of what Claes Oldenburg termed his "softenings". Wewerka, however, not only changed the materials but also practised constructive destruction: "Cutting things up became for me the epitome of radicalism. I had to dismember, dissolve, get to the bottom of things, to get away from the decorative aspect. The razorblade was my weapon, although I once cut that in half too."[2]

Wewerka has also done installations of complete rooms with extremely distorted furnishings, such as the famous nursery for his "Ludwig van" project at the Neue Galerie, Aachen, in 1969 (pl. 326): a table, chairs, a musicstand, a cot, a chest-of-drawers, all in a crazy geometry that requires more than a passing glance to take it in; a room like a musical score, which fails to conform to the laws and conceptions of a conventional interior. Wewerka himself has frequently pointed out the correspondence between some of his object and drawings and the world of music: a 1977 etching, the *Strindberg Chair* (pl. 324), is another distorted structure of oblique angles, it appears to be made of folded manuscript-paper, and synaesthetically suggests musical structures like counterpoint, variation and dynamic modulation, here represented by the varying thickness of the lines.

A more tangible, though still highly surreal variation of the same theme is what later became known as the *Vertreterstuhl* ("Representative Chair", pl. 325); this object, alongside which the artist liked to portray himself (pl. 328), demonstrates his feeling for the necessity of unmasking conventional attitudes. In 1971 he made a whole classroom of these chair-objects at the Galerie Müller in Cologne, since when it has also been known as the "Classroom Chair" (pl. 330). The chair translates graphic fantasy into three-dimensional designs. Its associations range from the servile curtsy to the dressage figures of the Spanish Riding School in Vienna. When the chairs are grouped together in the satirical classroom setting, the associations become those of conformism and the law-and-order mentality. The incongruity of form, content and material in the *Vertreterstuhl* effectively mocks our basic conception of the functions of chairs, precisely because it uses the structural elements and materials of a "normal" chair. As part of a publicity campaign for the "Initiative of Creative Interior Designers" a competition was organised to see who could sit the longest on this "impossible" chair; one of the participants sat it out for over forty minutes. The six elongated, ultra-slim Chair Variations of 1976 (pl. 327) are more suggestive of children at the ballet class or Giacometti sculptures than the ontological image of a chair. An ordinary wooden table with turned legs is sawn in two and reassembled to create a stepped top (pl. 329):

it is now an abstract, alien object, unsure of its own "nature as a table". Wewerka cuts up everyday things such as records, flags, cameras, spoons, and coins, and then puts them together again in new ways: this is an analytic rather than a reconstructive process. In this respect his technique is a creative act of ontological awareness. His five-mark coin that can be folded in half on hinges perhaps says more about the psychology and the sociology of money than a host of academic treatises. His flags, cut into pieces and zipped together again, are a more incisive commentary on the pompousness of national symbols than any verbal statement, be it ever so socially critical. As well as going to work on everyday objects, Wewerka has also created distorted images of architectural monuments, questioning and cutting down to size their claim to durability and dignity, high cultural value and ideological significance. His critique of the force of habit becomes a critique of power itself, the power of architecture. In his work of the early seventies triumphal arches, lighthouses and skyscrapers lean alarmingly to one side or bulge erotically (pl. 331–335, 338). Telephone booths are piled on top of one another like an alternative Tower of Pisa and thus assume a quality of urban architecture far surpassing their normal role as street furniture (pl. 337). The *Polnisches Grenzklo* ("Polish Frontier Lavatory", pl. 336), is an interior in which the distortion of commonplace furniture is reminiscent of the "Ludwig van" nursery installation.

In 1974/75 Wewerka sliced up the facades of various cathedrals and reassembled them in new, surreal and subversive configurations that would have cost any Gothic mason his livelihood (pl. 339–345). Palladian villas, Ledoux's architecture of the French Revolution, historic buildings of the nineteenth century (pl. 346–353) – nothing is safe from Wewerka's critical eye, which dissects and analyses. Wewerka is particularly intrigued by Ledoux, whose revolutionary designs are without historical precedent: Wewerka suggests that the Frenchman was also a "vandal" after his own heart, dedicating to him a precariously inclined column and a monumental bed in rusticated masonry. Even his project for a new headquarters for the Deutsche Welle broadcasting corporation alludes specifically to Ledoux (pl. 354).

This early phase of Wewerka's work is also significant as a contribution to the exploration of the nature of design as a discipline in its own right. It is as important and fundamental as, for instance, Mendini's concept of Re-Design. Wewerka and Mendini want to shake up our perceptions of everyday objects, fossilised by years of habit, and to teach us to see things anew. Their methods differ, but their goal is the same.

Chairs, and the phenomenon of sitting in general, as one of the archetypal, culturally conditioned activities of mankind, have always interested Wewerka much more than the evolution of the chair and all its varieties in the history of design. His preference is for unsophisticated sitting – on plinths, steps, ledges – which is an expression of cultured

behaviour: the natural, spontaneous gathering of people for gossip, discussion, and the exchange of opinions. He quotes the example of the Greeks and Romans, for whom the bases of columns must have been natural places to sit – public architecture was thus appropriated for private use. This has been going on throughout history: today people sit on the pavement, the kerb, the rims of fountains. It is precisely these natural, non-purpose-built sitting facilities that Wewerka seeks to reactivate, he envisages public "islands" to which people can resort, rather than designed artefacts. This is of course something of a paradox, for as a contemporary designer he now has to make new suggestions for what is after all a matter of instinct. The idea of such "natural" seating is exemplified by Wewerka's unobtrusive yet accomplished attendant's chair for the 1987 "Documenta 8" exhibition in Kassel (pl. 357) and his "seat island" in the glass pavilion he designed for the same exhibition, erected in the Karlsaue meadow (pl. 358, 359). This "island" was the fruit of many observations of the phenomenon of "casual sitting", and there are also echoes of the early Dadaist objects, such as the bisected chair of 1961 and the corner-chair of 1966, and of the pragmatic seating combinations with exaggerated angles designed for Tecta (pl. 360). Wewerka himself describes it as follows: "It is uncomfortable, but the user does not expect comfort, he just sits down for a few minutes on any raised surface that happens to be convenient. For me, this sculpture with its interpenetrating forms, in wood, marble or bronze, is perfect. It enshrines great potentials for variation. The utility factor *per se* does not really interest me or the user: Thus, all the rubbish about comfort in seating is irrelevant, and the way is clear for a new approach, a fresh opportunity to reassess the whole question of furniture with a pure and untrammelled spirit."[3]

In 1977 Wewerka started designing production-line furniture and then, a matter of course for one who sees himself as a "world architect", almost immediately addressed himself to the whole spectrum of interior design. For Tecta (a relatively small firm normally orientated towards the Classical Modern style) he has designed cupboards, desks, tables, armchairs, sofas, side-chairs, couches, lamps, and ashtrays. On launching the programme in 1980, Tecta hoped for a new impetus from Wewerka's unconventional furniture and, above all, access to the younger consumer strata who appreciate wit, irony, and design that goes against the Classical Modern trend. Their expectations were fulfilled in the subsequent years for, despite the dearth of right-angles. Wewerka's designs have a constructive aesthetic that looks functional. *Domus*, the Italian design journal, said of these objects that Wewerka allowed them, in a sense, to move freely in all the dimensions of space.[4] Despite their "free form", which is reminiscent of the "new departures" attitudes of the fifties and of the banal, off-the-cuff Pop-style furniture of the sixties, Wewerka's utility furniture is characterised by its quality workmanship, its practicality, and its almost Bauhaus-like dignity. The designer labels it "multifunctional", to indicate the rejection of specialisation and of the narrow delineation of functions, and to emphasise the rich variety of potential uses.

Three items from the utility range have already made design history. First, the "M 1" fan-shaped table (pl. 356), which can accommodate seven or eight people for dinner or just two in a work situation; it is designed to discourage the formation of hierarchies, whether in the family or in the office context. It has been acclaimed as the first truly "democratic" table. Wewerka describes his motivation for the design: "When I create a diagonal relationship the psychological effect is completely different from that created by a face-to-face confrontation."[5]

The second object is the "B 1" three-legged chair (pl. 42, 355), which seems to break effortlessly with the thousand-year tradition of symmetrical chairs, a tradition deriving from the symmetry of the human form. The seat is an irregular pentagon, the arms are dissimilar: the right arm broadens into a flat rest, while the left arm is a continuation of the vertical backrest. The shape of the chair, which was created by sawing in half two existing chairs and then combining the disparate halves to make a new entity, takes into account the fact that people and their patterns of movement are not, or only very rarely, symmetrical. The stock of possible sedentary postures is infinite, and the stiff, dignified, conventionalised poses make up only a small part of the spectrum. The majority of actions performed when sitting are one-handed or asymmetrical: writing, reading, propping one's head up, telephoning, crossing one's legs, many eating motions, to name but a few. All these are facilitated by the three-legged chair in an unobtrusive but eloquent way. Although when it stands isolated in a room it is more like a sculpture, it is highly functional and practical – in a sense, an ergonomic sculpture.

Other furniture by Wewerka, such as the cupboards, sofas, sideboard-tables, writing benches, coffee-tables with refrigerators, tables with built-in acrylic glass lamps and coloured drawers, and paraphrases of Thonet wicker-seat chairs, demonstrate his multifunctional, multifaceted design strategy (pl. 360 – 364). Wewerka often works with oblique angles, and thus his furniture draws the surrounding space into its aesthetic.

His tables especially, whether fan-shaped, rectangular or pentagonal, create a place for communication, just as such public places as the marketplace, the well and the bakehouse used to do. "When I think about tables I am also thinking of town-planning . . . I create a fixed point in the home: like the old hearth or the village well."[6]

Textures, materials and colour schemes are derived from already existing styles but are consistent within themselves: they represent a reflected version of modernity. Wewerka feels that he owes a lot to the Bauhaus, though this is by no means self-evident, particularly when we consider his early, purely artistic works of alienation. He uses and adapts achievements and insights of the Werkbund, the Bauhaus, the Ulm school and Functionalism, yet is never merely nostalgic: he does not quote from history in order to historicise, but interprets historical ideas and applies them to the present.

The third piece that has made design history is the "B 5" chair, known as 'the Einschwinger' ('Uniflex chair', pl. 44, 361 b). One might think that the "free-swinging" chair without rear legs had been dealt with once and for all in the twenties by Mies van der Rohe (pl. 17), Le Corbusier, Marcel Breuer und Mart Stam (pl. 14), whose designs have a timeless validity. Wewerka has succeeded in adding a new variation to this supposedly exhausted theme. He bends a single, 3.5 m long piece of steel tubing seven times in three dimensions so that the single leg, backrest and arm all derive from one flowing movement. Although one-legged, the chair has three points of contact with the floor, so that despite some flexing it affords stability. It is notable for the freedom it allows one to sit in many different postures. It too stands out in a spatial context like a sculpture, though naturally looks more delicate than the three-legged chair. Jean Prouvé congratulated Wewerka on this chair, declaring that the last word had now been spoken on the subject of "free-swinging" chairs: Wewerka's "Uniflex" was both the high-point and the end of the line for chairs of this type.

Wewerka has always been interested in combination furniture, where different functions are encompassed within as small a space as possible. He has for example designed a "kitchen-column" which stands like a tree in the middle of the room (pl. 362). Various shelves and appliances branch out radially from the central stem, including the hob and the sink. In 1985 he designed the "Cella", which fuses cupboard, bed, work-surface and bookshelf into a compact block reminiscent of the combination furniture of the fifties. Such compact furniture has an extensive history going back beyond the fifties to the creations of Buckminster Fuller and Le Corbusier, and it is also related to the mini-units of the Japanese Metabolists of the sixties.

Wewerka uses the experience gained from his furniture work in his architectural formulations, and these, conversely, have influenced his furniture design. He studied architecture under Max Taut in Berlin, among others, and worked for a time in Hans Scharoun's practice. More significant was his membership of Team Ten, who played a major role among the critics of Functionalism in the sixties. Members of the group included Oswald Mathias Ungers, the Dutch architects Aldo van Eyck and Jacob Bakema, and Peter and Allison Smithson from England. Team Ten's main objection to Functionalism was their belief in an architecture that was not in itself absolute, but took into consideration the existing context. Wewerka had already used the same argument in the early commissions that he executed. These are good examples of his integrative approach, and served to set standards for others; they can also be read as furnishings on the urban scale. The same is perhaps also true of his Ruhwald and Frühauf housing estate projects for

Berlin in 1963 – 65 (pl. 365 – 367), and of the Kerssenbohm house in Pommern in the Eifel, which was designed as early as 1954 (pl. 368). The latter consists basically of five separate houses surrounding in U-formation an open-ended courtyard, which constitutes the centre proper of the layout. The estate projects, with their imaginative placing of architectonic accents within the rows, represented a new variation on the housing rows that had dominated city planning in Germany since the late fifties. In the Ruhwald plan Wewerka made the rows so long and so close together that they resemble streets in their own right. The tower-blocks create a completely different rhythmic effect than that of the conventional open housing rows, especially from the perspective of the pedestrian. Wewerka's intention with such designs was "to put an end to the row as such" by reducing it to absurdity.[7]

His interpretation of the doctrines of classical Modernism, which were being increasingly abused in the fifties, was both sensitive and intelligent, as can be seen in his plans for civic centres. The dramatic, collage-like grouping of buildings round a central space for the Mehlem suburb of Bonn in 1956 (pl. 369) looks like an early anticipation of Charles Moore's 1973 concept for Kresge College, Santa Cruz, California. On the other hand, the civic centre for Radertal in Cologne (pl. 370), designed at about the same time, consists of rectangular, block-like buildings circumscribing a square, like the Kerssenbohm house of two years earlier. Similar layouts were used for the civic centre in Britz, Berlin, in 1964 (pl. 371) and for the crematorium complex in Ruhwald in 1963 (pl. 372).

Wewerka calls the strategy that links his ground-plans for Kerssenbohm Cologne-Radertal and Berlin-Britz "peripheral grouping". "By this he means the grouping of buildings, parts of buildings or rooms round a square or a courtyard. The house or the group of houses is planned as though it were a town in miniature, a concept reminiscent of Alberti's hallowed formulation of the house as city and the city as house, and also of Scharoun's idea of the 'farmstead' model. Wewerka goes a step further by extending the idea of the heart of the house (or of the town), which represents the archetypal image of shelter and security, from urban planning via his residential buildings (which are reminiscent of Mediterranean atrium houses) to his furniture, where it particularly affects the status of the table."[8]

One of the important buildings by Wewerka that have actually been constructed is a youth hostel on Bonn's Venusburg hill (1954). Wewerka was the first to allow in his plans for the rapidly growing motorisation among youth hostellers, and this project won him several prizes.

The fifties also saw his first "earth architecture" projects (pl. 373 – 377), pioneer work in which nature was seen as the architect's friend rather than his foe; here, the buildings were integrated with the landscape long before the concept of ecological or "green" architecture came into vogue. Most of these drawings were made between 1955 and 1958, and it is no coincidence that at this time

Wewerka was in touch with Friedensreich Hundertwasser, whose 1958 *Mildew Manifesto* attacked the tyranny of the right-angle. Wewerka makes the same protest in his work, but does so within the idiom of Modernism. Hundertwasser, in contrast, resorts to a sort of regressive architectural language that gives priority to the participation of the residents and users in the planning process, even when this results in a child-like or indeed infantile vocabulary.

Wewerka's earth architecture is, again, a kind of "landscape furniture". It is a design for living with nature and in nature, in houses like mushrooms or dolmens that obtrude as little as possible; they are not foreign bodies, artificial implants, but organic growths integrated into their environment right from the start. This earth architecture can be seen as a prophetic anticipation of today's eco-architecture, an increasingly important trend exemplified by the do-it-yourself clay houses of New Mexico, the mushroom-like dwelling projects of Christian Hunzinger, the energy-saving designs of such as Vladimir Nikolic and Bernd Faskel, or the subsidised housing of Otto Seidle.

The designs for a house in Sardinia (pl. 378, 379) profit from Wewerka's experience with earth architecture and from his theory of "natural" seating, here construed as the exploitation of topographical projections and height differences. Wewerka transforms these existing features into terraces, with steps and benches to sit on and other items of "furniture". He anticipates what Charles Moore, fifteen years later, was to call "Building for memorable places".[9] All these projects have however received little publicity: the earth architecture for example, was not exhibited as a series until 1984, in Munich.

A recent example of this landscape furniture is the glass pavilion for the "Documenta 8" (pl. 358, 359), Based on a similar construction erected in the grounds of the Tecta works, it is an enclosed room in the middle of an open space: the all-over glazing reveals the structure of braced, prefabricated girders; the bases of the girders, like the "seat island" inside the pavilion, serve as natural seats and again illustrate the dialectic between house and furniture. Wewerka has fitted out numerous interiors, apartments, conference rooms, galleries and bookshops, always with furniture of his own design and often with customised creations. For Aedes, an architecture gallery in Berlin, he prescribed man-high glass panels for the display of the exhibits: propped against the wall these would make a more efficient use of the restricted space than conventional picture frames and create a transparent, uncramped ambiente. In 1987, at the Frankfurt trade fair, he created a reception lounge for the Hoechst company (pl. 380 – 383). This was an integrated multipurpose room with "conference trees" and "catering trees" and leather cubes as seats: in this way a number of discreet conference areas were created without compromising the spatial coherence of the room.

Since 1977 Wewerka has also been designing clothes, although his work is far removed from the trendy designs of couturiers who have to come up with a new collection season each. Like so much of his other work, his garments are asymmetrical, fruits of his observations of the manifold movements of human beings and not artefacts which dictate, through the coercions of fashion, what patterns of movement are allowed. Thus, Wewerka reverses the whole strategy of fashion. Some of his creations, such as a crêpe-de-chine dress and a white dinner-jacket of the thinnest silk, can be compressed to the size of a cigarette packet without creasing. Thus one can always have one's cocktail-dress or tuxedo at hand, "prêt-à-party". This fits in with Wewerka's conviction that elegance and natural grace can only be achieved with the minimum of trappings, which should be designed with the realities of life in mind. He has made jackets of thick furnishing fabric with brightly coloured silk linings and leather patches on the elbows, collarless and, of course, asymmetrical in concept. His clothes come in two sizes only, they have distinct contours, and are attractive not for their perfect fit but for the way they hang: "The material must embrace the body: that is what makes a design, not affected fripperies. There's no getting away from it... For me, a jacket is also a sculpture... In the designing of a house, [too,] there must be a rapprochement between the ideas of the client and the architect, so that they fit like a made-to-measure jacket."[10]

Wewerka wants to give us more freedom of movement, in the broadest sense of the term, and to this end he applies all his talents, in all the disciplines in which he works. No man – and, for Wewerka, no sphere of activity – is an island. With his sawn-up chairs, his utility furniture, his architecture, fashion, painting, films, or sculpture, he is always chipping away at the power of convention, changing the way we behave and relate to objects by means of subversive surprises. Despite its nonlinear evolution, the caesuras and the (always justified) repetitions, Wewerka's work is remarkably consistent; for all its multiplicity, it is not extravagant, it has an inner coherence. Notwithstanding the volatility of his personality, Wewerka shows great tenacity; he hates to be categorised, type-cast, prejudged. In all his work, not least in his furniture designs, he has followed the maxims: Do little, but do it well: Let it mature and develop slowly, and, above all: Don't follow trends that are fundamentally alien to your nature merely in order to be "up-to-date". Wewerka, despite – or maybe because of – all his contradictions, is a true pioneer.

319 Stefan Wewerka
Halved chair, 1961

320 Stefan Wewerka
Corner chair in column,
1966

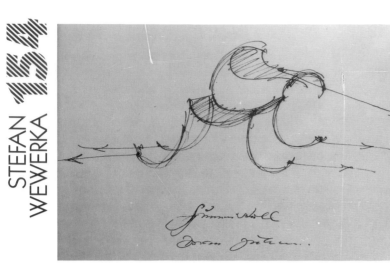

321

322

323

324

325

321 Stefan Wewerka
Rubber chair, 1965

322 Stefan Wewerka
Rubber chair, 1965

323 Stefan Wewerka
Rubber chair, 1965

324 Stefan Wewerka
"Strindberg" chair, 1977

325 Stefan Wewerka
"Vertreterstuhl" ("Rep-
resentative's Chair"),
1970

326 Stefan Wewerka
"Kinderzimmer" (Chil-
dren's Room"), installa-
tion for the "Ludwig
van" project, 1969

326

327 Stefan Wewerka
Chair variations, 1976

328 Stefan Wewerka
Title-page for the
magazine "md" (Maga-
zin Design), No. 1, Janu-
ary 1980, with
silhouette of Stefan
Wewerka and the "Rep-
resentative's Chair"

329 Stefan Wewerka
Painted table, 1976

330 Stefan Wewerka
"Lecturing Hall", 1971,
installation in the
Galerie Müller, Cologne

328

329

327

330

331

332

333

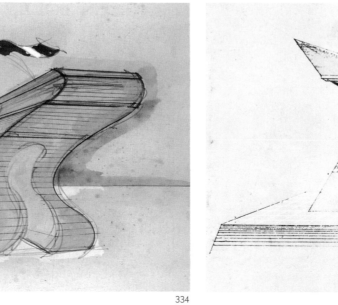

334

335

336

337

338

Münster zu F...
Weste...
...res Freiburg i. B.
...sicht.
...Gr.

340

Frauenkirche zu Nürnberg[...]

341

339

342

339–345
Stefan Wewerka
Kathedralen ("Cathed-
rals"), 1974/75

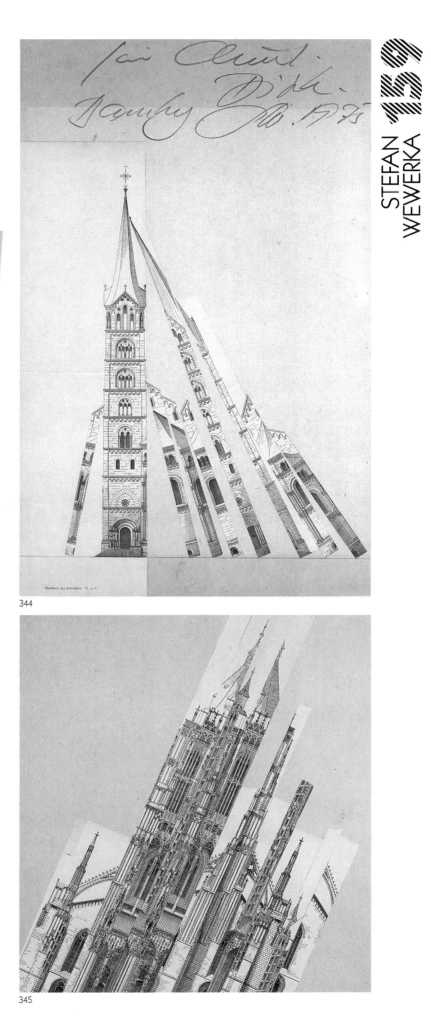

344

343

345

Palladio – Vicenza   346

Palladio – Vicenza   347

348

349

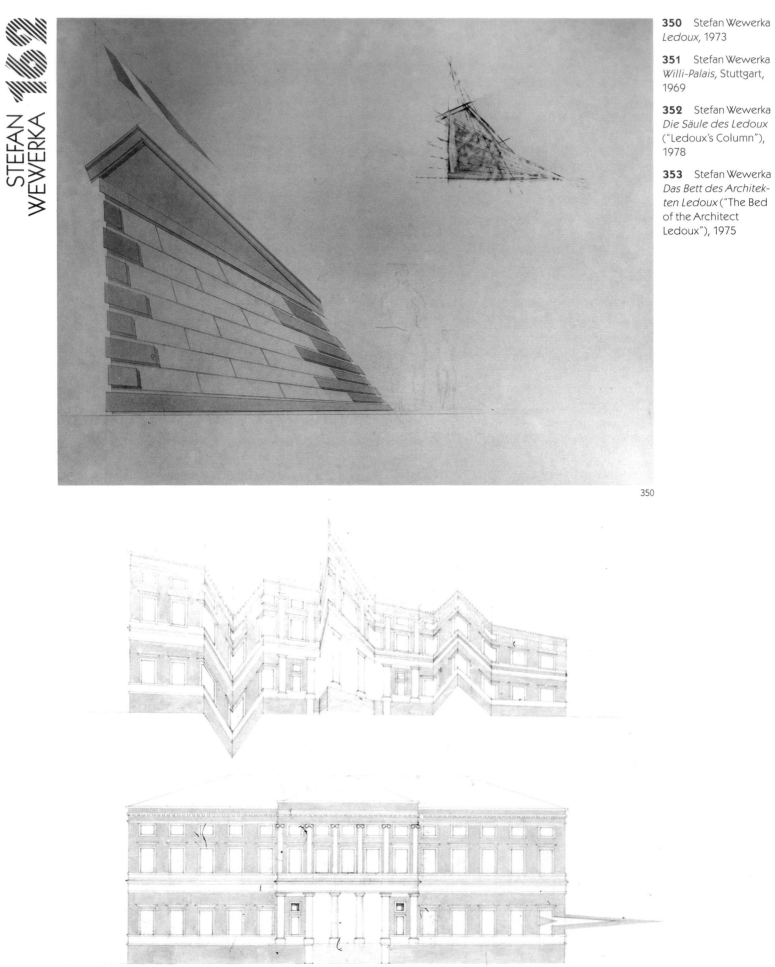

350 Stefan Wewerka
Ledoux, 1973

351 Stefan Wewerka
Willi-Palais, Stuttgart,
1969

352 Stefan Wewerka
Die Säule des Ledoux
("Ledoux's Column"),
1978

353 Stefan Wewerka
Das Bett des Architekten Ledoux ("The Bed
of the Architect
Ledoux"), 1975

350

351

352

353

354

355

356

357

354 Stefan Wewerka
New headquarters for
the Deutsche Welle
broadcasting corpora-
tion, 1980 (project)

355 Stefan Wewerka
"B 1" chair, 1977–79,
with preliminary ver-
sion

356 Stefan Wewerka
"M 1" fan-shaped
table, 1979

357 Stefan Wewerka
Attendant's chair for
the Documenta 8 in Kas-
sel, 1987

358, 359
Stefan Wewerka
Seating islands and
glass pavilion for the
Documenta 8 in Kassel,
1987

358

359

360
Stefan Wewerka
"F 2" sofa, "K 1" com-
mode-table, "S 04"
cupboard-base, "B 1"
chair, 1979

361 a
Stefan Wewerka
"B 2" asymmetrical can-
tilever chair, 1980

361 b
Stefan Wewerka
"B 5" one-legged chair
("Einschwinger") and
"M 5" desk, 1982

362   Stefan Wewerka
Kitchen column, 1983

360

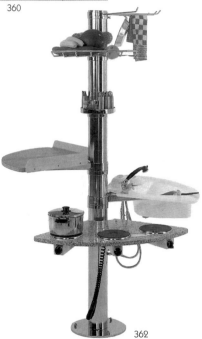

361a

361b

362

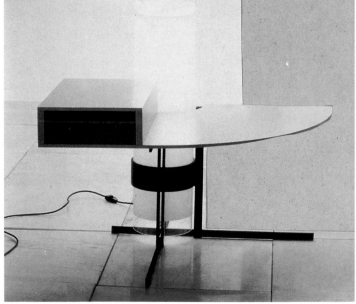

363

364

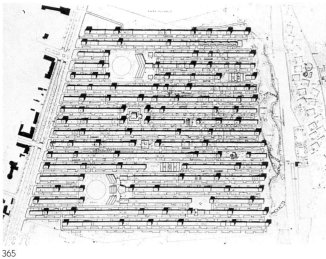

365

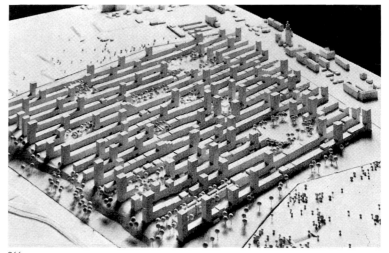

366

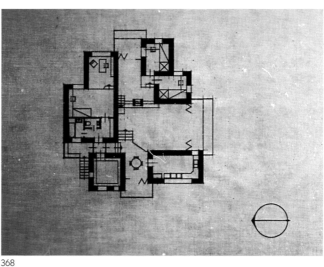

367

368

363 Stefan Wewerka
"S 01", "S 02", "S 03", "S
04" cupboards, 1979/
80 (limited)

364 Stefan Wewerka
"K 6" lamp-table, 1980
(limited)

365 Stefan Wewerka
Ruhwald, 1965

366 Stefan Wewerka
Ruhwald, 1965

367 Stefan Wewerka
Frühauf, 1963/64

368 Stefan Wewerka
Haus Kerssenbohm,
1954/55

369 Stefan Wewerka
Community centre for
Mehlem, Bonn, 1956

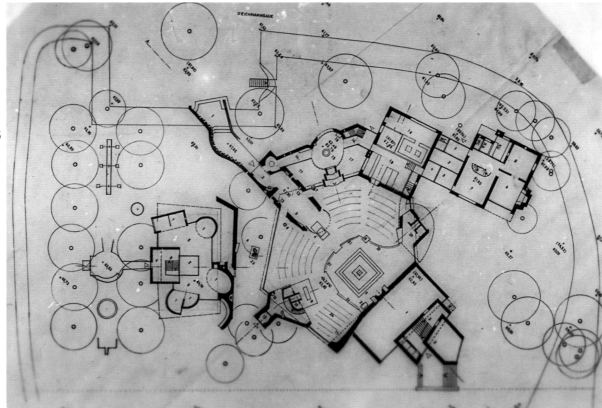

369

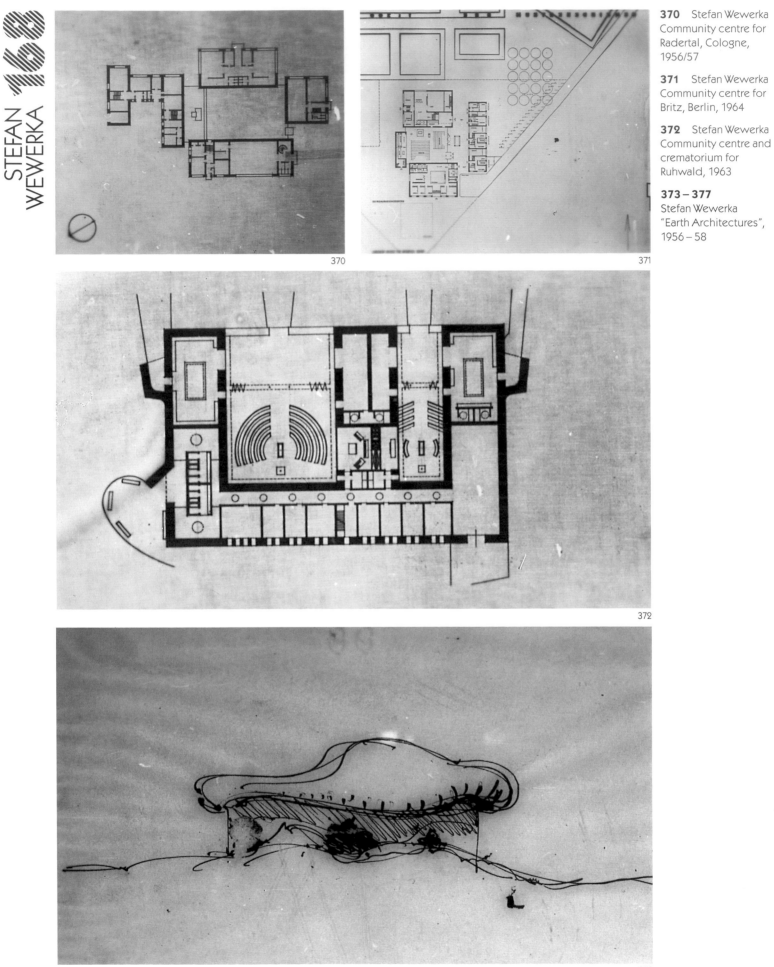

370

371

370 Stefan Wewerka
Community centre for
Radertal, Cologne,
1956/57

371 Stefan Wewerka
Community centre for
Britz, Berlin, 1964

372 Stefan Wewerka
Community centre and
crematorium for
Ruhwald, 1963

373 – 377
Stefan Wewerka
"Earth Architectures",
1956 – 58

372

373

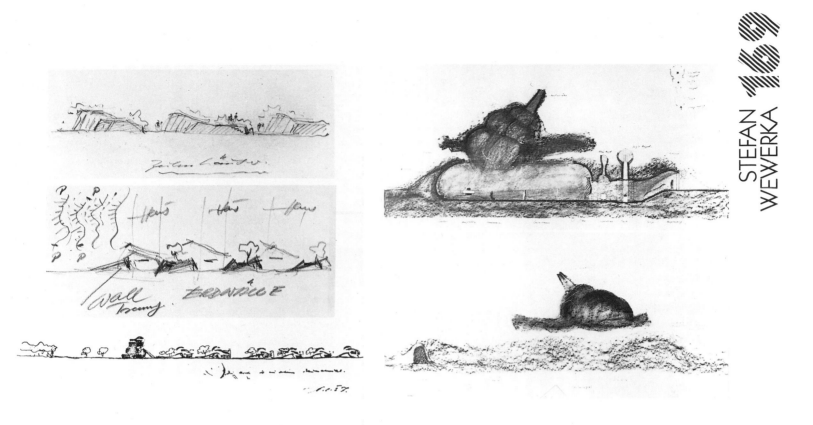

374

375

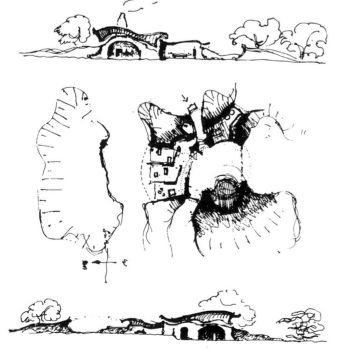

376

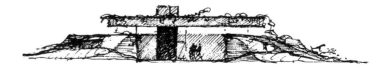

377

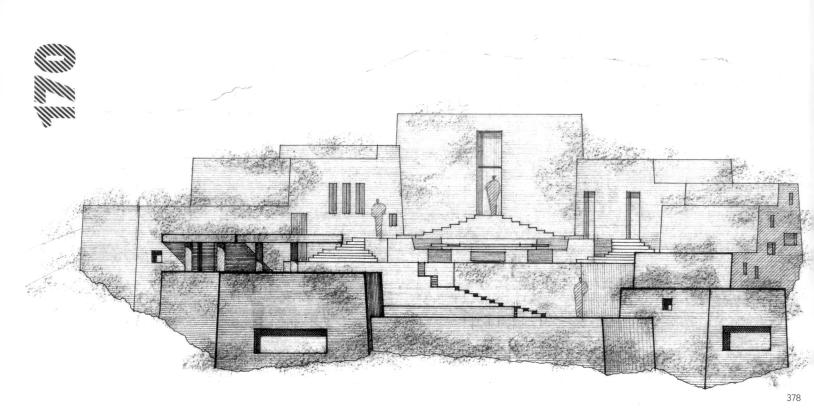

378

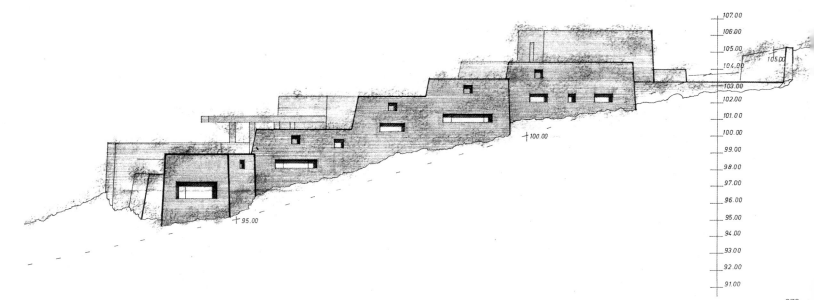

107.00
106.00
105.00
104.00
103.00
102.00
101.00
100.00
99.00
98.00
97.00
96.00
95.00
94.00
93.00
92.00
91.00

379

378 Stefan Wewerka
House on Sardinia,
1976/77

379 Stefan Wewerka
House on Sardinia,
1976/77

380 Stefan Wewerka
Hoechst lounge at the
Frankfurt Trade Fair with
"conference-trees" and

cubic leather hassocks,
1987

381 Stefan Wewerka
Hoechst lounge at the
Frankfurt Fair, 1987
Drawings of various
"trees", from left to
right: "snack-tree",
"loudspeaker-tree",
"table-tree"

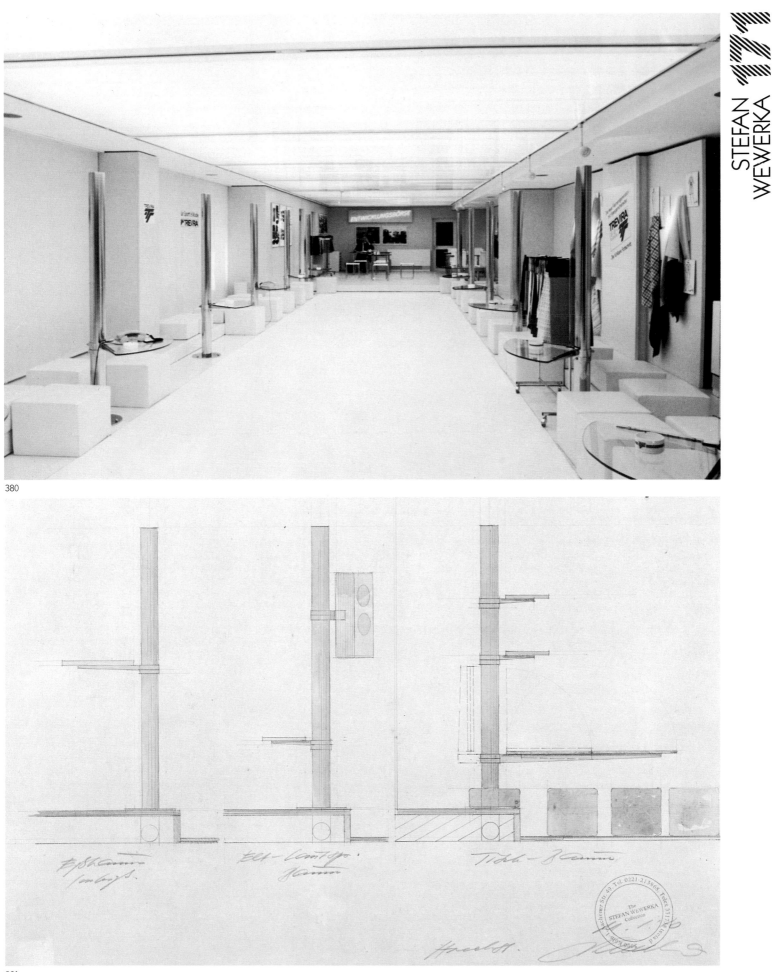

380

381

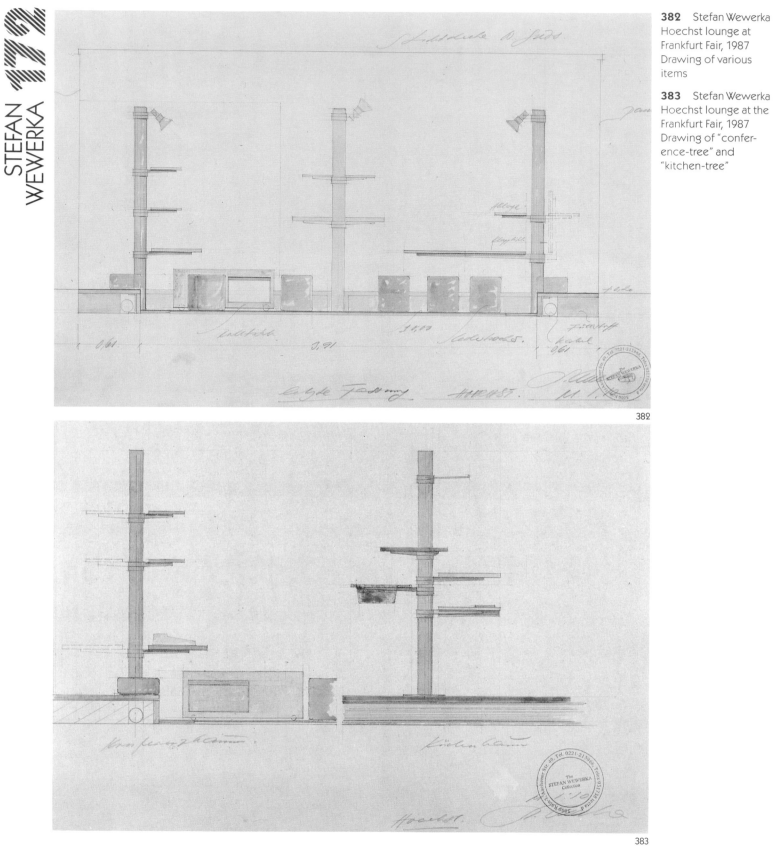

382 Stefan Wewerka
Hoechst lounge at
Frankfurt Fair, 1987
Drawing of various
items

383 Stefan Wewerka
Hoechst lounge at the
Frankfurt Fair, 1987
Drawing of "confer-
ence-tree" and
"kitchen-tree"

382

383

Among the younger designers in Germany, Holger Scheel from Stuttgart is one of the most intriguing figures: although he confines himself to a limited field of interior design – chairs and tables (recently, he has also turned his attention to glassware), his work over the years has, unlike that of most other designers, revolved around a few fundamental questions of form. Since the mid-seventies he has designed a number of series comprising more than fifty variations on these themes. Some have been produced in limited editions, and some of the more recent designs have been taken up by the German manufacturers Kill and Draenert, but many did not get beyond the prototype stage. The problems of form which Scheel investigates are of general relevance, almost archetypal. In one series of easy-chairs, for instance, he examines the relationship of voluminous upholstery to slender structural elements or to sharply defined flat surfaces. Another series features stark interfaces with negligible differentiation between structural elements and "upholstery". A third series combines both approaches.

After serving his apprenticeship as a carpenter in the early sixties, Holger Scheel studied interior design at the College of Applied Arts in Berlin. He worked for some years as an interior designer in Berlin and then moved to Stuttgart. As member of a team he designed functional furniture on ergonomic principles, including a series of office chairs to primarily economic and technical specifications. At the same time he worked on a complex scheme for the outfitting of a new university building in Stuttgart, where he became acutely aware of the gulf between architect, interior designer and client, and of the compromises that are unavoidable when one has to furnish such large-scale projects from a range of stock products. The experience of alienation between planner and product led him – like others in the late sixties – to forsake designing for a time in favour of theoretical planning in the fields of operational analysis, estimation of requirements, optimal use of available space, and costing.

But Scheel loves the material element too much, almost to the point of fetishism, not to feel an urgent need to express his ideas about the immediate sensuality of objects and to test these ideas as soon as possible in practice. On his own initiative he designed "Table 1" (pl. 387) and "Chair 3" (pl. 384), which owe a lot to the experiences of his student days. The table is clearly influenced by the Bauhaus in its combination of wood and steel, the leather seat of "Chair 3", however, is fashioned in a deliberately natural, asymmetrical, petal-like shape which goes beyond Bauhaus thinking. At the same time, this chair seems to be a paraphrase of Eileen Gray's famous asymmetrical tubular steel chair of 1926 (pl. 13); it reveals Scheel's fascination with the "Non-Conformist", while ironically "correcting" it.

HOLGER SCHEEL

In contrast however to Gray's elegant, coolly understated creations, Scheel's objects are also light-hearted, clearly ironical comments on early landmarks of modern design history. On the other hand, the chairs he designed shortly afterwards (pl. 385, 386), for the Rosenthal company (although they never went into production) give the impression of a very subjective process of discovery of a personal position through the reproduction of forms introduced by Scandinavian designers such as Alvar Aalto in their laminated wood furniture. All these early designs (there was another table and two more chairs) are characterised by Scheel's fascination with the dialectic of dissimilar materials, such as leather and wood or metal and fabric. Ergonomic requirements are harmonised with the sensuality of visual and tactile qualities.

The "Toga II" armchair of 1978 (pl. 388) is a stark seat-cube, even more sober than Le Corbusier's famous "LC 2" (pl. 12). The arms, seat and back of the "Toga II" are made of cool, absolutely smooth blocks of wood covered with varnished fabric, an element of tension is introduced by the cloth draped asymmetrically, seemingly haphazardly, across the arms and seat. The tactile and optical contrasts of the materials both veil the form of the chair and comment on it. Like Christo's art it is a form of "packaging": the essential shape and volumetric qualities of an object whose form we no longer register through long familiarity are rediscovered by being covered. This expansive cubic block is a kind of ironic distillation of the Classical Modern style: in addition to Le Corbusier, various other important examples of this uncompromisingly stereometric tradition are here reflected, ranging from Peter Keler's "D 1" Bauhaus cube of 1925 with its cavalry twill covers to Willie Landel's "Throw-Away" of 1965. However, these exemplary objects and the associations they evoke are deprived of all seriousness and dignity by the casual adjunct of the cloth. The name "Toga" is well-chosen: the chair positively drapes itself with the cloth in a grand rhetorical flourish worthy of a Roman senator. The appellation refers not only to the strategy of "veiling" a form in order to draw our attention to it, but also – as an ironic example of dignified classical nomenclature – to the currently popular Post-Modern style, which gives objects a new aura through historical allusions. An additional factor is the mutability of the design, the way it can be transcended, so to speak, by continual variations in use. The cloth can be draped round the sitter, so that a part of this static piece of furniture becomes dynamic, it can be worn as a cloak, so that the chair is not necessarily directly involved. The idea of clothing as a second skin is extended to include the chair as a third.

Scheel can be classed as a Post-Modern designer because he alludes to historical forms, reworking them in new, forward-looking ways which deny neither their debt to the past nor their intrinsic element of newness: both are combined in a creative dialectic. There is more to sitting, for him, than the purely ergonomic pandering to our backside. "Sitting is not merely the satisfying of the need for so-called comfort or of the criteria of ergonomics or of economic productivity: sitting is primarily a cultural act. The type of chair chosen for this act reveals which criterium has been given priority. Sitting is not, in itself, 'good for the body', nor are the economic considerations involved of universal validity; the key factors are the cultural dimension and the subjective relationship to materials. These are the things that influence the personal choice of a mode of sitting, which is a decision about oneself and one's relationship to the external world, a declaration of attitude."[1]

We should pause to reflect on what has gone before, what we now take for granted, and thus maybe gain an insight into the way things evolve – this is for Scheel the lesson to be learnt from history, this explains his dalliance with the formal elements of historical styles, a strategy that we might at first find irritating. Historical allusions are also evident in the series of chairs and a table that he designed in 1978/79 (pl. 389 – 393); here, however, he paraphrases the vocabulary of past styles, instead of quoting verbatim like many Post-Modern designers. The juxtaposition of constructivist sector-shapes, visually fragile arcs of sectional steel, and geometric solids of wood seems to reflect a view of history that is consciously related to the present.

This historical perspective governs the design of the various components, the way in which the piece of furniture is composed of its constituent parts, and also its relationship to the spatial environment: it not only occupies space but, in a way, creates space by its very presence. The resolutions Hoger Scheel finds for these basic questions call to mind not only the work of Eileen Gray but also fifties designs and the Pop Art era of the mid-sixties; there is also an element of Alchimia or Memphis philosophy in the "additive" structuring of his furniture, the unabashed use of colour (the upholstery is in leather or fabric, in soft tones of pink, turquoise, mauve, or lilac), and the contrasting of linear and solid geometry, curves and right-angles, soft and hard. Yet the new Italian school can hardly have influenced Scheel directly, for Alchimia was only just beginning to take shape when these designs ware created. A series of minimalistic, virtually stenographic sketches (pl. 394 – 405) presents variations on this concept, in which the delicacy of the fine linear framework is emphasised by the sturdy yet dynamic supports, suggestive of ABC sculptures of the sixties; from a repertoire of a few morphemes the possibilities of meaningful combinations are here explored. Thus, wooden elements in basic geometrical shapes, such as rectilinear or cylindrical sections, are related to arcs and other linear forms of tubular steel at various points of contact.

The scale models reveal further aspects of Scheel's strategy: it can be seen, for instance, that "Table 3" relates formally to "Armchair 9" (pl. 389). The irony that informs "Armchair 13" (pl. 393) is intended to set us thinking: the black block that serves as base and backrest is in paradoxical relationship to the seat hollowed out of it, for when the block is optically in a stable position the seat is tipped up, and vice versa; *both ways it is the sitter who will feel unsteady.* This perplexing construction can help us to discover new ways of perceiving and experiencing things, it challenges us to try and resolve the contradiction by setting the chair "straight" and thus turning it into a visually static object. The Bauhaus maxim "Less is more" applies to none of the designs in this series, they fuse together asceticism and emotionality, earnestness and irony, severity and luxury to form a new unity. The juxtaposition of marked structural elements and geometrical volumes results in exciting, individualised objects which are almost sculptures, though they never ignore the ergonomic criteria of "sitting properly".

This phase of Scheel's stylistic development may remind us of the Italian "Novecento" movement of the late twenties and the thirties, but the next series (pl. 406 – 411) evokes, much more directly, associations with Art Deco. These *Mobilien*, as the designer calls them in a linguistic allusion to the "immobile" environment of nature and buildings, suggesting that they are meant to interact even more than their predecessors with the surrounding space – these "mobile" objects are stylistically a synthesis of plush Art Deco upholstery and sober, Bauhaus-inspired structures of wood or metal that support, enclose and define the upholstered elements. The colour schemes are also dictated by the Art Deco and – more pronouncedly – the Pop Art aesthetics: an opalescent blue-violet, a rich gold or an opaque rosé combines with the starkly contrasting black or metallic silver of the structural elements to create a picture of blasé luxury and severe elegance at one and the same time.

Here are echoes of the tinselly glamour of Hollywood, its superficial charm and sensuality as unmasked in Friedemann Hahn's film-clip paintings, or of the debonair world of high society between the wars as captured by Tamara de Lempicka.

The first two models of the *Mobilien* series are the most important and formally convincing: the "La Matrice" easy-chair is arrogant and distinguished, with sensual undertones (pl. 406), and the "Villa R." chair (pl. 407) creates a similar effect, but with an archaic, hierarchical component as well. Both designs are architectonic in that they embody definite spatial concepts which of necessity impose themselves on their surroundings. As a rule, furniture subordinates itself to the room in which it is used: its materials and dimensions must be appropriate for the average house or flat; adaptability, mobility and neutrality are called for rather than an imposing presence. A creative designer will find his style cramped if he has to bear such factors in mind. Scheel has gone through this experience, too – there was just no suitable room to accommodate some of his creations. But instead of "cutting his furniture down to size" so that it would fit in with the conventional environments where it might be placed, he found a productive way out of the dilemma by subversively turning the tables: his objects would create their own setting, would define the spatial environment in defiance of traditional architectonic concepts. What might sound like arrogance is borne out by the results: "It has always been said that furniture can only have a complementary or, at best, interpretative function in relation to architecture; I find this attitude superficial and narrow-minded."[2]

"La Matrice", along with the "19", "22", "24", and "30" chairs, revolves around the formal tension between the visual austerity or the cool, sharply delineated surfaces of wood, painted black or dark blue, and the burgeoning, almost decadent luxuriance of the upholstery. There is a strong current of sensuality dammed up within these forms – not for nothing a name like "La Matrice" ("the womb"); the point was not lost on the newspaper critic who declared with relish: "Unconventional design makes itself perfectly clear in Scheel's corner-chair: the fulsome fleshiness of the shimmering violet upholstery with its vertical clefts evokes for the sitter highly pleasurable associations."[3] A piece of furniture like this just asks to be possessed, with all the erotic implications of the word: first comes the haptic experience, in which one "gets the feel" of the object, then the act of possessing, a word whose very root connotes sitting. The French structuralist Roland Barthes, in his famous *Myths of Everyday Life*, illustrates this process of taking possession by describing the presentation of a new model of car: "At the motor show the new car is inspected eagerly, intensely, lovingly. It is the important phase of tactile exploration, the moment when the visual wonder must undergo the test of touch (for of all the senses, the sense of touch is the most demystifying, whereas sight is the most magical sense); the bodywork is felt, the welds fingered, the upholstery palpated, the seat tried out, the doors caressed, the backrests patted. The object is totally prostituted and taken into possession."[4] Thus, once one has penetrated the hard "shell" of the chair, the soft centre is waiting to be enjoyed. The erotic component is nevertheless confined, conditioned, contained; it is this tension between the enclosing and the disclosing moments that sets Scheel's high-back easy-chair apart from such creations as Dalí's "Lips" sofa of 1936. "La Matrice" is available in mirror-image versions, so that two or four of these chairs can be grouped together to form self-contained spatial structures within the room. A particularly strong impression of being cut off from the surrounding space is created by the ensemble of four chairs facing inwards (pl. 406 e).

The idea behind the "Villa R." chair (pl. 407) might also appear vainglorious to some: Scheel envisaged setting up two facing rows of these chairs in the great domed hall of Palladio's Villa Romana in Vicenza, to counterbalance the classical architecture of this Renaissance villa. A black, con-

vex, cypress-like backpiece, very tall and narrow, is combined with a voluminous padded seat of rich golden material that sweeps down to the floor over a T-shaped steel base. It is more of a throne than a chair, evocative of prehistoric times when power and religion were still one, when the judgement seat, by its size and its majesty, raised the sovereign above the common people as he pronounced over life and death. The "thing"-thrones of the ancient Germans and the statue-seats of Rameses or Akhnaten in Egyptian temples are echoed in the "Villa R." chair. The posture it invites, indeed dictates, is one of ritualised solemnity – anything less would be sacrilege.

The sketches for this chair illustrate something of the evolution of the design. It is Scheel's practice to construct small models at an early stage in the creative process, the better to visualise his ideas and subsequent modifications; a full-scale mock-up of cardboard then serves as basis for the working drawings from which the prototype is built. In this particular example we can see how the process of clarification in three dimensions (whereby the precise relationship of materials to surfaces – textures, colours, etc. – is only determined in the final stages) has produced ideal proportions, an almost classical form. The original plan was modified so that the black parts are now made of sheet steel, which offers two distinct advantages: the structurally necessary cleft in the back could be made very fine, thus giving the lofty, cool, sharp-edged form a new dynamic quality; and the use of metal makes the T-shaped base more stable than one would expect from a structure of this type.

Also designed along the same lines are the chairs "19", "22", "24" and "30" (pl. 408 – 411). The "22" is a *récamière*, or rather a Post-Modern, pastel-coloured paraphrase of the famous chaise-longue of the early nineteenth century; named after the wife of one of Napoleon's bankers, it has continued to fascinate artists over the years, from Jacques-Louis David to Kurt Schwitters – Scheel calls his version a "re-Récamière", a remake, as it were, of the historical prototype. As in "La Matrice" and "Villa R.", the keynote of these designs is the voluptuous sweep generated by the juxtaposition of arc, sector and segment forms, the whole effect being enhanced by the contrasting of opulent upholstery and the smooth finish of the clear-cut frame elements. Sometimes a shape will burgeon to exaggerated proportions, as in "Chair 24" (pl. 408), which is almost a parody of a wing-chair. And one is never quite sure whether the diverse formal elements have not just been put together from a kit, like a children's toy. For all its sculpturality and sensuality, this furniture is functional, much thinking and experimentation having gone into the quest for optimal comfort. Yet such considerations do not mean that a design cannot also be provocative and self-assured, as eye-catching as the work of Alchimia and Memphis or the Post-Modernists; in Scheel's case, however, the formal contrasts are more aggressive, stemming from a "gut" feeling rather than the intellectual insights of a Mendini, Sottsass, or Guerriero. Again it is the dialectic of cool rationalism and unrestrained emotionality that makes these objects so interesting, that arouses our elementary instincts and challenges us to penetrate the severe, uncompromising exterior and enjoy the tactile delights within.

During these years of experimentation with the idea of "conditioned sensuality" Scheel was also working on a series of black-and-red chairs in which he used hard, flat surfaces for the seats and backrests, and not just for the frame (pl. 412–419). These creations are more like minimalistic sculptures than comfortable easy-chairs. Two models, "Armchair 26" and "Chair 7" (pl. 417, 418), have been produced in limited gallery editions. The backs – there are normal and high-back variants – and the seat supports are black, while red distinguishes the arms and seat surfaces. Forerunners of these constructivist designs can be seen in Rietveld's De Stijl furniture and in some of the Alchimia and Memphis chairs. These stark, calvinistic objects are the antithesis of the sensuous, luxurious creations that we have already seen in Scheel's œuvre.

"A Place for O." (pl. 421), custom-designed for a flagged hallway in a Renaissance castle, is something of an anticlimax. This "throne" seems to be an agglomeration of previously used design principles, but for all the ingenuity and sophistication of the composition it fails to achieve that degree of self-evidence so impressive in the earlier series. Nor can the "Scultura" chair (pl. 420) really be said to stand in the same line of continuous evolution as previous Scheel designs. Now manufactured in series by the Kill company, this lounge-chair has a hint of the Post-Modern, and the abstract geometry of the upholstered elements is reminiscent of George Sowden's easy-chairs for Memphis. The incorporation of historical allusions in a contemporary design here seems to lack logic and sophistication, although in this case marketing considerations may have dictated economies.

The designs created in 1985 for the German Architecture Museum in Frankfurt, "Table 5" and "Chair 5" (pl. 423), offer numerous possibilities of combination, the side-table coming in mirror-image versions. Here Scheel returns once again to his design repertoire of the late seventies.

Since 1985 Scheel has also been working for Draenert, furniture manufacturers in southern Germany. The first fruit of this collaboration was the "Armchair 31" (pl. 425), another attempt to counterpoise voluminous opulence and quasi-constructivist severity in suspenseful equilibrium. The morphological concept is intriguing: in both the sketch and the model one can clearly see the stylised likeness of a duck swimming on a pond, with the armrest representing the head and the back in the form of a wing; basically, this is another *recamière*, of reduced proportions. The full-scale version, though, with its shiny leather covers, is somewhat disappointing: one can imagine from looking at the model that a more dramatic effect might have been achieved with the shot quality of matt leather. The dialectic of ascetic

geometry and epicurean fulsomeness is further explored in "Chair 8" (pl. 422, 424), designed in symmetrical versions with or without armrest for the German Architecture Museum. Here again the dynamics of contrasting form are less evident in the final version than in the sketches and models. Typical Scheel features reappear in this design, too: the petal motif as archetypal metaphor of consummate chair comfort; the sharp contrasting of lascivious ease and calvinistic severity; and the psychologically irritating "incompleteness" of an object that only when complemented by its "other half" presents a symmetrical, "classical" form to our perception.

Another series of designs is concerned with the statics and tectonics of stone as a material. In tables and chairs Scheel builds up a repertoire of forms with which he demonstrates, magnifies, or seeks to neutralise these properties. The first experiment, "Table 4" (pl. 426), is a tongue-in-cheek combination of a monolithic wedge and two spheres of different sizes, whereby the thin end of the wedge rests on the larger sphere, which is in turn attached by a steel cable to the smaller sphere embedded in the slab – an ensemble with its own internal equilibrium, ironically illustrating the forces of mass, pressure, and tension. There is an immanent instability in the construction, for the large sphere, on which the edge of the slab rests at a critical point, seems about to break free at any moment – this counteracts the visual impression of solidity and ponderousness created by the material. The paradoxical optics of this design set it on a par with the sculptures of Richard Serra, whose giant steel plates are almost always precariously tilted, or with designs by architects such as the Haussmanns and Hans Hollein, who have attempted to set a pyramid on its apex. The popular conception of stone as something hard, heavy, and static rather than dynamic is further queried in "Table 7" and "Chair 9" (pl. 427, 428), both designed for Draenert in 1986. "Chair 9" revives the idea of the casually draped cloth as integral constituent of the chair itself, a motif familiar from the "Toga II" chair. In "Table 7" there is something odd about the way the hyperboloid table-top rests on the two monolithic legs: the bearing surfaces of these are hollowed out, so that the table-top is only supported at one point on each leg; thus, the volume of the legs is statically and rationally out of all proportion to the actual area of contact. The way he handles problems of form in a material like stone shows Scheel to be a designer capable of bringing home to us with disturbing clarity how fragile reality is; in this respect he has certain affinities to the Trans High Tech school, and to contemporary painters and sculptors like Hannsjörg Voth or Ben Willikens.

In "Table 10" and its companion chair (pl. 430, 429) Scheel pursues the same end of endowing a material with a dynamic flexibility, this time in wood; he applies to both objects his "principle of the striding legs". In this furniture with its "pleated" legs, however, there might be just a touch of preciosity, of all-too-facile elegance; yet, though it might appeal to the snobs, there is no denying the positively mischievous sophistication of the formal concept. Scheel has lately been designing glassware for Lobmeyr of Vienna: drinking-glasses, cups, boxes, even door-handles (pl. 431–434). Here, too, he seeks to bring out the latent organic sensuality of the material. The forms he creates may have their precedents in Art Nouveau, where nature served as inspiration, or in the work of such as Gaudí or Luigi Colani, but Scheel manages to invest this predominantly organic formal vocabulary with his personal touch.

The quality of Scheel's œuvre is admittedly sometimes uneven. Yet one must place on record that he was one of the first German interior designers – if not the very first – to embark in the mid-seventies, patiently and uncompromisingly, on the process of revising the ascetic concept of the object as taught by Functionalism. In confining himself to the painstaking, long-term exploration of just a few questions of form, but fascinating and controversial ones, he has produced designs that cannot be ignored. What could however give grounds for concern – and this is not a problem peculiar to Scheel – is his liaison with the world of mass production, in which questions of marketing strategy and economic viability are almost invariably at odds with the designer's original conception. As recently as 1983 he was bewailing just this state of affairs: "For reasons inherent in their genesis, these objects cannot be expected . . . to appeal to the public at large. I have no objection to series production on principle – after all, Rolls-Royce limousines are not one-off jobs. In saying this I am laying myself open to the charge of elitism; that, it would appear, is the price that has to be paid when one cuts down on the compromises."[5]

Scheel too has now had to make compromises between creative independence and the hard facts of reality when it comes to production on a large scale. It is to be hoped that he will not lose that individualism that made the early designs so remarkable – that balance between the luxuriance of Art Deco and the structural vocabulary of the Bauhaus – and will continue to combine sensuality and severity, emotion and elucidation. This would be quite in keeping with Matteo Thun's provocative description of the style of the eighties: "Bauhaus Baroque".

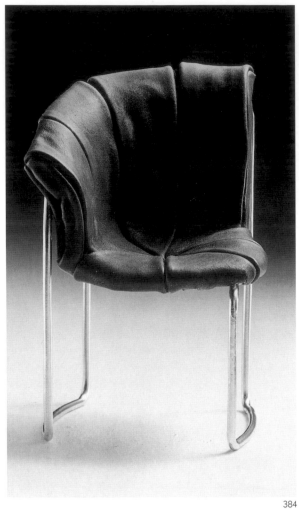

384 Holger Scheel
"Chair 3", 1978 (model)

385 Holger Scheel
Armchair for Rosenthal,
1979 (model)

386 Holger Scheel
Armchair for Rosenthal,
1979 (model)

387 Holger Scheel
Table 1, 1977 (model)

388 Holger Scheel
"Toga II" armchair, 1978

389 Holger Scheel
Table 3, 1979, and
Armchair 9, 1979 (models 1 : 7.5)

384

385

386

387

388

389

390

391

392

393

390 Holger Scheel
Chair 4, 1979 (model
1 : 7.5)

391, 392
Holger Scheel
Armchair 16, 1979
(model)

393 a, b
Holger Scheel
Armchair 13, 1979
(model)

394 –405
Holger Scheel
Sketches for chairs and
armchairs, 1979

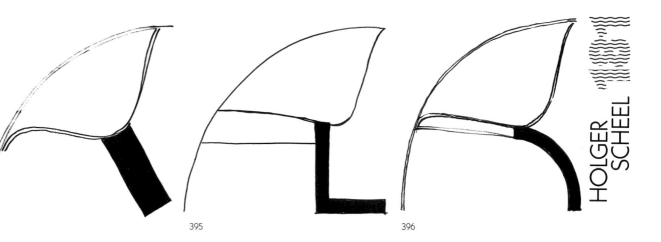

394

395

396

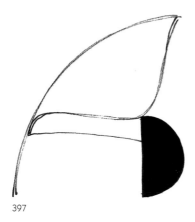
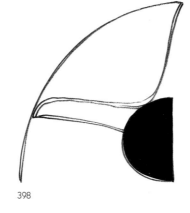

397

398

399

400

401

402

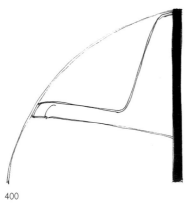
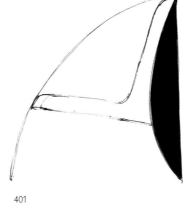

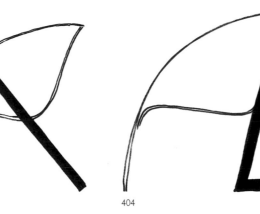
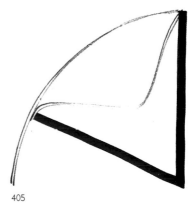

403

404

405

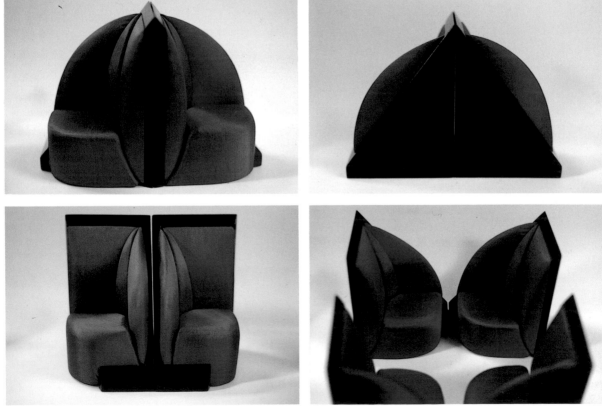

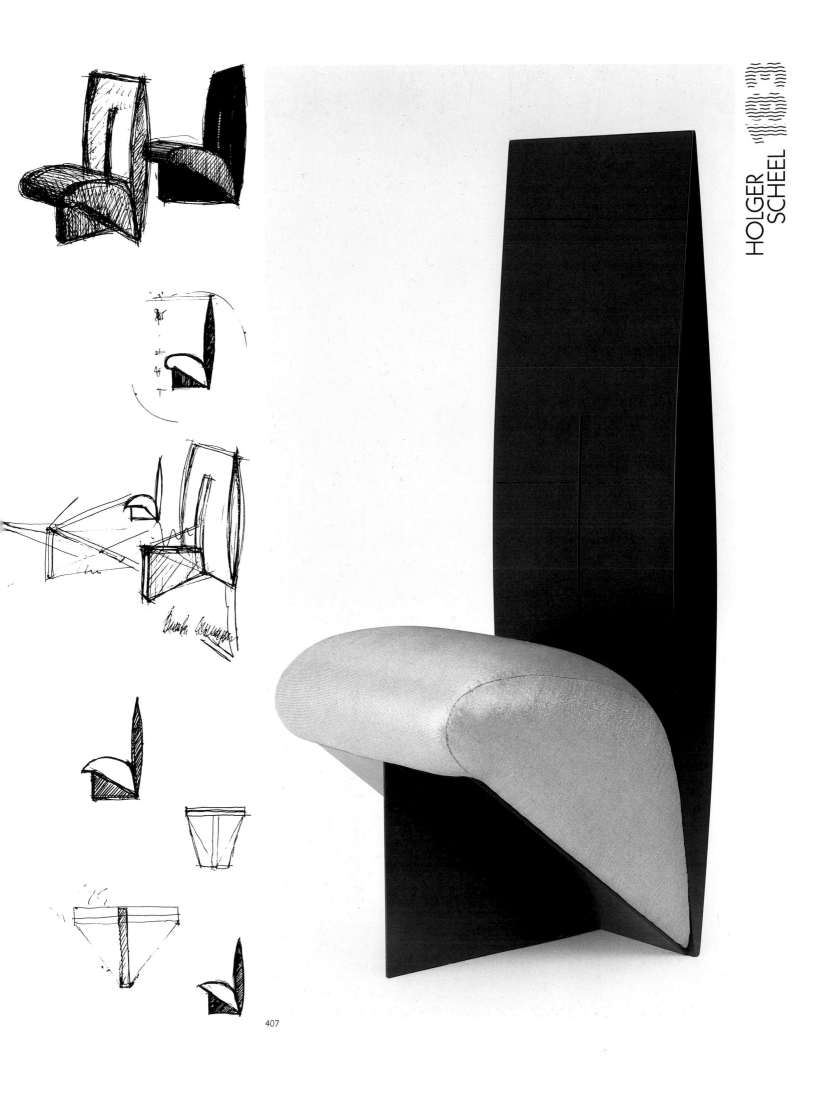

407

408

409

410

411

HOLGER SCHEEL

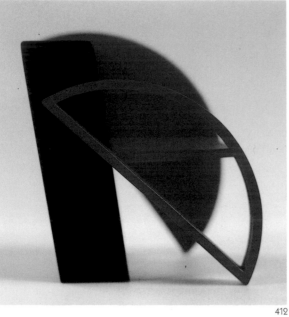

412

413

412–416, 419
Holger Scheel
7 variants of "Black/ Red" series (models)

417 Holger Scheel
Armchair 26, 1983

418 Holger Scheel
Chair 7, 1984

414

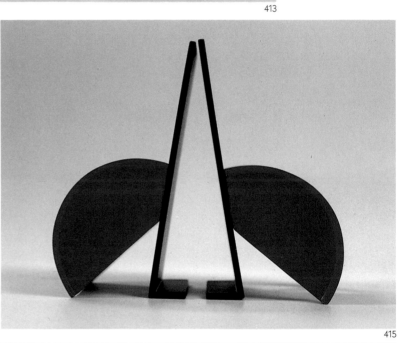

415

416

417

418

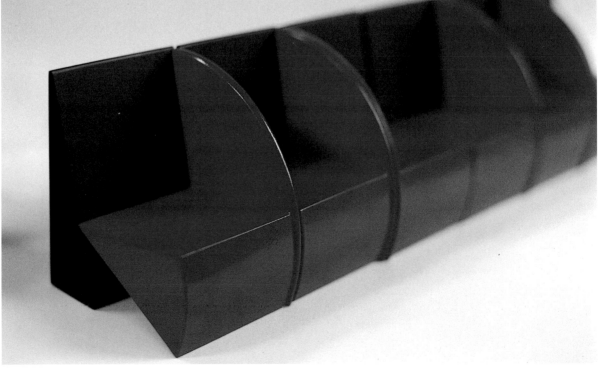

419

HOLGER
SCHEEL

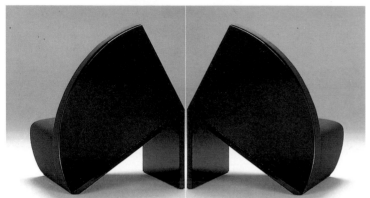

420 a–e
Holger Scheel
"Scultura" armchair,
1986

421 Holger Scheel
Ein Ort für O. ("A Place
for O."), 1986 (model)

420

421

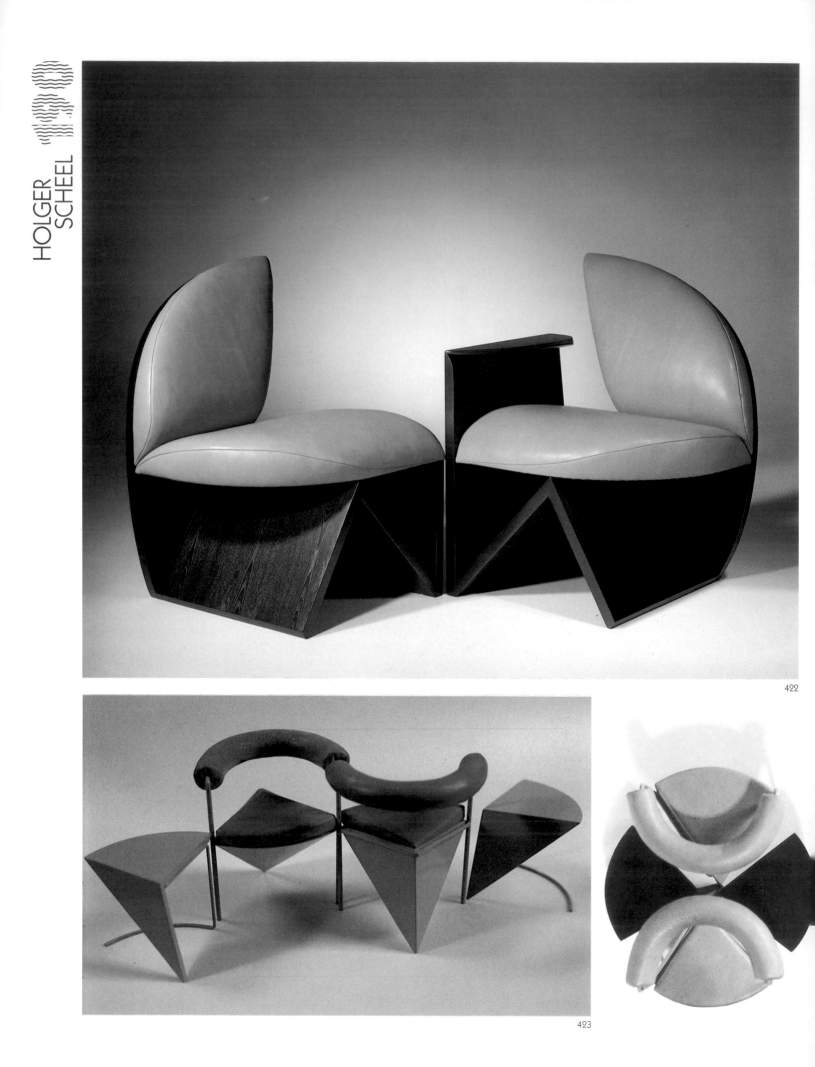

422

423

422 Holger Scheel
Chair 8, 1987, for Ger-
man Architecture
Museum

423 a, b
Holger Scheel
Chair 5 (and Table 5,
1985 (models 1 : 7.5)

424 a Holger Scheel
Chair 8, 1986

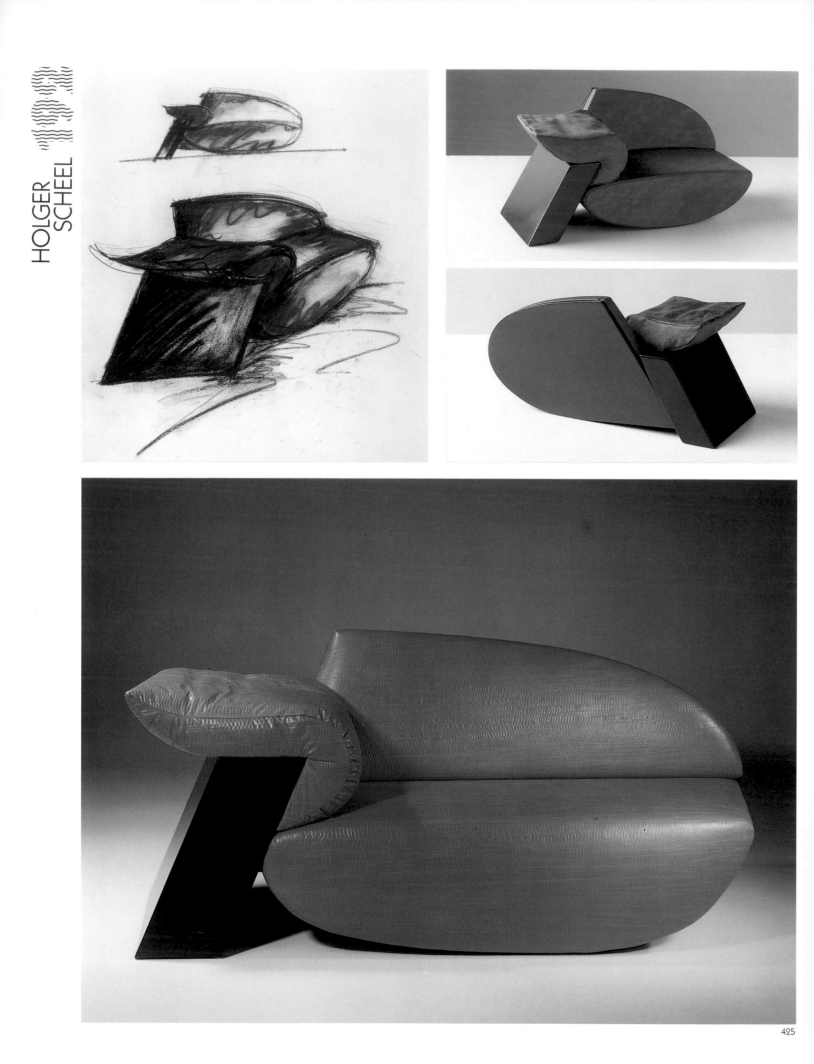

426

427

428

429

430

429 Holger Scheel
Chair 10, 1987 (model)

430 a, b
Holger Scheel
Table 10, 1987 (model)

431–434
Holger Scheel
Glassware designs,
1987

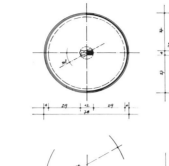

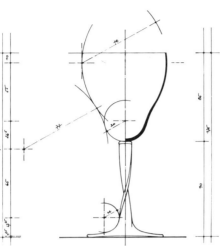

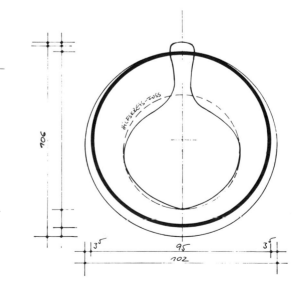

431

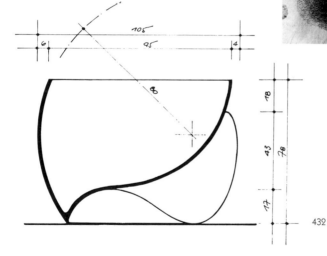

432

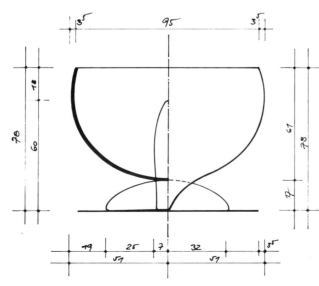

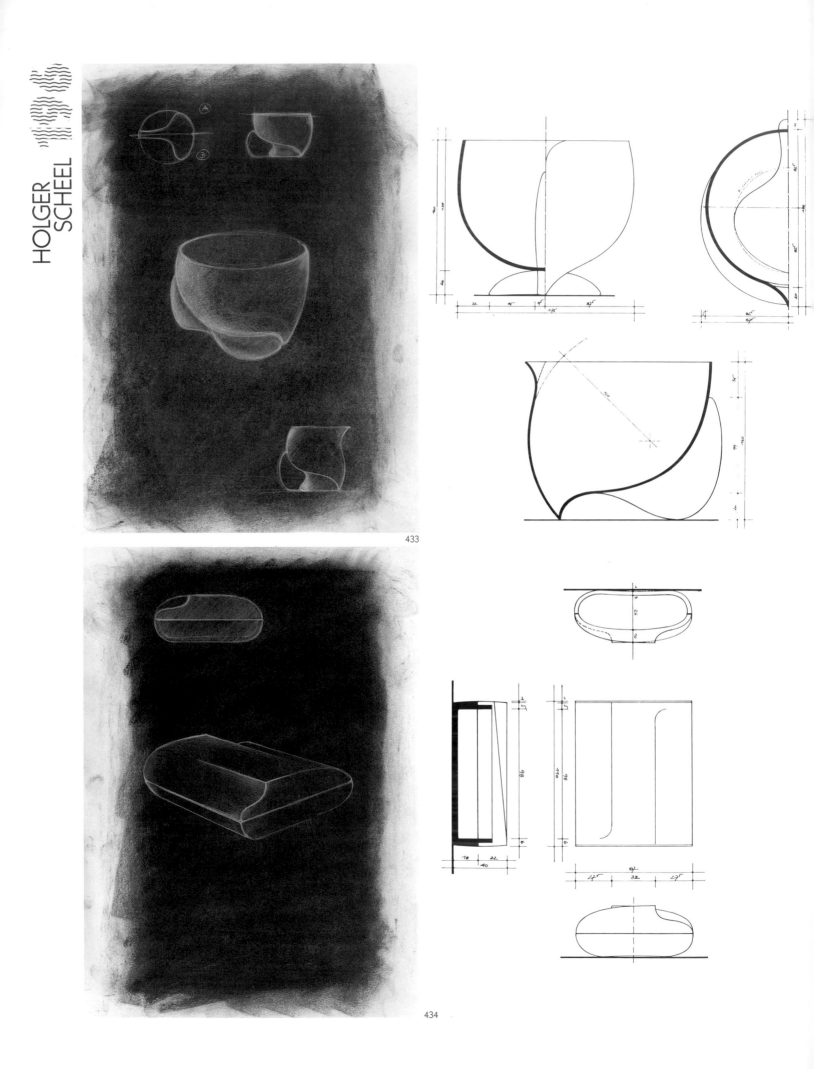

433

434

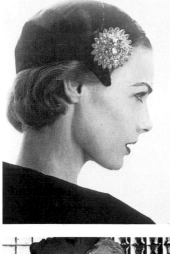

1

2

3

4

5

6

Fig. 1: Archetype-Purism
Fig. 2: Post-Modernism
Fig. 3: Minimalism
Fig. 4: High Tech
Fig. 5: Trans High Tech
Fig. 6: High-Touch/Memphis/
Alchimia

As one who likes to juggle with yardsticks, I am particularly interested in the theme of this exhibition, which I consider to be higly topical. I would like to contribute a few "anagrammatic signs". Not complete sentences, i. e.:
not a scholarly dissertation on interdisciplinary demarcation disputes – not just another statement by a designer-architect on the blurring of distinctions between the professions – not an inquiry into whether the sign-language of architecture is receiving new impulses from the yardsticks applied in object designs or rather, whether the small-scale designers draw their inspiration from the big boys.
Academic opinions on these matters will no doubt continue to clash in the future. It is my basic conviction that a holistic design dynamic is breaking down barriers now that Post-Modernism is on the wane. Today, those who are creatively

Matteo Thun

NEO-BAROQUE YARDSTICKS

minded can choose from a clearly articulated range of approaches which, as far as I am concerned, are practically identical with the "style-concepts" presented in this exhibition:

1. Archtetype-Purism (Rossi- Ungers, Botta, . . .) (Fig. 1)
2. Post-Modernism (Graves, Hollein, Venturi, . . .) (Fig. 2)
3. Minimalism (Kuramata, Stark, Zeus, . . .) (Fig. 3)
4. High Tech (Foster, Rogers, Piano, . . .) (Fig. 4)
5. Trans High Tech (Castiglioni, Maurer, Pesce, . . .) (Fig. 5)
6. High Touch/Memphis/Alchimia (Sottsass, Mendini, Art & Industry, . . .) (Fig. 6)

So much for the hyped-up game of names, institutionalised by experts, popularised, marketed. Is there common denominator in all the cultural ferments that derive from these concepts, a forward-looking curiosity that they share? I believe there is.

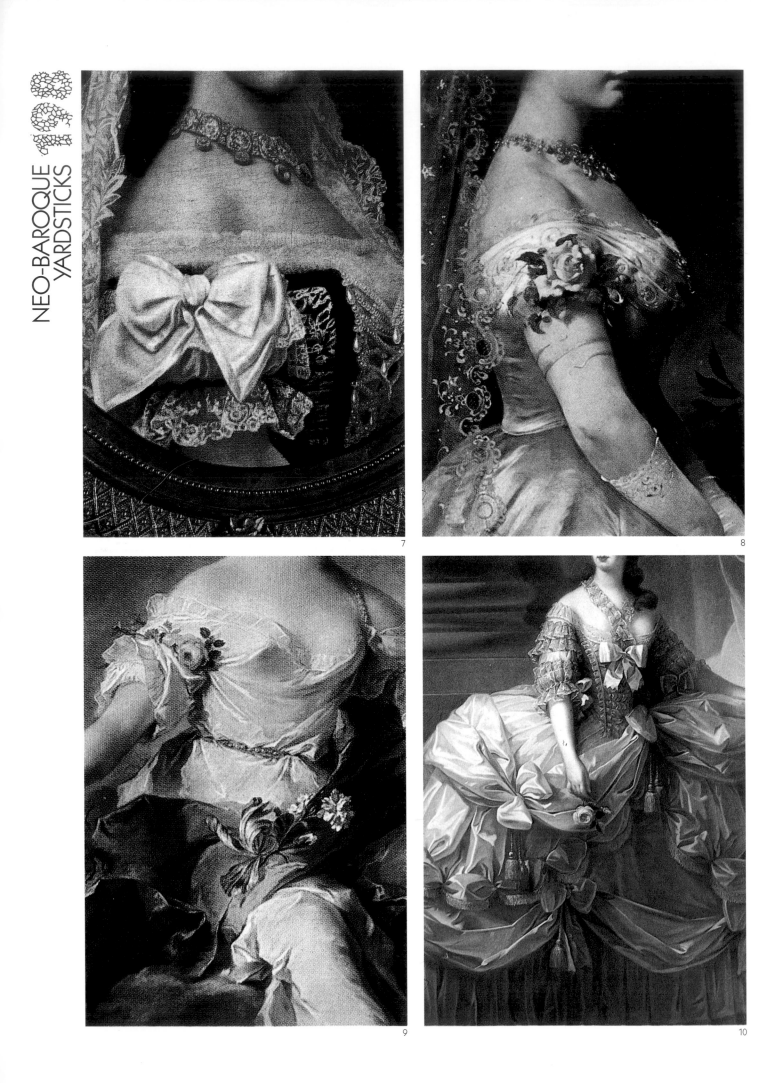

7

8

9

10

Fig. 7–10:   Neo-Baroque

Fig. 11:   Temple facade, Paestum (elevation)

Fig. 12:   Theatre in Schönbrunn Palace,
Vienna (interior)

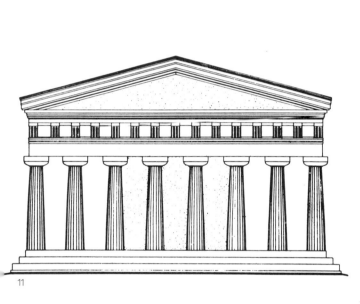

11

12

It seems to me that "Neo-Baroque" would do as a collective label: an intuitive analysis of the theme, not a "return" to Baroque, nor does it mean that the majority of the aesthetic statements of today's society are Neo-Baroque.

Neo-Baroque is a trend that links many of today's cultural phenomena in all fields and is thus quite different from all the cultural phenomena that have gone before.

The typical elements of Neo-Baroque are: the search for antiholistic forms, forms which substitute instability and complexity for systematic order. No scientific theory can accommodate such fluctuating and turbulent phenomena (Fig. 7–10).

Perhaps I can clarify my understanding of the "Neo-Baroque" nexus analytically through the following axioms, presented as parallel assertions from various fields – science, mass communications, philosophy, art, and behaviour.

1. Classical and Baroque

The formal constants of Classical and Baroque are antithetic, as Wölfflin showed at the beginning of the century: on the one hand linearity, on the other painterliness, surface plane versus depth; closed forms versus open forms, multiplicity versus unity, absolute clarity versus relative clarity (Fig. 11, 12).

What is more, the evolutionary stages of the successive eras can be seen as "experimental", "classical", and "baroque", with a progression towards perfectionism. These three stages are morphological transformations in the sense of Focillon's logic of morphogenesis and are valid for every stylistic period of history, applying to the origin and development, the perfection, and the degeneration of forms. The architectonic principles of order and symmetry in the classical phase are replaced by disharmony and asymmetry in the baroque phase.

Conclusion: Baroque, in this sense, is a term of analogy.

13

14

2. Rhythm and Repetition

Where the classical idea of originality emphasises the uniqueness of the object of art to the extent that it becomes virtually indescribable, the baroque approach tends towards the aesthetic of repetition. I am thinking for instance of the aesthetic of the Replicants in Ridley Scott's film *Blade Runner* (Fig. 14). Their feelings are superior to those of their classical forerunner, man. Rhythm and repetition also structure the narrative mode of TV series like *Dallas* or *Dynasty*: recurring patterns include the chase, the hold-up, the kiss. The astronomer Kepler was one of the first to grasp the structures of baroque dynamics. The new cosmology he created not only destroyed the Galilean notion of centrality but also introduced the predilection for the elliptical form into the Baroque ethos. This form was always both real and virtual centre (Fig. 13).

Conclusion: The Integrative elements of Neo-Baroque aesthetics are polycentrism, ordered disorder, organised variants, and accelerated rhythm.

Fig. 13: Andy Warhol: *Marylin Monroe*, serigraphs

Fig. 14: Still from Ridley Scott's *Blade Runner* (USA 1982)

Fig. 15: Collage: Lacroix – Sun King. Styles of the late Baroque period, around 1700, bear resemblances to the 1988 collection of Christian Lacroix.

15

3. Limited and Unlimited

The threshold of a house is a natural "limit" or borderline between inside and outside, the private sphere and the public. If we "go beyond the limit" we are in a sense breaking out of a closed system.

Examples of "going beyond the limit" are the paintings of the late Renaissance, Mannerism, and the Baroque period. In the construction of perspective the vanishing point wanders beyond the limit, boundaries fall away, in contrast to the enclosed pictorial space of the Renaissance created by the use of artificial perspective. This treatment of space is demonstrated, for instance, in Tiepolo's portrait of Louis XIV. At the court of the Sun King, around 1700, fashions and entertainments were also becoming eccentric, both went beyond the limit. Bridging the historical gap, the clothes of the couturier Christian Lacroix (1988) are based on similar ideas: the spectacular dominates, has become the rule, jeans are worn to ceremonial events, evening dress for strolls (Fig. 15).

The desire to totally transgress the limits finds fulfilment in eccentricity. In contrast to centrality, which is based on aesthetic and emotional roots, eccentricity is concerned with the externals of the work and with a pseudo-aesthetic formalism.

Conclusion: Static epochs are characterised by centralism and limitation, dynamic epochs on the other hand operate at the limit and with exaggeration. Neo-Baroque taste is volatile and continually in a state of excitement and turmoil, without however necessarily aiming at the abrogation of cultural values.

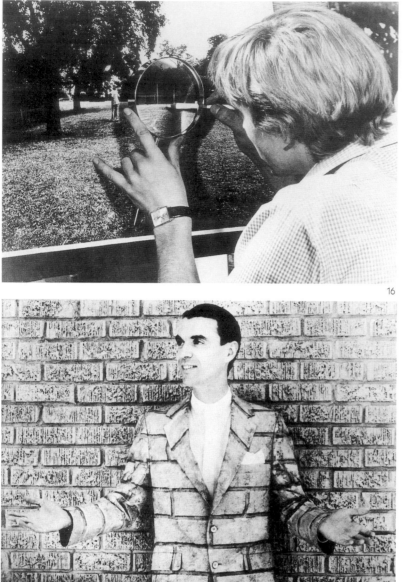

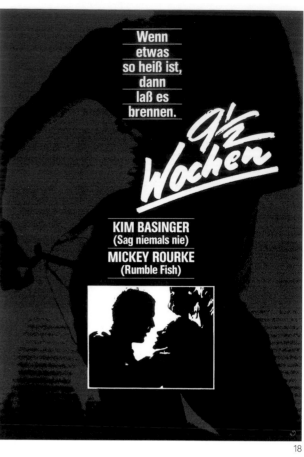

Fig. 16: Still from Michelangelo Antonioni's *Blow-Up* (GB 1966)

Fig. 17: Still from David Byrne's *True Stories* (USA 1986)

Fig. 18: German poster for Adrian Lyne's *9 ½ Weeks* (USA 1986)

4. Detail and Fragment

Details are developing towards ever increasing autonomy and away from the holistic model. I use the word "detail" here in the sense of the French roots *dé-tail*, "cutting off". Nowadays fragments increasingly emphasise their break-away from the whole – as far as we can see, nobody is going to put the fragments together again. In contemporary films such as Adrian Lyne's *Flashdance* or *9 ½ Weeks* the time-sequence of details has a clearly aesthetic function; in Antonioni's *Blow Up* the detail of a crime becomes the theme of the film; in David Byrne's *True Stories* the ideology of the fragment replaces the conventional film narrative (Fig. 16–18). Roland Barthes said some time ago that contradictoriness was to be preferred to an order that deformed. In architecture, people like Carlo Scarpa and Franco Albini use fragments and quotations from the past, setting them against the backcloth of a neutral construction. In this way both compose their individual poetry of design.

Conclusion: Neo-Baroque also means the decline and fall of the holistic approach.

Fig. 19:   Still from
Woody Allen's *Zelig*
(USA 1982)

Fig. 20:   Still from
Jean-Jacques Arnaud's
The Name of the Rose
(D/I/F, 1986)

Fig. 21:   SITE: "Notch"
showroom for Best
products, Sacramento
(1977)

5. Instability and Metamorphosis

In Woody Allen's film *Zelig* the principal character seems
to have neither an individual personality nor looks of his
own. Mentally and physically he adapts himself to his environment: Zelig becomes thin, fat, rich, poor, an athlete, a
politician, or whatever (Fig. 19).

Umbertos Eco's novel *The Name of the Rose* (1980)
employs the principle of metamorphosis structurally. Very
disparate texts are combined in a montage into a new text
and hence acquire new expressive power (Fig. 20).

In Salvador Dalí's painting *Cycle of Catastrophes 1981*,
instability is made the main theme of a work of art. In the
Best Showrooms designed by the American team of
architects SITE the monotonously recurrent box shape of
big stores has been given a characteristic instability
through various metamorphoses of the exterior (Fig. 21).

Conclusion: In our culture a mechanism of formal turbu-
lence is making itself felt: stable, ordered, regular, symmetrical forms are being succeeded by unstable, unor-
dered, irregular, unsymmetrical forms.

This is a sequence of fluctuating phenomena which destabilise the current system of values. In the main, however, our cultural universe is moulded by very traditional, stable, and ordered substructures. Hence, irregular forms and extremely stable forms confront each other in conflict. The Neo-Baroque culture I have outlined gives rise to a contrast programme, a new flowering of the classical ethos.

The various classicisms were never a simple return to the past. Every classicism consists both of configurations that belong directly to the past and of others that apparently have no such connections. The only thing that never changes is the inner morphology and structure of the value judgements. Normally, such a "classical" system is highly prescriptive and norm-setting: the Bauhaus and the Ulm School are impressive – and problematic – examples.

In contrast, "anticlassical" or "baroque" systems emerge from the collapse of symmetries and the appearance of fluctuations within the various categories and orders.

In the age of Neo-Baroque, however, the gulf between the two systems seems to have narrowed; the instability is the result of a blurring of categories. Such diverse phenomena as bodybuilding, the bronze figures of Riace, Gianni Versace advertisements, all depend on a classical neo-con-

Fig. 22: Collage
"Floating Particles"

Fig. 23: Lincoln
convertible (1950)

Fig. 24: Fiat Uno
(1980)

servatism for their system of reference. In contrast, there is a "cabriolet" culture which ranges from Ralph Lauren to Michael Graves's Portland Building.

Contemporaneously with classical neoconservatism, there is an increasingly important cluster of "floating particles" that together create a continuum: fashion designers such as Azedine Alaia, Zoran, Romeo Gigli, and Comme des Garçons; Japanese consumer goods, U. S. West Coast packaging, Foster's Shanghai Bank skyscraper; the world-wide chain of Esprit boutiques fitted out by Ettore Sottsass; Philippe Starck's Manin restaurant in Tokyo; suburban "No Names", and the "flexible manufacturing systems" of such firms as Fiat, Mirafiori, Volkswagen, and the Detroit car industry (Fig. 22).

In the age of Neo-Baroque, a 1980 Fiat Uno stands next to a 1950 Lincoln convertible (Fig. 23, 24), a dinner-jacket hangs next to a pair of jeans, a Tizio lamp stands next to a Tiffany lamp in Art Nouveau look, an exclusive shopping-bag from Vuitton next to a plastic carrier-bag . . .

A new cultural model appears on the occidental horizon: the "Neo-Baroque Bauhaus". Two lungs breathe and com-plement each other in one and the same organism, more oxygen than ever before is pumped into the creative processes – and into the personal experience of the objects created, too. This cultural model is motivated by the future, cosmopolitan and open-minded; yardsticks are no use here . . .

And so – surprise, surprise – the question posed by this exhibition – the relative roles of art and design in the creation of form – almost answers itself: it depends upon what the practitioners do.

NEO-BAROQUE YARDSTICKS

Appendix: "The small scale also follows the archtetype of house-building". (A comparison of scales with regard to the Ungers house).

The aesthetic disciplines of architecture and design are in many ways basically comparable. In acknowledgement of the *genius loci*, the following set of comparisons attempts to adapt to the discipline of design the morphological method used by Oswald Matthias Ungers in his plans for the German Architecture Museum, with the super-cypher of the "house within the house". The "house within the house" symbolically illustrates three aspects of the theoretical discipline of architecture. The level with the four open supports and the detached rectangular cornice is a sort of abstract representation of the idea that architecture always has something to do with loads and support, that is, with statics – this might be regarded as a form of grammar. On the next level, this structure is built up on the same modular system to create an enclosed space that relates to the space sur-

rounding it. This is again an abstract representation: the theme is the problem of the ground-plan, and the different approaches to this problem through the ages – a problem of changing conceptions of space, i. e. a problem of syntax. On the third level, finally, stands an abstract building with a saddle-roof. This stands for the sequence of categories and typologies in the development of architectural history, a "primal house", a temple, a hut – hence a problem of typology, of semiotics. When read as an abstract epistemology, this morphological model can be transferred to the discipline of design, where it presents parallels, again on three levels. I have tried to show how this could be applied to actual designed objects by taking three examples derived from contrasting life-style models (Fig. 25 – 30); there is a shift of proportions with this "house within the house" model according to where the main emphasis is placed.

ARCHITECTURE
(things you can walk about in)

3. TYPOLOGY (SEMIOTICS)

2. SPACE (SYNTAX)

1. STATICS: loads, supports (GRAMMAR)

" UNGERS HAUS "

DESIGN
(things you can't walk about in)

3. STYLE ELEMENT (use of style to state a position)
2. DIALOGUE WITH THE ENVIRONMENT (volumetric concept)
1. FUNCTIONALLY PRACTICABLE PRODUCTIONALLY PRACTICABLE

Example: three objects derived from three contrasting life-style models.

Fig. 25 Biedermeier life-style model (1900)
Fig. 26 Memphis (Schwarzenberg)

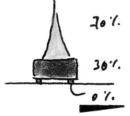

70%.

30%.

0%.

SEMIOTICS 70% repositioning of classical style elements produces a new "table-type"
SYNTAX 30% strong dialogue with the environment
STATICS 0% (one category absent) functionally impracticable productionally impracticable

Fig. 27 Bauhaus life-style model (1920)
Fig. 28 Braun shaver

5%.
30 %.

65%

SEMIOTICS 5% (flat roof) type: low semiotic profile does not permit positioning through style elements
SYNTAX 30% volumetrically "rounded" concept
STATICS 65% optimisation of functional practicability and productional practicability

Fig. 29 Pop Art life-style model (1960)
Fig. 30 Memphis ("Carlton")

40%

40%

20%

SEMIOTICS 40% balanced ratio of style elements
SYNTAX 40% to volumetric concept pushes functional practicability into the background
STATICS 20% support semiotics: the semantic profile becomes a semiotic profile

From about 1978 onwards there is evidence of a new stylistic diversification in the field of product design, comparable to the process that has been taking place in interior design. This phenomenon is particularly apparent in the context of Post-Modernism and Alchimia/Memphis, and to a lesser extent in other movements of recent years such as High Tech. In the design of utility objects the agglomerative approach, which has no qualms about "attaching" decorative elements to a basic shape or highlighting the various constituent parts, is rapidly gaining ground over the integrative approach of Functionalism, which seeks to present the image of an organic whole without extraneous ornament. In the case of electrical appliances, such as clocks, radios, pocket calculators and percolators, or even irons and vacuum-cleaners, this trend is encouraged by the miniaturisation of the technical components (pl. 185 – 191); and with articles of "table culture" – tea and coffee sets, trays, crockery, centrepieces, vases, candlesticks, fruit-dishes, cutlery – it is only the problems of working such materials as glass, earthenware, porcelain or metal that may impose limitations on the agglomerative designer. For the first time since the twenties and thirties, the heyday of Bauhaus and Art Deco, questions of form and style are being approached with an adventurousness that adds a new cultural dimension to mundane objects, brings the designer back into the public eye, and effectively polishes up corporate images.

Architectonic principles are evident in the design of many of these "table-top" accessories, hence the increasing acceptance of the term "Micro-Architecture", which was originally coined in Italy.[1] Scale and proportion are here as important as in the design of a building, and it is not surprising that most of the leading figures in the field are architects, Post-Modern paladins like Graves, Hollein, Tigerman and Venturi, Sottsass and Thun from the Memphis camp, or Late-Modernists like Richard Meier and Gwathmey & Siegel. There is furniture that can equally well be classified as Micro-Architecture – we have already encountered the "skyscraper" bureaux (pl. 204 – 208); in the field of tableware the movement began with an idea of Alessandro Mendini's that was taken up by the Italian metal goods manufacturers Alessi. The Officina Alessi, the firm's experimental division, commissioned a series of "Tea and Coffee Piazzas" (pl. 435 – 445) from eleven internationally renowned architects and designers: Venturi, Graves, Tigerman, Jencks, Meier, Rossi, Portoghesi, Mendini, Yamashita, Hollein, and Tusquets. Produced in a limited edition of ninety-nine sets of each design, and priced at around £ 12,000 each, these multiples were premiered in 1983 on two continents simultaneously – at the Brera gallery in Milan and at the Max Protetch architecture gallery in New York, the choice of such institutions as channels of distribution serving to emphasise the "cultural" quality of these wares.

The silver "Tea and Coffee Piazzas" are in the tradition of similarly ambitious projects of the Vienna Workshop, where Josef Hoffmann and Otto Wagner were the leading lights, and of Art Deco tableware of the thirties. For the first time in many years, the theories and principles that govern industrial design are again the same as those applied in architecture. The very term "piazza" implies a tectonically defined arrangement of the tea and coffee pots, sugar basin, and milk jug.[2] The early eighties also gave birth to the ceramic objects, now virtually classics of their kind, of Matteo Thun, founder-member of the Memphis organisation and undoubtedly along with Ettore Sottsass and Andrea Branzi one of the most successful contemporary Italian product designers. For the first Memphis collections in 1981/82 he created tableware that appeals unashamedly to the emotions, borrowing elements from the cultures of ancient Egypt and the Mayas or zoomorphic in its imagery, evoking lizards, dinosaurs, and birds (pl. 446, 447). The ornithological theme is elaborated in a series of tea and coffee pots for Alessio Sarri (pl. 448 – 453), and the lamps, cupboards and glassware (pl. 454, 455) of this period are in a similar vein.[3]

Thun belongs to the new international network of "iconophiles", for whom the intermingling of the various fields of culture and their experience therein constitutes a semiotic continuum: boundaries begin to dissolve, and it is but a small step from fashion to graphic art, and thence to design, architecture, film . . . There is a similar blurring of the distinction between reality and its interpretation, between facts and opinion or comment. The power of images has subverted the power of reality, at least when it comes to formulating aesthetic ideals and convictions. The flood of clashing, heterogeneous experiential possibilities in our postindustrial society makes it seem arbitrary and reactionary to distinguish between facts, opinions, symbols and attitudes; and Thun often speaks with relish of the "semantic chaos" that we have to accept, but to which we should attempt to give some sort of structure. The historical procession of styles has resulted in the accumulation of a rich diversity of forms, which we today can delve into, combining and exploiting for our own purposes. Sottsass paved the way, and Thun shows us where it could lead: the product designer should avail himself of this repertoire, without becoming bogged down in nostalgia; paying no regard to the significance that may have been attached to particular forms in their historical contexts, he should create new combinations that are meaningful in our day and age.

Thun's products also demonstrate how desirable, indeed necessary it is today that big manufacturing companies

MICRO-ARCHITECTURE

should rethink their commercial strategies to take account of the growing general prosperity and the emergence of new social strata, such as the yuppies, who are prepared to pay good money for the requisites they need to define their particular "life-style". Among the "sophisticated items" that reflect exquisite taste and discernment it is quite natural that the objects we are here concerned with, the "table landscapes", should be as sought-after as clothes, jewellery, houses and exotic holidays. Such products will subsume a variety of idioms, traditions and attitudes.

New market segments demand new approaches in company policy; as Thun puts it: "We need an industry that renews itself on the basis of the culture it has itself helped to create".[4] It is a sign of the times that, in addition to working as a designer, Matteo Thun has in recent years been retained as corporate identity consultant by several German firms, both large and small, whose image has always tended to be rather conservative. It is evidently due to his influence that some of these firms have since made interesting reappraisals of their product ranges. A case in point is the old-established Württembergische Metallwarenfabrik, WMF: probably the world's biggest manufacturers of domestic hardware and cutlery, they had hitherto virtually ignored the field of contemporary avant-garde design. (In 1927 they did create a department for experimental and artistic design as opposed to market-oriented mass production, but this was discontinued after the war.) Then, from about 1984 onwards, a few designers set about modifying the WMF image, or at least broadening its scope. As well as Matteo Thun, people like Jo Laubner, Angelo Cortesi, Mario Vivaldi, Vito Noto, Franz Otto Lipp, and Danilo Silvestrin have been involved (pl. 456 – 462, 464 – 468). "La Galleria" is a range of artistic accessories for the home in signed and limited editions: bottle-coolers, ice-buckets, trays, vases, candlesticks, centrepieces, the sort of things that are important in setting a stylish table. All the pieces in the series are made from brass and silver combined with marble and acrylate. Stylistically they are somewhere between "cool" neomodern design in the manner of the American East Coast and a narrative symbolic style based on Memphis. The visual differentiation of the various components underlines the architectonic structure of the objects. This agglomerative aesthetic derives from the stylistic strategies of Post-Modernism and Alchimia/Memphis: miniature columns function as supports, spheres link pyramids and cubes, rods and cylinders. The plethora of formal elements makes a sharp contrast to the compact, "off-the-peg" style of Modernism and the integrative design method of Functionalism.

The form language of these designers is however by no means homogeneous. While Jo Laubner inclines towards Art Deco shapes like the American skyscrapers of the thirties, or occasionally towards a Holleinesque vocabulary (pl. 460 – 462), Matteo Thun prefers to fuse the contrasts between different epochs and periods, as he indicated in his aphoristic manifesto of 1986, *Das barocke Bauhaus:* the time has come again for the language of myth to supersede that of logic, for a creative method that transcends the boundaries imposed by scale, that engages in dialogue with fashion (pl. 456 – 459). Stylistically, "Bauhaus Baroque" stands for the paradoxical combination of aristocratic extravagance, i. e. gold and ornamentation, with the austere formal discipline of classical Modernism. For this, a degree of emancipation is required that has most nearly been achieved in milieus where design is open to the influence of mass media such as advertising and film, California or Japan rather than in Europe; accordingly, Thun advocates the enrichment of European design with a "fresh breeze of Pacific fragrances".[5]

The idea of designing objects on architectonic principles can also be seen in the work of the other new WMF designers. Angelo Cortesi's creations are architecture in a nutshell (pl. 466), while Vito Noto and Danilo Silvestrin (pl. 464, 467) have used in their designs a pseudo-archaic idiom like that of Aldo Rossi in his famous Alessi espresso pots (pl. 463). Mario Vivaldi and F. O. Lipp also owe a debt to these archaic primary forms (pl. 465, 468).[6] Recently, within the overall concept of the "La Galleria" range, WMF have been experimenting with the large-scale production of "exclusive" articles aimed at particular sectors of the market. These objects must necessarily be keenly priced and suitable for marketing in department stores and High Street outlets; compromises have evidently had to be made. "Domus", a table ensemble in neon colours by Jo Laubner, Matteo Thun's "Tavola" range, effectively presented as a cityscape in the WMF catalogue (pl. 469), and the new plastic trays by the same designer (pl. 470, 471) have production runs of 60,000 to 100,000 envisaged for each design. The surface decorations of Thun's trays are reminiscent of the floral Art Nouveau of the turn of the century and of the pattern designs of William Morris; the handles are Memphis-inspired. The discreet use of pastel tones both smacks of "chinoiserie" and lends a Post-Modern touch that puts the nostalgic element into perspective. We find exuberant, flowery designs side by side with sober geometric patterns à la Josef Hoffmann – here again that combination of opulence and abstinence that is the keynote of "Bauhaus Baroque".

The classic WMF product field, cutlery, has also been affected by the segmentation of the market and the new cultural role of household wares. Mario Vivaldi was the first German designer to create a Post-Modern style for cutlery with "Solo" (pl. 473, 474). The handles of the knives, forks and spoons are decorated with an inlaid half-circle and an elegant side-bar; a great deal of experimentation was necessary to find a lamination process that would render the cutlery dishwasher-proof. The half-circles on the knife and fork complement each other, so when the table is laid they form a complete circle. Stylistically the decoration is reminiscent of the Abet laminates used by Memphis and their followers. Even the basic metal shape, without decoration, has a greater formal tension than conventional cutlery, but this "anticlassical" primary outline in the tradition of Hollein, Graves or Isozaki is most impressive in the coloured version. While other cutlery designs in the new "Ambiente" range are relatively unadventurous variants of the traditional spectrum of conventional cutlery, Matteo Thun's "Hommage à Madonna" set (pl. 472) is quite something else. The pop-star's erstwhile predilection for adorning herself with masses of jewellery – of gold, silver, brass, metal, even dog chains and sado-masochist accoutrements – is paraphrased in the flashy rings of diverse stylistic and cultural provenances that encrust the matt black handles. Evocative of the fat cigars and beringed fingers of Mafia bosses, they illustrate how the glittering world of show-biz and the shadowy world of crime are often closely related, as evidenced by the underworld connections of Frankie-Boy (Sinatra). This is cutlery that scotches all preconceived ideas about the genre, charged as it is with blasé nonchalance, oh-so-profound symbolism, extravagance, super-cool eroticism and mannered self-assurance.

Thun's glasses of the "Sherry Netherlands" series for Quartett's "Anthologie" collection (pl. 454, 455) are stylistically close to his early zoomorphic ceramics. The intricate forms pose severe problems for the glass-blower, as do the famous creations of the Czech Borek Sipek, also produced by Quartett. Originally German distributors of other firms' products, Quartett now also manufacture their own lines, including designs by the proprietor. Since 1986 they have been associated in a joint venture with Italian, French, English and Spanish avant-garde design groups; the activities of design, production, advertising and selling tend to become more and more interconnected, economically a factor of the increasing concentration on target segments within the broad market spectrum. Besides glass and ceramics, Quartett are also involved in cupboards and upholstered furniture. Because the big German manufacturers have, so far at least, given little thought to the setting up of experimental studios of their own, the organisational structure of Quartett is conducive to a relatively rapid economic success both in Germany and internationally.

In 1984 the American company Swid Powell appeared on the scene with a 54-piece collection of porcelain, crystal and silver, also destined for the "table landscape". Here, too, the management had decided to commission "the most glittering stars of the contemporary architectural firmament", so it is hardly surprising that over twenty percent of the series has since found its way into the permanent design collection of the Metropolitan Museum of Art in New York. Today, the Swid Powell range comprises more than one hundred objects. The table accoutrements include work by the most important contemporary American architects of Post Modernism, such as Michael Graves, Robert Venturi, Stanley Tigerman, Robert Stern, and Gwathmey & Siegel, as well as by internationally famous non-American architects like Hans Hollein, Arata Isozaki,

Ettore Sottsass, and the Swiss husband-and-wife team Robert and Trix Haussmann (pl. 476–487, 489). The crockery makes extensive use of patterns, symbols and motifs, often in combination, reflecting the stylistic impulses that the architects have formulated in their buildings; these echoes from the realm of architecture give the objects an additional aura. The Post-Modern predilection for decoration and ornament makes some of these plates more like display pieces, while in others it does not militate against their use at the dinner-table. Besides these ceramics, Swid Powell make table silver (pl. 490–495), which is conceived architectonically like the WMF and Alessi items. The tray by Vittorio Gregotti, the candlesticks by the Haussmanns and by Sottsass, and the various creations by Meier and Stern are luxurious pieces which, like Alessi's "Tea and Coffee Piazzas", look back on the rich tradition of table silver of the twenties and thirties. Robert Venturi and Stanley Tigerman/Margaret McCurry have also designed porcelain tea sets for Swid Powell whose iconography is a prime example of Micro-Architecture. Venturi (pl. 488) deconventionalises the almost "normal" shapes of his pots and bowls in Pop Art fashion by painting architectural motifs on them, while Tigerman and McCurry (pl. 475) take a different approach, reproducing in simplified form some of the traditional American architectural types of the Great Plains, such as the grain elevator of the Mid-West; the result is a sort of sarcastic inversion that creates elegant icons. The salt and pepper dispensers exemplify this aesthetic strategy most directly, because it is only when they are put together that they form a complete motif – and the sectional profiles are the only surfaces that are colour-enhanced.

The Viennese painter and sculptress Heide Warlamis seeks to latch onto the Vienna Workshop traditions of Josef Hoffmann and Koloman Moser with her architectonically construed porcelain. About three years ago she founded in Austria a small, family-run manufactory in which all her designs are produced in limited editions. In the "Vienna Collection" both the "Secession" bowls and the variants of the "Skyscraper" and "Metropolitan Tower" vases (pl. 496–500) are distinguished by diverse combinations of basic form and surface decoration. If in the "Skyscraper" vases there is still an attempt to establish a logical connection between the stepped volumetric outline of the porcelain and the applied verticals of the architectural decoration, in the "Metropolitan Tower" vases this connection becomes surreal, even by the standards of the Memphis doctrine of the independence of form and function, material and decoration. The craquelure pattern of the first of the pair of vases might have been conceived by Sottsass, Thun, or Natalie de Pasquier, while the decoration of the second has affinities either to the painting of the Neo-Fauves or – to pursue the architectural parallel – to the work of Coop-Himmelblau. The salt and pepper sets of the "Siena" series (pl. 501, 502) and the oil and vinegar sets of the "Skala" series (pl. 503) similarly present two options:

one variant is based on Hoffmann's aesthetic of black-and-white simplification while the other comes from Pop Art and seems almost a paraphrase of Venturi's Micro-Architecture for Swid Powell. Finally, the "Belvedere" candle-holder (pl. 504) could, with its symmetrical architectonic form and its decoration, almost have been designed by Josef Hoffmann himself, were it not a little too "soft" along the edges. This soft-line aesthetic may be dictated by the production process, but it still means that we cannot see Heide Warlamis's designs as direct translations of architecture in the same way that we might, for example, see sharp-edged objects of gold or silver; this "blunting" of forms gives them more of a whimsical air. Some of these miniature house-sculptures remind one in fact of the architecture of Greek islands such as the Cyclades or of whitewashed clay houses.

How architectural associations can be pushed into the background by the choice of material and technique can be seen at first glance in the next series of small objects (pl. 505 – 515). Franklyn Gerard and Piero Vendruscolo are both pupils of Aldo Rossi; their marble table-lamps are sharp-edged "houses" on small spherical feet, often with "windows" cut into the four walls. In each design a second, translucent house-form of Murano glass, culminating in a stepped pyramid, is set within the first, so that the light shines through the inner wall and then through the cut-out openings in the outer stone wall. Some of the models are based on the cube, others have the shape of a rectangular tower; one version incorporates a clock. Archetypal reductionism in the manner of Rossi and Ungers is a characteristic feature of these lamp designs. Some of them also exploit the translucency of very finely honed marble; hence they recall objects by Carlo Scarpa, who revived this technique that had been practised by medieval craftsmen. Two further examples of clocks show that table top architecture can also serve as a medium for designers of other stylistic persuasions. George J. Sowden's "Metropole" clock from the second Memphis collection (pl. 516) reflects the sort of additive aesthetic and "appliqué" use of decoration and primary colours seen in Memphis furniture. The wake of Memphis has spawned many designs along the same lines, not only "in-the-round" table clocks, but also wrist watches and wall clocks. The almost inexhaustible variety of dials of the "Swatch" watches or the clocks of the Italian firm of Lorenz (pl. 517) are typical examples.

Table lamps are also included in the "Stillight" range designed in 1985 by Matteo Thun and Andrea Lera for Bieffeplast (pl. 518). As in the three standard-lamps (pl. 113 – 115), it is interesting to note in the smaller table versions that the High-Tech aesthetic of perforated patterns in sheet metal is here an extrinsic and thus stylistic device. Since the holes are no longer perfect circles, but drilled by laser in a highly precise pattern of tiny rhombi, they have become an artistic form of decoration determined by aesthetic rather than technological criteria.

"These lamps, ranging in scale from the bedside model to the man-size standard-lamp, are a form of metal architecture in miniature, the shields being made of laser-perforated industrial sheet metal. The 'Stillight' collection displays a dynamic typical for Mattheo Thun: the design process is a similar one both for objects and for buildings – this is the dialectic of scale. What is more, the illuminated small-scale buildings create the illusion that one might enter them; the consumer's imagination is fired. The visual appreciation requires an emotional relationship between man and object (house on stilts, skyscraper, light-house, etc.)"[7]

Also in the High Tech idiom are the accessories of the Munich designer Andreas Weber, including vases, fruit-dishes, trays, cheese-boards and paper-trays (pl. 519 – 523). Like his brushed aluminium or steel furniture (pl. 106 –109) they represent a sophistication of the original High Tech idea of using relatively down-to-earth elements from the industrial world in the private sphere. Weber's designs are close to the classic Modernism of the twenties. His crystal, aluminium or steel surfaces show no trace of use, they are not factory-soiled as one might expect High Tech objects to be. They are the perfect complement to an interior by Mies van der Rohe or Le Corbusier. One might however regret the absence of poetic, literary, in fact, emotional qualities. These are more likely to be found in the Minimalist items of the Zeus group from Milan, whose trays, pencil-holders, and plant-stands with their black, calvinist geometrics are more emotionally stimulating than Weber's objects from the pantheon of classical Modernism.

In the field of Micro-Architecture jewellery has now come to occupy as important a place as items of table landscape. It is impossible to give full coverage here to the diversity of creations – the Cleto Munari collection alone, featuring gold and precious stones, comprises more than eighty pieces, the Acme range of fashion jewellery several hundred; both series were designed by leading Post- and Neo-Modern designers and architects. One project, however, exemplifies in such a prototypical fashion the adaptation of Micro-Architectural concepts to the field of jewellery that it deserves mention at the end of this chapter. In 1987 Masque, a New York architect duo (Douglas Frederick and Ann Cederna), in collaboration with a well-known goldsmith's workshop, produced a range called "Four Orders in Gold and Stone" in allusion to the classical architectural modes (pl. 524 – 528). The basic idea is both simple and intriguing: taking their inspiration from old plans of famous parks, the designers developed schematic forms to be worked in gold, while the surrounding topography was represented by a socle of black marble stepped to suggest the contours of the landscape, providing a suitably luxurious foil for the jewellery. Thus, the plan of Versailles became a ring and that of Blenheim a brooch; the gardens of Chantilly (architectonically a far cry from Blenheim park) gave rise to a pair of earrings; finally, a bracelet represents an abstract fusion of the first three orders to create a fourth order. The systems of reference and overlaps of the architectonic, spatial, structural and visual orders can hardly deny their debt to Ungers and Eisenman. Each piece costs about £ 5,000, so the "Four Orders" are not likely to sell like hot cakes; few yuppies or ultras would be prepared to pay that sort of price for the cultivation of their image. However, since Micro-Architecture is largely equated with "sophisticated items", we may be justified in noting the *non plus ultra* of the genre.

On the whole, it is characteristic of Micro-Architecture that here a new seriousness and thoughtfulness has become evident in the field of design. In view of this, one may express the hope that from these beginnings, which have so far largely been confined to the avant-garde, there will emerge a more consciously cultural attitude to the design of everyday products. We in the Western industrialised nations have it constantly hammered into us by the marketing-men, who are seconded by the mass media, that we need to define ourselves by buying and consuming, the "demonstrative consumer" being the ideal held up for emulation. Why then should this gospel concentrate on prestige products and avant-garde design? If equal energy were devoted to the stylistic enhancement of the mundane objects of everyday life, this life would be much more worth living.

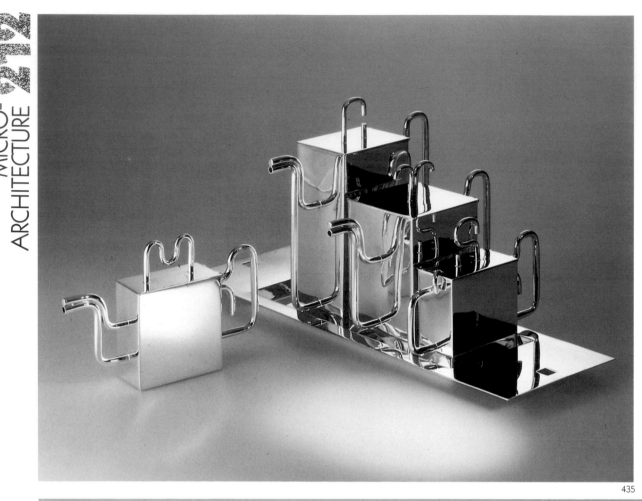

435
Kazumasa Yamashita
5-piece tea and coffee
set, 1983

436   Paolo Portoghesi
6-piece tea and coffee
set, 1983

437   Aldo Rossi
6-piece tea and coffee
set, 1983

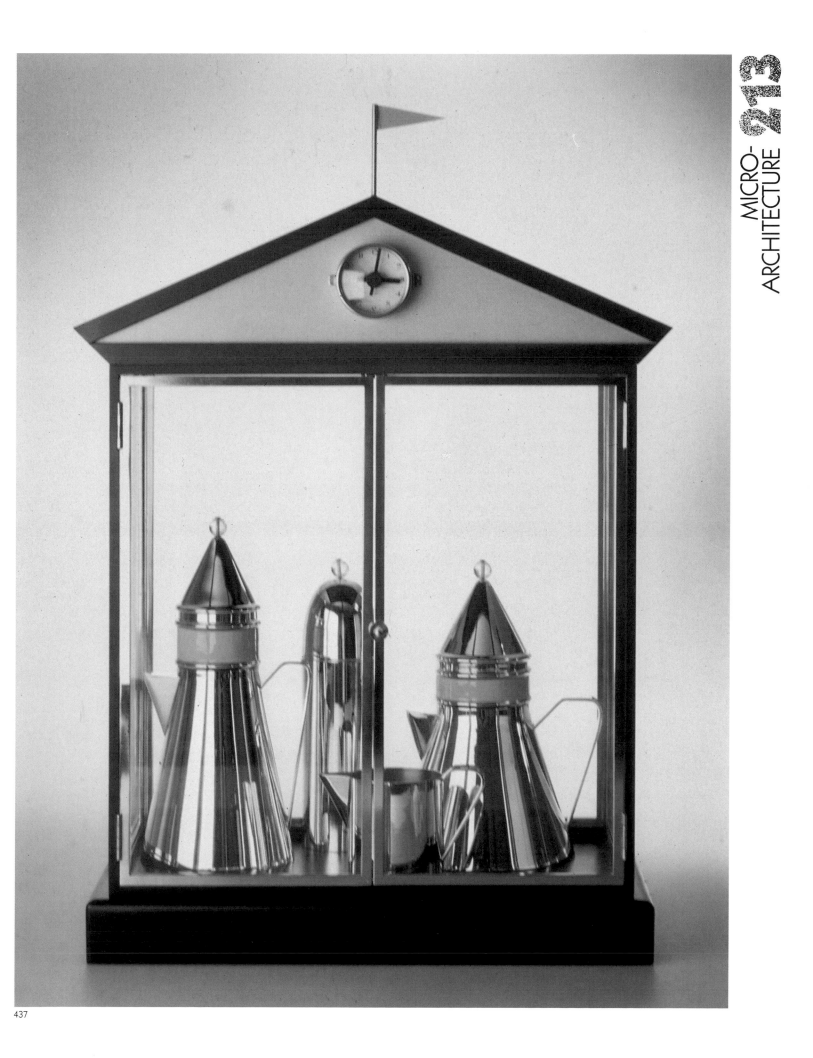

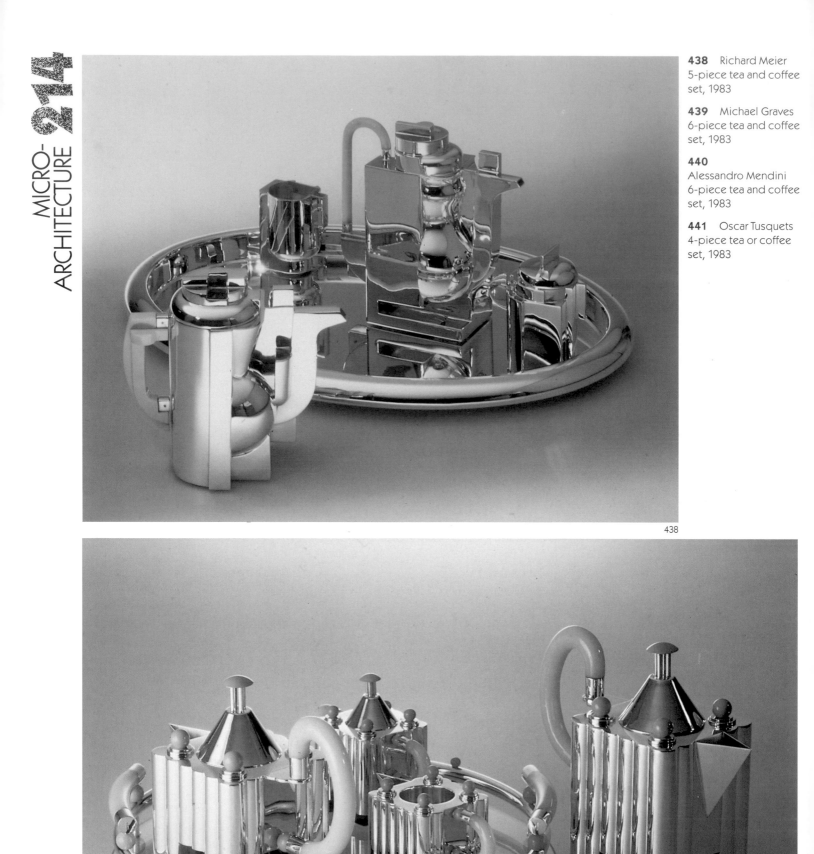

438 Richard Meier
5-piece tea and coffee
set, 1983

439 Michael Graves
6-piece tea and coffee
set, 1983

440
Alessandro Mendini
6-piece tea and coffee
set, 1983

441 Oscar Tusquets
4-piece tea or coffee
set, 1983

438

439

440

441

442

442 Stanley Tigerman
5-piece tea and coffee
set, 1983

443 Robert Venturi
5-piece tea and coffee
set, 1983

444 Charles Jencks
5-piece tea and coffee
set, 1983

445 Hans Hollein
5-piece tea and coffee
set, 1983

444

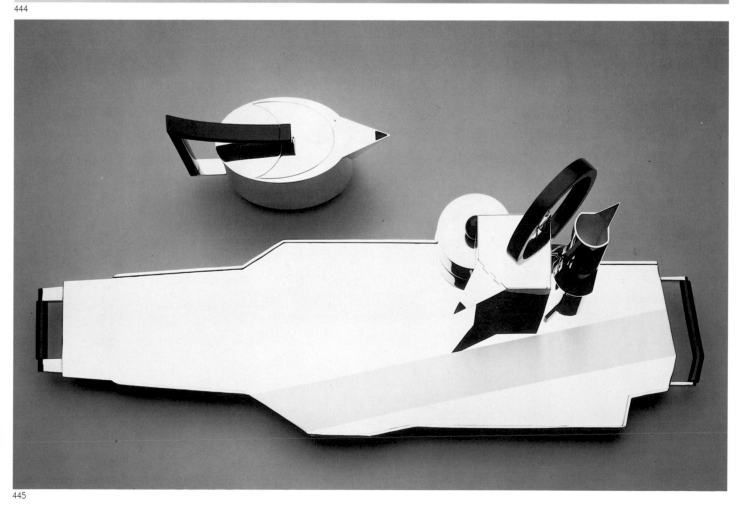

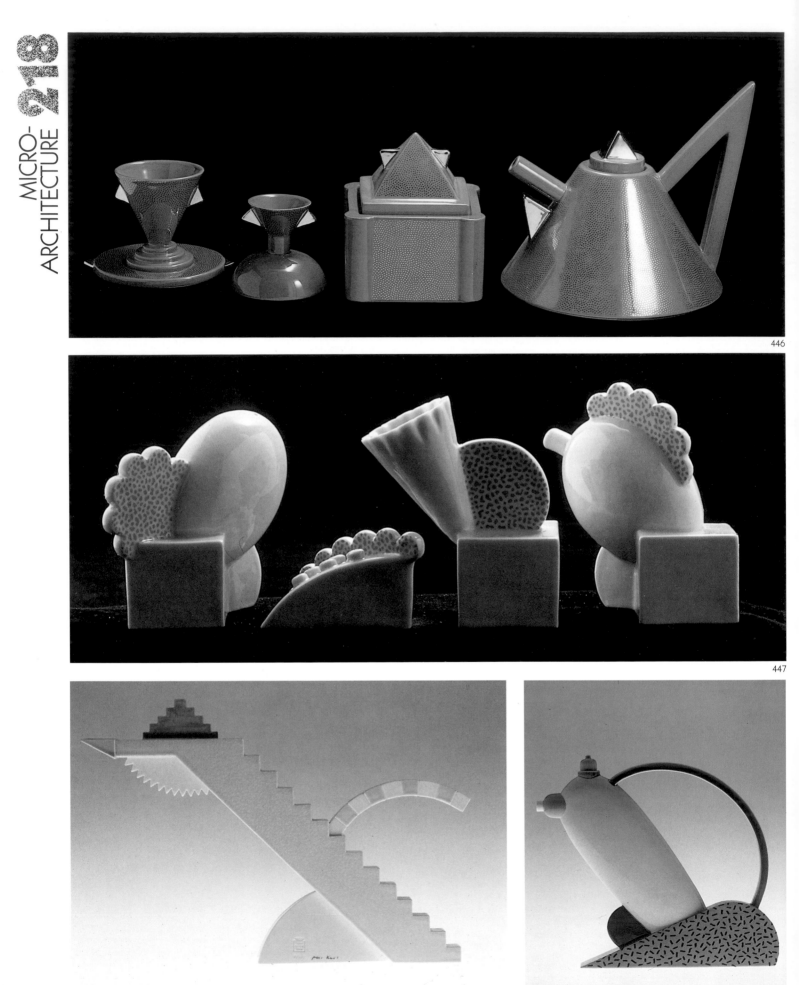

446

447

448

449

446 Matteo Thun
"Nefertiti" tea set and
egg-cup, 1981

447 Matteo Thun
"Ontario" pepper-pot,
"Erie" cocktail-stick
holder, "Superior"
toothpick holder,
"Michigan" salt-cellar,
1982

448 Matteo Thun
"Gallus Italicus" pot,
1982

449 Matteo Thun
"Lesbia Oceanica" pot,
1982

450 Matteo Thun
"Cuculus Canorus" pot,
1982

451 Matteo Thun
"Columbina Superba"
pot, 1982

452 Matteo Thun
"Passer Passer" pot,
1982

453 Matteo Thun
"Pelecanus Pontifex"
pot, 1982

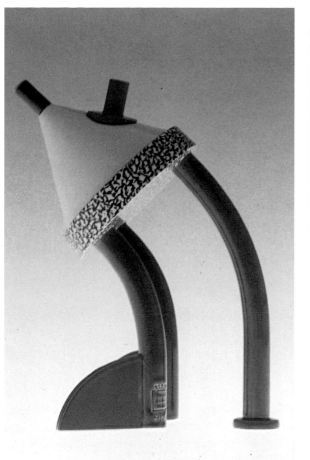

450

451

452

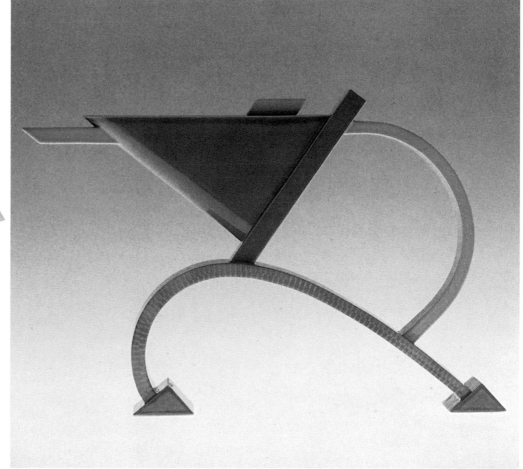

453

454

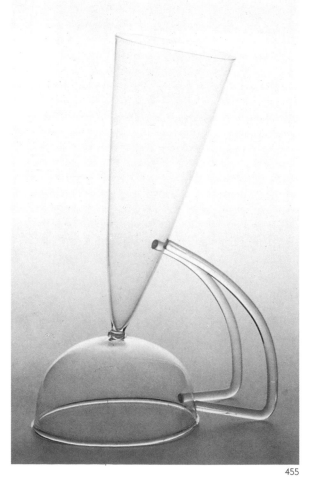

455

456

454 Matteo Thun
"Archetto" cham-
pagne-glass, 1984

455 Matteo Thun
"Manico" champagne-
glass, 1984

456 Matteo Thun
"Punta Raisi" candle-
stick, 1985

457 Matteo Thun
"Piazzetta di Capri"
tray, 1986

458 Matteo Thun
"Walking Coffee Pots/
Flicflac", 1986

459 Matteo Thun
"Taleggio" covered
dish, 1984

457

458

459

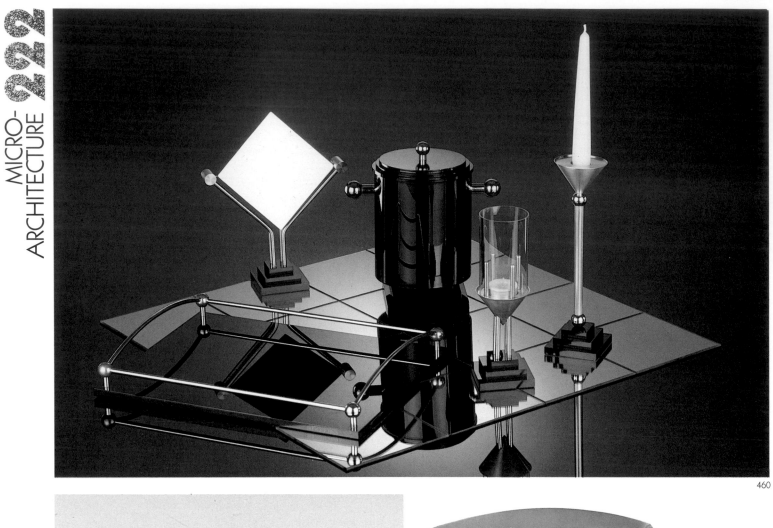

460

461

462

460 Jo Laubner
"Arena" tray, mirror, ice-
cooler, lamp and
candlestick, 1985

461 Jo Laubner
"Focus" champagne-
cooler, 1984

462 Jo Laubner
"Babylon Greetings"
vase, 1985

463 Aldo Rossi
"La Conica" espresso-
pots, 1984

464

465

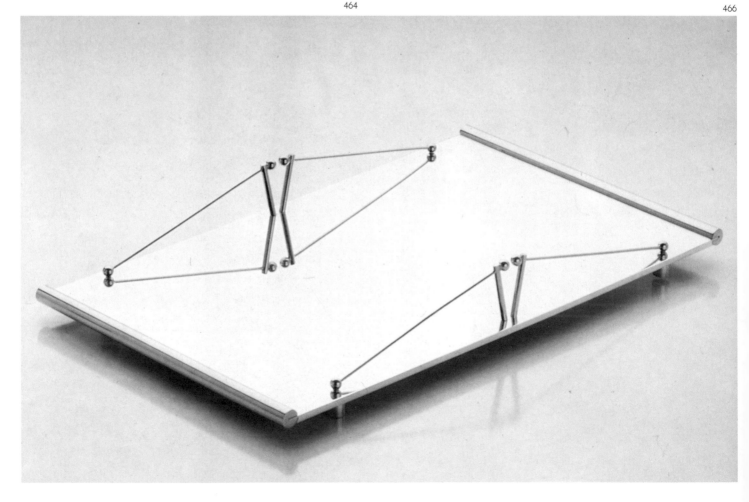

466

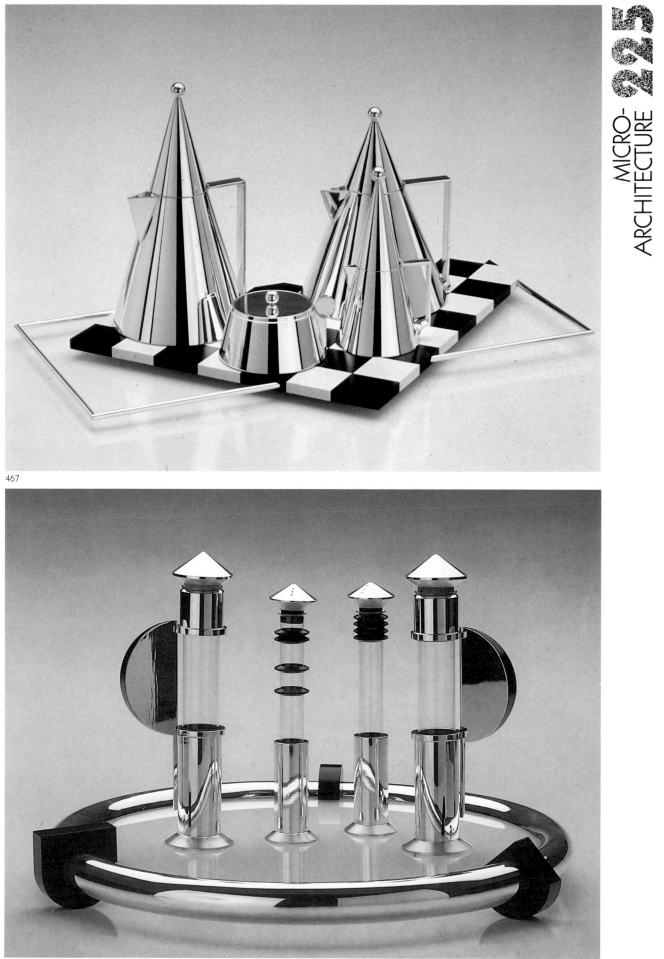

467

468

469

470

471

469 Matteo Thun
"Tavola" tableware,
1987

470 Matteo Thun
"Design Matteo Thun"
tray collection, 1986

471 Matteo Thun
"Design Matteo Thun"
tray collection, 1986

472 Matteo Thun
"Hommage à
Madonna" cutlery,
1985/86

473 Mario Vivaldi
"Solo" cutlery, 1986

474 Mario Vivaldi
"Solo" cutlery, 1986,
coloured variants

472

473

474

475

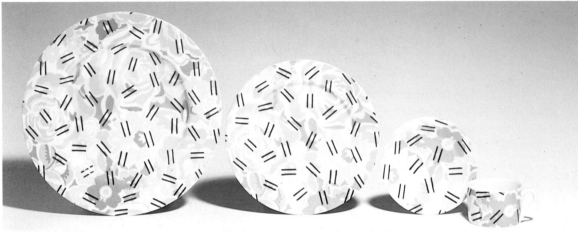

476

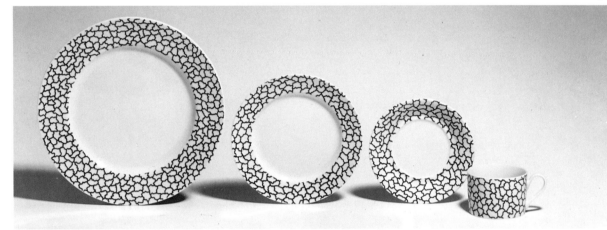

477

478

475 Stanley Tigerman
and Margaret McCurry
"Teaside" 7-piece crock-
ery set, 1985

476 Robert Venturi
"Grandmother" 4-
piece crockery set,
1984

477
George J. Sowden
"Montreal" 4-piece
crockery set, 1984

478 Robert Venturi
"Notebook" 4-piece
crockery set, 1984

479 Stanley Tigerman
and Margaret McCurry
"Sunshine" plate, 1985

480 Stanley Tigerman
and Margaret McCurry
"Pompeji" plate, 1986

481
Robert A. M. Stern
"Majestic" plate, 1985

482 Steven Holl
"Planar" plate, 1984

483 Arata Isozaki
"Stream" plate, 1984

484
Robert and Trix
Haussmann
"Stripes" plate, 1985

485 Hans Hollein
"Kaleidoscope" 4-
piece crockery, 1986

486 Ettore Sottsass
"Medici" 4-piece croc-
kery set, 1986

479

480

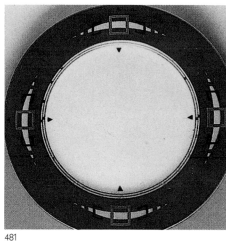

481

482

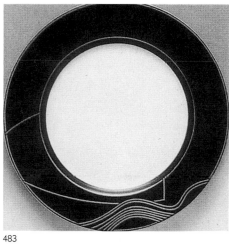

483

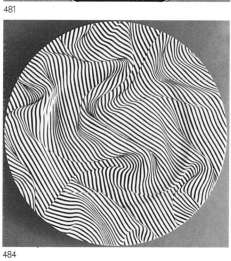

484

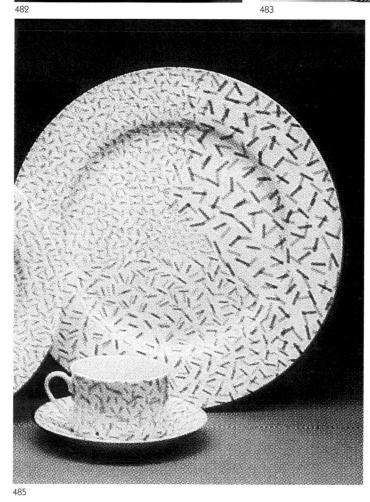

485

486

487

488

489

493
Robert A. M. Stern
"Century", "Metropoli-
tan" and "Harmonie"
candlesticks, 1984

494   Richard Meier
Candlestick, pepper-
mill and tray, 1986

495   Ettore Sottsass
"Starlight" and "Silver-
shade" candlesticks,
1986

490

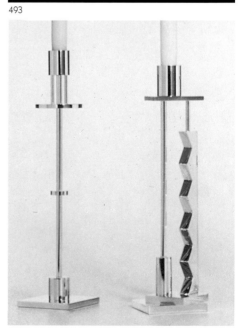

491

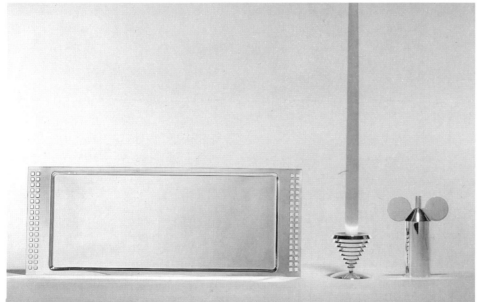

492

493

494

495

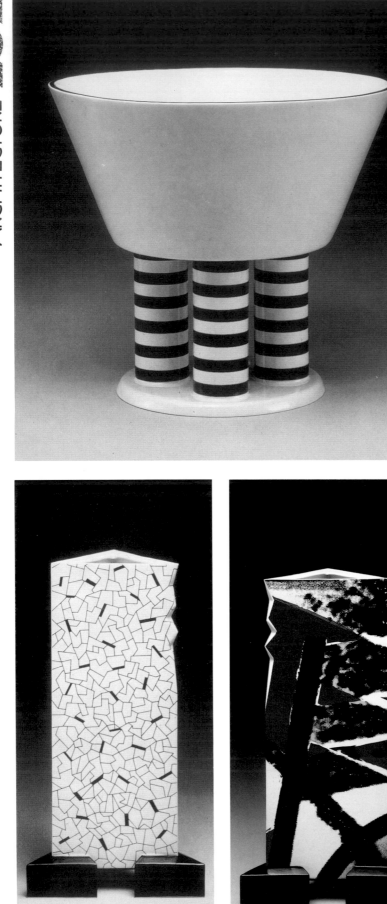

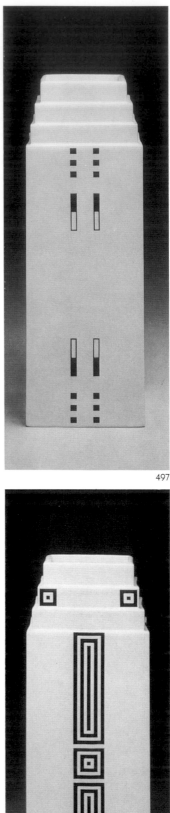

496 Heide Warlamis "Secession" bowl, 1984

497, 500 Heide Warlamis "Skyscraper" vases, 1984

498, 499 Heide Warlamis "Metropolitan Tower" vases, 1986

501, 502 Heide Warlamis "Siena" salt and pepper set, 1986

503 Heide Warlamis "Skala" oil and vinegar set, 1987

504 Heide Warlarmis "Belvedere" candle-stand, 1987

496

497

498

499

500

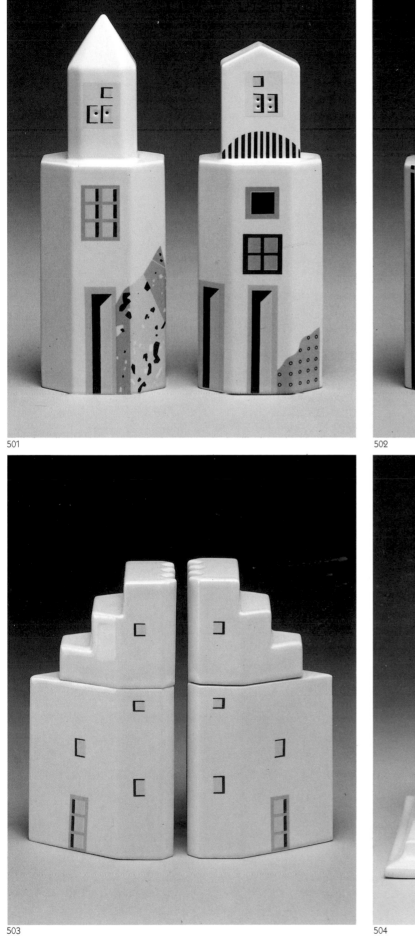

501

502

503

504

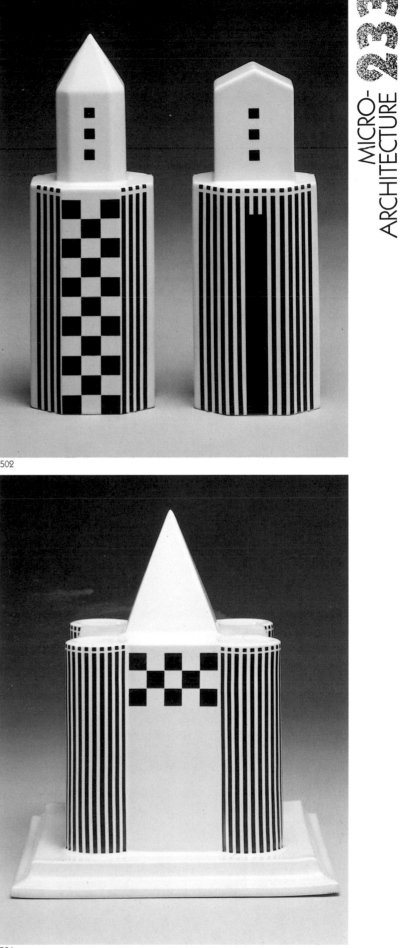

505

506

507

508

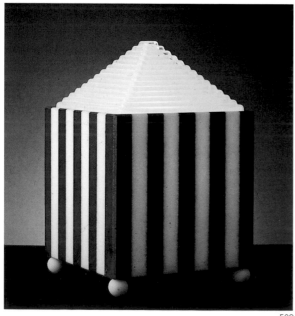

509

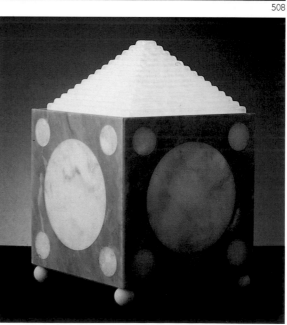

510

505
Piero Vendruscolo
and Franklyn Gerard
"Malamocco Lasa"
table-light, 1985

506
Piero Vendruscolo
and Franklyn Gerard
"Malamocco Rosa"
table-light, 1985

507
Piero Vendruscolo
and Franklyn Gerard
"Miracoli" table-light,
1986

508
Piero Vendruscolo
and Franklyn Gerard
"Trifora" table-light,
1986

509
Piero Vendruscolo
and Franklyn Gerard
"Regatta" table-light,
1986

510
Piero Vendruscolo
and Franklyn Gerard
"Codussi" table-light,
1986

511
Piero Vendruscolo
and Franklyn Gerard
"Murano Faro" table-
light, 1985

512
Piero Vendruscolo
and Franklyn Gerard
"Faro" table-light, 1985

513
Piero Vendruscolo
and Franklyn Gerard
"Torre Rosa" table-light,
1985

511

512

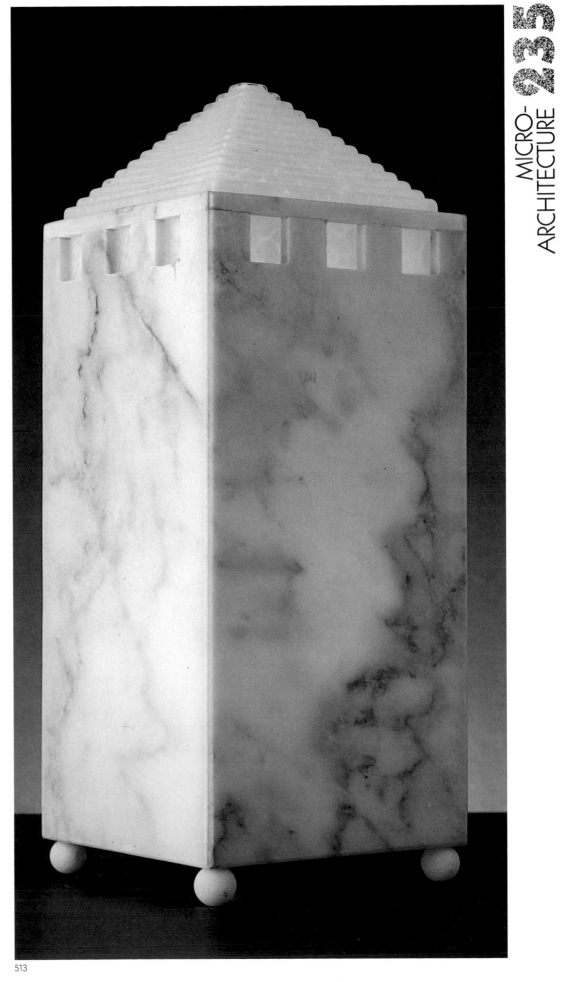

513

514

515

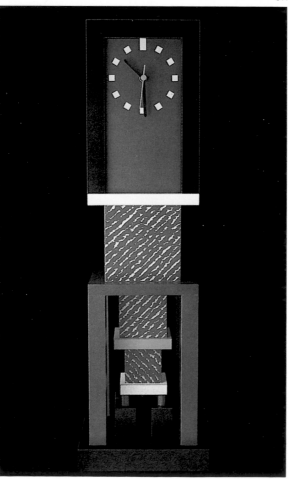

516   517

514
Piero Vendruscolo
and Franklyn Gerard
"Torre Nera" table-light,
1985

515
Piero Vendruscolo
and Franklyn Gerard
"Torre dell' Orologio"
table-light with clock,
1985

516
George J. Sowden
"Metropole" table-
clock, 1982

517
Nathalie de Pasquier
and George J. Sowden
Table-clock, 1987

518
Matteo Thun and
Andrea Lera
"Tobruk", "Zero Visibil-
ity", "Spargi", "Guar-
diano Giovanni", "Spar-
giotto" and "Mad-
dalena" table-lamps,
1985

519   Andreas Weber
Vase, 1986

520   Andreas Weber
Paper-tray, 1984

521   Andreas Weber
Tray, 1982

522   Andreas Weber
Fruit-dish, 1987

523   Andreas Weber
Cheese dish, 1984

518

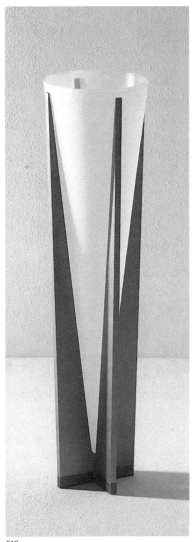

519

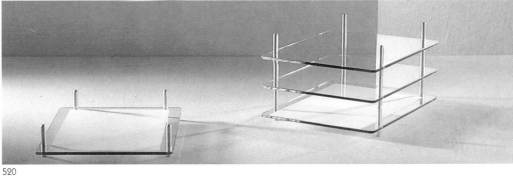

520

521

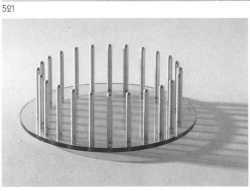

522

523

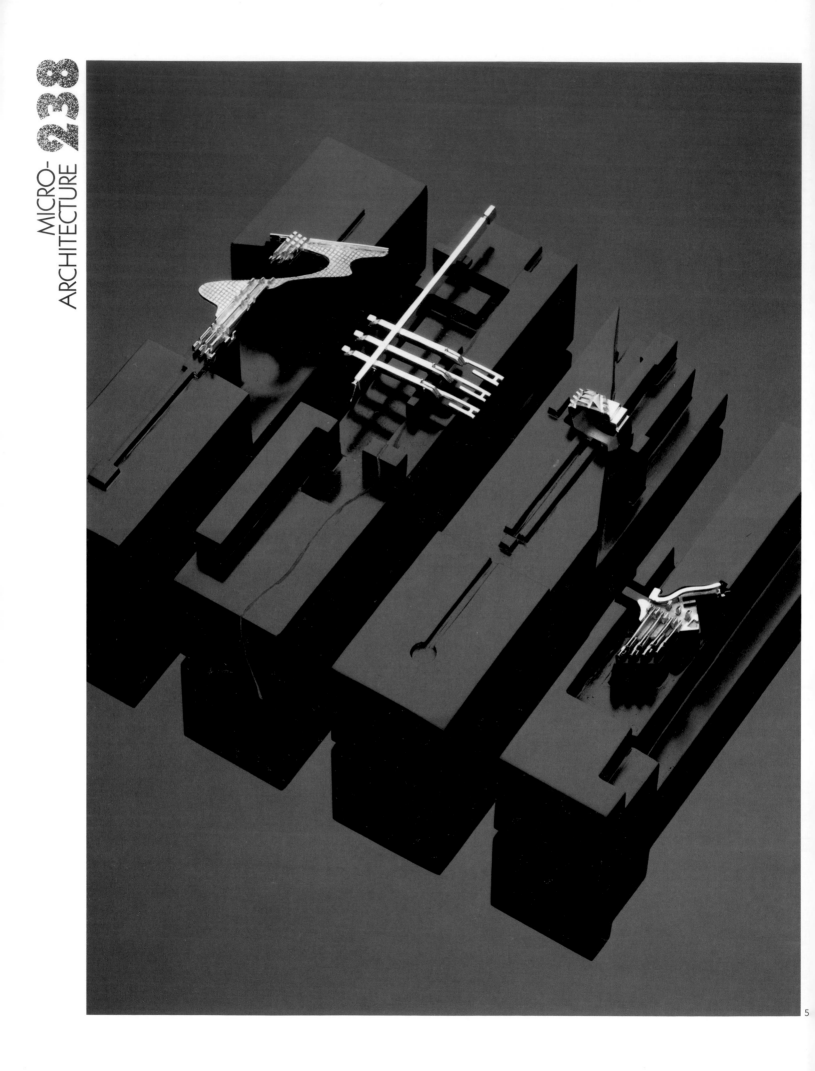

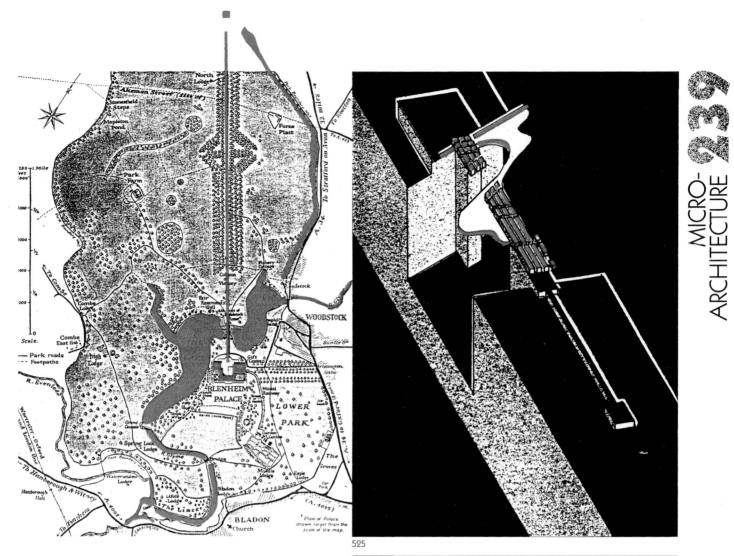

525

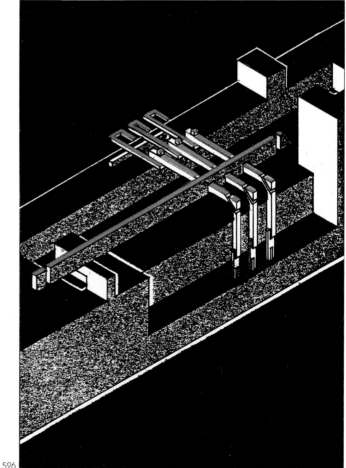

524 Masque
(Douglas Frederick/
Ann Cederna)
"Four Orders in Gold
and Stone", 1987

525 Masque
(Douglas Frederick/
Ann Cederna)
Brooch, 1987 (after the
ground-plan of
Blenheim)

526 Masque
(Douglas Frederick/
Ann Cederna)
Bracelet, 1987

526

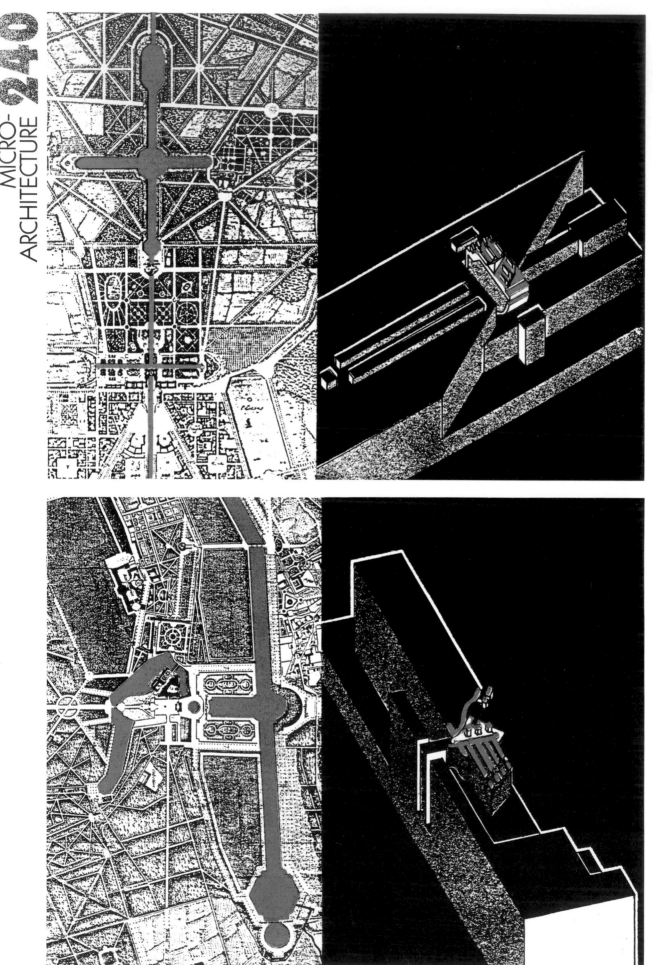

527 Masque
(Douglas Frederick/
Ann Cederna)
Ring, 1987 (after the
ground-plan of Versail-
les)

528 Masque
(Douglas Frederick/
Ann Cederna)
Earring, 1987 (after the
ground-plan of Chan-
tilly)

The aura of an object is produced by a combination of many factors. In addition to the brand image and the individual stamp of its designer, who may or may not be well known, it may display the characteristics of a particular style, and it will have its own biography, so to speak, in the form of its marketing history, its use in various contexts, etc. All this taken together will, ideally, make an object in a sense "representative" of its age. This is obviously true, for example, of exemplars of the interior and industrial design of the Bauhaus period; the passage of time, in any case, is often a material factor in establishing an aura. More often than not, however, some of these "auratic" factors are absent: many products have no particular brand character, let alone an "image", cannot be traced to a specific designer, have no identifiable "object history". Builders' hardware typically comprises such anonymous objects: door-handles, window-catches, wall-sockets, light-switches, mountings, radiators, even tap units and other bathroom fittings are seldom specially selected by the occupants of a house or flat. Marketing theorists have christened these "no name" or "low interest" products; when I speak of "banal" design, I refer merely to the mundane nature of these articles produced en masse by competing manufacturers – their design has by no means always been banal in the pejorative sense. During the whole of the nineteenth century and well into the twentieth, there was a rich tradition of individualistic forms within the genre, notwithstanding the Industrial Revolution and the consequent trend towards standardisation of technical design processes. Many artists and architects of the Bauhaus and Art Deco schools designed such objects, not to mention those of the Arts and Crafts movement, the Glasgow School and the Vienna Workshop. This is a tradition which includes such diverse figures as William Morris, C. R. Mackintosh, Peter Behrens, Walter Gropius, H. P. Berlage, Gerrit Rietveld, Eileen Gray and Charlotte Perriand. After the Second World War, however, with increasing rationalism of manufacturing processes and the need to keep labour costs down, individual design in the field of banal products gave way to anonymous mass production – attitudes to style had changed. In Italy, Scandinavia and the United States the end of the tradition was perhaps not so abrupt as in Germany, but even so only a few isolated examples recalled the great variety of former years.

The situation remained unchanged until the advent of Post-Modernism in architecture and the post-Functionalist innovations of Alchimia and Memphis in design. There was a renewed commitment to specific styles which, in an age of growing prosperity resulted in a general design euphoria and, not least, in a desire to rescue banal products from their cultural limbo. Internationally renowned designers of various stylistic persuasions are now prepared, along with

BANAL DESIGN

their engagement in the field of Micro-Architecture, to turn their attention to "no name" products.

Seeing the way the wind was blowing, the German hardware manufacturers Franz Schneider Brakel invited nine leading international architects and designers to make suggestions for the future shape of door-handles. Despite a rather modest fee and worldwide demand for their services, all the design-stars approached accepted the commission. Some two years later, in March 1986, Hans Hollein from Vienna, Mario Botta from the Ticino, Peter Eisenman from New York, Arata Isozaki and Shoji Hayashi from Tokyo, Alessandro Mendini from Milan, Peter Tuchy from Czechoslovakia, and Dieter Rams and Hans-Ulrich Bitsch from West Germany submitted their designs; after three months of close consultation the prototypes were ready. In September of that year, FSB invited the designers and representatives of the international trade press to a symposium in the sleepy Westphalian health resort of Brakel. After a learned round on the cultural aspects of the door-knob, a workshop was held with the designers; a rustic feast and a tour of the works rounded off this "FSB Designer's Saturday". (By a strange coincidence, this name was also given to events held in New York, London, Brussels, Amsterdam, Paris and Düsseldorf.) The door-handle had now emerged from "no name" obscurity to take its rightful place in contemporary culture. The last time anyone had thought seriously about the design of door-handles had been in the Bauhaus era – Gropius for instance; there was another flickering of interest at the Ulm School in the fifties. In the sixties and seventies the Hewi company set the aesthetic standard with their plastic tubing models in primary colours, which well exemplified the softline look typical of swaged artefacts.

It was a happy coincidence that none other than FSB had made Walter Gropius's metal door-handles for the Fagus works, already famous in their own day, for this gave Alessandro Mendini, the international "grand master" of Re-Design, the opportunity to do a revamped version; he also gave a new look to two of the company's models from the fifties and sixties (pl. 529 – 531). Hans Hollein miniaturises architectural details with precise elegance; one of his door-handles can be mounted either way up, and is called accordingly either *Storchenschnabel* ("Stork's Beak") or *Frauenschuh* ("Lady's Slipper") (pl. 532). Hans-Ulrich Bitsch, professor of product design in Düsseldorf, created models which, although supposedly inspired by the centuries-old door-handles of Sienna cathedral, give the impression of being rather long-in-the-tooth Hollein designs spiced with a touch of Memphis and a hint of Michael Graves (pl. 533). Both Mario Botta and Peter Eisenman, in accordance with their architectural doctrines, contributed geometrical exercises. Botta's handles, flat iron

bars either sharply bent to form a lever or worked into a full circle, are High Tech devices that draw our attention to the constructive process of building and, in their own small way, help to give it an aesthetic aura (pl. 539). For Peter Eisenman the dividing-line between small-scale door-handle and large-scale building is unsharp; proportion is neither anthropomorphic nor symbolic, least of all iconographic, but always abstract (pl. 538). The two Japanese emphasise the tactile element, the manner of grasping. Hayashi wants to prolong the sensation of hand/handle contact, and thus specifies hard pitted or soft "high-touch" surfaces (pl. 536). Isozaki charms both hand and eye with coloured handles of laminated wood (pl. 537); he believes that a door-handle, when it is touched, "becomes for a moment part of the body". The handles and knobs by Dieter Rams are as quietly elegant as his Braun products: they are ergonomic classics, even though, according to FSB, their manufacture is much more complicated than one would think from looking at them (pl. 534). Economy of form and function manifests itself here not so much in real terms as in fiction and symbol of the highest order. These Rams designs confirm our thesis that not even Modernism and Functionalism can get by without some sort of aesthetic dressing-up of their message, i. e. without formulating a "style-language". Tucny's models, on the other hand, are lacking in formal stringency (pl. 535): the soft edging of what are in other respects tectonic forms obscures the product-idiom, renders it imprecise; it matters little that, as Tucny has pointed out, extensive trials were carried out with various contour forms to find the optimal, most natural grip.

Press coverage of this door-knob project was so good that FSB enjoyed a degree of publicity that would have consumed the advertising budget of a multinational organisation.[1] A mass-produced article had at long last cast off the cloak of anonymity and re-emerged before the public eye; the prospective purchaser could now take account of form, could allow his choicer to be influenced by the cultural tradition or by contemporary styles.

The leaven of "culturel" is also at work in many other auxiliary items that are becoming ever more important in interior design for the structuring of "life-style" situations. Tiles, curtain-rods, wall-to-wall carpeting, picture-rails, fluorescent tubes, doors, the steps and bannisters of staircases, all are available in a wide variety of styles, often with references to historical examples that subtly evoke an aura of distinction. Post-Modern doors and light-switches are already available, skirting-boards along the same lines will no doubt soon follow. In the field of furniture hardware, which also has a long tradition going back to the Vienna Workshop, the West German firm Union Knopf of Bielefeld has been making a name for itself in the last few years. With the increasing anonymity of the standardised cupboard and wardrobe systems in monochrome laminated chipboard, the choice of a distinctive handle could provide a welcome touch of individuality. Union Knopf's range of "creative" handles comprises no less than four hundred variants, making them one of Europe's biggest specialists in the field. The extensive range is built up from a repertoire of basic forms in various combinations of materials and surface finishes. The "Terrazzo" series, for example, has only nine variations of mosaic finish, but these can be combined with a choice of twelve basic shapes and either a metal grip available in three colours or black or white plastic mountings, so that in all more than a hundred variants are possible (pl. 540 – 545). The design alludes not only to the Italian tradition of terrazzo flooring in the first forty years of the century but also, quite explicitly, to the revival of this decor by Alchimia and Memphis. The recent "Duron" series, on the other hand, displays stylistic connections with High Tech; in one of the models, a golf-ball serves as a knob (pl. 546). Two other series expressly pander to our nostalgia for styles of the past. The "Fifties" selection (pl. 547– 552) uses plastic, chrome and aluminium in forms reminiscent of the exuberant lines of American limousines or of the kidney-shaped table to recreate the feeling of the period. The "Art Deco" series (pl. 553 – 558) recalls the age of glamour and the charleston. The effects of rootwood veneer, marble or terrazzo are all achieved with the same plastic material, Duro-Horn. The manufacturers see the stylised ornamental air of their "Art Deco" range as a counterpoint to the "techno" look of, for example, the "Duron" series. In addition, they produce series of knobs which imitate marble, and softline handles in fruit-drop colours that look like ground glass and bear names like "Seaglass" or "Balloon". There is a promise of poetry: "A walk by the sea: sand, stones, flotsam, ceaseless movement. There, a piece of coloured glass: its sharp, jagged edges have become rounded, silken and smooth. 'Seaglass' – a creation that inspires." From these stylistic references we might guess that Union Knopf aims to supply the requirements of specific sectors of the market. And indeed, thanks to highly flexible production methods, the firm can undertake to produce prototypes of customers' own designs within six days. "You make a sketch. Our house designers will develop your idea and, in continuous consultation with you, bring it to production stage."

The company also works in close cooperation with furniture manufacturers to design fittings (pl. 559, 560). Last but not least, they took Mendini's "Terrazzo" Re-Design handle for the FSB competition (pl. 531) through to the prototype stage. It is surprising, though, that in all the marketing and publicity material the designers are never named.[2]

We may draw the same conclusion as we did when discussing Micro-Architecture: these small objects help us to develop an awareness of style; they enable us, maybe even compel us, to make personal stylistic preference the basis of our choices. Concomitantly, they serve as aids to the appreciation of cultural connections and lines of tradition, without the aloofness of "pure" art. Hence, they influence our experience of everyday life in a much more pervasive way than fine-art objects could ever do.

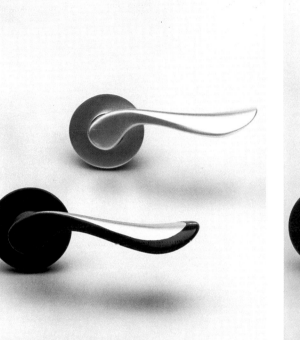

529

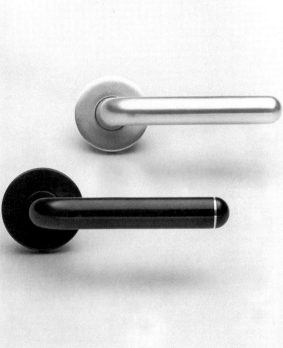

530

531

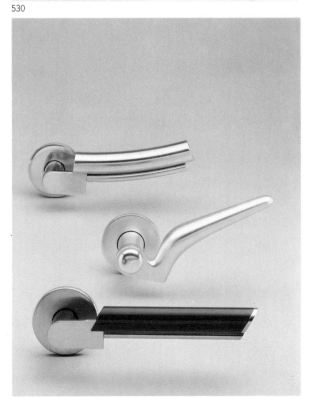

532

529
Alessandro Mendini
"Potente" door-handle
Re-Design, 1986

530
Alessandro Mendini
"Wittgenstein" door-
handle Re-Design, 1986

531
Alessandro Mendini
"Gropius" door-handle
Re-Design, 1986

532 Hans Hollein
Door-handle, 1986

533 Hans-Ulrich
Bitsch
Door-handles, 1986

534 Dieter Rams
Door-handles and
doorknobs, 1986

535 Petr Tucny
Door-handles, 1986

536 Shoji Hayashi
Door-handle and
doorknobs, 1986

537 Arata Isozaki
Door-handle,
doorknob and door-
pull, 1986

538 Peter Eisenman
Door-handle, 1986

539 Mario Botta
Door-handles, 1986

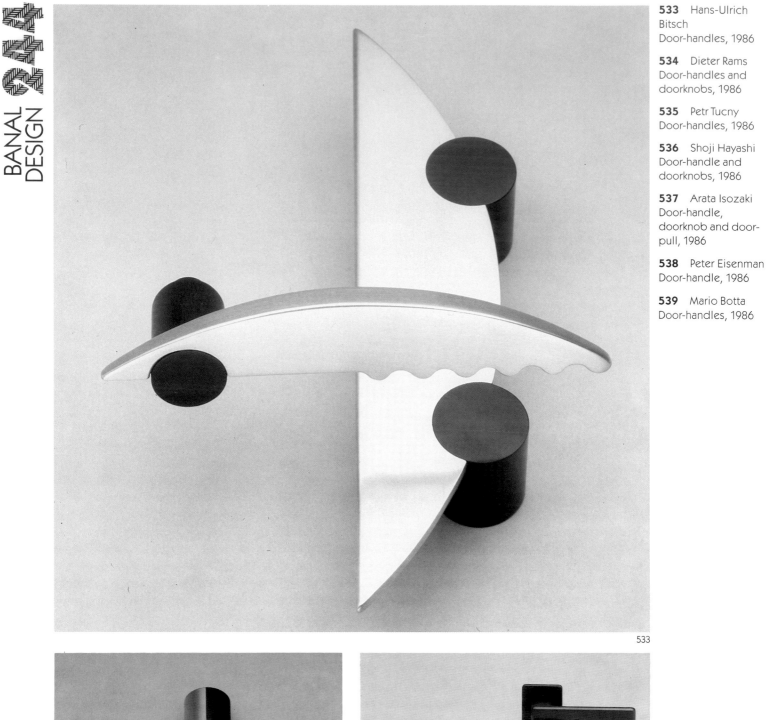

533

534

535

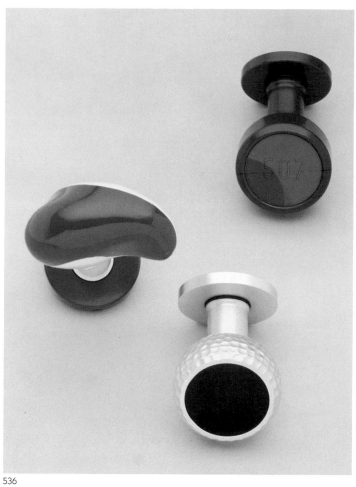

536

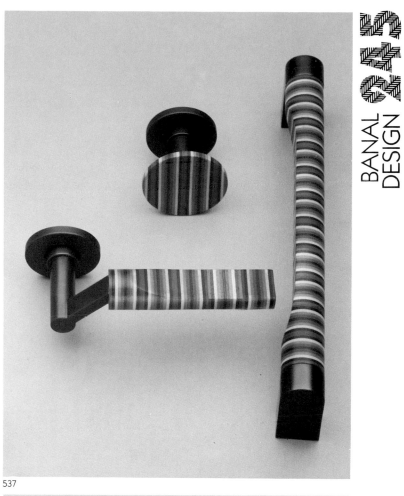

537

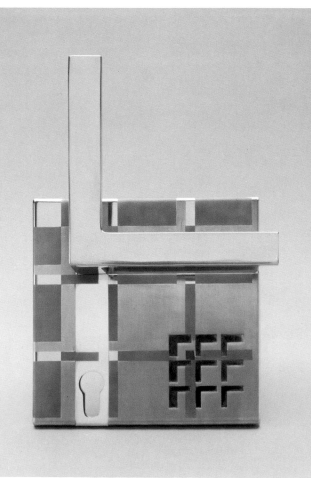

538

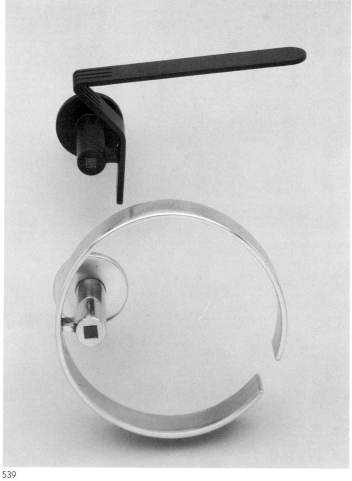

539

540

541

542

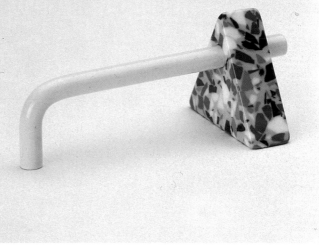

543

544

545

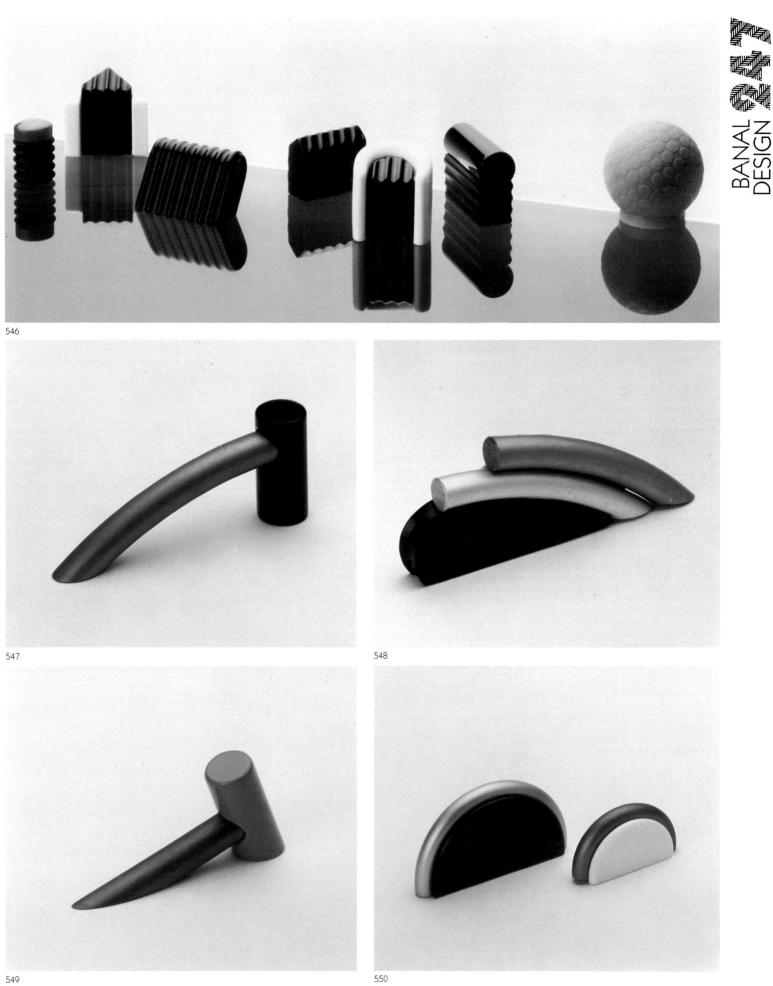

546

547

548

549

550

BANAL DESIGN 88

551

552

553

554

555

556

557

558

559

560

The advertising industry loves to use architecture in connection with products and services. First of all there are the well-known landmarks, such as the Eiffel Tower, Big Ben, or the Statue of Liberty, which stand unmistakably for internationalism and the yearning for faraway places; credit-card companies and tour operators are among the main exploiters of these symbols. Building societies, insurance companies, and window and door manufacturers on the other hand usually promote their products and services with the help of "desirable" detached residences, renovated timber-frame houses, or romantic cottages. Cool and unflamboyant, the car industry presents its prestigious limousines in front of a backcloth of geometric facades colour-matched in sober blues and greys.

The most popular of all architectural metaphors, however, is the tower block, especially the skyscraper we all know from the Manhattan skyline. No other type of building embodies more clearly the socially recognised values of power, wealth, and authority. But there is also no other type of building that is more controversial, representing as it does ruthlessness and speculation, not to mention the specific infrastructural, technical and climatic problems. Advertising campaigns that make use of the skyscraper metaphor not surprisingly emphasise only the positive features, playing down or simply ignoring any negative aspects.

Let us take a few examples of skyscraper advertising from the last ten years and examine the special strategies of this type of campaign.

In the first place, there are the advertisements which picture the skyline fairly realistically and accompany it with suitable slogans. South Manhattan with the obligatory World Trade Center is the "bridgehead to foreign markets" (West German State Bank, fig. 1). "Presence on the spot" guarantees access to one of the most important world markets (German Cooperative Bank, fig. 2). Here "money earns good money with security" (Karina Financial Management, fig. 3). A similar note is struck in adverts for transport companies, express couriers, and electrical engineering firms. The photographs are usually bird's eye or panoramic views from the south. The black-and-white reproduction underlines the respectableness of the advertisers. In contrast, companies appealing to tourists, such as British Airways or Airtours, evoke the holiday mood by using colour. Apart from the typical postcard look of the photographs, they too show Manhattan more or less realistically.

The choice of viewpoint in this group of advertisements is significant, as Andreas Adam has shown by comparing a typical postcard view with the Statue of Liberty in the foreground with panoramas from the east, the north and the west.[1] Monotonous tenement-blocks, the slums of Harlem and the no-man's-land to the east are not going to attract investors or tourists; but seen from the South, the Wall Street district is bathed in sunshine, the sea lapping at its shores. Who wouldn't enjoy making money here?

"The only way to see New York, circle it! 35 miles of famous sights" is the slogan of the Circle Line Sightseeing Yachts Inc. (fig. 4). The claim would appear to be justified, and is an apt commentary on the urban situation, since only the distant viewpoint permits one to see those up to 400-metre high giants in any sort of relationship to their surroundings, the neighbouring buildings, the traffic, the vegetation – where there is any.

And when one dives into what Siegfried Krakauer calls "this perpendicular ocean", the sightseeing panorama becomes a blur.[2] Elephantine base-blocks, gigantic portals, and curtain walls running straight into the ground obstruct any idea of a view. Perspectival distortions and the limited field of vision, which only presents a minimal segment of what from the sightseeing boat was perceived as a total prospect, lead to total confusion about size, articulation and texture, as does the vertical-horizontal illusion that tends to cause one to overestimate vertical as opposed to horizontal dimensions, especially when dealing with very tall objects.[3]

And, of course, if you crane your neck to try and get a better view of these skyscrapers you are immediately unmasked as a tourist.

In the heyday of American skyscraper architecture in the thirties, two- or three-dimensional models were provided to give an idea of the proportions, as height and projecting bases made this possible from the outside. In the lobby of the Empire State Building there is a huge metal relief of what in its day was vaunted as the "cathedral of the skies" (fig. 5). The silhouette of the Chrysler Building is embedded in the ceiling of its foyer. The portal of 60 Wall Tower, since demolished, was decorated with an exact three-dimensional replica of the building (fig. 6). To what extent these devices were deliberate attempts to make the dimensions of the building conceivable, as the American architecture historian Rosemarie Bletter maintains, or whether they were just typical examples of euphoristic Art Deco ornamentation, is a moot point.[4] Still, it appears that even in those days the proportions, articulation and dynamics of this sort of architecture could only be understood in miniature.

Nowadays more emphasis is put on the power of combination: as Paul Goldberger, architecture critic of the *New York Times*, writes: "The parts of the building may well serve different masters, the bottom serves the street and the top serves the skyline and they need not appear to be a fully unified object."[5]

Philip Johnson hopes à propos of his AT & T Building: "With the circle at the top and the arch at street level, your mem-

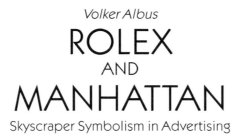

Volker Albus

ROLEX
AND
MANHATTAN

Skyscraper Symbolism in Advertising

ory will maybe prod you – That's the building whose top I saw twenty minutes ago from the Hudson Bridge."[6] It is thus left to the individual to relate the towers to the entrances – the city as picture-puzzle?

Johnson has overlooked the fact that the said AT & T Building does not catch the eye even from a distance, because it is simply not tall enough: its 197 metres is about average for midtown Manhattan, and besides, the neighbouring buildings are in the way. (The Empire State Building has never had this handicap, thanks to its relatively low-rise surroundings; there is no rival in the neighbourhood to spoil the view of or from "the most famous building in the world".) You really have to look hard to spot Johnson's Chippendale-style gable. The model for the project was a big media happening, more Post-Modern spectacle than architecture. But the actual building, because of its lack of commanding height and its unfortunate location, is only of

4

Fig. 1   Advertisement for the Westdeutsche Landesbank
Fig. 2   Advertisement for Deutsche Genossenschaftsbank
Fig. 3   Advertisement for Karina Vermögensgesellschaft mbH
Fig. 4   Advertisement for Circle Line Sightseeing Yachts Inc.
Fig. 5   Metal relief in the entrance hall of the Empire State Building (Shreve, Lamb & Harmon, 1931)
Fig. 6   Ornamentation over the entrance to 60 Wall Tower (Clinton & Russell, Holton & George, 1932)

5

6

Fig. 7   From left to right: McGraw-Hill Building (Harrison, Abramovitz & Harris, 1972); RCA Building (Reinhard & Hofmeister, Corbett, Harrison & MacMurray, Hood & Fouilhoux, 1933); Celanese Building (Harrison, Abramovitz & Harris, 1973). Photo: Reinhart Wolf

Fig. 8   Citicorp Center (Hugh Stubbins & Associates, Emery Roth & Sons, 1977). Photo: Reinhart Wolf

Fig. 9   United Nations Plaza (Roche, Dinkeloo & Associates, 1976). Photo: Reinhart Wolf

Fig. 10   Advertisement for Bank Vontobel, Zürich

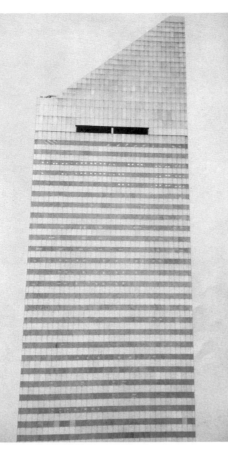

8

7

limited value as an advertising metaphor – at best as a caricature, or for the architect's visiting-card.

When the circumstances are right, however, the Manhattan skyscrapers can be employed very effectively. This is especially well shown in the book *New York* by the famous architecture photographer Reinhard Wolf (fig. 7–9).[7] The colour photographs reveal some interesting aspects of Wolf's method. Thus, he always chose a vantage-point on the roof of a neighbouring building, which allowed him to

photograph the skyscrapers in something like a "normal" perspective that an elevation or the photograph of a model would provide. Wolf was also very particular about getting the atmosphere he wanted: the emotive hour of gathering dusk or the sharp light of early morning provided the right conditions. His technical equipment was unusual: an 18 × 24 cm large-format camera with an extremely long-focus lens and supertelescopic attachment. Viewpoint, timing, equipment and framing have undoubtedly pro-

10

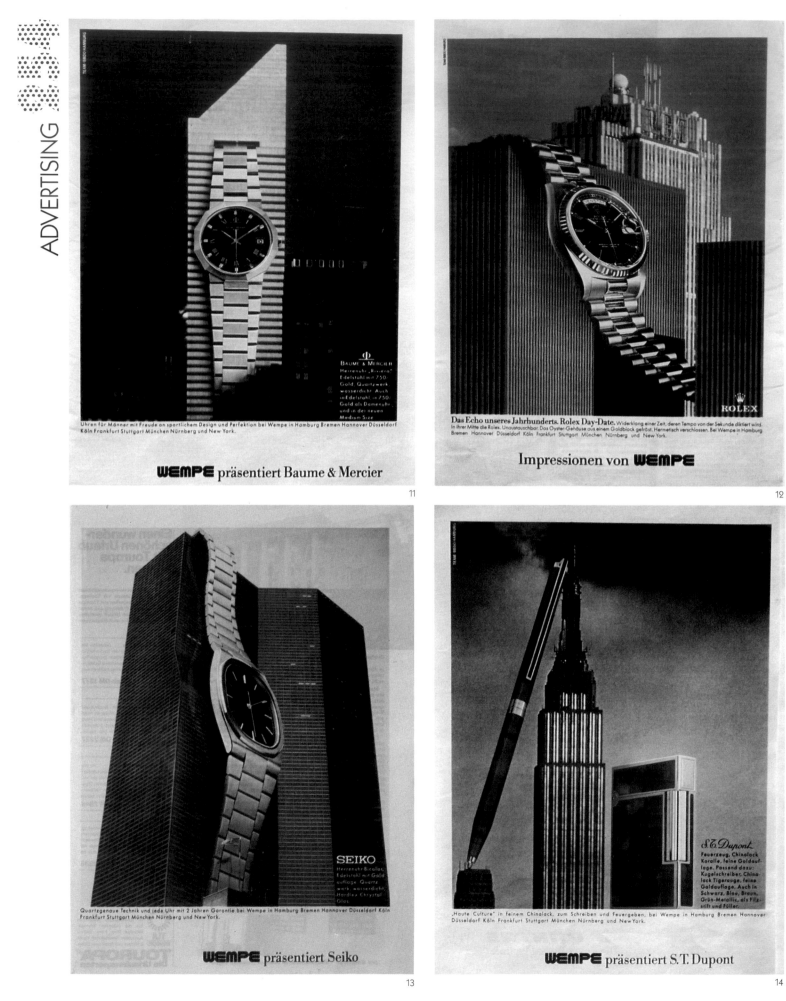

WEMPE präsentiert Baume & Mercier

Impressionen von **WEMPE**

WEMPE präsentiert Seiko

WEMPE präsentiert S.T. Dupont

duced results which *Die Welt* newspaper effusively called "technically brilliant colour photography of devastating sophistication". Wolf may be a "top" photographer, but showing the tops of buildings in isolation considerably detracts from the documentary value of his work: the viewer has no points of comparison by which to appreciate the size of the buildings and their relationship to their surroundings. From this point of view, Wolf's impressions are little more than stylish surrogates which have nothing to do with reality.

How thin the ice is on which Wolf skates is shown by an advertisement for the Vontobel Bank of Zürich, which in the present context could almost be a parody of Wolf's approach (fig. 10). A photograph of the Chrysler Building is accompanied by the caption "Is It or Isn't It?" and the following text: "Congratulations! You are one of the few who are not easily fooled. You realised that this Chrysler Building is only a cardboard model standing in solitary splendour, without the surrounding skyscrapers! Or did you?" The divergence between reality and model exemplified does not however seem to bother the advertising boys unduly. In 1982 a series of advertisements for the Wempe chain of jeweller's appeared in various German magazines (fig. 11–15). The Hamburg agency BRDO had the idea of presenting various items from the client's range in conjunction with well-known skyscrapers, and some fifteen arrangements were designed. In a clever manipulation of scale: the photographically reduced skyscrapers were hung with watches or used as foils for other prestige accessories. (A full-scale version of the idea was realised in 1984 when a giant wristwatch was hung over the full height of the Commerzbank building in Frankfurt.)

Thus, the luxurious Rolex "Day-Date" is draped casually over the fifty-one storeys of the McGraw-Hill Building; with the Celanese Building and the all-dominating RCA Building in the background, the gold oyster-case chronometer radiates its full cosmopolitan charisma. The same background, in mirror image, serves for the gold-with-diamonds "Lady-Date" watch. In another advertisement the Wempe "Fifth Avenue" watch hangs from the balustrade of the 82nd floor of the Empire State Building; or, leaning in King-Kong style against the aerial mast, a Dupont ball-pen flaunts its "tiger's-eye" Chinese lacquer and fine gold trim – the coral-lacquered cigarette-lighter a natural adjunct.

The twin towers of the World Trade Center are adorned by the jeweller variously with creations by Piaget ("the world's most expensive watches"), Cartier and Omega, and a 15-gram gold bar fashioned into the "Corun" gentleman's watch – "a fascinating idea of great originality", as the fulsome text of the advertisement has it. In similar lofty rendezvous the United Nations Plaza is coupled with the Seiko "Bicolor" watch, and the Citicorp Center with Baume & Mercier's "Riviera" watch.

ließlich Original-Créationen von Cartier bei Wempe in Hamb
t München Nürnberg und New York.

WEMPE präsentiert les

Fig. 11–15   Advertisements for Wempe

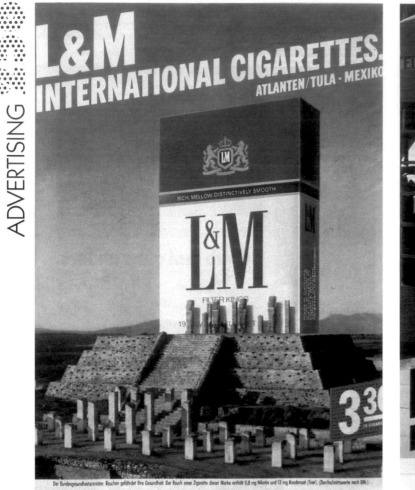

16

17

In order to make quite sure that the target-person makes the right associations, each of the advertisements incorporates a discreet text which reinforces the visual message. The "echo of our century" vies with "fascinating technology", "perfection", "chic ideas in jewellery", and above all: gold, gold, gold! Even the buildings often have a golden sheen in their *tête-à-tête* with the cool gold, platinum, and other precious metals, no matter whether it is the aluminium facade of the Citicorp or the Indian sandstone facade of the RCA Building.

In this technique architecture is processed in two stages: it is first interpreted through the eye of the photographer and then used as part of a collage. These steps highlight the qualities required by the advertising concept. In the final analysis, what we have are cloned replicas that are just big, beautiful or prestigious in a vague sort of way, but no longer have anything in common with the actual appearance of the buildings.

The L & M campaign (fig. 16 – 19) is in the same vein as the Wempe advertisements. The cigarette pack is also shown in topographical, mainly urban montages. Locations include: Tula, Mexico, with its atlas-columns; Avenida Paulista/Rua Bella Cintra in São Paulo; the Grand Master's Palace on Rhodes; Park Avenue in Garden Center, Toronto; the pond in Central Park, New York; Brooklyn Bridge, New York; the

Trans-America Building, San Francisco; and the "traditional" ambience of Berwick Street in London, with the familiar red telephone boxes in Georgian style.

The juxtaposition of pack and panorama reveals the true purpose of the sightseeing tour, which is to spread a message of the worldwide dissemination and international aura of the product. L & M are smoked in New York, San Francisco, London, and São Paulo. The accompanying price-list informing us how much 19 filter kings cost in Mexico or the Yemen underlines this message.

The composition of the individual montages is also interesting. Not only is exact co-ordination of scale important; special attention is also paid to the angle of photography and such features as perspectival distortion, particularly noticeable in the Brooklyn Bridge, and the way the pack is mirrored in the Central Park pond.

One may smile at these scenes and shrug them off as amusing advertising gimmicks. One would not like to imagine the crude hulk of the L & M box as a real building. And yet there exist thousands of buildings whose facades or overall forms are designed exclusively to serve the purposes of advertising. Take for instance the "fantasy" buildings of American origin, whose appeal stems largely from the unaccustomed scale on which the product is more or less realistically copied (fig. 20, 21) – The hot-dog as fast-food

Fig. 16–19
Advertisements
for L & M cigarettes

Fig. 20
Hot-Dog stand,
Los Angeles

ADVERTISING

stand, the truck-shop in the shape of a hamburger, and above all those "ducks" to which Robert Venturi referred in his book *Learning from Las Vegas*, when he coined the term "duck" for buildings which become cyphers in their own right; these Venturi contrasts with the "decorated shed", a building to which the insignia that characterise it are merely applied.[8]

For this aspect, advertisements on buildings, there are also innumerable examples. One need only think of the chains of petrol stations, which can be identified from hundreds of yards away by the distinctive colour scheme of the company graphics. More direct, even brutal in their effect, are the gigantic neon signs on the dreary tenements of the outskirts of Milan, where the blocks are little more than mountings for the Campari and Martini logos.

A synthesis of "duck" and "shed" is created by the simple and realistic concept of a Benson & Hedges advertisement (fig. 22). The World Trade Center, once again clothed in shimmering gold and merely overprinted with the brand name, looks remarkably like a couple of cigarette cartons. The use of buildings as and in advertisements exemplifies the versatility of the PR branch in their ceaseless quest for new visions and slogans, for in this business, too, "nothing is so out of date as yesterday's headline". The very ephemerality of this optical "fast food" is in a way consoling.

The creation of new functional contexts by modifications of scale relationships is not just a prerogative of the advertising agencies. The American Pop artist Claes Oldenburg, in his "Proposals for Monuments and Buildings" dating from 1960–1969, also used the manipulation of relative magnitudes as a basic formal strategy. Thus, for New York's Park Avenue he designed the "Good Humor Bar", a giant upside-down choc-ice with one corner bitten off to allow for the flow of traffic (fig. 23). For London he proposed a giant "knee"-monument (fig. 24), remarking: "I use my body to feel and come to know a city. In London I constantly felt cold in my knees – they always ached. It was aggravated by

Discover gold
BENSON & HEDGES

23

24

having to squat in those small English cars."[9] And again: "I think that my sculpture is by nature intimate and on a small scale. It is also indoor sculpture. This is underlined by the presentation of the intimate objects on a colossal outdoor scale . . . which has the effect for me of reducing the scale to the size and situation of an ashtray. My work is anti-heroic, anti-monumental, anti-abstract, anti-general and is best seen in an intimate situation."[10]

In contrast to the always identical L & M pack in its various settings, Oldenburg seeks to interpret the individuality and character of the place in question. In content and form the proposed baseball bats, doorknobs and electric plugs are the result of these deliberations. These projects, like what we have already seen, are of course the distillation of subjective experience, but where the international PR men are always seeking to gild the gingerbread, Oldenburg does not work ignorantly against, but consciously for the situation. He contributes something where the usual exercises in self-publicity push things out of the picture or destroy them; where L & M or Wempe "globalise" the situation, Oldenburg "localises" it.

Another example from the field of the visual arts is provided by the Swiss Peter Fischli and David Weiss. With their

Fig. 21   Big Duck, Long Island

Fig. 22   Advertisement for Benson & Hedges cigarettes

Fig. 23   Claes Oldenburg: Good Humor Bar, New York (1965)

Fig. 24   Claes Oldenburg: Knee, London (1966)

Fig. 25   Peter Fischli/David Weiss: Haus, Münster (1987)

25

Hofheim.

Frandfurt

26

Fig. 26 Mathäus
Merian: Hofheim,
engraving (1646)

Fig. 27 Advertisement
for Boss

Fig. 28 Advertisement
for Panasonic

27

"house" for the sculpture exhibition in Münster (fig. 25) they take issue with the conventional architecture of the international modern style, the type of building that was churned out ad nauseam all over the world and was brought to questionable perfection in West Germany in the fifties and sixties. On a plot surrounded by banal edifices of that period they erected a four-storey commercial building with shop, offices, goods lift and loading-ramp, horizontal strip windows, in its unalleviated grey tones an adequate reflection of the neighbourhood – but on a scale of 1:5. "In its curious in-between size the *House* underlines the devastating mediocrity and anonymity of its non-architecture, and at the same time resists being read as just a model of its genre; it is a concrete presence, this ›house‹, infinitely strange and yet of an almost daemonic familiarity. It is simply there, and it tells a tale. At once a profound mystery and a sublime joke, it tells the story of its absolutely meaningless existence, which fills the world though no-one notices it any more."[11] This Fischli and Weiss "sculpture" is a negative confirmation of the "It must be big" ideology. The reduction in scale robs the building they have portrayed of just about the only factor that gave it an identity, its size in relation to its peers. People only notice the big boys – which prompts the mischievous question: what would be left of a World Trade Center trimmed down to normal size? Two blocks in a common-or-garden style, anonymous off-the-peg stuff – that's all.

Talking of the WTC: from a purely commercial point of view one cannot deny that there is a touch of genius about the monster twins. In the course of the vertical expension of New York there were, for a long time at any rate, no glaring differences between the new skyscrapers; usually, the existing record was bettered by building just a couple of

Le Nouveau Monde électronique.

Panasonic

21 h 53. Nuit noire.
Choc des images. Éclat des sons.
Micro-télé, programme fiction. Arrêt.
Écran mural, scope 8 heures.
Touche lecture: plaisir, passion.
Panasonic, c'est du très bon.
Ascenseur, la rue, trafic dément.
Carry compo, ça balance dur.
Volume, puissance. Musique, fréquence.
Électronique des sens.
Panasonic vibre le Nouveau Monde
électronique.

storeys higher or adding as an afterthought a transmitter mast. But the WTC holds itself strictly aloof from any sort of dialogue, it dwarfs the entire neighbourhood. With these two towers the southwest tip of Manhattan looks like the blow-up of a sleepy village, its silhouette dominated by the familiar church spire (fig. 26). Paul Goldberger also came to a negative conclusion: "The complex was built to be big and it was set into motion by institutions that seem unable to see quality as anything but bigness."[12] And it is just this uncouth "bigness" that guarantees success and profitable publicity. Completed in 1973, the 412-metre World Trade Center could only hold onto the title of world's highest building for one year; but thanks to its eye-catching banality this palace of presumptuousness has become a favourite backdrop for products and services of all kinds. Whether for watches, cigarette-lighters, banks, or tour operators, the WTC stands for efficiency, size, and international reputation.

The real-estate tycoon Donald Trump has recognised the signs of the times. He is planning a Television City project with a veritable armada of eight skyscrapers, the highest of which at 509 metres will surpass the WTC by a cool 97 metres. But even this project pales into insignificance beside what the architects Robert Zobel and Emery, Roth & Sons have up their sleeve: the 500-floor Houston Tower will be two kilometres high. That would make it higher than such well-known winter sport resorts as Davos (1560 above sea level) and Zermatt (1616 m). Hard times to come for the World Trade Center.

This irrational obsession with height is explained by the engineer Vincent Desimone as follows: "Then why go taller? Because heroic structures capture the public's imagination and clients are intensely competitive. Ego is going to drive the next building higher."[13] Ada Louise Huxtable, the grand old lady of American architecture criticism, sums it up: "Admittedly the tall building works dramatically well for business and its satellite services; to deny this fact and its corollary, that the development of the skyscraper has logically served these characteristically twentieth-century needs, is to miss the real nature of the most conspicuous architecture of our time. The validity of the sybolism of the tall building for its age is intrinsic to its powerful imagery. Its single historical consistency has been its predictable penchant for setting records, for rising to ever greater heights."[5]

Let us return to the starting-point of our discussion. Having so far considered advertisements featuring skyscrapers that exist in the real world, we will now turn to a category that exploits high-rise features in advertising exclusively through the vehicle of models. The impression of a city panorama is achieved through special-effect photography, from a bird's-eye or head-on viewpoint, sometimes looking upwards with marked perspectival distortion, as in the Boss advertisement (fig. 27).

SIEMENS

Alles für die Elektronik Siemens

Willkommen zur »electronica '84«

Willkommen bei Siemens

29

Like Panasonic, Siemens and Philips create an urban panorama to convey the variety of their products and their numerous uses. In "Siemens City" (fig. 29) the firm shows its "whole range of components. From transistor to valve. From condenser to light diode. From microprocessor to customised integrated circuit. Everything for electronics – as the largest German manufacturers of electronic components we will show you the trends in these key technologies." It is interesting to note that the components are drawn to different scales: the resistors, for example, are in reality smaller – they are shown here greatly magnified; conversely, the high-voltage capacitors and switches which here symbolise high-rise buildings are much reduced in scale. The whole composition resembles a city perspective with trees, clearway, underpass, and tower-blocks in the centre.

The Philips scenario is in the same vein. Under the slogan "Building a safe future: Philips", the Alexander Demuth agency made montages of various items from the fields of office communications, glass fibre technology, traffic control systems, and automatics (fig. 30 – 32). The views of "office-blocks", "airports", and "oil-rigs" are suitably enlivened with helicopters whirring between the electronic skyscrapers, or a Concorde coming in to land on a microchip runway. Not only do these collages show what unfamiliar components look like, the use of different scales – extreme enlargement of chips, cables, etc., miniaturisation of helicopters, jets, and ships – emphasises the efficiency and structural superiority of these electronic systems. "The Philips Sophomation concept links up all office communications equipment and systems for access at a single work-station. Computer, printer, telephone, fax, teletext, word-processor, visual display unit, etc., are networked together. Data, speech, text and picture are correlated in intelligent networks by Philips for optimal communication between systems and system-operators."

Compared with the possibilities of these invisible communication systems, helicopters and jets really do seem rather puny and dated. The omnipotence of advanced technology is shown even more drastically in an advertisement for the business weekly *Wirtschaftswoche* in the *Frankfurter Allgemeine Zeitung* (fig. 33). A Neoclassical building is surrounded on all sides by gigantic and sinister-looking grid-pattern facades with built-in screens. The text comes straight to the point: "German stock-exchanges roll their sleeves up. The Big Bang has shaken up the stock-exchange scene here too. Liberalisation and computerisation will take us into the major league. The big German banks want to make Frankfurt the third-largest financial centre in the world. Will Bonn play along?" Here again, the text puts into words the associations the picture is intended to evoke. On the one side there is the old build-

"Le Nouveau Monde électronique" is the title of an advertisement for the Japanese electronics giant Panasonic featuring a cityscape reminiscent of Times Square, Piccadilly Circus, or the opening sequence of Ridley Scott's film *Blade Runner* (fig. 28). In front of a background of various shades of blue with a simulated sunset, loudspeakers, tuners, TV sets, walkmans, video-recorders and compact-disc equipment are arranged into an urban configuration. A lot of the items of horizontal design are stood on end so that they appear as miniaturised tower-blocks in computer-look. TV pictures, digital clocks, and the company name in bright lights suggest the bustle of city life. Down at street level red and yellow streams of light have been touched in to give the impression of busy traffic flow. Only the unmistakable texture of the hardware reveals that this is all audio and TV equipment.

The text of the advertisement complements the visual message and links urban impressions to the qualities of electronic entertainment. "21.53 hrs. Black night. Flood of images. Supersound. Micro-TV, dramatic story. Stop. Wall screen, 8 hours playing-time. Touch control: pleasure, passion. Panasonic, it's the best. Elevator, street, traffic unbelievable. Ghetto-blaster, turned up full. Volume, power. Music, frequency. Electronics of the senses. Panasonic shakes up the New World of electronics." Panasonic transmutes the city into one great media ritual, the city-as-sound, the "walkman-city".[15]

Fig. 29 Advertisement for Siemens

Fig. 30–31 Advertisements for Philips

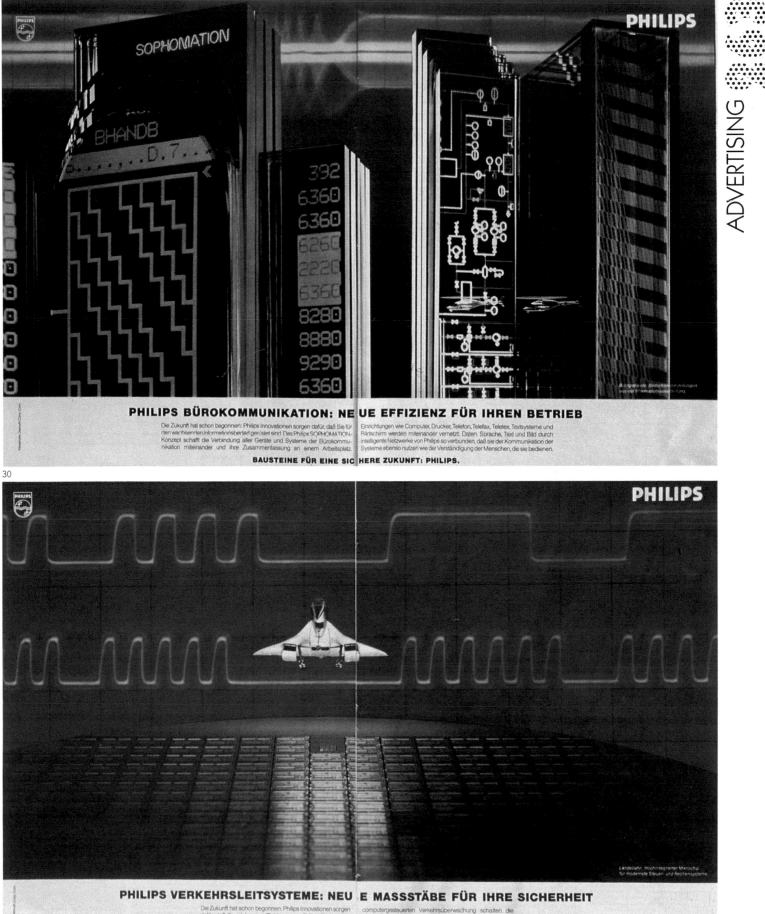

PHILIPS

SOPHOMATION

BHANDB
D.7

392
6360
6360
6260
2220
6360
8280
8880
9290
6360

PHILIPS BÜROKOMMUNIKATION: NEUE EFFIZIENZ FÜR IHREN BETRIEB

Die Zukunft hat schon begonnen: Philips Innovationen sorgen dafür, daß Sie für den wachsenden Informationsbedarf gerüstet sind. Das Philips SOPHOMATION-Konzept schafft die Verbindung aller Geräte und Systeme der Bürokommunikation miteinander und ihre Zusammenfassung an einem Arbeitsplatz.

Einrichtungen wie Computer, Drucker, Telefon, Telefax, Teletex, Textsysteme und Bildschirm werden miteinander vernetzt: Daten, Sprache, Text und Bild durch intelligente Netzwerke von Philips so verbunden, daß sie der Kommunikation der Systeme ebenso nutzen wie der Verständigung der Menschen, die sie bedienen.

BAUSTEINE FÜR EINE SICHERE ZUKUNFT: PHILIPS.

30

PHILIPS

PHILIPS VERKEHRSLEITSYSTEME: NEUE MASSSTÄBE FÜR IHRE SICHERHEIT

Die Zukunft hat schon begonnen: Philips Innovationen sorgen dafür, daß Sie sicher ans Ziel kommen. Philips Bodenradar schafft Übersicht auf den Start- und Landepisten, den Rollbahnen und dem Flughafenvorfeld. Philips Systeme zur

computergesteuerten Verkehrsüberwachung schalten die Ampeln zur rechten Zeit auf Grün. Philips Radarstationen sichern die Wasserwege in den wichtigsten Schiffahrtsrevieren des europäischen Festlandes.

BAUSTEINE FÜR EINE SICHERE ZUKUNFT: PHILIPS.

31

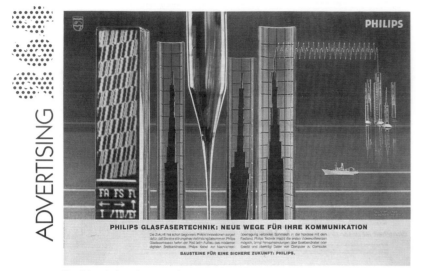

Fig. 32   Advertisement for Philips

Fig. 33   Advertisement for Wirtschaftswoche

ing as metaphor of provincialism, on the other the High Tech facades with their VDUs as image of new technology. Tradition is equated with backwardness, computerisation means international stature. Black and white are the only alternatives, as a facile oversimplification of a complex issue that would be more appropriate to the cheap tabloids.

In the overall effect, the images projected by the Siemens, Philips and *Wirtschaftswoche* advertisments could virtually be taken as prophetic warnings about the future development of our cities. Somewhat naively perhaps, but nevertheless vividly they show how information technology will transform the city and thus continue its modernisation by other means; the upshot will be that instead of storey being stacked upon storey, complex system networks will be accommodated in existing premises. Thus, there will no longer be any need for high-density building and urban agglomerations.[16]

The same applies to traffic, which, as in the Philips illustration, will be made obsolete and replaced by the mobilisation of images. Video interviews and conferences, viewdata, screen-shopping, even video "hostess" services are the first-fruits of this "brave new world".

In the advertisements presented here, superlatives are always symbolised by the familiar category of the skyscraper, which does duty both for the superficial prestige-spiel of Wempe, L & M, or Benson & Hedges with their evocations of international life-style and for the more abstract concepts of economic and technological power. We have noticed how the image of the skyscraper is subjected to more or less subtle modifications to make it serve its purpose in the various advertising campaigns: it is isolated, enlarged or reduced in scale, retouched in colour, in short it is manipulated at will to achieve the desired effect. This creates a "visual illusion which obscures the truth of the matter".[17] The skyscraper is thus reduced to a synthetic prop, whose information value consists at most in the semiotics of its attributes, often grossly exaggerated, but which otherwise oversimplifies the issues by presenting them in a deceptively rosy light. A lot of intelligence and creativity has undoubtedly gone into some of these advertising campaigns; and the exploitation of an object in advertising does not necessarily mean that it has to be endowed with positive (or negative) attributes. All the same, I will stick my neck out and say that these advertising campaigns are the propaganda wing of a trend which is getting more and more out of hand and spawning an "international style" of commercially oriented architecture that will in the end obliterate the diversity of our big cities under a cloak of monotonous uniformity.

Herbert Ohl once attempted to quantify the assessment of design. His thesis "Design is measurable" aroused great interest at the time,[1] but little came of it in the long run. True, qualitative criteria were for a time neglected and the concept of design reduced to the bare bones of arithmetical dimensions, a trend fostered by the German Design Council. From a present-day viewpoint it is easy to say that such a technocratic oversimplification of the issue was bound to come to nothing; but in his day Herbert Ohl's theory, though provocative, was really only a consequential elaboration of a position long established in the Functionalist camp, and thus broadly acceptable to the majority of German designers. Naive neo-Functionalists should bear this in mind. Leaving behind the debate on scientific and positivistic aspects we can today start from the premise that the search for orientation in design must take account of the complex interplay of quantitative and qualitative factors. Furthermore, although the Functionalists believed they had "abolished" style, it is now fairly obvious that all discussions of criteria in design can ultimately be reduced to the style question. This question has been crucial since the advent of Post-Modernism, if not before, and manifests itself today for example in the quest for distinctive corporate styles.

Not only the theoretical approach but also the motives of the design debate have changed considerably over the last ten years. At the time when Herbert Ohl was applying himself confidently to the refinement and pragmatisation of Functionalist criteria, anti-Functionalist critics had long been undermining the foundations of these criteria. Criticism of criteria has since been the general rule, up to the "new design" of today.

At the same time, the campaign against specific standards of "good form" has led to more and more instances of an anarchic refusal to design according to any norms whatsoever; the 1986 Düsseldorf exhibition "Emotive Collages" is evidence of this tendency. The rejection of norms is taken to its ultimate conclusion, "Anything goes". Some see this as a new creative freedom, others as a growing lack of orientation; many proceed from the one view to the other. This philosophy of "gut-centred design" played an avantgarde role in dismissing out-of-date notions of Functionalism, but now it often creates more uncertainty than it opens new perspectives, raises more questions than it can answer; having dispensed with the anchor, the ship is drifting on the open sea. Once the breakaway has been achieved, it serves little purpose to go on and on about the Functionalist bogeyman: the new freedom must be used constructively, otherwise it will go to seed and encourage reaction. Thus, Bazon Brock is now calling for a new "social commitment", and Jürgen Habermas is demanding "answers to recognisable problems of the future". Nor can we

Jochen Gros

SMALL
BUT
SOPHISTICATED
Microelectronics and Design

ignore the cultural repercussions of the new era of technology. All in all, to face up the new situation design will have to formulate new criteria.

The search for criteria in design today seems to be above all a search for orientation, which has been sparked off by "post-modern" changes in our life-style, and also perhaps by intimations of a new style of production. When we cannot see the wood for the trees we need new signposts, exemplars, and yardsticks. This does not mean that we should embrace them uncritically, but it does mean that the old "anti-authoritarian" urge to destroy criteria is passé. After the wild years of anarchy, however, things are now perhaps heading towards the opposite extreme: it begins innocuously enough in that every prominent exemplar is treated with exaggerated respect, even if it is only based on some fossilised tradition, private obsession, or "subjective myth"; but it could end in the sort of blind, unquestioning acceptance that greets a new "guru". As I see it, the new search for orientation in design is currently concentrated on three areas: the "reform" of Functionalism; the search for distinctive corporate styles; and the influence of microelectronics on design, which is the real theme of this essay. Before addressing the subject, we shall take a brief look at the first two phenomena.

New insights can be gained from Functionalism when it is considered against the background of Post-Modernism. I am not thinking of the regressive neo-Functionalism that sees a simple choice between Functionalism and Post-Modernism and plumps for the former, because that's the way it used to be. The present situation allows for a reform of the Functionalist ethos in keeping with the times, a new legitimation in which the arguments and experiences of the critique of Functionalism and those of Post-Modernism are not cast aside but absorbed. The only precondition is that the Functionalist claim to be the sole representative of design must be given up; in other words, Functionalism must stop believing that it is the only historically valid concept of design and that everything else is to be condemned as non-design, as mere styling. This would not only adapt the monocultural world of Functionalism to the pluralism of contemporary life-styles and – often overlooked – production-styles; some of the key arguments against Functionalism could also be countered in this way and the door be left open for future developments. If "good form" as preached by the Functionalists is seen as just one version of good form among others there could hardly be any objections. And when it is freed from the shackles of the dogma of a uniform cultural approach to everything "from the spoon to the suburb", Functionalism may well be acknowledged again to be the most appropriate solution in many product fields. Thus, a reform of the "good form" would depend on being able to see it as a relative concept; in sacrificing its exclusivity it would be confirmed as a force to be reckoned with in the post-modern era. This would, of course, be a "partial Functionalism", which would to a large extent correspond with Herbert Lindinger's notion of a "historical Functionalism" that has always existed alongside changing styles.

The new debate about style in design is most clearly exemplified by such catch-phrases as "corporate identity" and "corporate culture". In this field, it is claimed, design "is becoming increasingly important, not so much in terms of form but rather as regards the style and attitude of the organisation".[2] Where a reformed Functionalism still has to come to terms with the new stylistic pluralism, the search for a distinctive corporate image entails an *a priori* acknowledgement of the situation, which is reflected in the pluralism of company styles. There is room here not only for Rowenta and Erco but also for expressive displays of style, as in the corporate identity of firms like Quartett and subdivisions such as Interlübke-Duo and WMF-Galleria. "Target-group design" (with which companies whose philosophy is purely economic attempt to capture specific market segments) is rapidly evolving into "target-culture design", and the various subcultures are in turn beginning to influence the firms themselves more and more, even to the extent that a company may become identified with a particular "scene". In the last resort, the "trendy" company becomes a sub-culture in its own right. In the world of design, pluralism often works in quite distinct ways. Within the firm there is likely to be a tendency to increasingly strong stylistic cross-connections leading to design uniformity while externally, when designing for other firms, the pluralism of standards permits an ever greater pluralism of styles.

The results of these tendencies are, on the one hand, a growing consensus as regards the firm's particular style – up to the point of uniformity – and, on the other, an ever more varied palette of company styles. "Corporate culture" will presumably become something like a central forum, or even a catalyst, for the continuing growth of cultural pluralism; as regards the individual company, it means the application of the ultimate stylistic criterion – that a firm's products should be distinguishable from those of its competitors.

The technological revolution, particularly in the field of microelectronics, means that we must give renewed consideration to the question which gave birth to the Functionalist movement: that of the role of technological and material factors in design quality. We have all seen how most mechanical artefacts have become considerably smaller in the course of their development: precision engineering has reduced clock mechanisms from the church tower to the wristwatch format; more and more engine power is accommodated under car bonnets that have remained more or less the same size. In electronics, miniaturisation is proceeding at such a dizzy speed that it seems likely to reach the point of dematerialisation at any

moment. If one were to look at just a few years of development as if on speeded-up film one would see many electronic products practically implode. The shrinkage does not however proceed uniformly, like a deflating balloon: the telephone retreats into the receiver, on the portable radio only the loudspeakers seem to be still there (pl. 561), various elements have disappeared from the electric guitar (pl. 562).

From the cube to the plane: the increasing loss of the third dimension is one of the most obvious effects of electronic miniaturisation on design so far. This is not just an objective parameter of external dimensions: design has appropriated the phenomenon as a cypher, so that "flat" has come to signify advanced, high-quality, or simply electronic. With this in mind, designers attempt to make what volume is left at least appear to be two-dimensional: thus, the Loewe TV receiver has a casing that tapers off so markedly towards the back that it virtually appears to be just a flat screen (pl. 572). Thanks to electronics, the "Ulm cube", one of the major form-ideals of Functionalism, has lost its validity. As the quintessence of "good form" it used to be regarded, not without a measure of irony, almost as the *non plus ultra* of formal exemplarity, albeit hardly attainable in practice. As a present-day equivalent, one might take the "Siemens card" as key image for the design of electronic equipment. It is the humorous formulation of a serious idea: that if current trends continue it will be possible to reduce a personal computer to the dimensions of a standard sheet of paper and a telephone to the size of a credit-card (pl. 563). This seems in any case to be emerging as the standard format for electronic data-carriers that function as keys or payment-cards for photocopying or telephone charges, etc. (pl. 564, 589 – 593). Thus the plane, as the principal cypher of the "new technology", takes on more and more the role of a proto-form (pl. 565 – 571, 573, 574, 575 b). Even mechanical artefacts are looking flatter and flatter, just as in its day the streamline style was appropriated for objects which had no need to reduce wind resistance.

That the plane itself is to some extent exempt from the process of miniaturisation in microelectronics is largely due to the need for optical and mechanical handiness. If pocket calculators, for instance, were made as small as they could be, they would have to be held with princers and could only be read with a magnifying-glass. Convenience of operation is thus a classic ergonomic criterion that has lost none of its validity for the designer. In practice, his role is often reduced virtually to that of designing display and keyboard graphics (pl. 599 – 601). The design philosophy of Olivetti, for instance, exemplifies this by adopting as its central concept the "interface", which is defined simply as "the design of communication between man and machine".[3] The former connotation of the physical relationship of man to object has now been largely discarded: interface replaces interaction.

This does in fact reflect the evolution from mechanical

equipment, such as the loom, which often had to be worked with both hands and feet, to electronic apparatus, which makes so few demands on our bodies that we can really only think of it as a communication partner. Whether we like it or not, electronics is not a technology one can come to grips with in the literal sense; hence it is logical that eye contact should determine the new concept of design.

But, looking into the future, even the control-panel will one day cease to be a limiting factor in the vertiginous progress of electronic miniaturisation. When the products learn to speak and listen, the knobs, buttons and switches will atrophy under our fingers. The man-machine interface will then become the "voice interface". Once the resistance that the control-panel still offers to miniaturisation has been overcome, the electronic shrinking process will be able to continue practically ad infinitum. How big does a piece of equipment have to be that we operate merely by speaking?

Quality design has always tried to represent something of the "essence" of the product or of its technology. Daniel Weil's experiments in making the electronic components visible through an envelope of transparent plastic should perhaps be regarded as just a joke in this respect (pl. 578, 579). On the other hand, we may ask ourselves why it is that a fundamentally agglomerative technology like electronics is still in many cases housed, or rather hidden, in a classically integrative casing. For such an "additive" technology it would be much more appropriate to design an additive housing. This insight is now being reflected in a growing number of designs (pl. 575 a, 576, 577, 583, 616, 617, 619). The agglomerative concept of design is gaining ground not only in electronics; under such slogans as "breaking the box", even mechanical equipment is nowadays designed as an agglomeration of separate parts. In furniture too, e. g. Memphis, the "building-block" design is a distinctive feature.

Thus, two "super-cyphers" can be identified in the product-language of electronics: flatness, which refers to the trend towards "dematerialisation" (or at least to the loss of volume), and agglomerative design as a symbol of the new, similarly characterised technology. Advances in miniaturisation have also reduced some products to a state in which they literally "lose face"; but only at first glance do such products appear to be beyond the pale of design. It is of course a matter of some consequence as far as design is concerned when an object becomes so small that the naked eye can no longer recognise any distinctive feature. A micro-chip, for example, can only be really observed through a microscope, where it provokes the sort of strange fascination we get when looking at molecular chains or cell structures (pl. 580, 581). What we see here is a subvisual world without design in the sense that it has not been fashioned to appeal to our aesthetic sense.

But it is not just microelectronic components which are disappearing beneath the threshold of design: manufacturing processes can now be regulated with such precision that it is possible to reduce the size of mechanical parts to subvisual dimensions. Millimetre yardsticks are of little use in microengineering: already there is talk of new types of electric motors and cogwheel transmissions which will fit into the cross-section of a human hair (pl. 582). What used to be the fantasies of science fiction movies, such as electromechanical robots that operate in the blood-stream, are today quite realistic possibilities. Micromechanics is following in the footsteps of microelectronics.

"Loss of face" occurs not only when products are miniaturised to a subvisual level. It is also a consequence of the incorporation of components that may themselves be visible "under the skin" of another product, ie when, like an organ transplant, it becomes an invisible part of another body. So it is that within this built-in role, microelectronics plays a faceless, hidden part, rather like an undercover agent. In "smart buildings" electronic equipment is accomodated in the cellar or concealed behind the plaster. We already experience microtechnology at "first hand" in such gadgets as the glove calculator, the belt computer and the typewriter-camera-videophone waistcoat (pl. 584 – 588, 594); the time may not be so far away when we carry it around with us subcutaneously (pl. 595).

Finally there is yet another way in which technology has made it unnecessary for an object to possess an aesthetic identity. The age of remote control is just beginning. Already it reaches from kitchen stores to "Star Wars" and the growing use of remote control removes machines and processes from the visual field of the operator. Here too, design becomes invisible: under remote control, the heaviest machinery shrinks to the immaterial dimension of the control panel. But this is precisely where the designer again enters the field: the remote-controlled machine or process still has to be visualised by the operator, and thus it is given an artificial image on the display screen (pl. 599, 600). The railway signalman switches the points (pl. 597), the welder steers his acetylene torch, the farmer feeds his pigs – all without getting their hands dirty: the software provides the necessary optical guidance by "materialising" the field of operations where its image is really needed, before the eyes of the operator. In this context the aesthetic design of the hardware may well be subordinated to that of the software, which constitutes the real centre of attention.

In the early days of the computer, the "picture" which guided the operator was composed simply of rows of figures or code-words – a digital system can, after all, only process information that is capable of being reduced to mathematical terms. But more advanced models, for example the Apple "Macintosh", ushered in a new age of software design: instead of the prosaic representation of hard mathematical facts we could have the information presented to us in forms that were more easily assimilable and more pleasing to the eye. The role of the designer was now not so much to make the machine amenable to the operator, but primarily to make the data amenable to his visual capacities.

Let us consider how software design has affected the evolution of a familiar instrument, the calculator. We remember the bulky desk models of twenty or thirty years ago, and how they have become increasingly compacter and more streamlined over the years (pl. 596); in its most reduced form of materiality it has become little more than a plane field of operations (pl. 598); and in the immaterial dimension it is present as a function in many computer programmes. But it is with the "Macintosh" that the dematerialised calculator regains its visual form. By pressing keys on the keyboard we can, with the aid of the cursor, operate it just as we would a material calculator (pl. 599). One could of course go a step further and design this immaterial-visual representation in the Memphis look or as a Braun classic, according to taste. The idea is not so far-fetched: why should software design be particularly immune to the vagaries of style and the influence of kitsch? But first and foremost, the decisive factor in the acceptance of software, particularly by the nonprofessional user, is clarity and convenience.

The nonprofessional user, for instance, might well be concerned about energy-saving and wish to control his domestic heating via his home computer. But this will only be a realistic option if he does not have to learn keyboard combinations by heart or look up code-words; if, in effect, the "lost face" of the remote-controlled thermostat is restored through visual representation in the software graphics. A new and weighty dimension is thus added to the old design maxim of self-explanatoriness and self-evidence: software form explains software function!

"Nonprofessional" software users also include the mechanic, the doctor, or the ship's captain who is not a computer-buff. Thus, the control console of a milling machine that is linked via an "off-line" programme to a computer screen in the drawing office needs a good measure of designer attention. The design quality of capital goods in general will depend in future not only on the look of the hardware but increasingly on the visual qualities of the software. Siemens, for example, are already putting considerable efforts into software design (pl. 601).

The field of software appears at the moment to be the design area with the most potential for development. There are even calls for a special course of study for software designers, which would cover industrial design, informatics, and graphic design. The future will no doubt bring refinements of the rather banal graphics that currently reflect the infancy of the art. With only a modicum of fantasy one can imagine commercial software which will make "serious" programmes as exciting as contemporary video games and flight simulators. They could be further enhanced with video sequences and with such devices as videophones and voice activation. The new software

design, freed from the material constraints of the old forms of design and concerned with the mere representation of reality, has positively surreal possibilities.

While the three-dimensional world of "hard" products is rapidly vanishing from sight or so to speak imploding onto the computer screen, a new "soft" world of images is exploding thereon to provide these products with substitute forms. With the introduction of large-format 3D screen this indirect visualisation of our environment could become a deceptively real world. The sketch by the "Kunstflug" group gives some idea of these possibilities (pl. 602).

What we have so far considered constitutes one side of the picture: the effects of miniaturisation on the criteria of product design. There is another side that I find to be even more important for our industrial culture: the changes that technology has brought about in methods of production. The distinguishing characteristic of modern high-tech manufacturing is usually said to be its flexibility, whereby flexibility in production is regarded as coterminous with computer control.

Flexibility is however also one of the main features that distinguish handicraft from the industrial mode of production. Basic hand-tools such as the hammer and the plane are flexible in contrast to specialised industrial tools, whose most extreme example is the assembly line itself. Thus, computer-controlled manufacturing can in a way be seen as a revival of handicraft. The concept of manual production as represented by the craftsman does of course have many other characteristics besides flexibility, but all these are to a greater or lesser degree also seen in computer-controlled manufacturing, even if it is strictly speaking "untouched by human hand": there are for example the special organisational structures connected with the crafts, specific standards of training, and the special design criteria for short series and one-off production. The computer itself is in the Marxist sense, a craftsman's tool.[4] The old controversy about craft and industrial design thus appears on the agenda again, improbable though it might have seemed not so long ago that the shift from one-off manual production to industrial mass production could ever be reversed. (We cannot here consider the aspect of "alternative" handicraft.)

Traditional categories become blurred by the emergence of such concepts as the "industrial one-off", which seeks to underline the difference between single pieces manufactured with the aid of advanced technology and preindustrial handmade articles. At the same time, the process exemplifies the re-emergence of traditional structures and techniques in a futuristic setting, when the "robot craftsman" takes up his tools. Industrial robots can be seen as personifications of the whole concept of computer controlled production. Rather than confusing the highly complex categories of handicraft and industrial production, I would therefore suggest "postindustrial handicraft" as a more apt term to distinguish these new techniques from both industrial production and preindustrial handicraft.

The terms "industrial" and "handmade" stand for two systems of criteria, each with complex ramifications in our lives and our work, and naturally of great significance for design, too. Such concepts as "industrial society" and "handicraft – based society" give some sense of the significance of each particular form of production. Without industrialisation there would in fact be no "design" as we know it; the term "industrial design" is a tautology, though it might serve to differentiate against graphic, interior, hair design, etc. Our entire discussion of style in design is based on industrial premises. As industrial designers we tend, for instance, to see the "good form" of Functionalism as the true reflection of the transition from craft to industrial production. To do justice to "postindustrial handicraft" we must therefore reassess the entire history of style to date, paying special attention to the criteria derived from the advantages and disadvantages of handicraft as opposed to industrial production. In the light of advanced technology, with all its flexibility, we may discover new perspectives on old controversies, even such vexed questions as that of ornamentation.

An example of computer-assisted manufacture of single pieces is the Eyemetrics spectacle system (pl. 603), in which the customer's face is optically measured to provide the manufacturing data for what is somewhat awkwardly called the "mass production of unique pieces". The design of the Eyemetrics spectacles, however, still reflects a markedly industrial aesthetic: evidently the ergonomic advantages of the "industrial one-off" are the principal consideration here, and suffice to give the product the edge over the competition.

The Eyemetrics system only takes account of the physical features of the customer's face, and not (as yet!) his equally variegated psychosocial characteristics. But what will happen when flexible bespoke production becomes the rule rather than the exception? As with all mature technologies, the possibilities of aesthetic enhancement will then play an important role in product differentiation, targeting of market segments, etc. The history of spectacle design illustrates this particularly well. There will be a massive flowering of design variety, the flexible production technique will facilitate the expression of the customer's personality, aesthetic tastes, sensuality, etc., in the product to a much greater degree than with industrial mass production. Only in the one-off can design really create a work of art.

Against this background I cannot see it as entirely coincidental that the practitioners of "new German design" are again turning to handcrafted pieces and short-run series in reaction against the aesthetic norms of industrial mass production. It is regrettable that these exponents of Post-Modernism are still in the thrall of the traditional examplars of pre-industrial handicraft, and that their anti-High-Tech stance is so unsubtle as to amount to a virtual rejection of

industry. These attitudes moreover restrict the "new designers" to the genre of furniture; as exceptions we may note the designs for preamplifiers of the "Berliner Zimmer" group (pl. 604–606), which in my opinion represent a somewhat incongruous answer to the problems of miniaturisation and "loss of face" in micro-electronic equipment.

Industrial design in the narrower sense of the word has not made a special issue of either pre- or postindustrial handicraft; it has reacted more strongly to the technological revolution and more cautiously in terms of design than the "new German" design, but likewise with stylistic experimentation. This is primarily a reaction to the loss of orientation ensuing from the inapplicability of the old maxim "Form follows function" to the design of electronic equipment. The stylistic revolution in this sphere had no need of protagonists: it occurred automatically when even the most text-book designer found that nowadays technical functions no longer provide practical guidelines.

Rather, the microelectronic building blocks have themselves design potential and require their own organisational criteria. If at all, such criteria are going to be found only from outside the field of product design. Because of this insight, we have become accustomed to speaking about the design of electronic equipment in a very different way.

Realising that the world of microelectronics is governed by the whole new set of mostly quite inscrutable laws, we designers cannot apply our traditional precepts to this world. We no longer say that "good design" must be fashioned "from inside to outside" or that "honest" design must externally "reflect" the "functional essence" of a product, let it "shimmer through" so to speak. On the contrary, the internal anonymity of microelectronics engenders more and more attempts to seek external explanations. Form, the designable boundary between interior and exterior, is no longer treated as a transparent covering but as a screen onto which metaphorical interpretations of invisible technology can be projected. Here the designer can no longer think of himself as a neutral mediator who allows the beauty of technology to speak for itself; he must have something to say about this faceless technology in the form of "product-language" – otherwise the user will do it his own way (pl. 618). Thus, "Metaphor Design" has become the most important trend of recent years, at least it is certainly true of experimental industrial design (pl. 607–617, 619).

There are however some questions that still have to be resolved. Why does Metaphor Design as a rule concentrate on the interpretation of practical functions (ignoring such aspects as that of "corporate culture")? And why has no one publicly reflected on the scale of production on which such metaphors might be aesthetically acceptable and economically feasible? New questions of product style are not being studied enough from the point of view of a new production style to generate a truly new debate.

The situation may be provisionally summed up as follows: the technological upheaval in the field of microelectronics seems to be so far-reaching that it is certain to lead to revolutionary changes in our way of life and work; it is the third industrial revolution. Any form of stylistic evolution in design will therefore have to take the new technology into account. While the technological framework of this upheaval is gradually becoming more clearly defined, we still do not know what sort of spirit will or should imbue it.

The "Post-Modern" philosophy, without a forward-looking concept of technology, would hardly be suitable. Not surprisingly, most of the design experiments this philosophy has inspired present no real alternative to "good form", but are the somewhat pathetic manifestations of a stylistic limbo.

Still, we have long since become sceptical about the technological utopia: perhaps we should not be overimpatient to enter the stylistic utopia.

561 Thomas Stark
Portable radio, 1985/86
(model 1 : 1)

562 Seymour/Powell
"Blackhawk Stutz" elec-
tric guitar, 1987 (pro-
totype)

561

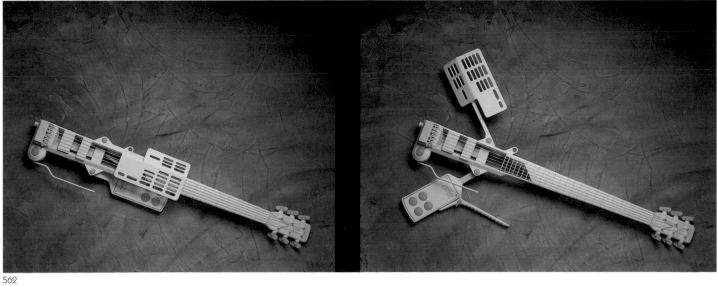

562

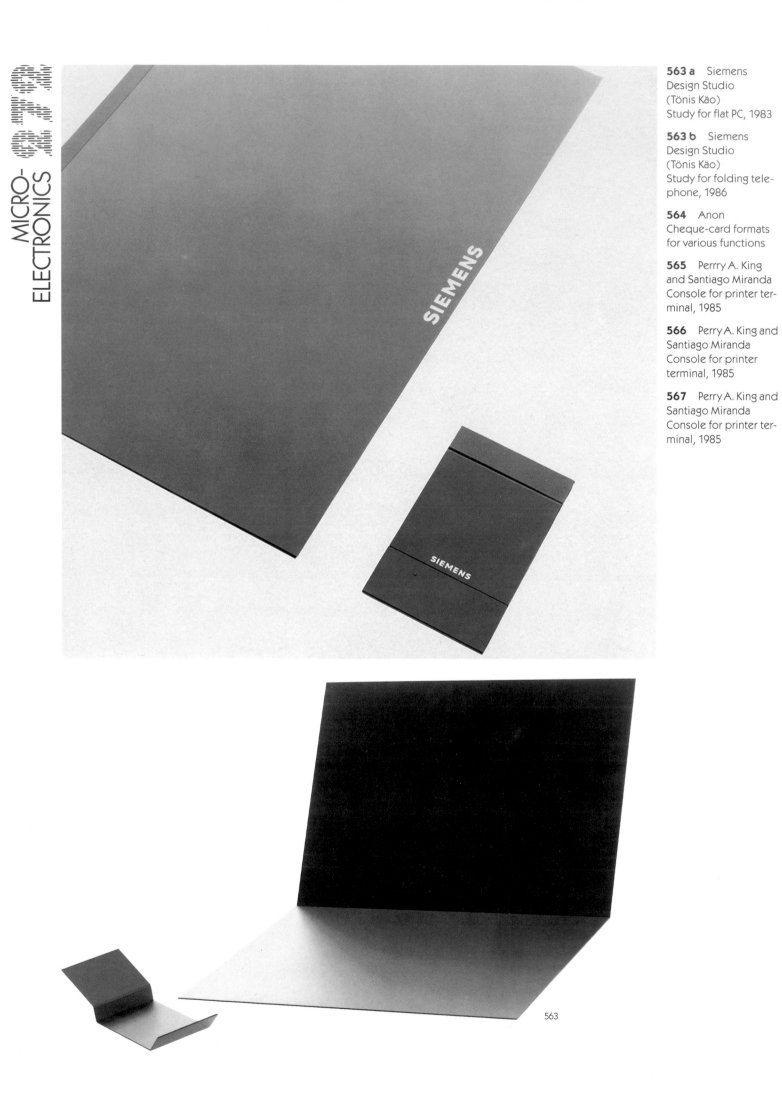

563 a Siemens
Design Studio
(Tönis Käo)
Study for flat PC, 1983

563 b Siemens
Design Studio
(Tönis Käo)
Study for folding tele-
phone, 1986

564 Anon
Cheque-card formats
for various functions

565 Perrry A. King
and Santiago Miranda
Console for printer ter-
minal, 1985

566 Perry A. King and
Santiago Miranda
Console for printer
terminal, 1985

567 Perry A. King and
Santiago Miranda
Console for printer ter-
minal, 1985

564

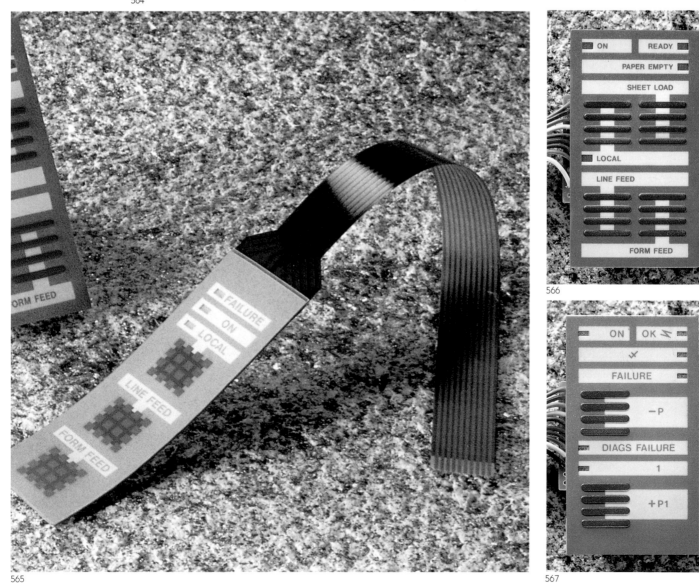

565

566

567

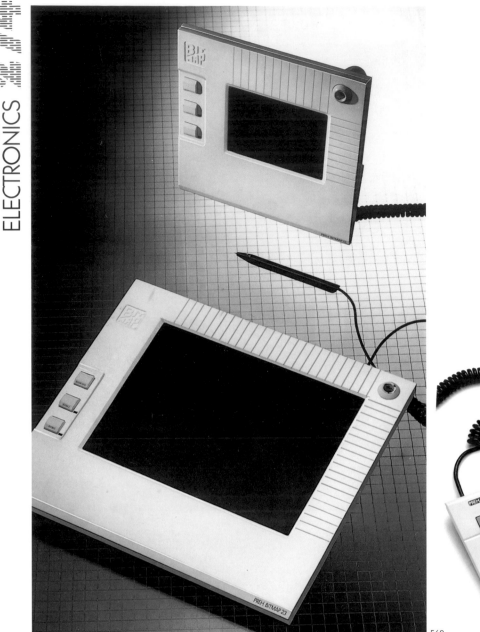

568 Hans-Jürgen and Helga Lannoch "Bitmap 12" graphics tablet, 1983/84

569 Hans-Jürgen and Helga Lannoch "Commander" keyboard, 1983/84

570 Siemens Design Studio (Christoph Böninger and Hans-Jürgen Escherle) Study for multifunctional communications panel, 1986

571 Frank Eisele and Heike Kuberg Personal computer, 1983 (mock-up)

572 Loewe "Art S 32" television, 1988

573 Frogdesign "Rotating Frogline" TV set with swivel screen, 1986 (prototype)

568

569

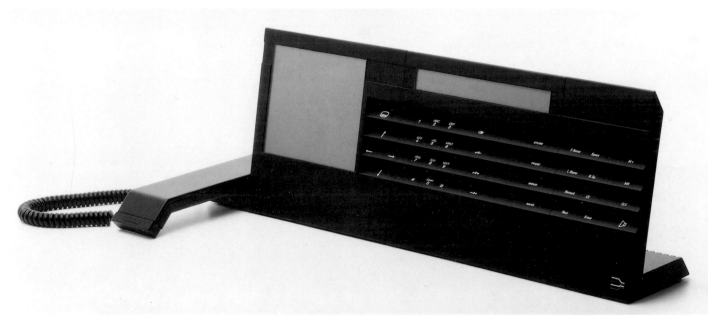

570

571

572

573

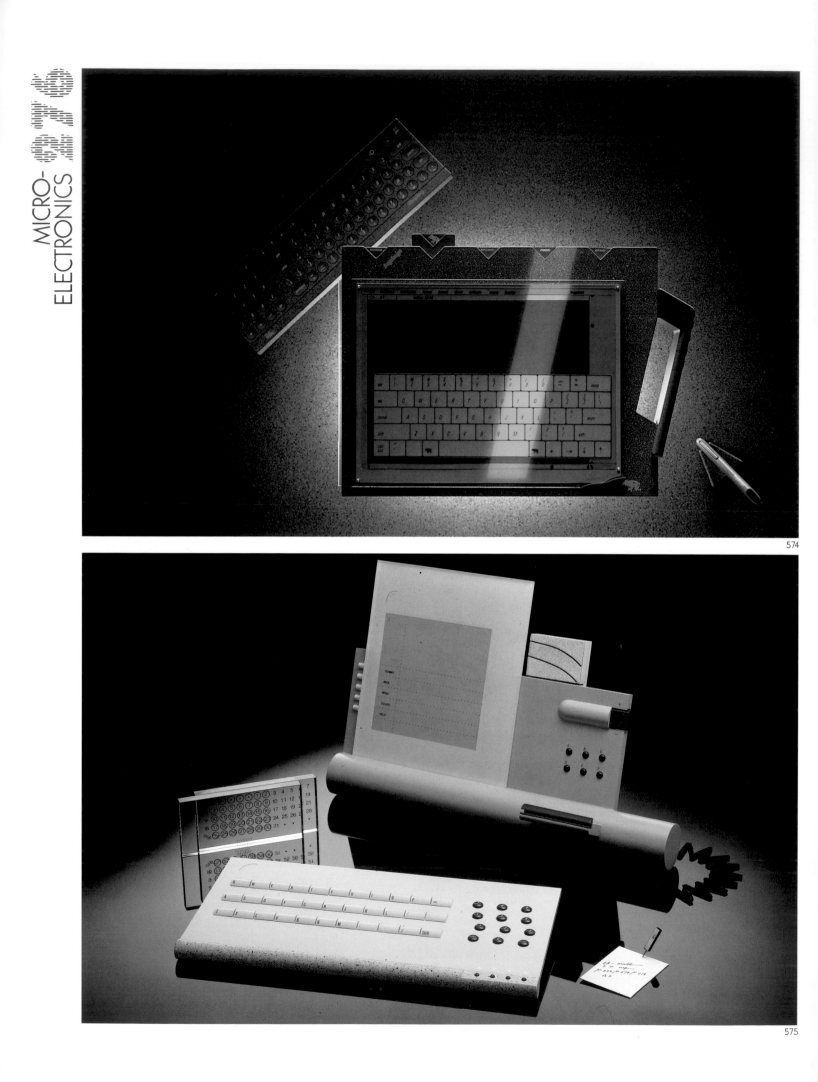

574 Frogdesign
"Office for the Future"
study for a workstation/
portable, 1986

575 a
Design Central Team
Personal electronic ter-
minal, 1986/87

575 b Frogdesign
"RCS 1" radio control-
led solar clock, 1986

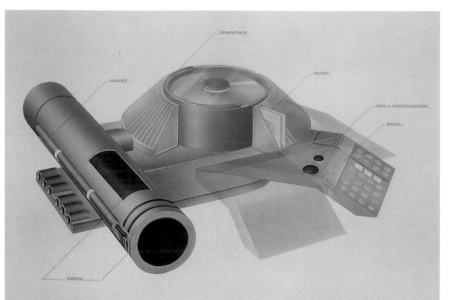

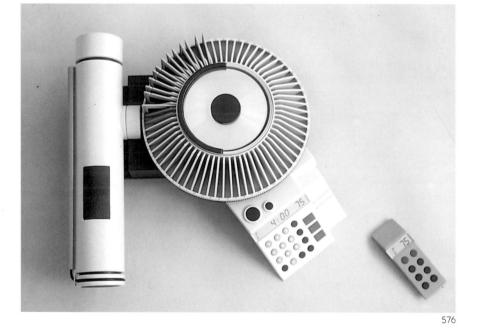

576

576 a, b Achim Pohl
and Stefan Imhof
Epidiascope, 1986
(prototype)

577 Peter Kienle and
Horst Pohlenz
Digital large-screen
projector, 1986 (pro-
totype)

578 Daniel Weil
"100 objects mirrors of
silenced time . . ." digital clock, 1982

579 Daniel Weil
"Verse" calculator, 1985

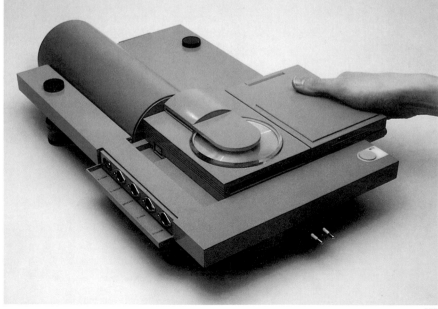

577

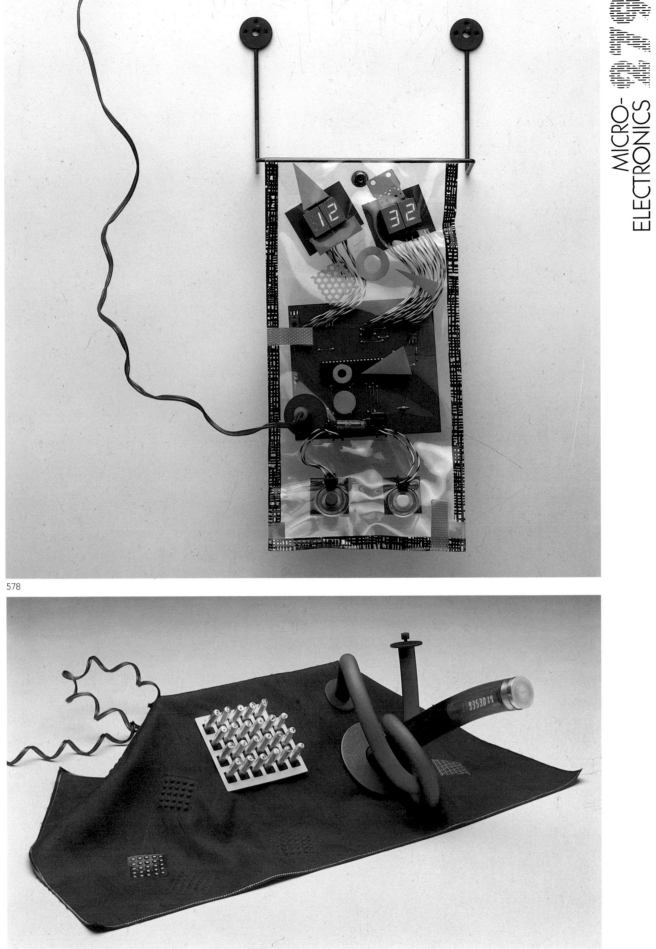

578

579

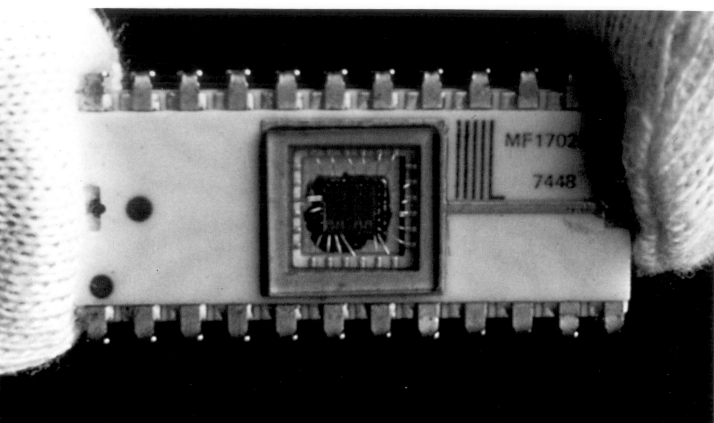

580

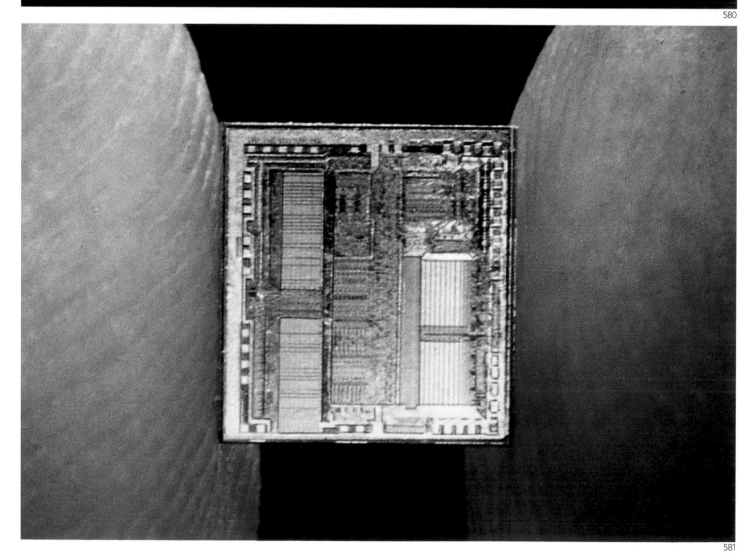

581

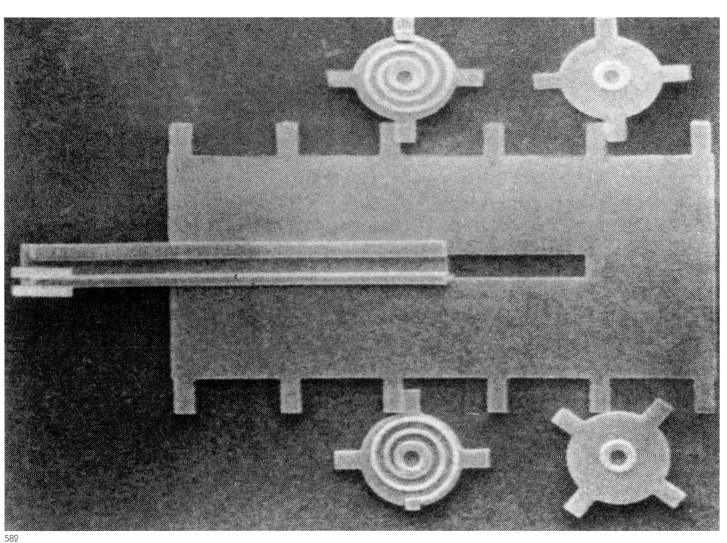

582

580 Olivetti
Microprocessor

581 Chip

582 a, b Micro-
mechanics (toothed
rack and pinions in the
diameter of a hair) 1988

583

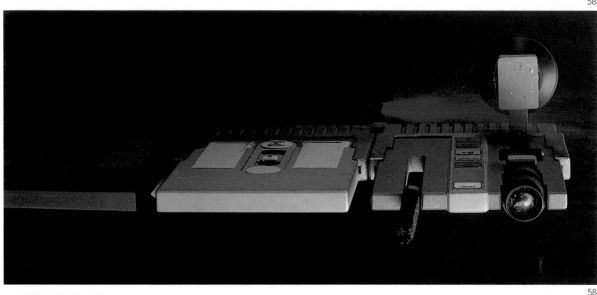

584

585

583 Frogdesign
"Office for the Future,
Workstation Eins", 1986
(prototype)

584 – 587
Uwe Berndt
Portable communica-
tions system, 1987

584 Camera

585 Typewriter

586 Portable com-
munication equip-
ment, waistcoat

587 Videophone

588 Hagai Shvadron
(under the direction of
Mario Bellini)
"Count Down 1990"
portable computer,
1987 (model)

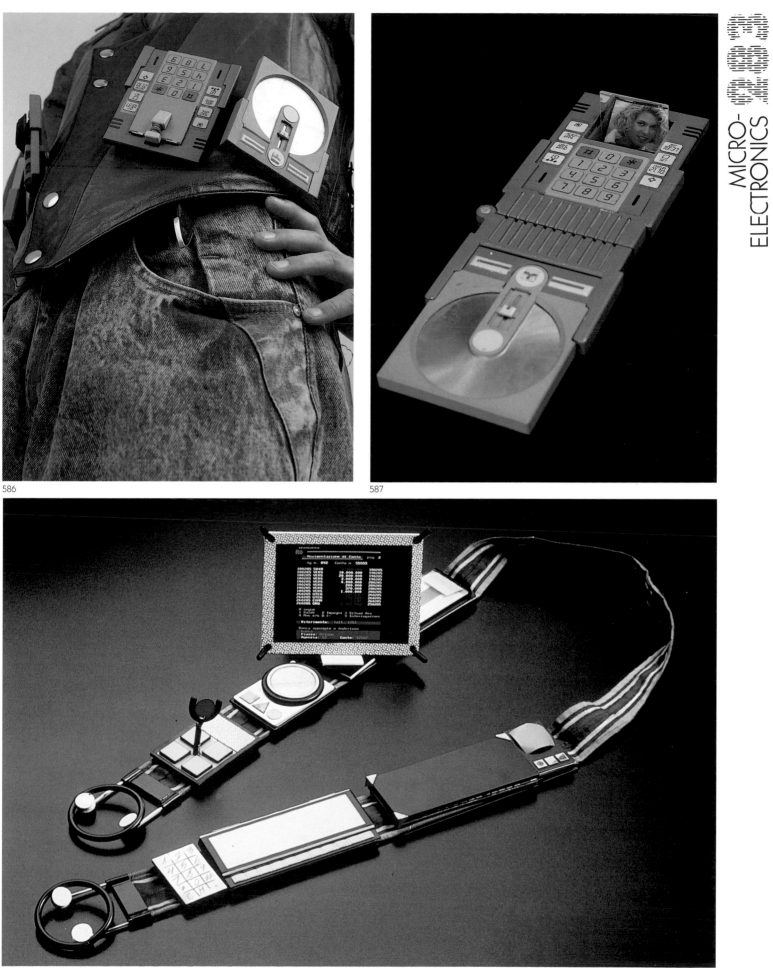

586

587

588

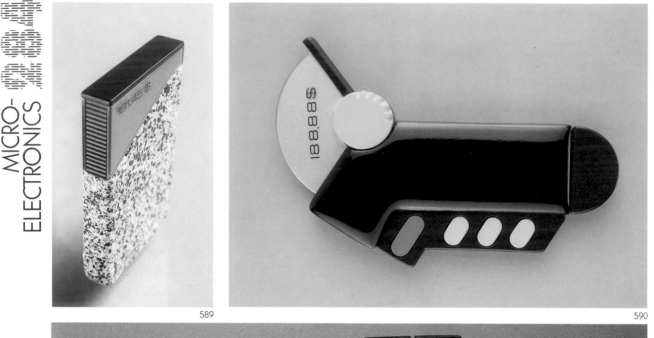

589

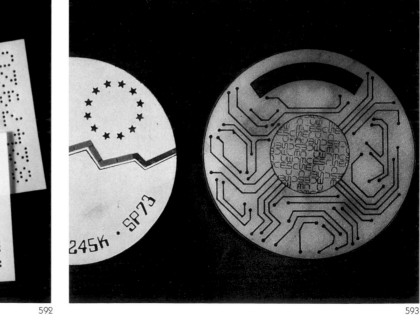

590

589 Manfred Nitsch
"Paymate" electronic
money, 1986 (pro-
totype)

590 Manfred Nitsch
"Paymate" electronic
money, 1986 (pro-
totype)

591 Stefan Pütz
"Paymate" electronic
money, 1986 (pro-
totype)

592, 593 "Electronic
Coins", coins and notes
of various denomina-
tions, 1987 (prototype)

594 Paolo Grasselli
Glove calculator, 1986

595 Kunstflug
Electronic finger cal-
culator, 1986/87

591

Generalitat de Catalunya
**Departament d'Economia
i Finances**

Generalitat de Catalunya
**Departament d'Economia
i Finances**

20 ECU

592

245K · SP73

593

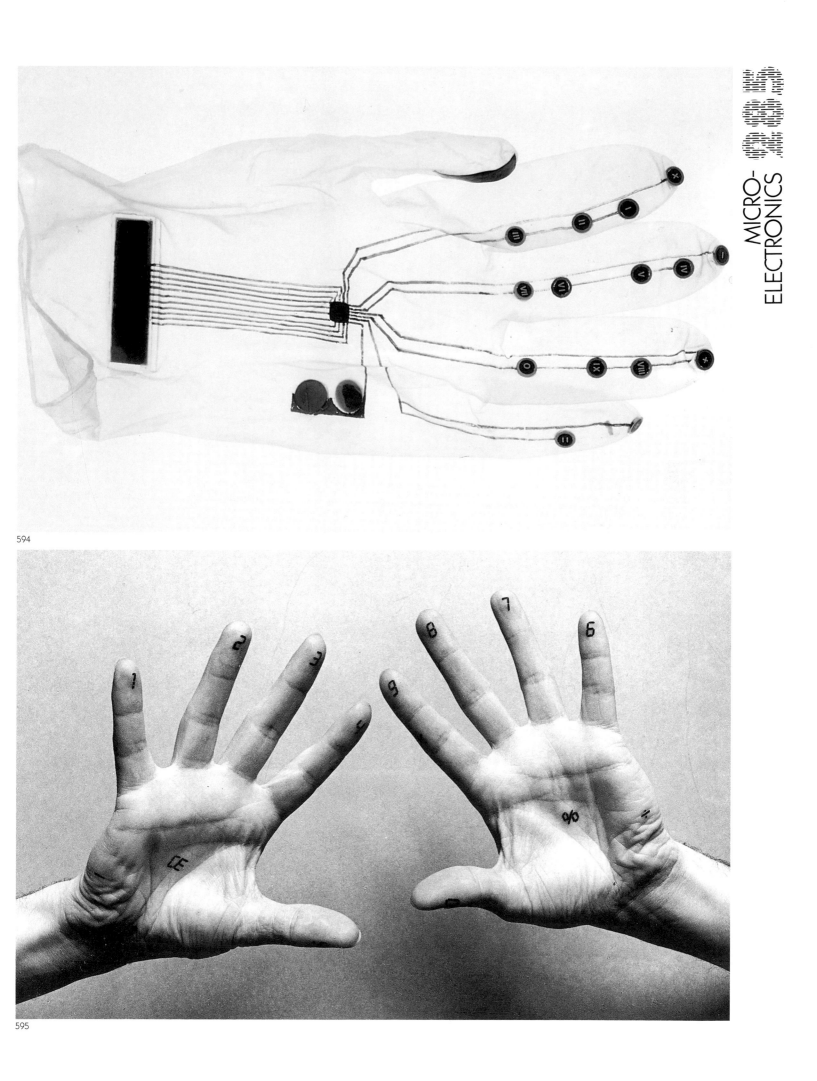

594

595

596 a, b
Marcello Nizzoli
"Divisumma 24" desk
calculator, 1956

596 c
Design Central Team
Desk calculator, 1986/87

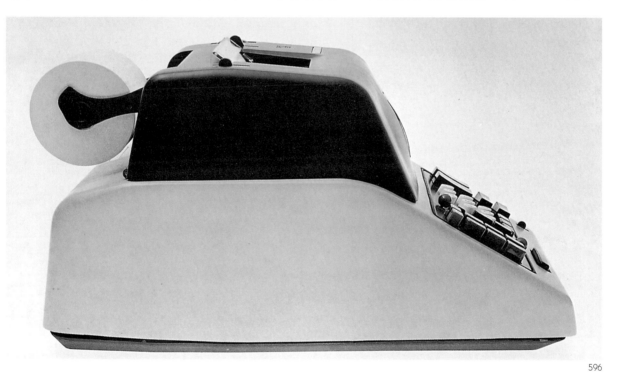

596

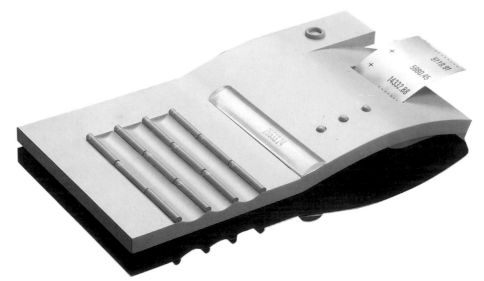

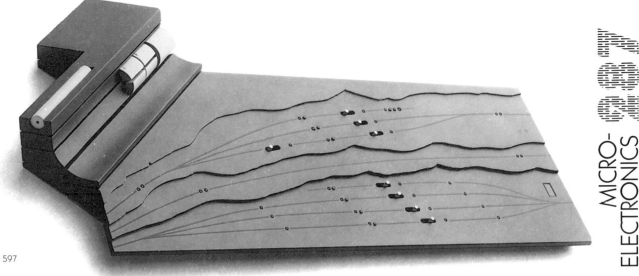

597 Siemens Design Studio (Jürgen Hitzler) Study for track terminal, 1986

597a Nele Ströbel PC keyboard with integrated cursor ball-control and neon-coloured programme masks, 1985/86

598 Anonymous "Quartz Cal 318SE" solar cell calculator

597

597a

QUARTZ CAL   SOLAR CELL CALCULATOR 318SE

598

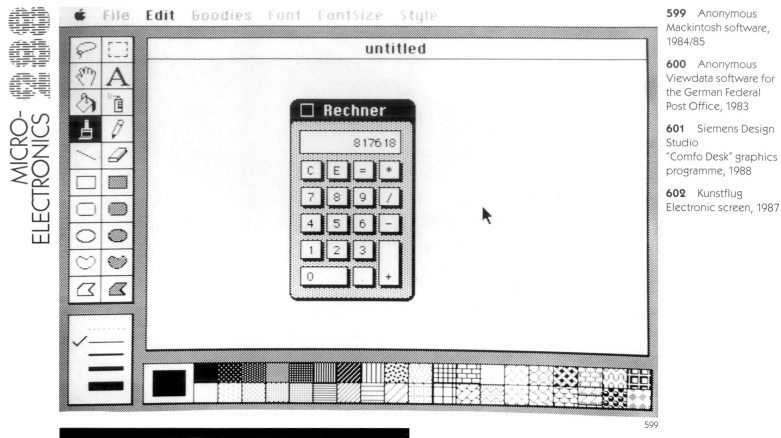

599

600

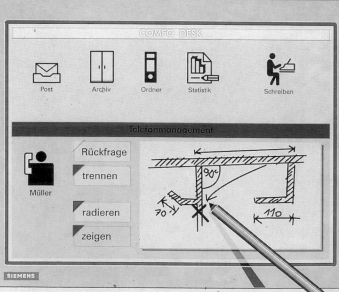

601

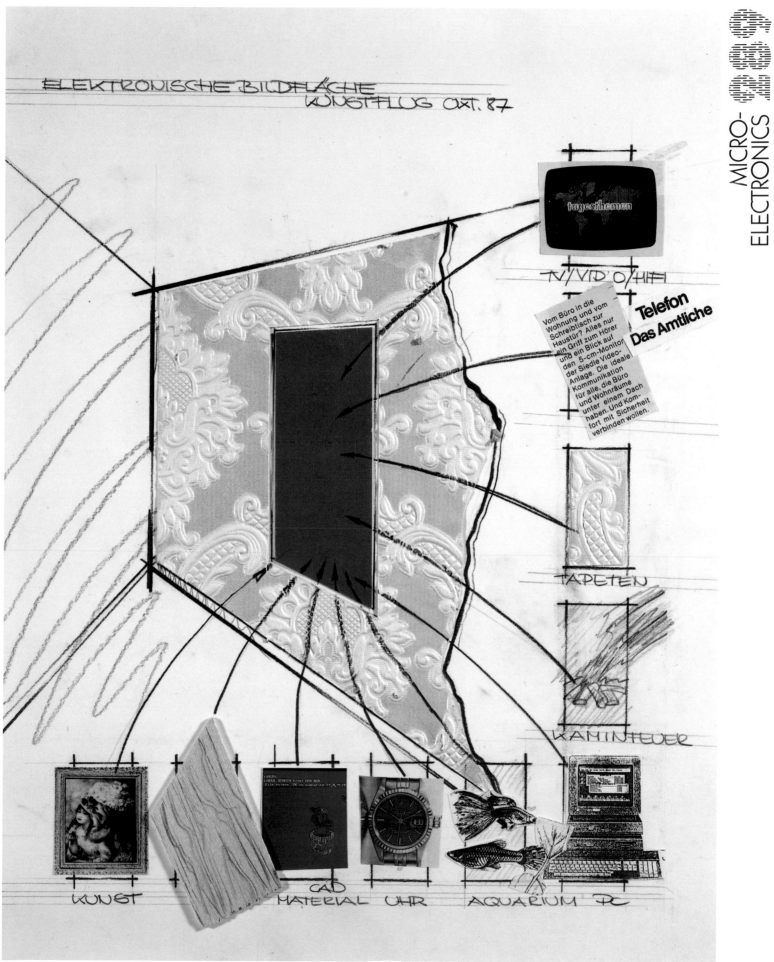

ELEKTRONISCHE BILDFLÄCHE
KUNSTFLUG OKT. 87

tagesthemen

TV/VIDEO/HIFI

Vom Büro in die Wohnung und vom Schreibtisch zur Haustür? Alles nur ein Griff zum Hörer und ein Blick auf den 5-cm-Monitor der Siedle Video-Anlage. Die ideale Kommunikation für alle, die Büro und Wohnräume unter einem Dach haben. Und Komfort mit Sicherheit verbinden wollen.

Telefon
Das Amtliche

TAPETEN

KAMINFEUER

KUNST   MATERIAL UHR   AQUARIUM PC

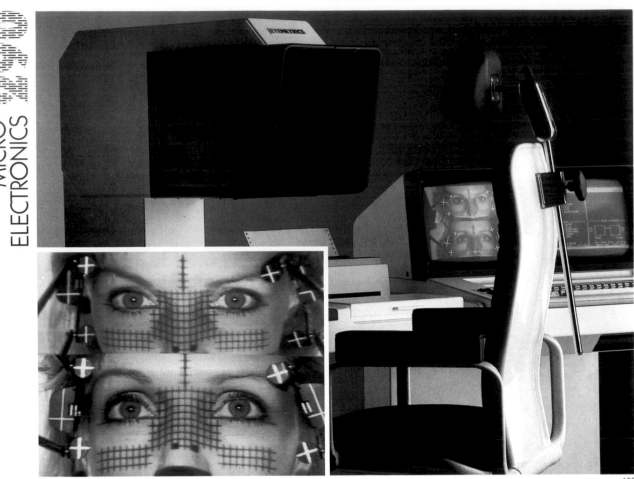

603 a, b
Wilhelm Anger
"Eyemetrics" systems,
1987

604   Bellefast
(Andreas Brandolini)
"Kalle" hi-fi pre-
amplifier, 1986

605   Bellefast
(Joachim B. Stanitzek)
"Play 846" hi-fi pre-
amplifier, 1986

606   Gelb Selectiv
(Christian Schneider-
Moll)
"Strata ZaZa" hi-fi pre-
amplifier, 1986

603

604

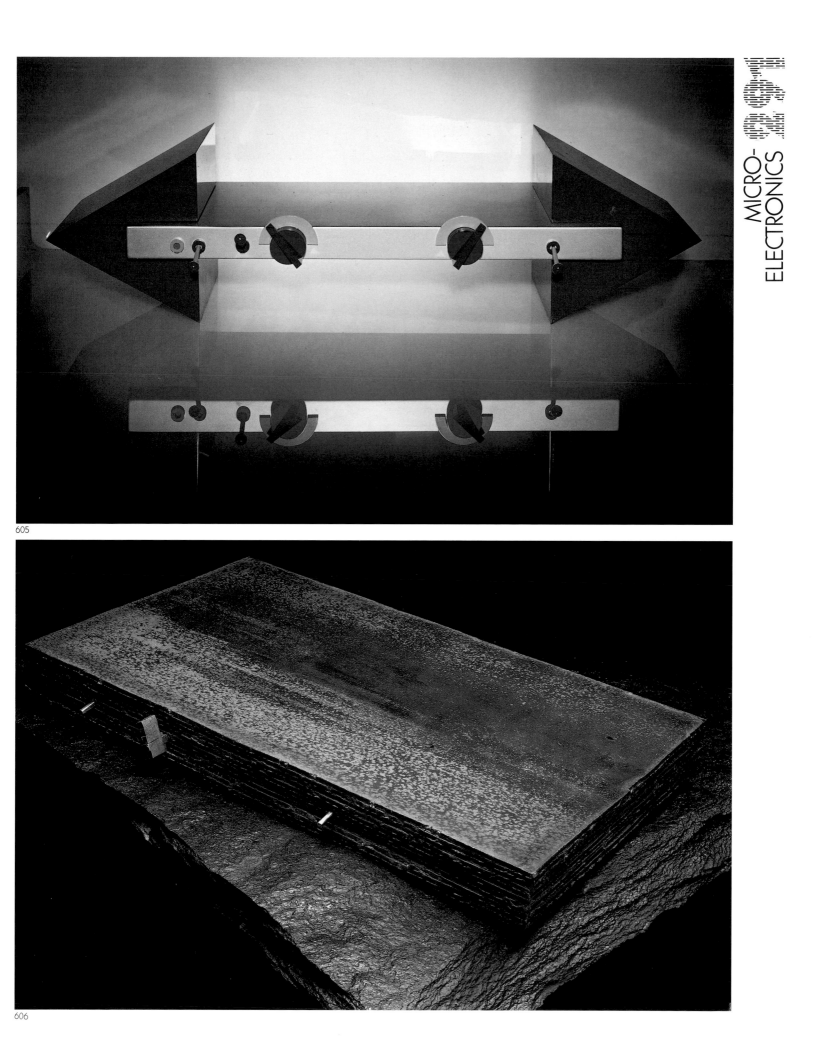

605

606

607

608

607 Robert Nakata
Stereo receiver 1984

608
Paul Montgomery
Electronic still-camera,
1987 (project)

609
Paul Montgomery
"Picture Phone", 1987

610 Lisa Krohn
Multifunctional tele-
phone answering
machine with thermal
printer, LCD display and
phonebook, 1987

609

610

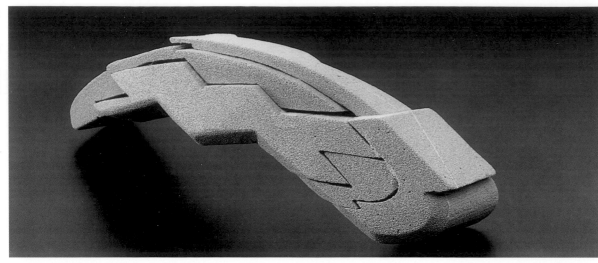

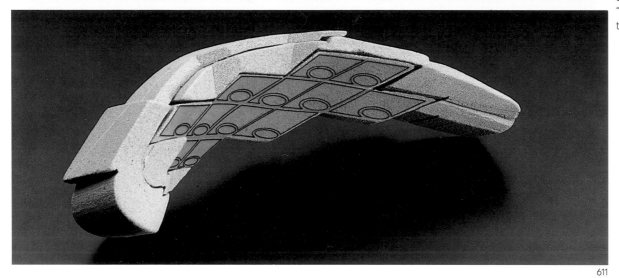

611

612

611 a, b Siemens Design Studio (Hatto Grosse) Study for compact telephone, 1986

612 Siemens Design Studio (Luitpold Hecht) "Plasma" study for a telephone, 1986

613 Siemens Design Studio (Jürgen Hitzler and Werner Schuss) Study for a telephone, 1986

614 Siemens Design Studio (Rolf Hering) "Lobster", study for a telephone, 1986

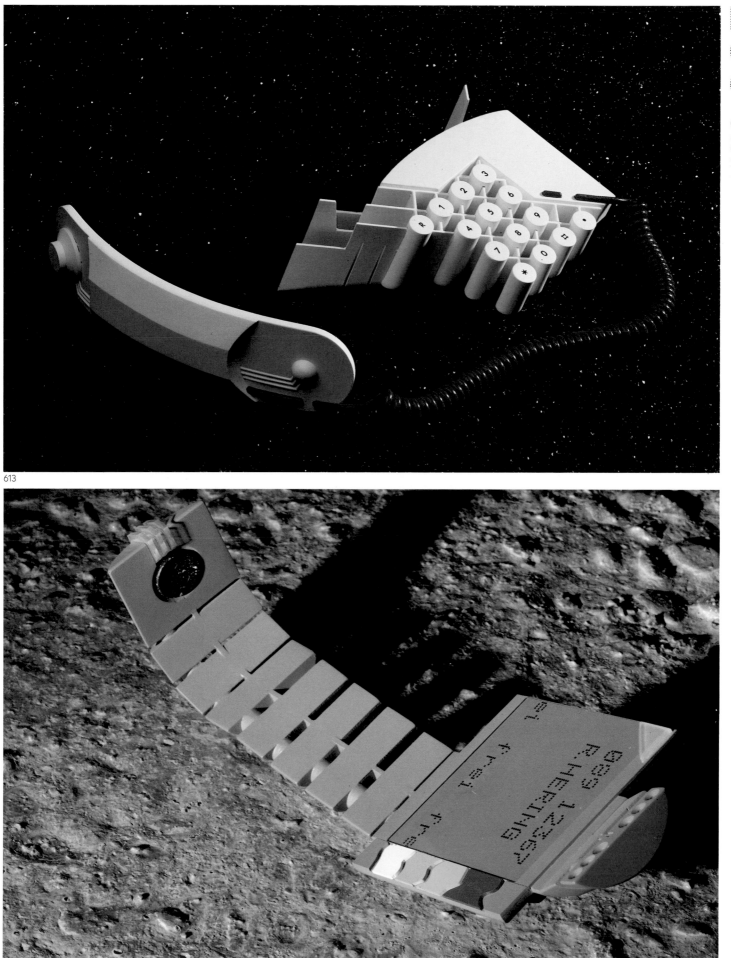

613

614

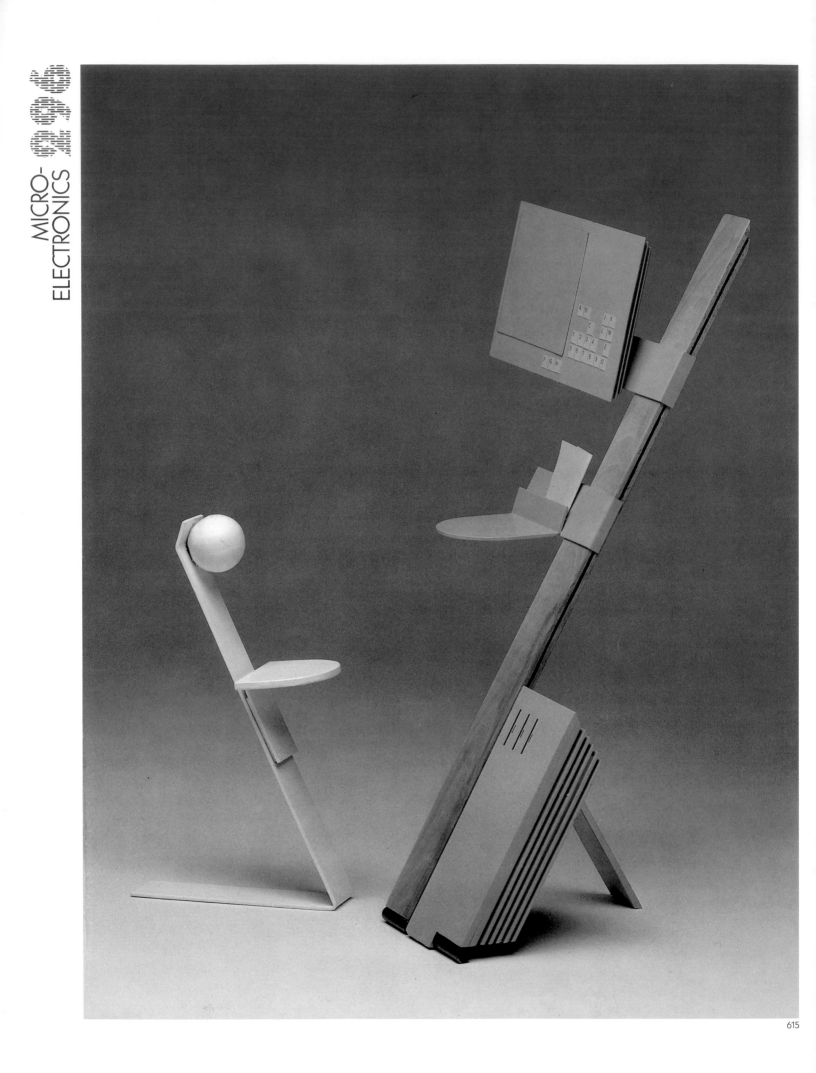

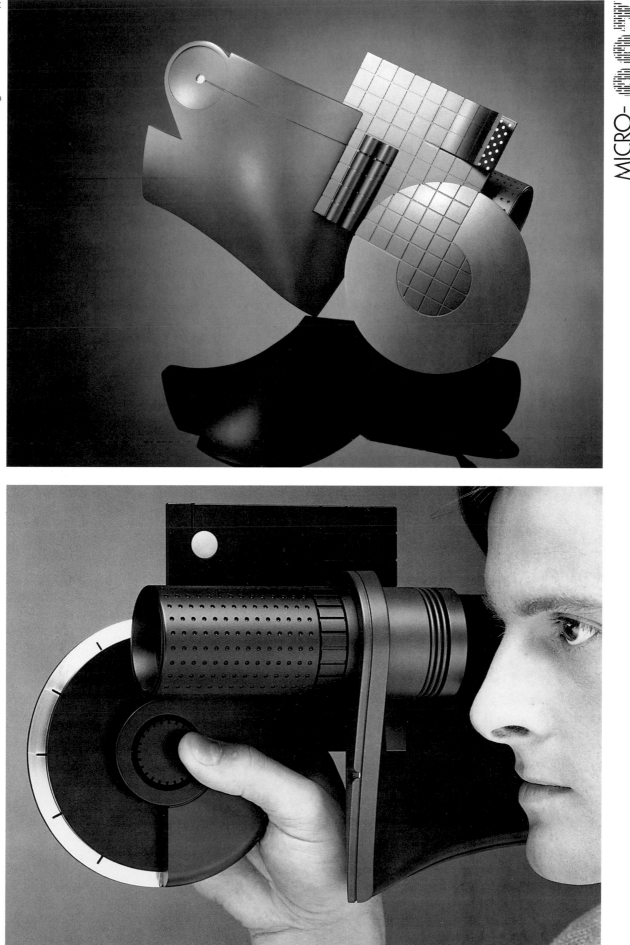

615 Alois Dworschak
Computer workplace,
1986/87 (model)

616 a, b D. M.
Gresham and Martin
Thaler
CD video-camera, 1986

616

617 D. M. Gresham
and Martin Thaler
Speaking slide-projec-
tor, 1985

618 VDU workplace

619 D. M. Gresham
and Hel Rinkleib
"Book" computer, 1985

617

618

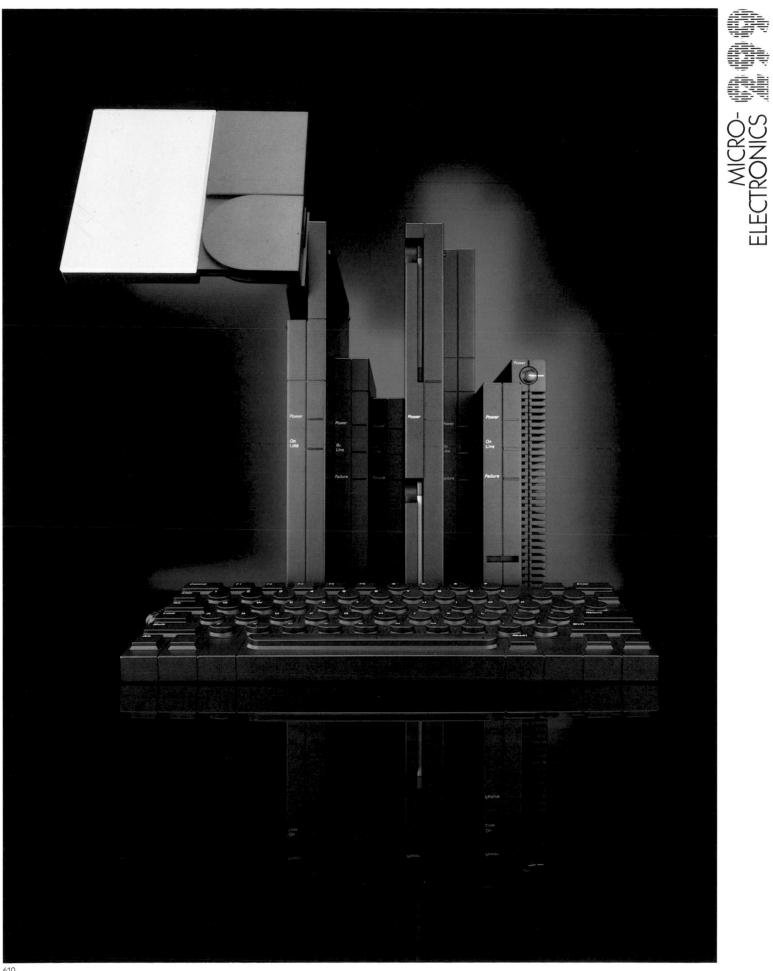

NOTES

Formal Concepts of Contemporary Design, pp. 45/46

1   Volker Albus et al. (ed.): *Gefühlscollagen. Wohnen von Sinnen,* catalogue of Düsseldorf exhibition. Cologne 1986.
2   Volker Fischer: "Technologie als Fetisch, High-Tech in Architektur und Design." In Heinrich Klotz (ed.): *Vision der Moderne. Das Prinzip Konstruktion.* Munich 1986, pp. 66–77.

High-Tech, pp. 47–49

1   Joan Kron, Suzanne Slesin: *High-Tech. The Industrial Style and Source Book for the Home.* New York 1978, London 1980³.
2   Susan Sontag: "Notes on 'Camp'." In: *Against Interpretation and Other Essays.* New York 1966, London 1967, pp. 275–292.
3   Volker Fischer, as in Note 2, Formal Concepts, p. 69 ff.
4   Volker Fischer, as in Note 9, Formal Concepts, p. 70 ff.
5   Press-release from Tecno for the product launch. Milan 1987.
6   "Der Raum wird zur Leuchte, Revolution der Innenarchitektur. Das neue Licht." Der Spiegel 12 (1987).
7   "Leuchtenakrobatik – das Licht auf den Seilen." Form 114, II (1986), pp. 44–47.

Trans-High-Tech, pp. 59–61

1   Volker Fischer, as in Note 2, Formal Concepts, pp. 66–77.

Alchimia/Memphis, pp. 73–75

1   Volker Fischer: "Interieurs der Zweiten Moderne." In: *Jahrbuch für Architektur 1983,* p. 186 ff., esp. p. 201.
2   Matteo Thun, one of the founder-members of Memphis, in conversation with the author.

Minimalism, pp. 101/102

1   Shiro Kuramata e Cappellini. *Progetti Compiuti.* Cappellini International Interiors, Carugo (Italy) 1986.

Archetypes, pp. 111/112

1   "Jene Sehnsucht nach den alten Tagen ..." Der Spiegel 5 (1973), pp. 86–99, esp. p. 90. See also Volker Fischer: *Nostalgie. Geschichte und Kultur als Trödelmarkt.* Lucerne/Frankfurt 1980. Wolfgang Schievelbusch: "Das nostalgische Syndrom. Überlegungen zu einem neuen antiquarischen Gefühl." Frankfurter Hefte 4 (1973), pp. 270–276.

2   Betty Cornfeld: *Quintessenz. Die schönen Dinge des Lebens.* Munich 1984.

Dieter Rams, pp. 125–129

1   Rudolf Schönwandt: "Beschreibung des Designers Dieter Rams." In: François Burkhardt, Inez Franksen (eds.): *Design. Dieter Rams.* Berlin 1980/81, pp. 17–30, esp. p. 18.
2   Burkhardt, Franksen, as above.
3   Instant 22 (issue devoted to Braun), Frankfurt/Wiesbaden 1987. Der Braun-Sammler 1–9 (mimeographed magazine published by "collectors"), Hamburg, 1984–1988.
4   Richard Hamilton: opening address at the IDZ exhibition, Berlin 1980. Quoted in Burkhardt, Franksen, as above, inside cover.
5   Michael Schneider. Instant 22, as above, p. 3.
6   Dieter Rams: "Funktionales Design ist eine Zukunftsausgabe." In Design-Dasein, exhibition catalogue. Hamburg 1987, pp. 155–159.
7   Dieter Rams, Roland Ullmann: "Gute Form ist nie vollendet." Form 108/109 (1984/1985), pp. 38–41.
8   Dieter Rams, as in Note 6 above, p. 157.
9   Dieter Rams interviewed by Gina Angress and Inez Franksen: "Zurück zum Einfachen, zum Puren." In Burkhardt, Franksen, as in Note 1 above, p. 207.
10   Dieter Rams, as in Note 1 above, pp. 207 ff.
11   Product information from the Vitsoe company.
12   Dieter Rams, as in Note 1 above, p. 209.
13   François Burkhardt, Inez Franksen: Introduction. As in Note 1 above, p. 9.
14   Dieter Rams, as in Note 6 above, p. 158.

Stefan Wewerka, pp. 149–153

1   Verrückte Welten. Die Karrieren des Stefan Wewerka. Film by Lothar Spree.
2   Erna Lackner: "Rätsel auf schiefen Stühlen. Stefan Wewerka." Frankfurter Allgemeine Zeitung, Suppl. 350 (14. 11. 86), pp. 62–72, esp. p. 68.
3   Stefan Wewerka: typescript notes on the "seating island" for the exhibition.
4   Francesco Raggi: "The Designer Tries." Domus 617 (1981), Suppl. Domus Moda, pp. 17–19.
5   Stefan Wewerka. Brochure of Tecta Co., Lauenförde 1973.
6   From an unpublished interview with Heinrich Klotz, 1982.
7   Andrea Gleiniger: "Zu den Arbeiten von Stefan Wewerka", typescript of lecture, Werkbund, Hannover 20. 4. 85. I am indebted to Dr. Andrea Gleiniger, Frankfurt, for valuable insights on Wewerka's oeuvre.
8   Andrea Gleiniger, as above.
9   Kent C. Bloomer, Charles W. Moore, with a contribution by Robert J. Yudell: *Body, Memory and Architecture.* New Haven 1977.
10   Erna Lackner, as in Note 2 above, p. 68.

Holger Scheel, pp. 173–177

1   Volker Fischer: "Sitzen ist Setzung." Interview mit dem Stuttgarter Designer Holger Scheel. *Jahrbuch für Architektur 1983,* pp. 202–222, esp. p. 208.
2   Holger Scheel in Fischer, as above, p. 218.
3   "In den Stuttgarter Gallerien", Stuttgarter Zeitung, 25. 2. 83.
4   Roland Barthes, tr. by Annette Lavers: *Mythologies.* London 1972, pp. 88–90.
5   Holger Scheel in Fischer, as Note 1 above, p. 220.

Microarchitecture, pp. 209–211

1   This term was first suggested by Alessandro Mendini in 1978/79 with reference to Alessi's "Tea and Coffee Piazza" project.
2   *Tea and Coffee Piazza.* Officina Alessi, Crusinallo (Italy) 1983.
3   V. Fischer: "High Rise Application. Der Architekt als Visagist der Metropolen." In *The Heavy Dress. Die Oberfläche als Manifest,* Matteo Thun, exhibition catalogue. Vienna 1986.
4   Matteo Thun: "Das barocke Bauhaus. Aphorismen zu einem Manifest." Frankfurt 1986 (on the occasion of a WMF trade show in the Frankfurt Museum für Kunsthandwerk).
5   Matteo Thun, as in Note 4 above.
6   In this connection, F. O. Lipp's "Triga" fruit-dish gives the impression of being a belated reaction to similar designs for table culture objects with multicoloured marble elements by Ettore Sottsass, Mario Bellini and Andrea Branzi for the Italian firm Up & Up.
7   Matteo Thun. In Volker Albus, Michael Feith, Rouli Lecatsa, Wolfgang Schepers, Claudia Schneider-Esleben (eds.): *Gefühlscollagen, Wohnen von Sinnen.* Cologne 1986, p. 272.

Banal Design, pp. 241–243

1   Siegfried Gronert: "Design: Weltstars in Brakel. Der Zeitgeist in der Klinke. Ein Fabrikant und die Kultur des Greifens – ein origineller Einfall." Die Zeit 40 (26. 9. 86), p. 3. "Türklinken: Zeitgeist im Griff." Häuser 11 (1986): "Die Form des Banalen." Frankfurter Allgemeine Zeitung (8. 10. 86): "Klinkenputz." Form 11 (1986): "Banales als Thermometer der Kultur." Magazin Design 12 (1986): "Klinke im Designer-Griff." Der Stern 4 (1987).
2   The designers are sometimes named, if only in passing, in exhibitions of these fittings: for instance Hans Jürgen Bauer for the "Terrazzo" range at the Haus der Industrieform, Essen.

Measuring Up: Rolex and Manhattan, pp. 249–264

1   Archithese 17 (1976), p. 11.
2   Siegfried Krakauer: "Feet First" (film review), 1931.

3   M. D. Vernon: *Perception through Experience.* London 1970, p. 124.

4   Rosemarie Bletter: "Metropolis réduite." Archithese 18 (1976), pp. 22–27.

5   B. Karpf: "Form Follows Form – Philip Johnsons Hochhausprojekte." Bauwelt 5 (1985), p. 187. Paul Goldberger: *The Skyscraper.* New York 1981, p. 153.

6   B. Karpf, as note 5.

7   *New York. Fotografien von Reinhart Wolf.* Cologne 1980.

8   Robert Venturi, Denise Scott Brown, Steven Izenour: *Learning from Las Vegas.* Cambridge (Mass.) and London 1972.

9   Claes Oldenburg: *Proposals for Monuments and Buildings 1965–1969.* Chicago 1969, p. 19.

10   *Claes Oldenburg: Mouse Museum/Ray Gun Wing,* catalogue of exhibition at the Kröller-Müller Museum, Otterloo. Cologne 1979, p. 60.

11   Patrick Frey. In Kaspar König (ed.): *Skulptur-Projekte in Münster 1987.* Münster 1987, p. 88.

12   Paul Goldberger: *The City Observed – New York.* New York 1979, p. 11.

13   Ada Louise Huxtable: *The Tall Building Artistically Reconsidered: The Search for a Skyscraper Style.* New York 1984, p. 117.

14   Ada Louise Huxtable, as note 13, p. 116. See also *Skyscrapers,* a film by Bernhard Leitner, including a conversation with Gerald D. Hines, who describes himself as a developer who "coordinates the wishes and energies of the most varied people in order to produce an optimal end-product, in this case a building." Slogan: "A Building is a product."

15   Wolfgang Kabisch, Felix Zwoch: "Die Stadt am Clip." Stadtbauwelt 93 (1987), pp. 445–49.

16   Georg Franck: "Die informationstechnische Transformation der Stadt – Fortsetzung ihrer Modernisierung mit anderen Mitteln." Bauwelt 78 (1987), pp. 1158–72.

17   Michel de Certeau: "Umgang mit Raum. Die Stadt als Metapher." Bauwelt 48 (1978), pp. 1750–65.

Technology of Miniaturisation, pp. 265–270

Form 78, II (1977).

2   Kurt Weidemann: Introduction. In: *Erkundungen,* catalogue of the International Design Congress. Stuttgart 1986, p. 7.

3   Gianni Barbacetto: *Design Interface. How Man and Machine Communicate.* Olivetti Design Research, Milan 1987.

4   Michael J. Piore, Charles F. Sabel: *Das Ende der Massenproduktion.* Berlin 1985.

APPENDIX

List of Objects

Data are given in the order: designer, object, year, material, dimensions (height × length × depth), manufacturer.
Unless otherwise stated, the manufacturer (or distributor in the Federal Republic of Germany) is also the lender. The photographer is only named where the picture is not a works photograph.

1
Thonet brothers
"Modell 209" chair, original c. 1900, present form 1965. Steam-bent beech frame, wicker seat
75 × 54 × 57 cm, height of seat 46 cm
Thonet, Frankenberg, FRG

2
Charles Rennie Mackintosh
"Hill House 1" chair, 1902, in production again since 1973
Black-stained ash, upholstered seat
141 × 4 × 39 cm, height of seat 45 cm
Cassina, Milan

3
Josef Hoffmann
"Purkersdorf" armchair, 1903
Ash with white rubbing-varnish, back-cushion and webbed seat in black and white geometric pattern
84 × 61 × 61 cm, height of seat 42 cm
Wittmann, Etsdorf am Kamp, Austria

4
Charles Rennie Mackintosh
"Willow 1" chair, 1904, in production again since 1973
Black-stained ash, upholstered seat
119 × 94 × 41 × cm, height of seat 39 cm
Cassina, Milan

5
Frank Lloyd Wright
"Robie" chair, 1908, in production again since 1986
Natural cherry, padded seat covered in leather or fabric
133 × 40 × 45 cm, height of seat 46 cm
Cassina, Milan

6
Josef Hoffmann
"Fledermaus" chair, 1909
Steam-shaped beech, padded seat and back
74 × 53 × 46 cm, height of seat 47 cm
Wittmann, Etsdorf am Kamp, Austria

7
Walter Gropius
"D 51" chair, 1911
Black-stained ash, loose seat and back cushions
79 × 61 × 56 cm, height of seat 46 cm
Tecta, Lauenförde, FRG

8
Frank Lloyd Wright
"Midway 1" chair, 1914, in production again since 1986
Gloss-lacquered tubular steel, upholstered seat
88 × 40 × 46 cm, height of seat 46 cm
Cassina, Milan

9
Gerrit T. Rietveld
"Rood en Blauw" [Red and Blue] chair, 1918, in production again since 1973
Beech, stained black and yellow, seat painted blue, back painted red
88 × 65 × 83 cm, height of seat 33 cm
Cassina, Milan

10
Marcel Breuer
"Wassily" armchair, 1925
Chromium-plated tubular steel, seat, arms and back leather or sailcloth
72 × 79 × 70 cm, height of seat 42 cm
Knoll Deutschland, Murr, FRG

11
Le Corbusier, Pierre Jeanneret, Charlotte Perriand
"LC 1" armchair, 1925 –28, in production again since 1965
Tubular steel, chromium-plated or painted black, arms leather, covers sheepskin, leather or canvas
64 × 60 × 65 cm, height of seat 40 cm
Cassina, Milan

12
Le Corbusier, Pierre Jeanneret, Charlotte Perriand
"LC 2" armchair, 1925 –28, in production again since 1965
Tubular steel, chromium-plated or painted, loose cushions covered in leather or fabric
67 × 70 × 70 cm, height of seat 43 cm
Cassina, Milan

13
Eileen Gray
"Non-Conformist" armchair, 1926
Chromium-plated tubular steel, leather upholstery
57 × 63 × 78 cm, height of seat 45 cm
Vereinigte Werkstätten, Munich

14
Mart Stam
"S 32" chair, 1927
Tubular steel, shaped beech frames with wickerwork
80 × 45 × 57 cm, height of seat 44 cm
Thonet, Frankenberg, Austria

15
Le Corbusier, Pierre Jeanneret, Charlotte Perriand
"LC 7" swivel chair with armrests, 1929, in production again since 1978
Tubular steel, chromium plated or painted, backrest and seat cushions upholstered in leather or fabric
73 × 60 × 56 cm, height of seat 50 cm
Cassina, Milan

16
Ludwig Mies van der Rohe
"Barcelona" easy-chair, 1929
Special sprung steel, polished chromium plating, seat and back foam rubber upholstered in leather
77 × 75 × 76 cm, height of seat 43 cm
Knoll Deutschland, Murr, FRG

17
Ludwig Mies van der Rohe
"Brno" armchair, 1929
Special sprung steel, polished chromium plating, foam cushions with leather covers
78 × 55 × 59 cm, height of seat 42 cm
Knoll Deutschland, Murr, FRG

18
Renè Herbst
Nickel-plated chair, 1930
Tubular steel, nickel-plated, seat and back with black, white, blue, red or yellow rubber springs
81 × 43 × 40 cm, height of seat 47 cm
Écart, Paris

19
Jean Prouvé
"D 80" high-backed armchair, 1930
Sheet steel, chromium-plated and partly painted
99 × 67 × 110 cm, height of seat 45 cm
Tecta, Lauenförde, FRG

20
Giuseppe Terragni
"Follia" chair, 1934, in production again since 1972
Black-painted wood, back-support of chromium-plated steel
80 × 50 × 60 cm, height of seat 41 cm
Zanotta, Milan

21
Gerrit T. Rietveld
"Zig-Zag" chair, 1934, in production again since 1973
Wood, untreated
74 × 37 × 43 cm, height of seat 44 cm
Cassina, Milan

22
Alvar Aalto
"69" chair, 1933 –35
Legs and seat unvarnished birch, back laminated wood
72 × 38 × 44 cm
Artek, Helsinki

23
Hans Coray
"Spartana" chair, 1938, in production again since 1971
Aluminium alloy
76 × 54 × 64 cm, height of seat 43 cm
Zanotta, Milan
(formerly Blattmann, Wädenswil, Switzerland, marketed as the "Landi" chair)

24
Charles Eames
"Plywood" chair, 1946
Chromium-plated round bar steel, seat and back laminated wood
79 × 47 × 56 cm
Vitra, Weil am Rhein, FRG

25
Frank Lloyd Wright
"Taliesin" armchair, 1949, in production again since 1986, "I Maestri" collection
Laminated wood, cherry veneer, inner surfaces upholstered in leather or fabric
77 × 94 × 90 cm, height of seat 38 cm
Cassina, Milan

26
Charles Eames
"Dax" armchair, 1949/51
Chromium-plated or coated metal, seat polyester, also available with upholstery
82 × 65 × 62 cm, height of seat 45 cm
Vitra, Weil am Rhein, FRG

27
Harry Bertoia
"420" chair, 1952, "Diamond" series
Round bar steel, steel wire, padded cushion
55 × 76 × 50 cm, height of seat 45 cm
Knoll Deutschland, Murr, FRG

28
Arne Jacobsen
"3107" chair, 1955
Chromium-plated tubular steel, seat shaped laminated wood
Various sizes
Hansen, Alerød, Denmark

29
Eero Saarinen
"151" chair, 1956
Rilsan-coated cast aluminium, seat moulded polyester, white, loose foam cushion
81 × 51 × 54 cm, height of seat 47 cm
Knoll Deutschland, Murr, FRG

30
Achille and Piergiacomo Castiglioni
"Sella" telephone stool, 1957, in production again since 1983
Bicycle saddle on metal column, hemispherical cast iron base
Height 71 cm, Ø 33 cm
Zanotta, Milan

31
Achille and Piergiacomo Castiglioni
"Mezzadro" stool, 1957, in production again since 1970
Foot beech, supporting bar chromium-plated steel, seat chromium-plated or painted metal
51×49×51 cm
Zanotta, Milan

32
Gio Ponti
"Superleggera" chair, 1957
Painted or unpainted ash, seat of cane, twined cord, fabric or leather
83×41×47 cm, height of seat 45 cm
Cassina, Milan

33
Charles Eames
"Ea 105" aluminium chair, 1958
High-gloss aluminium, fabric or vinyl covers
84×53×60 cm, height of seat 47 cm
Vitra, Weil am Rhein, FRG

34
Dieter Rams
"602" easy-chair, 1960
Aluminium frame, seat fibreglass-reinforced polyester, cover black leather
74×60×65 cm, height of seat 39 cm
Wiese Vitsoe, Frankfurt am Main

35
Verner Panton
"Panton" chair, 1960
Plastic
82×50×60 cm, height of seat 42 cm
Vitra, Weil am Rhein, FRG

36
Dieter Rams
"620" armchair, 1962
Light grey or black polyester panels on swivel base, cover black leather
70×86×77 cm, height of seat 39 cm
Wiese Vitsoe, Frankfurt am Main

37
Helmut Bätzner
"BA 1171" ("Bofinger"), chair, 1966
Fibreglass-reinforced polyester
75×53×40 cm, height of seat 44 cm
Menzolit, Menzingen, FRG

38
Gian Carlo Piretti
"Plia" folding chair, 1968
Metal frame, chromium-plated, painted or coated, seat and backrest Cellidor plastic
75×46×50 cm, height of seat 45 cm
Castelli, Bologna

39
Pierro Gatti, Cesare Paolini, Franco Teodoro
"Sacco" easy-chair, 1968
Canvas, leather or imitation leather filled with polystyrene balls
68×80×80 cm
Zanotta, Milan

40
Archizoom (Paolo Deganello)
"Aeo" armchair, assembled from kit, 1973
Base grey urethane, frame light grey stove-enamelled steel, cushions polyurethane foam and polyester wadding, covers fabric or leather
107×79×70 cm, height of seat 46 cm
Cassina, Milan

41
Rodney Kinsman
"Omkstack" chair, 1974
Tubular steel frame, seat and back perforated sheet steel, painted
75×50×53 cm
Bieffeplast, Selvazzano (Padua), distributed in FRG by Werner Schmitz Collectionen, Düsseldorf

42
Stefan Wewerka
"B 1" chair, 1977–79
Painted wood, seat covered in leather or fabric
74×68×48 cm, height of seat 46 cm
Tecta, Lauenförde, FRG

43
Toshiyuki Kita
"Wink" easy- chair, 1980
Steel frame on dish castors, polyurethane foam padding, covers fabric or leather, back and two-part headrest adjustable
95×78×90 cm, height of seat 38 cm
Cassina, Milan

44
Stefan Wewerka
"B 5" ("Einschwinger") chair, 1982
Chromium-plated or painted tubular steel, leather upholstery
79×62×54 cm, height of seat 46 cm
Tecta, Lauenförde, FRG

45
George J. Sowden
"Palace" chair, 1983
Painted wood
95×49×45 cm
Memphis, Milan

46
Michele de Lucchi
"First" chair, 1983
Metal and wood, painted
90×69×50 cm
Memphis, Milan

47
Philippe Starck
"Costés" chair, 1985, "Aleph Ubik" series
Black-painted tubular steel, back of moulded laminated wood in black satin-frosted finish, cushions with synthetic stuffing, covered in black leather
80×47×55 cm
Driade, Fossadello di Caorso, Italy

48
Mario Botta
"Seconda" chair, 1982
Galvanised steel frame with silver-metallic or matt black epoxy coating, seat perforated sheet steel, backrest soft black polyurethane
72×52×58 cm
Alias, Milan

49
Mario Botta
"Quinta" chair, 1985
Epoxy-coated metal frame, seat and backrest of epoxy-coated perforated sheet steel
92×46×55 cm
Alias, Milan

50
Philippe Starck
"Miss Wirt" chair, 1987
Epoxy-coated tubular steel, black linen
110×60×47 cm, height of seat 48 cm
Disform, Barcelona

51
Anonymous
"Opal" hanging lamp, 1920
Chromium-plated metal, opal glass
Height 120 cm, ∅ 20 cm
Tecnolumen, Bremen

52
Gerrit T. Rietveld
Hanging lamp for Dr. Hartog, 1920 (numbered edition)
3 pendants, tube-holders black wood
165×40×40 cm
Tecta, Lauenförde, FRG

53
Anonymous
De Stijl lamp, c. 1923
Nickel-plated metal, aluminium tube, painted wood
22×13×10 cm
Tecnolumen, Bremen

54
Wilhelm Wagenfeld
Bauhaus lamp, 1924
Metal, opal glass
Height 36 cm, ∅ 18 cm
Tecnolumen, Bremen

55
Eileen Gray
"Tube Light" standard-lamp, 1927
Chromium-plated steel, fluorescent tube
Height 102 cm, ∅ 25 cm
Vereinigte Werkstätten, Munich

56
Christian Dell
"15-1192-21-20" wall light, 1930
Painted metal
Max. extension 90 cm, ∅ 21 cm
Kaiser, Arnsberg, FRG

57
Gio Ponti
"0024" hanging light, 1931
Clear crystal glass, central tube frosted glass, socket chromium-plated brass
Height 53 cm, ∅ 53 cm
Fontana Arte, Milan

58
Jac Jacobsen
"Luxo L 1" desk lamp, 1937
Tubular steel, reflector aluminium, plastic or steel
Max. extension 122 cm, reflector ∅ 20 cm
Luxo (Jac Jacobsen), Hildesheim, FRG

59
Pietro Chiesa
Table lamp, 1939
Crystal glass, brass, adjustable opal glass shade
22×44×20 cm
Fontana Arte, Milan

60
Isamu Noguchi
"Akari" hanging light, 1952
Bamboo, paper
Height 175 cm, ∅ 53 cm

61
Max Ingrand
"Fontana" table lamp, 1954
Opal glass, white
Height 78 cm
Fontana Arte, Milan

62
Arne Jacobsen
"AJ Diskus" wall lamp, 1956
Opal glass, metal base
Depth 11.5 cm, ∅ 22 cm,
Depth 12 cm, ∅ 35 cm,
Depth 13 cm, ∅ 45 cm,
Poulsen, Copenhagen

63
Poul Henningsen
"PH Cone" hanging lamp, 1958
Copper laminate matt or glossy white, undersides matt white
Height 47, 63 or 69 cm, ∅ 60, 72 or 84 cm
Poulsen, Copenhagen

64
Gino Sarfatti
"2097/30", "2097/50" chandeliers, 1958
Chromium-plated or brass-covered metal
Height 66 cm, ∅ 88 cm (2097/50: height 87 cm, ∅ 100 cm)
Arteluce-Flos, Brescia, Italy

65
Arne Jacobsen
"AJ Pendulum" hanging lamp, 1960
Painted metal
Height 22 cm, ∅ 49 cm
Height 16 cm, ∅ 37 cm
Poulsen, Copenhagen

66
Achille and Piergiacomo Castiglioni
"Toio" standard-lamp, 1962
Base painted steel, shaft nickel-plated brass
Height 170–200 cm, base 21×20 cm
Flos, Brescia, Italy

67
Achille and Piergiacomo Castiglioni
"Taccia" table lamp, 1962
Base black metal or anodised
aluminium, sleeve and reflector
painted metal, diffuser clear glass
Height 54 cm, Ø 49 cm
Flos, Brescia, Italy

68
Achille and Piergiacomo Castiglioni
"Arco" standard-lamp, 1962
Base marble, shaft steel, reflector
aluminium
Height 250 cm, max. extension 200
cm
Flos, Brescia, Italy

69
Robert Haussmann
"C 300" light-structure, 1964/65
Aluminium or bronze finish, plastic
connectors, bulb Ø 80 or 120 mm
Swisslamps, Zurich

70
Enzo Mari, Anna Fasolis
"Polluce" standard-lamp, 1965
Matt nickel-plated brass, opal glass
globe
Height min. 115 cm, max. 180 cm,
base Ø 30 cm
Artemide, Milan

71
Gino Sarfatti
"600 P" table lamp, 1966
Base imitation leather, bulb-holder
and shade painted metal
Height 18 cm, Ø 9 cm
Arteluce-Flos, Brescia, Italy

72
Joe Colombo
"Colombo 281" table lamp, 1966
Base painted metal, body acrylic
glass
24×26×3 cm
O-Luce, Milan

73
Tito Agnoli
"Agnoli 387" standard-lamp, 1967
Base marble, metal parts matt nickel-
plated
Height 190 cm, base Ø 17 cm
O-Luce, Milan

74
Tobia Scarpa
"Biaggio" table lamp, 1968
Marble
34×38×38 cm
Arteluce, Brescia

75
Aldo van den Nieuwelaar
"TC 6" wall or table lamp, 1969
Fluorescent tube, metal
Height 40 cm
Eikelenboom, Ouderkerk aan de
Amstel, Netherlands, distributed in
FRG by Teunen & Teunen,, Geisenheim

76
Vico Magistretti
"Chimera" standard-lamp, 1969
Opal-white metal acrylate
Height 180 cm, width 22 cm
Artemide, Milan

77
Elio Martinelli
"Foglia" table lamp, 1969
Methacrylate, opal-white (in one
piece)
Height c. 45 cm, Ø 45 cm
Martinelli, Lucca, Italy

78
Marco Albini, Franca Helg, Antonio
Piva
"AS41Z" ceiling light with swivel arm,
1970
Chromium-plated or gilt metal
Swivel arm 100 cm, shade Ø 45 cm,
extension and height variable
Sirrah, Imola, Italy

79
Pio Manzù, Achille Castiglioni
"Parentesi" standard-lamp, 1970
Stainless steel rope, base and tube
chromium-plated or painted
Max. height 400 cm
Flos, Brescia, Italy

80
Livio Castiglioni, Gianfranco Frattini
"Boalum" table, floor and wall light,
1970
Metal and synthetic resin
Max. length 200 cm, Ø 6 cm
Artemide, Milan

81
Isao Hosoe
"Hebi" table lamp, 1970
Metal tubing covered with PVC,
reflector painted aluminium
Max. height 140 cm
Valenti, Milan

82
Richard Sapper
"Tizio" table lamp, 1970
Synthetic resin and metal, black
Max. height 113 cm, max. width 108
cm
Artemide, Milan

83
Verner Panton
"Panthella" table or standard-lamp,
1971
Shade opal acrylic glass, stand white
plastic or steel
Height 127 cm, Ø 50 cm; height 67 cm,
Ø 50 cm; height 53 cm, Ø 40 cm
Poulsen, Copenhagen

84
Achille Castiglioni
"Noce 1" wall or ceiling light, 1972
Painted aluminium, moulded glass
18×36×25 cm
Flos, Brescia, Italy

85
Örni Halloween
"Macumba 117" hanging lamp, 1974
Matt nickel-plated metal
Height 63 cm, Ø 80 cm
Artemide, Milan

86
Tobia Scarpa
"Papillona" standard-lamp, 1976
Shade metallised glass, base and
shaft painted aluminium
Height 192 cm, Ø 26 cm
Flos, Brescia, Italy

87
Kazuhide Takahama
"Kazuki 2" standard-lamp, 1976
White fabric on wire frame
159×55×41 cm
Sirrah, Imola, Italy

88
Marcello Cuneo
"Calla" standard-lamp, 1976
Synthetic fabric, painted metal
height 110, 160 or 210 cm
Valenti, Milan

89
Vico Magistretti
"Atollo 233" table lamp, 1976/77
Painted metal
Height 70 cm, base Ø 20 cm, reflec-
tor Ø 50 cm
O-Luce, Milan

90
Achille Castiglioni
"Frisbi" hanging light, 1978
Reflector high-gloss chromium-
plated metal, inner surface painted,
diffuser methacrylate, steel wires
Arteluce, Brescia, Italy, distributed in
FRG by Flos, Euskirchen

91
Gianfranco Frattini
"Megaron" standard-lamp, 1979
Gloss-painted moulded aluminium,
steel base covered with black rubber
Height 181 cm, base Ø 31 cm
Artemide, Milan

92
Achille Castiglioni
"Gibigiana" table lamp, 1980/81
Painted sheet metal and aluminium,
reflector metal with mirrored surface
Height 41 or 52 cm Ø 10 cm
Flos, Brescia, Italy

93
Martine Bedin
"Super" table or floor lamp, 1981
Fibreglass, sheet steel, painted in
various colours, plastic wheels
40×50 cm
Memphis, Milan

94
Ettore Sottsass
"Callimaco" standard-lamp, 1982
Metal painted in various colours
Height 200 cm, base Ø 40 cm
Artemide, Milan

95
Ron Arad
"Aerial Light" remote-control lamp,
1982
Metal, rubber, plastic, halogen lamp
Height up to joint c. 40 cm, swivel
arm extending to c. 70 cm
One Off, London
Photo: Howard Kingsnorth

96
Livio and Piero Castiglioni
"Scintilla" lighting system, 1982/83
Room lighting system with exposed,
peg-shaped halogen lamps mounted
on cables slung from wall to wall,
additional elements attachable
directly to ceiling, series connection
Fontana Arte, Milan

97
F. A. Porsche
"Kandido" table lamp, 1982/83
Die-cast metal, plastic, telescopic
arms
Height 28–86 cm
Luci, Cinisello (Milan)

98
Ingo Maurer & Team
"YaYaHo" low-voltage lighting system, 1984
Wall to wall mounting with variable
arrangement of lighting elements:
glass, porcelain, ceramic, metal, plastic, multimirror reflectors, halogen
bulbs
Design M, Munich

99
Matteo Thun, Andrea Lera
"Chigao Tribune" standard-lamp,
1986
"Stillight" series
Painted perforated metal
190×30×30 cm
Bieffeplast, Selvazzano (Padua), dis-
tributed in FRG by Werner Schmitz
Collectionen, Düsseldorf

100
Mario Bellini
"Eclipse" spotlight, 1987
Runner lighting system with transformer and adapter for 220 V or 12 V,
low voltage runners, basic unit with
various lamp attachments, accessories (filters, lenses, honeycomb
louvres, antiglare attachments)
Lamp Ø 90 or 125 mm
Erco, Lüdenscheid, FRG

101
Rodney Kinsman
"Omkstack" chair, 1974
Tubular steel frame, seat and back
perforated sheet steel, painted
75×50×53 cm
Bieffeplast, Selvazzano (Padua), dis-
tributed in FRG by Werner Schmitz
Collectionen, Düsseldorf

102
Haigh Space
"Tux" chair, 1984
Tubular steel, seat and back perfo-
rated sheet steel
74×49×54 cm
Bieffeplast, Selvazzano (Padua), dis-
tributed in FRG by Werner Schmitz
Collectionen, Düsseldorf

103
Rodney Kinsman
"Tokyo" chair, 1985
Tubular steel, painted black, seat upholstered in vinyl, backrest moulded polyurethane
70×43×43 cm
Bieffeplast, Selvazzano (Padua), distributed in FRG by Werner Schmitz Collectionen, Düsseldorf

104
Rodney Kinsman
"Tokyo" bar-stool, 1985
Tubular steel, painted black, seat upholstered in vinyl, backrest moulded polyurethane
88×43×37 cm
Bieffeplast, Selvazzano (Padua), distributed in FRG by Werner Schmitz Collectionen, Düsseldorf

105
Rodney Kinsman
"Tractor" stool, 1969
Tubular steel, chromium-plated, seat chromium-plated
75×40×49 cm or 53×40×49 cm
Bieffeplast, Selvazzano (Padua); distributed in FRG by Werner Schmitz Collectionen, Düsseldorf

106
Andreas Weber
Couch table, 1985
High-grade steel, crystal glass
35×100×100 cm
Weber

107
Andreas Weber
Roller container, 1985
High-grade steel, black glass top
69×50×47 cm
Weber

108
Andreas Weber
Chest-of-drawers, 1985
High-grade steel
160×50×47 cm
Weber

109
Andreas Weber
Container cupboard, 1985
High-grade steel, laminated surface, black and grey; adjustable glass shelves
150×80×50 cm
Weber

110
Matteo Thun
"Madia" sideboard, 1985
Epoxy-coated steel, glass, perforated doors, shelf element laminated, black and white or red and black
209×100×65 cm
Bieffeplast
Lent by Werner Schmitz Collectionen, Düsseldorf

111
Matteo Thun
"Settimanale" container cupboard, 1985
Epoxy-coated steel, front of drawers perforated
45×62×160 cm
Bieffeplast
Lent by Werner Schmitz Collectionen, Düsseldorf

112
Matteo Thun
"Comodino", container cupboard, 1985
Epoxy-coated steel, front perforated
48×40×40 cm
Bieffeplast
Lent by Werner Schmitz Collectionen, Düsseldorf

113
Matteo Thun and Andrea Lera
"Chicago Tribune", standard-lamp, 1985
"Stillight" series
Perforated metal, painted
190×30×30 cm
Bieffeplast
Lent by Werner Schmitz Collectionen, Düsseldorf

114
Matteo Thun and Andrea Lera
"WWF Tower", standard-lamp, 1985
"Stillight" series
Perforated metal, painted
93×37×37 cm
Bieffeplast
Lent by Werner Schmitz Collectionen, Düsseldorf

115
Matteo Thun and Andrea Lera
"Joseph", standard-lamp, 1985
"Stillight" series
Perforated metal, painted safetyglass diffusor
53×26×26 cm
Bieffeplast
Lent by Werner Schmitz Collectionen, Düsseldorf

116
Urs Gramelsbacher
"Corda d'Arco" standard-lamp, 1983
Tubular steel, bracing wire, halogen low-voltage system
Height 183 cm
Teunen & Teunen

117
Hans Dinnebier
"Clip" standard-lamp, 1980
Chromium-plated tubular steel, 5 or 8 halogen lamps clipped on, adjustable
Height 150 cm, base Ø 15 cm
Light im Raum

118
Jean-Marc da Costa
"Basis" standard-lamp, 1984
Anodised or powder-coated aluminium, nickel-plated steel, integrated dimmer switch for 300/500 W halogen bulb
190×20×20 cm
Serien

119
Jean-Marc da Costa
"Lift" hanging lamp, 1983
Nickel-plated round bar steel, thermo-painted sheet steel, two 9-watt fluorescent lamps
Height adjustable from 90 to 145 cm (115–195 cm, 135–230 cm), width 36 cm
Serien

120
Mario Botta
"Prima" chair, 1982
Frame galvanised steel, epoxy-coated metallic silver or matt black, backrest black polyurethane, seat perforated steel
72×48×58 cm
Alias

121
Mario Botta
"Seconda" chair, 1982
Frame galvanised steel, epoxy-coated metallic silver or matt black, seat perforated steel, backrest soft black polyurethane
72×52×58 cm
Alias

122
Mario Botta
"Tesi" table, 1986
Steel frame, perforated, black epoxy coating, glass top
Height 70 cm, top 180/240/300×86 cm
Alias

123
Bruce Burdick
"Burdick-Tech-Group" office workplace system, 1982
Chromium-plated steel frame, girder supports, worktop glass, wood and plastic, shelves and filing boxes plastic
Vitra

124
Mario Botta
"Quarta" chair, 1985
Aluminium, hard PVC, backrest polyurethane
67×98×65 cm
Alias

125
Mario Botta
"Latonda" chair, 1987
Frame galvanised steel, epoxy-coated metallic silver or matt black, seat perforated steel
77×63×60 cm
Alias

126
Mario Botta
"Quinta" chair, 1985
Epoxy-coated metal frame, seat and backrest epoxy-coated perforated sheet steel
92×45×55 cm
Alias

127/128
Norman Foster
"Nomos" office furniture system, 1987
Steel, table-top glass, marble, wood or laminate, interlinking system with horizontal and vertical adjustment, shelving and drawers plastic, integrated lighting system
Height adjustable 64–72 cm
Tecno

129
Kunstflug (Heiko Bartels, Harald Hullmann)
"Baumleuchte" I and II standard-lamps, 1981
Natural oak trunk, hammer-effect enamelled, on steel base, neon ring or tubes
Height as desired 175–260 cm, Ø c. 20 cm
Kunstflug

130
Gerard Kuijpers, Désirée Verstraete
"Zigzag" chair, 1984
Steel frame, seat slate or wood, rubber
70×50×60 cm
Kuijpers

131
Gerard Kuijpers, Désirée Verstraete
Telephone stand, 1984
Steel, slate, granite
130×40×33 cm
Kuijpers

132
Gerard Kuijpers, Désirée Verstraete
Lounge table, 1983
Steel, glass, marble
45×90×23 cm
Kuijpers

133
Gerard Kuijpers, Désirée Verstraete
Japanese étagère, 1984
Steel, glass
150×180×40 cm
Kuijpers

134
Gaetano Pesce
"Green Street Chair", 1984/86/87
Vitra-Edition
Plastic, metal
94×61×55 cm
Vitra

135
Gaetano Pesce
"Sansonedue" table, 1987
Top coloured epoxy resin with injected metal trelliswork, legs PVC, feet semistiff polyurethane
Height 73 or 41 cm, top square 130×130 or 120×120 cm, rectangular 200×90 or 160×80 cm, round Ø 130 cm
Cassina Lent by Leptien 3, Frankfurt am Main
Photo by Bella e Ruggeri

136
Gaetano Pesce
"Feltri" armchair, 1987
Felt with quilted textile cover, down
filling, hemp bands
140×74×64 cm or 98×74×64 cm
Cassina
Lent by Leptien 3, Frankfurt am Main
Photo by Bella e Ruggeri

137
Ron Arad
"Concrete" Sound system, 1985
Stereo systems embedded in rein-
forced concrete
Record-player 75×46×38 cm
Loudspeaker 89×20×20 cm
Amplifier 20×30×25 cm
One Off
Photo by Howard Kingsnorth

138
Ron Arad
"Cone" chairs and "Cone" table, 1986
Steel and glass, chair seats steel,
aluminium or glass
Table height 70 cm, Ø c. 70 cm
Chairs c. 180×30×50 cm
One Off
Photo by Peter Wood

139
Ron Arad
"Rover" chair, 1985
Rover V 8 front seats, leather cover, on
epoxy-coated tubular steel frame
c. 70×70×70 cm
One Off
Photo by Howard Kingsnorth

140
Ron Arad
"Horns" armchair, 1986/87
Aluminium, springs, galvanised with
plastic coating
c. 90×70×70 cm
One Off
Photo by Howard Kingsnorth

141
Ron Arad
"Well-tempered" chair, 1986/87
Vitra-Edition
Sheet steel
85×91×83 cm
Vitra
Photo by Howard Kingsnorth

142
Ron Arad
"Aerial Light", remote-control lamp,
1982
Metal, rubber, plastic, infra-red con-
trolled, extending swivel arm, halo-
gen lamp
Height to joint c. 40 cm, swivel arm
extends to c. 70 cm
One Off
Photo by Howard Kingsnorth

143
Ron Arad
Paper-shredder, 1986 one-off
Aluminium, steel
123×175×30 cm
One Off
Lent by Trust Werbeagentur, Frankfurt
am Main
Photo by Howard Kingsnorth

144
Ron Arad
"Deep" screen, 1987
Opaque glass, aluminium, steel,
silicone
c. 200×200 cm
One Off
Photo by Peter Wood

145
Shiro Kuramata
"How High the Moon" armchair,
1986/87
Vitra-Edition
Metal mesh
72×95×82 cm
Vitra

146
Marie-Therese Deutsch and Klaus Bol-
linger
Desk, 1986
Spring steel, concrete top, tension
cables with tightening screws
77×150×75 cm
Deutsch & Bollinger
Photo by Waltraud Krase

147
Wolfgang Laubersheimer for Pentagon
Braced shelving, 1985
Unfinished steel, welded, bracing
wire
250×30×27 cm Pentagon

148 a, b, c
Gin-Bande
"Tabula Rasa" pull-out table-and-
bench combination, 1987
Metal and wood
78×125×89 cm (extends to 500 cm)
Vitra (from 1988/89 on)

149
Ingo Maurer & Team
"BaKa-Rú" low-voltage halogen lighting system, 1985/86
Wall-to-wall mounting, lighting elements attachable as desired, glass,
porcelain, ceramics, metal, plastic,
multimirror reflectors
Design M

150
Ingo Maurer & Team
"YaYaHo" low-voltage halogen lighting system, 1984
Wall to wall mounting (up to 600 cm),
lighting elements to be hung as
desired, glass, porcelain, ceramics,
metal, plastic, multimirror reflectors,
halogen bulbs
Design M

151
Ingo Maurer, Franz Ringelhan
"Ilios" standard-lamp, 1983
Metal and glass
190×18×18 cm
Design M

152
Till Leeser
"Viola" standard-lamp, 1985
Steel
Height 200 cm
Anta
Lent by Till Leeser, Hamburg

153
Alessandro Mendini
"Kandinsky" sofa, 1978
"Bau-Haus" collection
Painted wood, leather and fabric
130×200×90 cm
Studio Alchimia
Lent by Galerie Kaess-Weiss, Stuttgart

154
Alessandro Mendini
"Proust" armchair, 1979
"Bau-Haus" collection
Wood and fabric, hand-painted
115×105×80 cm
Studio Alchimia
Lent by Galerie Kaess-Weiss, Stuttgart

155
Alessandro Mendini
Redesign of the Thonet "214" chair of
1859, 1973
Steam-shaped beech, stained black,
wickerwork, coloured appliqués
Height 90 cm, seat Ø 41 cm
Lent by Museo Alchimia, Milan, Italy

156
Alessandro Mendini
Redesign of the Breuer "Wassily"
armchair of 1925, 1973
Tubular steel, leather, coloured
appliqués
80×80×70 cm
Lent by Museo Alchimia, Milan, Italy

157
Alessandro Mendini
Shoes from the "Robot Sentimentale"
series, "Set for the Gentleman", pro-
ject 1983
Mixed media
50×70 cm
Lent by Museo Alchimia, Milan, Italy

158
Alessandro Mendini
Helmet from the "Robot Sentimentale" series, "Set for the Gentleman"
project
1983
Mixed media
50×70 cm
Lent by Museo Alchimia, Milan, Italy

159
Alessandro Mendini
Redesign of a chest-of-drawers from
the 50s, 1980/81
Painted wood with appliqués
c. 90×160×40 cm
Lent by Museo Alchimia, Milan, Italy

160
Alessandro Mendini
Redesign of a chest-of-drawers from
the 50s, 1980/81
Painted wood with appliqués
c. 130×120×70 cm
Lent by Museo Alchimia, Milan, Italy

161
Alessandro Mendini
Cupboard, 1981
"Il Mobile Infinito" series
Decor by Mimmo Paladino, Nicola de
Maria, Sandro Chia, feet by Denis San-
tachiara, handles by Ugo la Pietra
Wood, metal and plastic

c. 360×82×82 cm
Lent by Vitra International
Photo by Occhiomagico

162
Alessandro Mendini
Untitled, 1987
Lacquer on canvas
150×180 cm
Lent by Galerie Kaess-Weiss, Stuttgart

163
Alessandro Mendini
Untitled, 1986
Lacquer on wood
75×90 cm
Lent by Galerie Kaess-Weiss, Stuttgart

164
Bruno Gregori
"Fabric Pattern", 1984
Collection of winter fabrics for
Limonta
Tempera
50×70 cm
Lent by Museo Alchimia, Milan, Italy
Photo by Studio 30.40

165
Bruno Gregori
Design for a new kitchen, 1986
"The World in the Kitchen"
series for Salvarini
Tempera
50×70 cm
Lent by Museo Alchimia, Milan, Italy
Photo by Studio 30.40

166
Giorgio Gregori
Design for an alphabet, 1986
Badges for the Acme company
Tempera
50×70 cm
Lent by Museo Alchimia, Milan, Italy
Photo by Studio 30.40

167
Alessandro Guerriero
"Tiger" design for a carpet pattern,
1986
Tempera
70×100 cm
Lent by Museo Alchimia, Milan, Italy
Photo by Studio 30.40

168
Carla Ceccariglia
Design for tiles for Appiani, 1982
Tempera
70×50 cm
Lent by Museo Alchimia, Milan, Italy
Photo by Studio 30.40

169
Ettore Sottsass
"Carlton" bookcase, 1981
Laminated wood
196×190×40 cm
Memphis
Lent by Leptien 3, Frankfurt am Main

170
Ettore Sottsass
"Tahiti" table-lamp, 1981
Metal, laminated wood
Height 60 cm
Memphis

171
Martine Bedin
"Super" standard-lamp, 1981
Fibre-glass, sheet steel, painted, plastic wheels
40×50 cm
Memphis

172
Peter Shire
"Bel Air" armchair, 1982
Wood, wool or fabric upholstery
125×115×110 cm
Memphis
Lent by Objektform, Kronberg im Taunus

173
Ettore Sottsass
"Treetops" standard-lamp, 1981
Painted sheet steel, chromium-plated metal tubing, halogen lamp
Height 200 cm
Memphis

174
Peter Shire
"Brazil" table, 1981
Painted wood
72×205×80 cm
Memphis

175
George J. Sowden
"Palace" chair, 1983
Painted wood
95×49×45 cm
Memphis

176
Michele de Lucchi
"First" chair, 1983
Metal and wood, painted
90×69×50 cm
Memphis
Lent by Leptien 3, Frankfurt am Main

177
George J. Sowden, fabric by Nathalie de Pasquier
"Oberoi" armchair, 1981
Cotton upholstery in red or blue, patterned cotton cover
101×93×72 cm
Memphis

178
Ettore Sottsass
"Le Strutture Tremano" table, 1979
"Bau-Haus" collection
Metal, laminated wood, crystal glass
115×50×50 cm
Formerly made by Studio Alchimia
Now made by Belux
Lent by Prof. Friedrich Friedl, Frankfurt am Main

179
Michele de Lucchi
"Sinerpica" lamp, 1979
"Bau-Haus" collection
Painted metal
Height 75 cm, Ø 17 cm
Formerly made by Studio Alchimia
Now made by Belux

180
Ettore Sottsass
"Quisisana" ceiling light, 1979
Laminated wood, plastic
c. 60×30×15 cm
Memphis

181
Ettore Sottsass
"Seggiolina da Pranzo" chair, 1980
"Bau-Haus" collection
Chromium-plated frame, laminated wood
84×45×32 cm
Formerly made by Studio Alchimia
Now made by Belux

182
Collage of laminate patterns
Abet

183
Ettore Sottsass
"Teodora" chair, 1986/87
Vitra-Edition
Wood with hardboard surface, backrest safety-glass
82×56×47 cm
Vitra
Photo by Balthasar Burkhard

184
Ettore Sottsass
"Cargo" multifunctional unit, 1981
"Bau-Haus" collection
Laminated wood
180×200×80 cm
Studio Alchimia

185
Michele De Lucchi
Hair-dryer (prototype), 1979
Made for the 1979 Milan Triennale
Laminated wood
Photo by Giorgio Molinari

186
Michele De Lucchi
Iron (prototype), 1979
Made for the 1979 Milan Triennale
Laminated wood
Photo by Giorgio Molinari

187
Michele De Lucchi
Vacuum cleaner (prototype), 1979
Made for the 1979 Milan Triennale
Laminated wood
Photo by Giorgio Molinari

188
Jörg Hieronymus
Travelling iron set, model, 1986/87
Made at a student design seminar (3rd semester) in Prof. Friedbert Obitz's class in cooperation with Krups & Co.
Lent by the University of Essen
Photo by Ralf Peter Passmann

189
Marcus Botsch
"Toaster-Horse", model, 1986/87
Made at a student design seminar (3rd semester) in Prof. Friedbert Obitz's class in cooperation with Krups & Co.
Lent by the University of Essen
Photo by Ralf Peter Passmann

190
Michael Matuschka
Toaster, model, 1986/87
Made at a student design seminar (3rd semester) in Prof. Friedbert Obitz's class in cooperation with Krups & Co.
Lent by the University of Essen
Photo by Ralf Peter Passmann

191
Stefan Ambrozus
3 small toasters, models, 1986/87
Made at a student design seminar (3rd semester) in Prof. Friedbert Obitz's class in cooperation with Krups & Co.
Each 13×12×5 cm
Lent by Robert Krups Stiftung, Solingen
Photo by Ralf Peter Passmann

192
Robert Venturi
"Chippendale" chair, 1984
Laminated plywood, "Grandmother" decor
95×65×60 cm
Knoll International
Lent by Deutsches Architektur-museum, Frankfurt am Main

193
Robert Venturi
"Queen Anne" chair, 1984
Shaped plywood, laminated or veneered in maple
98×67×60 cm
Knoll International
Lent by Deutsches Architektur-museum, Frankfurt am Main

194
Robert Venturi
"Art Deco" chair, 1984
Shaped plywood, laminated or veneered in maple
80×60×61 cm
Knoll International
Lent by Deutsches Architektur-museum, Frankfurt am Main

195
Robert Venturi
"Sheraton" chair, 1984
Shaped plywood, laminated or veneered in maple
86×59×61 cm
Knoll International
Lent by Deutsches Architektur-museum, Frankfurt am Main

196
Michael Graves
"MG 1" chair, 1984
"Michael Graves" collection
Natural maple, cornerpieces black ebony, seat cushion polyurethane, covered in leather or fabric
83×44×53 cm
Sawaya & Moroni

197
Michael Graves
"MG 2" chair, 1984
"Michael Graves" collection
Natural maple, armrests black ebony,
seat cushion polyurethane, covered in leather or fabric
84×58×52 cm
Sawaya & Moroni

198
Michael Graves Collection
"MG 3" chair, 1984
"Michael Graves" collection
Natural maple, black ebony inlays, polyurethane, padding covered in leather or fabric
77×85×76 cm
Sawaya & Moroni

199
Hans Hollein
"Marilyn" sofa, 1981
Maple-root, veneered, polyurethane padding, satin cover
85×238×95 cm
Nuovo Poltronova
Lent by Melodrom, Frankfurt am Main

200
Michael Graves
"MG 4" sofa, 1984
"Michael Graves" collection
Natural maple, black ebony inlays, polyurethane padding, covered in leather or fabric
83×136×78 cm
Sawaya & Moroni

201
Charles Jencks
"Sun Chair", 1985
Maple, veneered black ebony inlays
99×60×48 cm
Sawaya & Moroni
Photo by Ron Forth, Cincinnati

202
Norbert Berghof, Michael A. Landes, Wolfgang Rang
"F 3" chair
"Sternensessel", 1985/86
"Frankfurter Kunstmöbel" series
Bird's eye maple with punched-out stars, veneer inlays in ebony and maple, blue and black, front legs ash with ebony and maple mosaic, back leg wengé (African oak) with brass base, leather upholstery
83×63×54 cm
Draenert

203
Michael Graves
"Ingrid" standard-lamp, 1987
Wood, onyx
Sawaya & Moroni

204–206
Norbert Berghof, Michael A. Landes, Wolfgang Rang
"F 1" bureau, 1985/86
Bird's eye maple, ebony, briar, root grain, solid maple, bubinga, ivory, horn, brass, gold leaf, Lasa and Aosta marble, Bahia-Blue granite
230×75×40 cm
Draenert

207
Norbert Berghof, Michael A. Landes, Wolfgang Rang
"F 2" ("Vertiko") Frankfurt cupboard, 1986
Bird's eye maple, ebony columns with brass elements, horn handles, walnut drawers, baldachin gilt with 10 small lights, white, green and black marble, enamel
175 × 75 × 40 cm
Draenert

208 a, b
Nobert Berghof, Michael A. Landes, Wolfgang Rang
"F 1" bureau, 1987 (one-off)
Black lacquer, paintings on some surfaces
230 × 75 × 40 cm
Draenert

209/210
Norbert Berghof, Michael A. Landes, Wolfgang Rang
"F 5" chair and "F 7" table, 1985/86
Chair: stained bird's eye maple, anatomically contoured seat in plywood, front legs with brass elements and friezes in Lasa and Aosta marble
114 × 42 × 40 cm
Table: stained bird's eye maple, brass stars on legs, friezes in Lasa and Aosta marble
74 × 250 × 120 cm
Draenert

211
Frank Gehry
"Little Beaver" armchair, 1980
Vitra-Edition
Corrugated cardboard
87 × 81 × 86 cm
Vitra

212 a, b
Stanley Tigerman
"Tête-a-Tête" double easy-chair, 1983
Colorcore laminate, brass studs
122 × 122 × 122 cm
Schmidt
Photo by Harry Hedrich-Blessing, Chicago

213
Matteo Thun
"Rainer" sofa, 1983
Wood, veneered, metal, fabric upholstery
95 × 220 × 88 cm
Anthologie Quartett

214
Dakota Jackson
Console, 1983
"New Classic" series
Cherry and leather, metal
80 × 190 × 52 cm
Jackson
Photo by Jan Fisher Studio

215 a, b
SITE (James Wines and Alison Sky)
Door, 1983
Colorcore laminate, doorknob porcelain, brass hinges
228 × 178 × 89 cm

SITE and David Geise
Photo by Harry Hedrich-Blessing, Chicago

216
Dakota Jackson
Table, 1983
"New Classic" series
Cherry, leather, glass, painted
69 × 180 × 80 cm
Jackson

217
Dakota Jackson
Cupboard, 1984
"New Classic" series
Bird's eye maple, charry, marble, glass, painted
225 × 140 × 55 cm
Jackson

218
Philippe Starck
"J" armchair, 1986
"Lang" series
Leg aluminium, polyurethane padding, black leather upholstery
86 × 60 × 66 cm
Driade
Photo by Ballo & Ballo, Driade

219 a
Philippe Starck
"Pratfall" armchair, 1982
"Aleph Ubik" series
Tubular steel frame, painted black, back moulded plywood, painted matt black, seat cushions filled with synthetic foam, black leather upholstery
86 × 61 × 78 cm
Driade
Photo by Ballo & Ballo, Driade

219 b
Elysée Palace, Paris: François Mitterand's conference room with "Pratfall" chairs

220 a, b
Philippe Starck
"Tippy Jackson" table, 1982
"Aleph Ubik" series
Three-legged folding frame of tubular steel, top of sheet steel, painted dark grey metallic
height 71 cm, Ø 120 cm
Driade
Photo by Ballo & Ballo, Driade

221 a, b
Philippe Starck
"Titos Apostos" table, 1985
"Aleph Ubik" series
Three-legged folding frame of tubular steel, top of sheet steel, painted gold or silver metallic
height 71 cm, Ø 85 cm
Driade
Photo by Ballo & Ballo, Driade

222
Philippe Starck
"Dole Melipone" table, 1981
Frame tubular steel, epoxy-coated or nickel plated, top glass, transparent or granular
Height 74 cm, Ø 137 cm
XO

223
Philippe Starck
"Mickville" table, 1983
"Aleph Ubik" series
Three-legged, folding, tubular steel frame, top sheet steel, lacquered azure metallic and matt black
Overall height 80 cm, height of table-top 48 cm, Ø 38 cm
Driade
Photo by Ballo & Ballo, Driade

224 a, b
Philippe Starck
"Sarapis" stool, 1985
"Aleph Ubik" series
Frame square-profile steel, seat steel mesh, painted dark grey metallic
85 × 35 × 45 cm
Driade
Photo by Ballo & Ballo, Driade

225
Philippe Starck
"Von Vogelsang" chair, 1984
"Aleph Ubik" series
Tubular steel frame, sheet steel seat, painted silver-grey
71 × 54 × 51 cm
Driade
Photo by Ballo & Ballo, Driade

226
Philippe Starck
"Pat Conley No. 1" armchair, 1983
Frame and backrest tubular steel, seat PVC
60 × 55 × 71 cm
XO

227
Philippe Starck
"Dr. Sonderbar" chair, 1983
Frame and backrest tubular steel, seat perforated sheet steel, epoxy-coated
63 × 92 × 47 cm
XO

228
Philippe Starck
"Mister Bliss" kneeling-stool, 1982
Frame tubular steel, epoxy-coated black, covers black canvas, removable
75 × 51 × 40 cm
XO

229
Philippe Starck
"M" table, 1986
"Lang" series
Legs aluminium, top glass or wood, stained mahogany
Height 73 cm, Ø 130 cm
Driade
Photo by Ballo & Ballo, Driade

230
Zeus (Maurizio Peregalli)
"Poltroncina" chair, 1982
Squared tubular steel, black, seat rubber knubs, black, backrest rubber-coated, black
85 × 56 × 58 cm
Zeus
Lent by Quartett, Hanover
Photo by Bitetto Chimenti Fotografia s.r.l., Milan

231
Zeus (Maurizio Peregalli)
"Savonarola" chair, 1984
Squared tubular steel, black, armrests rubber-coated, seat rubber knubs
71 × 39 × 55 cm
Zeus
Lent by Quartett, Hanover
Photo by Bitetto Chimenti Fotografia s.r.l., Milan

232
Abdenego and Anna Anselmi
"Sardegna" chair, 1984
Frame tubular steel, painted black, seat perforated sheet steel, painted black
83 × 47 × 47 cm
Bieffeplast
Lent by Werner Schmitz Collectionen, Düsseldorf

233
Shiro Kuramata
"Apple Honey" chair, 1986
Tubular steel, chromium-plated or epoxy-coated, arms and back bent tubing, chromium-plated, seat wood with foam padding and vinyl or leather cover
72 × 48 × 51 cm
XO

234
Shiro Kuramata
"Sing Sing Sing" armchair, 1986
Frame tubular steel, seat and back metal slats
89 × 54 × 59 cm
XO

235
Zeus (Roberto Marcatti)
"Arcade" standard-lamp, 1985
Metal, epoxy-coated, matt black
130 × 66 × 20 cm
Zeus
Lent by Quartett, Hanover
Photo by Bitetto Chimenti Fotografia s.r.l., Milan

236
Zeus (Vincenzo Javicoli and Maria Luisa Rossi)
"Batista" clothes-rack, 1986
Tubular steel on iron base, painted black
172 × 47 × 39 cm
Zeus
Lent by Quartett, Hanover
Photo by Bitetto Chimenti Fotografia s.r.l., Milan

237
Aldo Rossi
"AR 1" cupboard, ("Cabina di Elba"), 1982
Polished beech, pink, light blue, aniline yellow or pnk and light blue, base brass-plated
240 × 93 × 67 cm
Longoni

238
Aldo Rossi
"AR 2" chair, 1983

Polished beech, aniline yellow, black, pink or light blue, backrest with steel disc
82×38×38 cm
Longoni

239
Aldo Rossi
"AR 3", chest-of-drawers, 1983
Polished beech, aniline yellow, black, pink or light blue, top marble or wood, base brass-plated
109×103×50 cm
Longoni

240
Aldo Rossi
"AR 6", kitchen cupboard, 1983
Wood painted white, black, blue, aniline yellow or pink, base and handles brass, polished Portuguese onyx or green Beola, marble top with brass trim in white or yellow wood frame
90×208 (142)×50 cm
Longoni

241
Aldo Rossi
"AR 4" tallboy, 1983
Polished, aniline yellow, black, pink or light blue, base and topboard brass-plated, drawer handles and columns solid brass, "cathedral green" glass, marble slab with brass trim in wood frame
205×78×50 cm
Longoni

242–245
Oswald Mathias Ungers
Chair, table and desk programme for the German Architecture Museum in Frankfurt, 1982/83
Beech, stained black, backrests and seats with white leather panels
Height 70.5, 94.0 or 117.5 cm
Height of seat 47.0 cm, seat area 50.5×50.5 cm
Rosenthal

242
Office

243
Exhibition area

244
Exhibition area

245
Lecture room

246 a– d
Oswald Mathias Ungers
"Cabinet Tower", 1986 (prototype)
Designed for the 27th Triennale in Milan
Base black marble, body wood, mirror-glass, alabaster and black tiles, flap wood lined with black leather, diffusor opal glass
219×36.4×36.4 cm
Lent by O. M. Ungers, Cologne

247 a, b
Oswald Mathias Ungers
"Candelabrum" standard-lamp, 1986 (prototype)
Base brass and wood, black, highly polished, body wood lined with "Granit 90" coloured "Rosso svezia", diffusor opal glass in brass frame
196×56×56 cm
Lent by O. M. Ungers, Cologne

248
Oswald Mathias Ungers
Easy-chair No. 1 b, 1987
Frame and panels glazed mahogany, black leather cushions, legs lined with high-grade sheet steel
72×72×72 cm, height of seat 43.2 cm
Lent by O. M. Ungers, Cologne

249
Oswald Mathias Ungers
Easy-chair No. 1, 1987
Frame and panels glazed mahogany, black leather cushions, legs lined with high-grade sheet steel
72×72×72 cm, height of seat 43.2 cm
Lent by O. M. Ungers, Cologne

250
Oswald Mathias Ungers
Easy-chair No. 3, 1987
Frame and panels glazed mahogany black leather cushions, legs lined with high-grade sheet steel
72×72×72 cm, height of seat 43.5 cm
Lent by O. M. Ungers, Cologne

251
Oswald Mathias Ungers
Easy-chair No. 2, 1987
Frame and panels glazed mahogany, black leather cushions, legs lined with high-grade sheet steel
72×72×72 cm, height of seat 43.2 cm
Lent by O. M. Ungers, Cologne

252 a, b, c
Oswald Mathias Ungers
"Neue Klassik" tea and coffee service, 1987/88
a: Proportional diagram of all items
Pen and ink on transparent paper
Lent by O. M. Ungers, Cologne
b: Coffee-pot
c: Arrangement on tray

253
Oswald Mathias Ungers
Coffee-pot from the "Neue Klassik" service, 1987/88
Sterling silver 925, ebony
22.5×18.7×10 cm
Wilkens

254
Oswald Mathias Ungers
Teapot from the "Neue Klassik" service, 1987/88
Sterling silver 925, ebony
15.3×20×15 cm
Wilkens

255
Oswald Mathias Ungers
Sugar-bowl from the "Neue Klassik" service, 1987/88

Sterling silver 925, ebony
8.4×14.5×10 cm
Wilkens

256
Oswald Mathias Ungers
Milk-jug from the "Neue Klassik" service, 1987/88
Sterling silver 925, ebony
5.6×13×10.5 cm
Wilkens

257
Oswald Mathias Ungers
Tray from the "Neue Klassik" service, 1987/88
Sterling silver 925, ebony
7.5×62.5×18.7 cm
Wilkens

258
Re-Design HFG Ulm – Braun Produktgestaltung
"Exporter 2" radio, 1955
Plastic
12×17.5×5 cm
Recharging unit (not shown)
20.2×2.6×7.5 cm
Braun

259
Braun Produktgestaltung (Dieter Rams)
"L 02" loudspeaker, 1958
Wood, anodised aluminium mesh
18×18×18 cm
Braun

260
Braun Produktgestaltung (Dieter Rams)
"Atelier 1/2/3" radio, 1957 and "L 2" loudspeaker, 1958 Radio: veneered and painted wood
30×58×29 cm
loudspeaker: wood, front with plastic coating, tubular steel frame
72×43×32 cm
Braun

261
Braun Produktgestaltung (Hans Gugelot, Dieter Rams)
"SK 4" radio and record-player ("Phonosuper"), 1956
Veneered wood, painted sheet steel, acrylic glass
24×58×29 cm
Braun

262
Braun Produktgestaltung (Dieter Rams)
"EF 2" flash attachment, 1958
Plastic
20×20.6×8 cm
Braun

263
Braun Produktgestaltung (Dieter Rams)
"CE 11" radio, 1959 (later stereo version)
Sheet steel, front anodised aluminium
11×20×32 cm
Braun

264
Braun Produktgestaltung (Dieter Rams)
"TP 1 Phonokombination" with "T 4" pocket receiver, 1959
Plastic, holder anodised aluminium
23.3×15×4.3 cm
Braun

265
Braun Produktgestaltung (Dieter Rams)
"T 41" pocket receiver, 1959
Plastic
15×8.3×4 cm
Braun

266
Braun Produktgestaltung (Dieter Rams)
"H 1/H 2" fan heater, 1959
Plastic, sheet steel
9×26.5×13.5 cm
Braun

267
Braun Produktgestaltung (Dieter Rams)
"T 1000" short-wave receiver, 1962
Wood with artificial leather and anodised aluminium
24×36×13.5 cm
Braun

268
Braun Produktgestaltung (Dieter Rams)
"D 40" remote-control slide projector, 1961
Die-cast aluminium, painted
18×11×27 cm
Braun

269
Braun Produktgestaltung (Dieter Rams)
"RT 20" ("Tischsuper") radio, 1961
Wood, front painted sheet steel
26×50×18 cm
Braun

270
Braun Produktgestaltung (Alfred Müller, Hans Gugelot)
"Sixtant" mains shaver, 1962
Plastic, metal frame
9.9×7.1×3.5 cm
Braun

271
Braun Produktgestaltung (Dieter Rams)
"TG 60" tape-recorder, 1963
Sheet steel, safety-glass cover
11×42×28 cm
Braun

272
Braun Produktgestaltung (Dieter Rams)
"TS 45" control unit, 1965
Sheet steel, anodised aluminium
11×65×28 cm
Braun

273
Braun Produktgestaltung (Dieter Rams)
"CE 500" tuner, 1966
Sheet steel, anodised aluminium
10×26×32 cm
Braun

274
Braun Produktgestaltung (Dieter Rams)
"CSV 250" amplifier, 1966
Sheet steel, anodised aluminium
10×20×32 cm
Braun

275
Braun Produktgestaltung (Dieter Rams)
"FS 80" television set, 1964
Wood with plastic coating, anodised aluminium
66×59×34 cm
Braun

276
Braun Produktgestaltung (Dieter Rams)
"FS 1000" television set, 1967
Wood coated with plastic, anodised aluminium
54×78×54 cm
Braun

277
Braun Produktgestaltung (Dieter Rams, Jürgen Greubel)
"Lectron" experimental and learning system, 1967
1.5×42×30 cm
Braun

278
Braun Produktgestaltung (Dieter Rams)
"T 2/TFG 2" table lighter, 1968
Plastic or metal
Height 8.7 cm, Ø 5.5 cm
Braun

279
Braun Produktgestaltung (Dieter Rams)
"KMM 2" coffee-grinder, 1969
Plastic
Height 20 cm, Ø 12 cm
Braun

280
Braun Produktgestaltung (Dieter Rams)
"TG 1000" tape-recorder, 1970
Sheet steel, painted
14×45×32 cm
Braun

281
Braun Produktgestaltung (Dieter Rams)
"TG 1020" tape-recorder, 1970
Sheet steel, painted
14×45×32 cm
Braun

282
Braun Produktgestaltung (Dieter Rams)
"F 111" flash attachment ("Hobby"), 1970
Plastic, front aluminium
8.3×2.9×6.3 cm
Braun

283
Braun Produktgestaltung (Dieter Rams)
"Cockpit 250/260" record-player with radio, 1970
Plastic, safety-glass cover
21×57×35 cm
Braun

284
Braun Produktgestaltung (Dieter Rams)
"mactron F 1 Linear" lighter, 1971
Metal
7×3.2×1.4 cm
Braun

285
Braun Produktgestaltung (Dieter Rams)
"HLD 4" hair-dryer, 1970
Plastic
14×5×8.5 cm
Braun

286
Braun Produktgestaltung (Dieter Rams)
"Phase 1" alarm-clock, 1971
Plastic
7.5×17.8×9.8 cm
Braun

287
Braun Produktgestaltung (Dieter Rams, Jürgen Greubel)
"MP7 9" lemon-squeezer, 1972
Plastic
Height 21.5 cm, Ø 16 cm
Braun

288
Braun Produktgestaltung (Dieter Rams, Jürgen Greubel)
"DS 1" tin-opener, 1972
Plastic, metal
21×11×10.5 cm
Braun

289
Braun Produktgestaltung (Dieter Rams, Florian Seiffert, Robert Oberheim, Peter Hartwein)
"Sixtant 8008" mains shaver, 1973
Plastic, metal frame
11.3×6.4×2.8 cm
Braun

290
Braun Produktgestaltung (Dieter Rams)
"Regie 308" radio, 1973
Plastic, safety-glass cover
16.7×46×34.5 cm
Braun

291
Braun Produktgestaltung (Dieter Rams, Peter Hartwein)
"RS 1" studio system, 1977
Die-cast aluminium, sheet steel, painted
5.5×60.5×33 cm
Braun

292 a–d
Braun Produktgestaltung (Hartwig Kahlcke)
"Aromaster 10 KF 40" coffee-maker, 1987
Plastic
33×17.5×22 cm
Braun

292 e
Braun Produktgestaltung (Hartwig Kahlcke)
"Aromaster 10-plus KF 45" coffee-maker, 1987
Plastic
33×17.5×22.5 cm
Braun

293
Braun Produktgestaltung (Ludwig Littmann)
"Vario 6000" lightweight, 1987
Plastic, aluminium base
13.5×27×12 cm
Braun

294
Braun Produktgestaltung (Dietrich Lubs)
"Quartz ABW 30" battery wall-clock, 1983
Casing plastic, face plastic-coated metal
Ø 20 cm, depth 2.4 cm
Braun

295
Braun Produktgestaltung (Dietrich Lubs)
"voice control AB 312 vsl" battery alarm-clock, 1985
Plastic
6.5×8.5×2 cm
Braun

296
Braun Produktgestaltung (Dietrich Lubs)
"voice control AB 45 vsl" battery alarm-clock, 1984
Plastic
9×10.5×5 cm
Braun

297
Braun Produktgestaltung (Dietrich Lubs)
"quartz AG 46 –24 h mains and battery alarm-clock, 1985
Plastic
9×10.5×5 cm
Braun

298
Braun Produktgestaltung (Dieter Rams, Dietrich Lubs)
"control ET 55" pocket calculator, 1981
Plastic
13.7×7.7×1 cm
Braun

299
Braun Produktgestaltung (Dietrich Lubs)
"Solar card ST 1" cheque-card pocket calculator, 1987
Plastic, steel
5.4×8.5×0.2 cm
Braun

300 a, 302–305
Braun Produktgestaltung (Roland Ullmann)
"micron vario 3" electric shaver, 1987
Hard and soft plastic
13×5.4×3 cm
Braun

300 b
Braun Produktgestaltung
Design studies for the "micron vario 3" electric shaver, 1987

301
Braun Produktgestaltung (Roland Ullmann)
"exact universal" beard-trimmer, 1986
Plastic
15.5×3.5×3 cm
Braun

306
Braun Produktgestaltung (Robert Oberheim)
"Silencio travel-combi PI 1200", 1987 (combining hair-dryer and travelling-iron with case for iron attachment and spray-flask)
Plastic
14×22×9 cm
Braun

307
Braun Produktgestaltung (Peter Hartwein, Dieter Rams)
"Atelier" hi-fi stack (on disc pedestal), 1987
Steel, aluminium, plastic
83×44.5×36 cm
Braun

308, 309
Braun Produktgestaltung (Peter Hartein, Dieter Rams)
"Atelier" TV stack, 1987
Steel, aluminium, plastic
308: horizontal arrangement on cabinets
Photo by a/d/s
309: vertical arrangement on cabinet
Photo by Coder Team Gräbner Wernig
Braun

310
Dieter Rams
"570" table programme, 1957
(in background "571/572" wall-unit system, 1957)
Desk with shelf, top coated with melamine resin, light grey or matt black, aluminium legs anodised natural or matt black
73×120 –200×65 –114 cm
Semicircular table: radius 65 – 90 cm
Wall-unit: sides and floors faintly textured, a shade darker than light grey or beech veneer, doors front and back light grey or matt black, fronts of drawers light grey or matt black, edges and floors matt black
44 –205 cm×114×25/44/60 cm
Wiese Vitsoe
Photo by Ingeborg Rams, Kronberg im Taunus

311
Dieter Rams
"601/602" easy-chair, 1960
Frame aluminium, painted natural
aluminium colour or polished, shell
fibre-glass-reinforced polyester, light
grey or matt black, upholstery leather
or fabric
70×60×65 cm
105×60×70 cm
Wiese Vitsoe
Photo by Ingeborg Rams, Kronberg
im Taunus

312
Dieter Rams
"606" shelving system, 1960 (originally wall shelving, from 1970 on free-
standing, from 1973 on space-struc-
turing programme and "710" auxiliary
units, 1971
Shaped vertical elements of
anodised aluminium, into which
items such as shelves, drawers or
tables can be inserted
Wiese Vitsoe
Photo by Ulfert Beckert, Frankfurt am
Main

313
Dieter Rams
"610" cloakroom programme, 1961
(perforated metal panels, to which
cloakroom accessories can be
attached as desired)
Metal, stove-enamelled light grey or
matt black, aluminium, plastic, light
grey or matt black
Wiese Vitsoe
Photo by Ulfert Beckert, Frankfurt am
Main

314 a, b
Dieter Rams
"620" armchair range, 1962
Solid wood frame with sprung core,
panels and trim fibre-glass-reinforced polyester, painted light grey
or matt black, down filling, leather or
fabric upholstery, castors, fixed legs
or swivel base
70×66×77 cm
90×66×80 cm
Wiese Vitsoe
Photo by Ulfert Beckert, Frankfurt am
Main

315
Dieter Rams
"690" sliding-door system, 1969
Slatted doors of plastic and
aluminium, shelving variable
Dimensions variable
Wiese Vitsoe
Photo by Ulfert Beckert, Frankfurt am
Main

316
Dieter Rams
"rundoval 860" table, 1986
Plastic, painted light grey or matt
black
71×120/185×110 cm
Wiese Vitsoe
Photo by Gotthart A. Eichhorn,
Frankfurt am Main

317
Dieter Rams, Jürgen Greubel
"862" chair range, 1986
Frame solid ash, stained or painted,
anodised or polished aluminium,
shaped plywood shells, available
with or without upholstered
armrests, cover fabric or leather
80×55×61 cm
Wiese Vitsoe

318
Dieter Rams, Jürgen Greubel
"850" conference-table, 1985
(model)
Plastic, painted light grey or matt
black
71×120/185×110 cm
Wiese Vitsoe
Photo by Ingeborg Rams, Kronberg
im Taunus

319
Stefan Wewerka
Halved chair, 1961
Lent by Stefan Wewerka, Cologne

320
Stefan Wewerka
Corner chair in column, 1966
Lent by Stefan Wewerka, Cologne

321
Stefan Wewerka
Rubber chair, 1965
Sketch
Lent by Stefan Wewerka, Cologne

322
Stefan Wewerka
Rubber chair, 1965
Lent by Stefan Wewerka, Cologne

323
Stefan Wewerka
Rubber chair, 1965
Sketch, pen and ink
Inscription: Gummi-Stuhl Radier-
gumme StW 65
Lent by Stefan Wewerka, Cologne

324
Stefan Wewerka
"Strindberg" chair, 1977
Coloured etching
Lent by Deutsches Architektur-
museum, Frankfurt am Main

325
Stefan Wewerka
"Vertreterstuhl" ("Representative's
Chair"), 1970
Lent by Deutsches Architektur-
museum, Frankfurt am Main

326
Stefan Wewerka
"Kinderzimmer" ("Children's Room"),
installation for the "Ludwig van" pro-
ject, 1969
In the Neue Galerie, Aachen
Photo by Sammlung Ludwig, Aachen

327
Stefan Wewerka
Chair variations, 1976
Wood
91×170×20 cm
Lent by Galerie Ruth Maurer, Zurich

328
Stefan Wewerka
Title-page for the magazine "md"
(Magazin Design), No. 1,
January 1980, with silhouette of Ste-
fan Wewerka and the "Representa-
tive's Chair"
Photos by md, Leinfelden-Echter-
dingen

329
Stefan Wewerka
Painted table, 1976
Wood
98×75×61 cm
Lent by Galerie Ruth Maurer, Zurich

330
Stefan Wewerka
"Lecturing Hall" installation 1971, in
the Galerie Müller, Cologne
Photo by W. Penkert, Stuttgart

331
Stefan Wewerka
Arc de Triomphe, 1971
Screenprint
41×51 cm
Lent by the Von-der-Heydt Museum,
Wuppertal

332
Stefan Wewerka
Arc de Triomphe, 1971
Gouache on cardboard
Private collection

333
Stefan Wewerka
Arc de Triomphe, 1971
Gouache on cardboard
Private collection

334
Stefan Wewerka
Arc de Triomphe, 1971
Charcoal on tempera on cardboard
Private collection

335
Stefan Wewerka
Leuchtturm Alexandria ("Alexandria
Lighthouse"), 1973
Lent by Bengt Adlers Collection,
Malmö, Sweden

336
Stefan Wewerka
Polnisches Grenzklo ("Polish Border
Loo"), 1969
Lent by Schmitter-Media-Agentur,
Hamburg

337
Stefan Wewerka
Prospekt für einen Telefonzellen-Turm
("Prospect for a Telephone-Kiosk
Tower"), 1971
Coloured pen-and-ink drawing over
pencil
50×70 cm
Lent by Kunsthaus Lempertz, Cologne

338
Stefan Wewerka
Hochhausvariation ("Tower-Block
Variation"), 1969
50×66 cm
Lent by Sammlung Ludwig, Neue
Galerie, Aachen
Photo by Ann Münchow

339–345
Stefan Wewerka
Kathedralen ("Cathedrals"), 1974/75
Lent by Deutsches Architektur-
museum, Frankfurt am Main

346–349
Stefan Wewerka
Palladio – Vicenza, 1975
Charcoal and watercolour on paper
40×54 cm each
Lent by Galerie Jule Kewenig, Frechen
Photo by Lothar Schnepf, Cologne

350
Stefan Wewerka
Ledoux, 1973
Watercolour and ink on paper
Private collection
Photo by Schmitz-Fabri, Cologne

351
Stefan Wewerka
Willi-Palais, Stuttgart, 1969
65×90 cm
Private collection

352
Stefan Wewerka
Die Säule der Ledoux ("Ledoux's Col-
umn") 1978
Coloured etching
Lent by Deutsches Architektur-
museum, Frankfurt am Main

353
Stefan Wewerka
Das Bett des Architekten Ledoux
("The Bed of the Architect Ledoux"),
1975
Gouache
Lent by Deutsches Architektur-
museum, Frankfurt am Main

354
Stefan Wewerka
New headquarters for the Deutsche
Welle broadcasting corporation,
1980 (project)
Lent by Deutsches Architektur-
museum, Frankfurt am Main

355
Stefan Wewerka
"B 1" chair, 1977–79, with preliminary
version
Wood, painted black, white or red,
cotton or leather upholstery
74×68×48 cm
Tecta or Wewerka
Lent by Stefan Wewerka, Cologne

356
Stefan Wewerka
"M 1" fan-shaped table, 1979
Ash, white or black
Tecta or Wewerka
Stone version: Broby Granit

357
Stefan Wewerka
Attendant's chair for the Documenta
8 in Kassel, 1987
Lent by Stefan Wewerka, Cologne

358, 359
Stefan Wewerka
Seating islands and glass pavilion for
the Documenta 8 in Kassel, 1987
Lent by Stefan Wewerka, Cologne

360
Stefan Wewerka
"F 2" sofa, "K 1" commode-table, "S 04" cupboard-base, "B 1" chair, 1979
Sofa: red cavalry twill
Table: wood, stained black
Cupboard-base: wood, stained or painted
Tecta or Wewerka

361 a
Stefan Wewerka
"B 2" asymmetrical cantilever chair, 1980
Tubular steel, chromium-plated, wood, wickerwork in natural colour, stackable
Tecta or Wewerka
Lent by Deutsches Architektur-museum, Frankfurt am Main

361 b
Stefan Wewerka
"B 5" one-legged chair ("Einschwinger") and "M 5" desk, 1982
Chair: frame tubular steel, chromium-plated or painted, seat and backrest leather
Desk: beech plywood, stained or painted
Tecta
Table (from 1988): Broby Granit
Lent by Stefan Wewerka, Cologne

362
Stefan Wewerka
Kitchen column, 1983
Tubular steel, chromium-plated, safety-glass, granite, plywood
Height 196 cm, Ø 120 cm
Tecta or Wewerka
Lent by Stefan Wewerka, Cologne

363
Stefan Wewerka
"S 01", "S 02", "S 03", "S 04" cupboards, 1979/80 (limited)
Wood, painted
Tecta or Wewerka

364
Stefan Wewerka
"K 6" lamp-table, 1980 (limited)
Tecta or Wewerka

365
Stefan Wewerka
Ruhwald, 1965
Site plan
Lent by Stefan Wewerka, Cologne

366
Stefan Wewerka
Ruhwald, 1965
Competition model
Private collection

367
Stefan Wewerka
Frühauf, 1963/64
Model view
Photo by Stefan Wewerka, Cologne

368
Stefan Wewerka
Haus Kerssenbohm, 1954/55
Ground-plan
Lent by Stefan Wewerka, Cologne

369
Stefan Wewerka
Community centre for Mehlem, Bonn, 1956
Ground-plan
Lent by Graphische Sammlung, Neue Staatsgalerie, Stuttgart

370
Stefan Wewerka
Community centre for Radertal, Cologne, 1956/57
Ground-plan
Lent by Stefan Wewerka, Cologne

371
Stefan Wewerka
Community centre for Britz, Berlin, 1964
Ground-plan
Lent by Stefan Wewerka, Cologne

372
Stefan Wewerka
Community centre and crematorium for Ruhwald, 1963
Ground-plan
Lent by Stefan Wewerka, Cologne

373 – 377
Stefan Wewerka
"Earth Architectures", 1956 – 58
Pen and ink on paper
Lent by Graphische Sammlung, Neue Staatsgalerie, Stuttgart

378
Stefan Wewerka
House on Sardinia, 1976/77
View from the east
Lent by Graphische Sammlung, Neue Staatsgalerie, Stuttgart

379
Stefan Wewerka
House on Sardinia, 1976/77
View from the north
Lent by Deutsches Architektur-museum, Frankfurt am Main

380
Stefan Wewerka
Hoechst lounge at the Frankfurt Trade Fair with "conference-trees" and cubic leather hassocks, 1987
Interior view
Photo by Hoechst AG

381
Stefan Wewerka
Hoechst lounge at the Frankfurt Fair, 1987
Drawings of various "trees", from left to right: "snack-tree", "loudspeaker-tree", table-tree"
Pen and ink, coloured, signed
Scale 1:10
Lent by Malte Kindt, Hoechst AG, Frankfurt am Main

382
Stefan Wewerka
Hoechst lounge at the Frankfurt Fair, 1987
Drawing of various items
Pen and ink, coloured, signed, inscribed "final version"
Scale 1:10
Lent by Malte Kindt, Hoechst AG, Frankfurt am Main
Photo by Lothar Schnepf, Cologne

383
Stefan Wewerka
Hoechst lounge at the Frankfurt Fair, 1987
Drawing of "conference-tree" and "kitchen-tree"
Pen and ink, coloured, signed
Scale 1:10
Lent by Malte Kindt, Hoechst AG, Frankfurt am Main

384
Holger Scheel
"Chair 3", 1978 (model)
Tubular steel, leather upholstery
85 × 65 × 66 cm
Lent by Deutsches Architektur-museum, Frankfurt am Main

385
Holger Scheel
Armchair for Rosenthal, 1979 (model)
Wood, upholstered elements
75 × 100 × 90 cm
Lent by Holger Scheel, Stuttgart

386
Holger Scheel
Armchair for Rosenthal, 1979 (model)
Wood, upholstered elements
78 × 98 × 89 cm
Lent by Holger Scheel, Stuttgart

387
Holger Scheel
Table 1, 1977 (model)
Tubular steel, wood
72 × 150 × 75 cm
Lent by Holger Scheel, Stuttgart
Photo by Chris Meier, Stuttgart

388
Holger Scheel
"Toga II" armchair, 1978
Frame wood, high-gloss painted, sprung-core upholstery, taffeta covers, woollen drape
65 × 100 × 89 cm
Schurr
Model lent by Deutsches Architektur-museum, Frankfurt am Main

389
Holger Scheel
Table 3, 1979, and Armchair 9, 1979 (models 1:7.5)
Table: laminated wood, painted matt, steel sections
49 × 165 × 80 cm
Chair: painted laminated wood, steel sections, upholstered elements, leather covers on elastic fabric
64 × 76 × 82 cm
Lent by Deutsches Architektur-museum, Frankfurt am Main

390
Holger Scheel
Chair 4, 1979 (model 1:7.5)
Laminated wood, painted matt, steel sections, elastic fabric
140 × 62 × 91 cm
Lent by Holger Scheel, Stuttgart

391, 392
Holger Scheel
Armchair 16, 1979 (model)
Laminated wood, painted matt, steel sections, elastic fabric
92 × 74 × 98 cm
Lent by Holger Scheel, Stuttgart

393 a, b
Holger Scheel
Armchair 13, 1979 (model)
Hollow wooden body, steel sections, elastic fabric
Lent by Holger Scheel, Stuttgart

394 – 405
Holger Scheel
Sketches for chairs and armchairs, 1979
Felt pen on transparent paper
30 × 20 cm
Lent by Holger Scheel, Stuttgart

406 a
Holger Scheel
"La Matrice" easy-chair, 1981
Frame wood, high-gloss painted, corded upholstery, silk covers
142 × 100 × 85 cm
Schurr

406 b–e
Holger Scheel
"La Matrice" easy-chair, 1981
Combinations in twos and fours (models)
Lent by Holger Scheel, Stuttgart

407 a
Holger Scheel
"Villa R" easy-chair, 1981
Sketches, ball-pen on paper
Lent by Holger Scheel, Stuttgart

407 b
Holger Scheel
"Villa R" easy-chair, 1981
Frame wood and steel, satin-matt painted, corded upholstery, gold lamé covers
141 × 50 × 59 cm
Schurr

408
Holger Scheel
Armchair 24, 1983 (prototype)
Laminated wood, high-gloss painted, corded upholstery, viscose covers
190 × 105 × 75 cm
Lent by Holger Scheel, Stuttgart

409
Holger Scheel
Armchair 30, 1984, and Table 6, 1984
Chair: wooden frame, high-gloss painted, corded upholstery, silk covers
136 × 171 × 108 cm
Table: steel frame, matt painted, top wood, high-gloss painted
63 × 83 × 38 cm
Schurr

410
Holger Scheel
Armchair 19, 1983 (prototype)
Laminated wood, high-gloss painted, corded upholstery, silk covers
85 × 119 × 80 cm
Schurr

411
Holger Scheel
Armchair 22, 1983
Wooden frame, high-gloss painted,
corded upholstery, silk covers
84×180×105 cm
Schurr

412–416, 419
Holger Scheel
7 variants of "Black/Red" series
(models)
Laminated wood frames painted matt
black and high-gloss red
Lent by Holger Scheel, Stuttgart

417
Holger Scheel
Armchair 26, 1983
Wooden frame, painted high-gloss
and satin-matt
96×90×63 cm
Schurr

418
Holger Scheel
Chair 7, 1984
Wood, back painted matt, seat
painted high-gloss
48×59×75 cm
Schurr

420 a–e
Holger Scheel
"Scultura" armchair, 1986
Wooden frame, painted high-gloss,
shaped elements of foam material
lined with wadding, silk covers
Chair: 120×105×75 cm
Stool: 48.8×63.8×63.8 cm
Kill, Fellbach bei Stuttgart

421
Holger Scheel
Ein Ort für O. ("A Place for O."), 1986
(model)
Original in Haigerloch Castle, West
Germany
Laminated wood (shaped), ebony
veneer, stele lime-wood with gold
leaf, drape crêpe satin
225×120×93 cm
Lent by Holger Scheel, Stuttgart

422
Holger Scheel
Chair 8, 1987, for German Architecture
Museum
Laminated wood, stained, shaped
upholstery elements, leather covers
90×64×68 cm
Draenert

423 a, b
Holger Scheel
Chair 5 and Table 5, 1985 (models
1:7.5)
Chair: tubular steel, hollow wood
body, painted, shaped upholstery
elements, leather covers
86×75×56 cm
Table: Tubular steel and wood,
painted
45×45×45 cm
Lent by Deutsches Architektur-
museum, Frankfurt am Main

424 a
Holger Scheel
Chair 8, 1986
Charcoal, coloured chalk on paper
c. 55×75 cm

424 b, c
Holger Scheel
Chair 8, 1986 (models with and with-
out armrests)
Laminated wood, painted, shaped
upholstered elements, silk covers
87×60×66 cm
Lent by Holger Scheel, Stuttgart

425 a
Holger Scheel
Armchair 31, 1985
Charcoal, coloured chalk on paper
c. 75×55 cm

425 b, c
Holger Scheel
Armchair 31, 1985 (model)
Laminated wood, painted, corded
upholstery, painted silk covers
95×185×83 cm
Lent by Holger Scheel, Stuttgart

425 d
Holger Scheel
Armchair 31, 1987
Frame painted wood, shaped
upholstered elements, leather covers
87×196×80 cm
Draenert

426
Holger Scheel
Table 4, 1981 (models)
Polished flamed granite, non-elastic
wire cable
25×150×125 cm
Lent by Holger Scheel, Stuttgart

427
Holger Scheel
Table 7, 1986 (model)
Polished flamed granite
70×192×135 cm
Lent by Holger Scheel, Stuttgart

428
Holger Scheel
Chair 9, 1986 (model)
Flamed polished granite, V2A seat
and connecting tubes, fabric drape
with padding
86×58×62 cm
Lent by Holger Scheel, Stuttgart

429
Holger Scheel
Chair 10, 1987 (model)
Wood, stained dark, shaped wooden
seat
90×48×55 cm
Lent by Holger Scheel, Stuttgart

430 a, b
Holger Scheel
Table 10, 1987 (model)
Laminated wood, stained dark
72×200×100 cm
Lent by Holger Scheel, Stuttgart

431–434
Holger Scheel
Glassware designs, 1987
Wine-glass, cup, milk-jug, butter-dish
Sketches, charcoal and crayon, tech-
nical drawings
42×29 cm
Lobmeyr
Lent by Holger Scheel, Stuttgart

435
Kazumasa Yamashita
5-piece tea and coffee set, 1983
Signed and numbered edition of 99
"Tea and Coffee Piazza series"
Silver 925/1000
Coffee-pot 22.5×24×7.5 cm
Teapot 19.5×24×10 cm
Milk-jug 14.5×23×5 cm
Sugar-basin 15×20×5 cm
Tray 1.5×51×16 cm
Officina Alessi

436
Paolo Portoghesi
6-piece tea and coffee set, 1983
Signed and numbered edition of 99
"Tea and Coffee Piazza series"
Silver 925/1000, ebony, black and
white engravings
Coffee-pot 16.5×16.5×8 cm
Teapot 16.5×23.5×16 cm
Milk-jug 9.5×15×8 cm
Sugar-basin 11×12×8 cm
Ashtray 3×9.5×8 cm
Tray 2×42.5×20.5 cm
Officina Alessi

437
Aldo Rossi
6-piece tea and coffee set, 1983
Signed and numbered edition of 99
"Tea and Coffee Piazza series"
Silver 925/1000, stove enamel, quartz
Coffee-pot 26×13.5×12 cm
Teapot 22.5×17×15 cm
Milk-jug 8.5×13.5×7.5 cm
Sugar-basin height 22.5 cm, Ø 6.5 cm
Spoon 17 cm
Display box 64×43.5×29 cm
Officina Alessi

438
Richard Meier
5-piece tea and coffee set, 1983
Signed and numbered edition of 99
"Tea and Coffee Piazza series"
Silver 925/1000, ivory
Coffee-pot 22.5×21×9.5 cm
Teapot 20.5×22×11 cm
Milk-jug 9.5×8×7 cm
Sugar-basin 12.5×10.5×7.5 cm
Tray 4.5×66.5×36 cm
Officina Alessi

439
Michael Graves
6-piece tea and coffee set, 1983
Signed and numbered edition of 99
"Tea and Coffee Piazza series"
Silver 925/1000, black bakelite bases,
ivory, aluminium, crystal glass
Coffee-pot 24.5×26.5×12 cm
Teapot 20.5×26.5×12 cm
Milk-jug 10×16×8 cm
Sugar-basin 14.5×17.5×8 cm
Spoon 9.5 cm
Tray height 7 cm, Ø 41 cm
Officina Alessi

440
Alessandro Mendini
6-piece tea and coffee set, 1983
Signed and numbered edition of 99
"Tea and Coffee Piazza series"
Silver 925/1000
Coffee-pot 24×21.5×12.5 cm
Teapot 21.5×23×13.5 cm
Milk-jug 18×9×7 cm
Sugar-basin height 8 cm, Ø 11 cm
Spoon 11 cm
Tray height 3 cm, Ø 45 cm
Officina Alessi

441
Oscar Tusquets
4-piece tea or coffee set, 1983
Signed and numbered edition of 99
"Tea and Coffee Piazza series"
Silver 925/1000, inside surfaces gold-
plated (since 1984 also available in
silver-plated brass), ebony, crystal
Teapot 19×21×13.5 cm
Milk-jug 12×13×10 cm
Sugar-basin 8×12×10 cm
Tray 6×52.5×31 cm
Officina Alessi

442
Stanley Tigerman
5-piece tea and coffee set, 1983
Signed and numbered edition of 99
"Tea and Coffee Piazza series"
Silver 925/1000
Coffee-pot 19.5×14.5×9 cm
Teapot 15.5×14.5×9 cm
Milk-jug 11.5×17×9 cm
Sugar-basin 8.5×10.5×9 cm
Tray 4×47.5×34 cm
Officina Alessi

443
Robert Venturi
5-piece tea and coffee set, 1983
Signed and numbered edition of 99
"Tea and Coffee Piazza series"
Silver 925/1000, engravings with gold
leaf, ebony
Coffee-pot 21.5×20×14.5 cm
Teapot 15×26×15 cm
Milk-jug 10×12×7 cm
Sugar-basin height 13 cm, Ø 9.5 cm
Tray 1.5×42.5×35.5 cm
Officina Alessi

444
Charles Jencks
5-piece tea and coffee set, 1983
Signed and numbered edition of 99
"Tea and Coffee Piazza series"
Silver 925/1000
Coffee-pot 22×7.5×7.5 cm
Teapot 21×7.5×7.5 cm
Milk-jug 17.5×7.5×7.5 cm
Sugar-basin 14×7.5×7.5 cm
Tray 2×45×18.5 cm
Officina Alessi

445
Hans Hollein
5-piece tea and coffee set, 1983
Signed and numbered edition of 99
"Tea and Coffee Piazza series"
Silver 925/1000, methacrylate
Coffee-pot 17×15.5×13.5 cm
Teapot 18×28×10.5 cm
Milk-jug 13×9.5×7 cm
Sugar-basin height 7 cm, Ø 10 cm
Tray 4.5×92.4×31 cm
Officina Alessi

446
Matteo Thun
"Nefertiti" tea set and egg-cup, 1981
Ceramic
Teapot height 20 cm, Ø 20 cm
Sugar-basin 14×13×13 cm
Teacup height 9 cm, Ø 8 cm
Egg-cup height 9 cm, Ø 9 cm
Memphis

447
Matteo Thun
"Ontario" pepper-pot, "Erie"
cocktail-stick holder, "Superior"
toothpick holder, "Michigan" salt-cel-
lar, 1982
White porcelain, decorated
Height 10 cm, 2.5 cm, 10 cm, 10 cm
Memphis

448
Matteo Thun
"Gallus Italicus" pot, 1982
"Rara Avis" series
Ceramic
36×48×13 cm
Sarri
Lent by Anthologie Quartett, Bad
Essen
Photo by Fabio Zonta

449
Matteo Thun
"Lesbia Oceanica" pot, 1982
"Rara Avis" series
Ceramic
31×30×7 cm
Sarri
Lent by Anthologie Quartett, Bad
Essen
Photo by Fabio Zonta

450
Matteo Thun
"Cuculus Canorus" pot, 1982
"Rara Avis" series
Ceramic
25×19×13 cm
Sarri
Lent by Anthologie Quartett, Bad
Essen
Photo by Fabio Zonta

451
Matteo Thun
"Columbina Superba" pot, 1982
"Rara Avis" series
Ceramic
c. 25×20×15 cm
Sarri
Lent by Anthologie Quartett, Bad
Essen
Photo by Fabio Zonta

452
Matteo Thun
"Passer Passer" pot, 1982
"Rara Avis" series
Ceramic
25×27×8 cm
Sarri
Lent by Anthologie Quartett, Bad
Essen
Photo by Fabio Zonta

453
Matteo Thun
"Pelecanus Pontifex" pot, 1982
"Rara Avis" series
Ceramic
28×41×8 cm
Sarri
Lent by Anthologie Quartett, Bad
Essen
Photo by Fabio Zonta

454
Matteo Thun
"Archetto" champagne-glass, 1984
"The Sherry Netherlands" series
Mouth-blown glass
Height 29.2 cm, Ø 6.2 cm
Barovier & Toso
Lent by Anthologie Quartett, Bad
Essen

455
Matteo Thun
"Manico" champagne-glass, 1984
"The Sherry Netherlands" series
Mouth-blown glass
Height 28.5 cm, Ø 15.8 cm
Barovier & Toso
Lent by Anthologie Quartett, Bad
Essen

456
Matteo Thun
"Punta Raisi" candlestick, 1985
Silver-plated brass, base black Mar-
quinha marble, acrylic dish
Height 49 cm (without candle)
WMF

457
Matteo Thun
"Piazzetta di Capri" tray, 1986
Silver-plated brass, gold-leaf decora-
tion, gold-plated brass
7×42×30 cm
WMF

458
Matteo Thun
"Walking Coffee Pots/Flicflac", 1986
Silver-plated brass, solid wood
22×31 cm, 25×23 cm, 20×18.5 cm
WMF

459
Matteo Thun
"Taleggio" covered dish, 1984
Black Belgio marble, base elements
polished white, cover acrylic glass
25×36×36 cm
WMF

460
Jo Laubner
"Arena" tray, mirror, ice-cooler, lamp
and candlestick, 1985
Acrylic glass, metal parts chromium-
plated, spherical elements gilt
Tray 37×23 cm, mirror height 26 cm,
ice-cooler height 26 cm, lamp height
22 cm, candlestick height 26 cm
WMF

461
Jo Laubner
"Focus" champagne-cooler, 1984
"La Galleria" art-object, signed and
numbered
Silver-plated, gilt
Height 35 cm, Ø 34 cm
WMF

462
Jo Laubner
"Babylon Greetings" vase, 1985
"La Galleria" art-object, signed and
numbered
Brass, silver- and gold-plated,
base elements black acrylate
Height 52 cm
WMF

463
Aldo Rossi
"La Conica" espresso-pots, 1984
Steel, with copper base, for 6 or 3
cups
Height 30.5 cm, Ø 8.5 cm; height 24
cm, Ø 7.5 cm
Officina Alessi

464
Vito Noto
"Como" table centrepiece, 1984
"La Galleria" art-object, signed and
numbered
Brass, silver- and gold-plated
WMF

465
Franz O. Lipp
"Triga" fruit-dish, 1985
"La Galleria" art-object, signed and
numbered
Brass, silver-plated matt, base ele-
ments black marble
Ø 38 cm
WMF

466
Angelo Cortesi
"Ponte" tray, 1985
"La Galleria" art-object, signed and
numbered
Brass, silver-plated, edges gold-
plated
51×31 cm
WMF

467
Danilo Silvestrin
"Scacco Matto" 5-piece coffee and
tea service, 1985
"La Galleria" art-object, signed and
numbered
Brass, silver-plated, serigraph on
foam material
25×53×32 cm
WMF

468
Mario Vivaldi
"Collegium Tabulae" oil and vinegar
set, 1985
"La Galleria" art-object, signed and
numbered
Silver-plated brass, acrylic glass
Tray Ø 45 cm
WMF

469
Matteo Thun
"Tavola" tableware, 1987
"La Galleria" series
From left to right: salt-mill, jam-pot,
cruet, serviette-ring, jam-pots, ser-
viette-ring, cruet, jam-pot, pepper-
mill

Acrylised plastic, chromium-plated
metal parts, crystal glass
Dimensions from left to right
(height×Ø) height 17.5 cm, 17×12.5
cm, 6×9 cm, Ø 3.5 cm, 12.5×20 cm,
Ø 3.5 cm, 6×9 cm, 17×12.5 cm,
height 17.5 cm
WMF

470
Matteo Thun
"Design Matteo Thun" tray collection,
1986
"La Galleria Design International"
series
"Flora" and "Linea" decors
Acrylised plastic, flower handles
plastic, curved handles metal
Rectangular trays 42×30 cm, round
trays Ø 35 cm
WMF

471
Matteo Thun
"Design Matteo Thun" tray collection,
1986
"La Galleria Design International"
series
"Golden Gate", "Comet", "Black and
White" decors
Acrylised plastic, handles metal
42×30 cm
WMF

472
Matteo Thun
"Hommage à Madonna" cutlery, 1985/
86
Matt black polyamide, decorative
elements gilt
WMF

473
Mario Vivaldi
"Solo" cutlery, 1986
"WMF-Ambiente" series
Cromargan (R) stainless steel, Mono-
bloc knife
WMF
Photo by Foto Design Schuhmacher,
Geislingen

474
Mario Vivaldi
"Solo" cutlery, 1986, coloured vari-
ants
"WMF-Ambiente" series
Cromargan (R) stainless steel, Mono-
bloc knife
WMF

475
Stanley Tigerman and Margaret
McCurry
"Teaside" 7-piece crockery set, 1985
Teapot, milk-jug, sugar-basin, tray,
biscuit-box, salt-cellar, pepper-pot
Porcelain
Swid Powell
Lent by Bestform, Arnsberg
Photo by Olof Wahlund

476
Robert Venturi
"Grandmother" 4 piece crockery set,
1984
Porcelain
Cup 5.1×7.6 cm, saucer 9.5 cm, plates
23.5 and 30.5 cm
Swid Powell
Lent by Bestform, Arnsberg

477
George J. Sowden
"Montreal" 4-piece crockery set, 1984
Porcelain
Cup 5.1 × 7.6 cm, saucer 9.5 cm, plates
23.5 and 30.5 cm
Swid Powell
Photo by Olof Wahlund

478
Robert Venturi
"Notebook" 4-piece crockery set,
1984
Porcelain
Cup 5.1 × 7.6 cm, saucer 9.5 cm, plates
23.5 and 30.5 cm
Swid Powell
Lent by Bestform, Arnsberg

479
Stanley Tigerman and Margaret
McCurry
"Sunshine" plate, 1985
Porcelain
30.5 cm
Swid Powell
Lent by Bestform, Arnsberg

480
Stanley Tigerman and Margaret
McCurry
"Pompeji" plate, 1986
Porcelain
30.5 cm
Swid Powell
Lent by Bestform, Arnsberg

481
Robert A. M. Stern
"Majestic" plate, 1985
Porcelain
30.5 cm
Swid Powell
Lent by Bestform, Arnsberg

482
Steven Holl
"Planar" plate, 1984
Porcelain
30.5 cm
Swid Powell
Lent by Bestform, Arnsberg

483
Arata Isozaki
"Stream" plate, 1984
Porcelain
30.5 cm
Swid Powell
Lent by Bestform, Arnsberg

484
Robert and Trix Haussmann
"Stripes" plate, 1985
Porcelain
30.5 cm
Swid Powell
Lent by Bestform, Arnsberg

485
Hans Hollein
"Kaleidoscope" 4-piece crockery
set, 1986
Porcelain
Cup 5.1 × 7.6 cm, saucer 9.5 cm, plates
23.5 and 30.5 cm
Swid Powell
Lent by Bestform, Arnsberg

486
Ettore Sottsass
"Medici" 4-piece crockery set, 1986
Porcelain, white with painted deco-
ration
Cup 5.1 × 7.6 cm, saucer 9.5 cm, plates
23.5 and 30.5 cm
Swid Powell
Lent by Bestform, Arnsberg

487
Ettore Sottsass
"Renaissance" 5-piece crockery set,
1986
Porcelain, white with painted deco-
ration
Cup 5.1 × 7.6 cm, saucer 9.5 cm, dish
23.5 cm, plates 23.5 and 30.5 cm
Swid Powell
Lent by Bestform, Arnsberg

488
Robert Venturi
"Village" 4-piece tea set, 1986
Porcelain
Swid Powell
Lent by Bestform, Arnsberg

489
Michael Graves
"The Big Dripper" coffee-pot, 1986
Porcelain
Swid Powell
Lent by Bestform, Arnsberg

490
Richard Meier
"Silver Boxes", 1987
Silver
Swid Powell
Lent by Bestform, Arnsberg
Photo by Olof Wahlund

491
Robert A. M. Stern
Salt and pepper set, 1984
Silver
Height 7.5 cm
Swid Powell
Lent by Bestform, Arnsberg
Photo by Olof Wahlund

492
Vittorio Gregotti
Tray, 1987
Silver
Robert and Trix Haussmann
Candlestick and "Mickey" pepper-
mill, 1986
Silver
Swid Powell
Lent by Bestform, Arnsberg
Photo by Olof Wahlund

493
Robert A. M. Stern
"Century", "Metropolitan" and "Har-
monie" candlesticks, 1984
Silver
Swid Powell
Lent by Bestform, Arnsberg

494
Richard Meier
Candlestick, pepper-mill and tray,
1986
Silver
Swid Powell
Lent by Bestform, Arnsberg

495
Ettore Sottsass
"Starlight" and "Silvershade" candle-
stick, 1986
Silver, platinum
Swid Powell
Lent by Bestform, Arnsberg

496
Heide Warlamis
"Seçession" bowl, 1984
"Vienna" Collection
Porcelain
Height 20 cm, Ø 24 cm
United Studios
Lent by Bestform, Arnsberg

497, 500
Heide Warlamis
"Skyscraper" vases, 1984
"Vienna" collection
Porcelain
Height 30 cm
United Studios
Lent by Bestform, Arnsberg

498, 499
Heide Warlamis
"Metropolitan Tower" vases, 1986
"Vienna" collection
Porcelain
Height 30 cm
United Studios
Lent by Bestform, Arnsberg

501, 502
Heide Warlamis
"Siena" salt and pepper set, 1986
"Vienna"
Porcelain
Height 17 cm
United Studios
Lent by Bestform, Arnsberg

503
Heide Warlamis
"Skala" oil and vinegar set, 1987
"Vienna" collection
Porcelain
Height 13 cm
United Studios
Lent by Bestform, Arnsberg

504
Heide Warlamis
"Belvedere" candle-stand, 1987
"Vienna" collection
Porcelain
10 × 16 × 16 cm
United Studios
Lent by Bestform, Arnsberg

505
Piero Vendruscolo and Franklyn
Gerard
"Malamocco Lasa" table-light, 1985
White Lasa marble, Murano glass
24 × 26.5 × 16.5 cm
Vendrusculo & Gerard
Lent by Electum Design Furniture,
Munich

506
Piero Vendruscolo and Franklyn
Gerard
"Malamocco Rosa" table-light, 1985
Pink Portugal marble, Murano glass
24 × 16.5 × 16.5 cm
Vendrusculo & Gerard
Lent by Electum Design Furniture,
Munich

507
Piero Vendruscolo and Franklyn
Gerard
"Miracoli" table-light, 1985
Red Verona marble, grey Bardiglio
marble, white Lasa marble, Murano
glass
24 × 16.5 × 16.5 cm
Vendrusculo & Gerard
Lent by Electum Design Furniture,
Munich

508
Piero Vendruscolo and Franklyn
Gerard
"Trifora" table-light, 1986
White Lasa marble, black Marquinia
marble, Murano glass
24 × 16.5 × 16.5 cm
Vendrusculo & Gerard
Lent by Electum Design Furniture,
Munich

509
Piero Vendruscolo and Franklyn
Gerard
"Regatta" table-light, 1986
White Lasa marble, black Marquinia
marble, Murano glass
24 × 16.5 × 16.5 cm
Vendrusculo & Gerard
Lent by Electum Design Furniture,
Munich

510
Piero Vendruscolo and Franklyn
Gerard
"Codussi" table-light, 1986
Grey Bardiglio marble, pink Portugal
marble, Murano glass
24 × 16.5 × 16.5 cm
Vendrusculo & Gerard
Lent by Electum Design Furniture,
Munich

511
Piero Vendruscolo and Franklyn
Gerard
"Murano Faro" table-light, 1985
Grey Bardiglio marble, Murano glass
42.5 × 16.5 × 16.5 cm
Vendrusculo & Gerard
Lent by Electum Design Furniture,
Munich

512
Piero Vendruscolo and Franklyn
Gerard
"Faro" table-light, 1985
Red Verona marble, white Lasa
marble, Murano galss
42.5 × 16.5 × 16.5 cm
Vendrusculo & Gerard
Lent by Electum Design Furniture,
Munich

513
Piero Vendruscolo and Franklyn
Gerard
"Torre Rosa" table-light, 1985
Pink Portugal marble, Murano glass
42.5 × 16.5 × 16.5 cm
Vendrusculo & Gerard
Lent by Electum Design Furniture,
Munich

514
Piero Vendruscolo and Franklyn
Gerard
"Torre Nera" table-light, 1985
Also available with clock
Black Portoro
marble, Murano glass
42.5×16.5×16.5 cm
Vendrusculo & Gerard
Lent by Electum Design Furniture,
Munich

515
Piero Vendruscolo and Franklyn
Gerard
"Torre dell'orologio" table-light with
clock, 1985
Grey Bardiglio marble, white Lasa
marble, Murano glass, quartz clock
42.5×16.5×16.5 cm
Vendrusculo & Gerard
Lent by Electum Design Furniture,
Munich

516
George J. Sowden
"Metropole" table-clock, 1982
Wood with plastic laminates
81×24×24 cm
Memphis

517
Nathalie de Pasquier and George J.
Sowden
Table-clock, 1987
"Neos" series
Wood, painted
27×16×6 cm
Lorenz
Lent by Watch Company, Bremen

518
Matteo Thun and Andrea Lera
"Tobruk", "Zero Visibility", "Spargi",
"Guardiano Giovanni", "Spargiotto"
and "Maddalena" table-lamps, 1985
"Stillight" series
Painted steel, glass or porcelain
20×25×24 cm, 35×19×19 cm,
20×20×20 cm, height 44× Ø 21 cm,
35×17×17 cm, 64×25×25 cm
Bieffeplast
Lent by Werner Schmitz Collectionen,
Düsseldorf

519
Andreas Weber
Vase, 1986
"Artwork" series
Aluminium, satinised glass
Height 50 cm, Ø 12 cm
Weber

520
Andreas Weber
Paper-tray, 1984
"Artwork" series
Crystal glass, aluminium, stackable
32.5×26 cm
Weber

521
Andreas Weber
Tray, 1982
"Artwork"
Granular aluminium, glass
65×42 cm
Weber

522
Andreas Weber
Fruit-dish, 1987
Aluminium
Height 6.5 cm, Ø 16.3 cm
Weber

523
Andreas Weber
Cheese dish, 1984
"Artwork" series
Crystal glass, aluminium
Height 19 cm, Ø 29 cm
Weber

524
Masque (Douglas Frederick/Ann
Cederna)
"Four Orders in Gold and Stone",
1987
From left to right: brooch, bracelet,
ring, earring
Stands Belgian black marble, jewel-
lery 18-carat gold, palladium
Masque
Goldsmith: Wattson & Wattson, New
York

525
Masque (Douglas Frederick/Ann
Cederna)
Brooch, 1987 (after the ground-plan
of Blenheim)
"Four Orders in Gold and Stone
Black Belgian marble, 18-carat gold,
palladium
Masque
Goldsmith: Wattson & Wattson, New
York

526
Masque (Douglas Frederick/Ann
Cederna)
Bracelet, 1987
"Four Orders in Gold and Stone"
Black Belgian marble, 18-carat gold,
palladium
Masque
Goldsmith: Wattson & Wattson, New
York

527
Masque (Douglas Frederick/Ann
Cederna)
Ring, 1987 (after the ground-plan of
Versailles)
Four Orders in Gold and Stone"
Black Belgian marble, 18-carat gold,
palladium
Masque
Goldsmith: Wattson & Wattson, New
York

528
Masque (Douglas Frederick/Ann
Cederna)
Earring, 1987 (after the ground-plan
of Chantilly)
"Four Orders in Gold and Stone
Black Belgian marble, 18-carat gold,
palladium
Masque
Goldsmith: Wattson & Wattson, New
York

529
Alessandro Mendini
"Potente" door-handle Re-Design,
1986
FSB Workshop 1986
Aluminium, black contrasting pieces
12 cm
FSB

530
Alessandro Mendini
"Wittgenstein" door-handle Re-
Design, 1986
FSB Workshop 1986
Aluminium coated black
13 cm
FSB

531
Alessandro Mendini
"Gropius" door-handle Re-Design,
1986
FSB Workshop 1986
Aluminium with Duro-Horn
12.5 cm
FSB

532
Hans Hollein
Door-handle, 1986
FSB Workshop 1986
Top: brass, 15.5 cm
Centre: aluminium, 15 cm,
Below: steel with
Duro-Horn, 16.5 cm
FSB

533
Hans-Ulrich Bitsch
Door-handles, 1986
FSB Workshop 1986
Aluminium 20 cm each
FSB

534
Dieter Rams
Door-handles and door-knobs, 1986
FSB Workshop 1986
Aluminium with plastic
Upper handle 13 cm, lower handle
14.5 cm, knobs Ø 4 cm
FSB

535
Petr Tucny
Door-handles, 1986
FSB Workshop 1986
Aluminium
c. 16 cm
FSB

536
Shoji Hayashi
Door-handle and doorknobs, 1986
FSB Workshop 1986
Left: porcelain, 8.5 cm
Below: aluminium,
coloured coating, Ø 5.5 cm
Above: aluminium and plastic,
Ø 5.5 cm
FSB

537
Arata Isozaki
Door-handle, doorknob and door-
pull, 1986
FSB Workshop 1986
Aluminium with coloured wood
Handle 16 cm, knob Ø 6.5 cm, door-
pull 30 cm
FSB

538
Peter Eisenmann
Door-handle, 1986
FSB Workshop 1986
High-grade steel
17×17 cm
FSB

539
Mario Botta
Door-handles, 1986
FSB Workshop 1986
Top: steel, coated black, 18 cm
Below: high-grade steel, Ø 16 cm
FSB

540
Hans Jürgen Bauer
Furniture-handle, 1986/87
"Terrazzo" series,
Plastic with metal bar
7.8×2.6 cm
Union Knopf

541
Hans Jürgen Bauer
Furniture-handle, 1986/7
"Terrazzo" series
Plastic in various colours
5×3.4 cm
Union Knopf

542
Hans Jürgen Bauer
Furniture-handle, 1986/87
"Terrazzo" series
Plastic
5×2.5×1.8 cm
Union Knopf

543
Hans Jürgen Bauer
Furniture handle, 1986/87
"Terrazzo" series
Plastic with metal bar
7.8×3.4 cm
Union Knopf

544
Hans Jürgen Bauer
Furniture-handle, 1986/87
"Terrazzo" series
Plastic
5×2.6 cm
Union Knopf

545
Hans Jürgen Bauer
Furniture-handle, 1986/87
"Terrazzo" series
Plastic
3.3×2.4 cm
Union Knopf

546
Furniture-handles and knobs, 1988
"Duron" series
Plastic in various colours
From left to right: 2.1× Ø 1.4 cm;
3×3.3 cm; 2×2.5 cm; 2.5×2.5 cm;
3×2.5 cm; 2.5×3.4 cm; 3.3×Ø 3.3
cm
Union Knopf

547
Furniture-handle, 1987
"Fifties" series
Plastic, white, black or grey, com-
bined with aluminium, painted
8.2×3.4×1.5 cm
Union Knopf

548
Furniture-handle, 1987
"Fifties" series
Plastic, white, black or grey, combined with aluminium matt or painted
9.9×4.0 cm
Union Knopf

549
Furniture-handle, 1987
"Fifties" series
Plastic, white, black or grey, combined with aluminium, painted
6.8×3.2×1.5 cm
Union Knopf

550
Furniture-handles, 1987
"Fifties" series
Plastic, white, black or grey, combined with aluminium, painted
5.4×3.0×1.0 cm; 4.8×2.1×1 cm
Union Knopf

551
Furniture-handles, 1987
"Fifties" series
Aluminium or metal
11.2×1.8 cm, or 15.2×2.9 cm, Ø 1 cm
Union Knopf

552
Furniture-handle, 1987
"Fifties" series
Aluminium or metal
15.2×2.2 cm, Ø 1 cm
Union Knopf

553
Furniture-handles, 1987
"Art Deco" series
Plastic, black and root effect
Height 2.7 cm, Ø 2.8 cm; height 2.4 cm, Ø 2.0 cm
Union Knopf

554
Furniture-handle, 1987
"Art Deco" series
Plastic, black and root effect
6×2 cm
Union Knopf

555
Furniture-handle, 1987
"Art Deco" series
Plastic, black and root effect
5.8×2.9 cm
Union Knopf

556
Furniture-handle, 1987
"Art Deco" series
Plastic, root and chromium effect
9.9×4.0 cm
Union Knopf

557
Furniture-handle, 1987
"Art Deco" series
Plastic, root and chromium effect, black
2.6×4.6×2.2 cm
Union Knopf

558
Furniture-handles, 1987
"Art Deco" series
Plastic, with chromium or gold effect
5.4×3.0×1.0 cm; 4.8×2.1×1 cm
Union Knopf

559
Furniture-handle
Plastic, combined with perforated metal
2.9×5.9 cm
Union Knopf

560
Furniture-handle
Plastic
3×Ø 2.2 cm
Union Knopf

561
Thomas Stark
Portable radio, 1985/86, (model 1:1)
Plastic, metal
100×50×23 cm (width and height variable)
Lent by Thomas Stark, Darmstadt

562
Seymour/Powell
"Blackhawk Stutz" electric guitar, 1987 (prototype)
Metal casting (magnesium alloy)
c. 90×50 cm (opened), c. 90×20 cm (folded)
Lent by Seymour/Powell Ltd., London

563 a
Siemens Design Studio (Tönis Käo)
Study for flat PC, 1983
Plastic
A4 and cheque-card formats
Lent by Siemens Design Studio, Munich

563 b
Siemens Design Studio (Tönis Käo)
Study for folding telephone, 1986
Plastic
A4 and cheque-card formats
Lent by Siemens Design Studio, Munich

564
Anon.
Cheque-card formats for various functions
Plastic, magnetic strip coding
c. 5.5×8.5 cm each
Lent by Illner & Teufel, Frankfurt am Main

565
Perry A. King and Santiago Miranda
Console for printer terminal, 1985
6.9×3.4 cm
Olivetti

566
Perry A. King and Santiago Miranda
Console for printer terminal, 1985
6.9×3.4 cm
Olivetti

567
Perry A. King and Santiago Mirando
Console for printer terminal, 1985
6.9×3.4 cm
Olivetti

568
Hans-Jürgen and Helga Lannoch
"Bitmap 12" graphics tablet, 1983/84
11.5×9.5 cm
Preh

569
Hans-Jürgen and Helga Lannoch
"Commander" keyboard, 1983/84
3.6×51.6×19.2 cm
Preh

570
Siemens Design Studio (Christoph Böninger and Hans-Jürgen Escherle)
Study for multifunctional communications panel, 1986
Plastic
23×50×18 cm
Lent by Siemens Design Studio, Munich

571
Frank Eisele and Heike Kuberg
Personal computer, 1983 (mock-up)
With screen, two diskette drives, flexible polyurethane mask and wireless keyboard with remote control
c. 50×40×40 cm, screen adjustable between 7° and 90°
Lent by Eisele/Kuberg und Partner, Gruppe für Gestaltung, Ulm

572
Loewe
"Art S 32" television, 1988
Flat square large-screen tube, 70 hi-fi stereo
98×77×56 cm; screen diagonal 82 cm
Loewe

573
Frogdesign
"Rotating Frogline" TV set with swivel screen, 1986 (prototype)
Designed for the Helen Hamlyn Foundation
Base 42×38 cm, Ø 52 cm
Lent by Frogdesign, Altensteig

574
Frogdesign
"Office for the Future" study for a workstation/portable, 1986
c. 35×50 cm
Lent by Frogdesign, Altensteig
Photo by Dietmar Henneka

575 a
Design Central Team
Personal electronic terminal, 1986/87
With flat-screen LCD display
28×42 cm
Lent by Design Central, Columbus, Ohio

575 b
Frogdesign
"RCS 1" radio controlled solar clock, 1986
Energy obtained through solar cells, time information from the transmitter at the Physico-Technical Institute in Braunschweig
30×20×5 cm
Junghans

576 a, b
Achim Pohl and Stefan Imhof
Epidiascope, 1986 (prototype)
Wood, safety-glass, Rohazell
12×37×29 cm
Lent by Achim Pohl, Mühltal/Trautheim

577
Peter Kienle and Horst Pohlenz
Digital large-screen projector, 1986 (prototype)
Combination of projector, floppy drive and video-disc player
13×53×30 cm
Lent by Design Manufaktur Pohlenz Kienle, Schwäbisch-Gmünd

578
Daniel Weil
"100 objects mirrors of silenced time . . ." digital clock, 1982
Soft PVC, transparent, with screen print, painted steel wire
28.5×14.5×5 cm
Quartett

579
Daniel Weil
"Verse" calculator, 1985
Plastic, fabric, metal
15×30×15 cm
Quartett

580
Olivetti
Microprocessor
Photo from Gianni Barbacetto: *Design Interface. How Man and Machine Communicate.* Olivetti Design Research, Milan 1987, p. 96
Olivetti

581
Chip
From a BMW advert entitled "Examples of New Thinking", 1986
0.225×0.225 cm
Photo by Creative Colour

582 a, b
Micromechanics (toothed rack and pinions in the diameter of a hair), 1988
Silicon, chemically etched out of discs
Pinion Ø c. 100 μm
Photo above by Berkeley Sensor and Actuator Center
Photo below by AT & T Bell Laboratories
From *Newsweek*, 30 Nov., 1987

583
Frogdesign
"Office for the Future, Workstation Eins", 1986 (prototype)
c. 70×190×90 cm
Lent by Frogdesign, Altensteig

584 – 587
Uwe Berndt
Portable communications system, 1987
Double-sided leather waistcoat with electronic foil in lining, press-buttons, transmitter and receiver unit in the lapel, and around the waist computer-aided teletext and telex apparatus, two diskette drives, videophone and digital camera
584: camera
585: typewriter
586: portable communication equipment, waistcoat
587: videophone
Lent by Uwe Berndt, Oberursel

588
Hagai Shvadron (under the direction of Mario Bellini)
"Count Down 1990" portable computer, 1987 (model)
Lent by Hagai Shvadron, Herzlia, Israel
Photo by Emilio Tremolada

589
Manfred Nitsch
"Paymate" electronic money, 1986 (prototype)
Made in the design faculty (Prof. Stefan Lengyel), of the University of Essen for the Italia's Cup, Milan
Acrylic glass and metal
c. 7×5×1 cm
Lent by Gesamthochschule Essen
Photo by Andreas Fein, Essen

590
Manfred Nitsch
"Paymate" electronic money, 1986 (prototype)
Made in the design faculty (Prof. Stefan Lengyel), of the University of Essen for the Italia's Cup, Milan
Plastic and metal
4×5 cm
Lent by Gesamthochschule Essen
Photo by Andreas Fein, Essen

591
Stefan Pütz
"Paymate" electronic money, 1986 (prototype)
Made in the design faculty (Prof. Stefan Lengyel), of the University of Essen for the Italia's Cup, Milan
Acrylic glass
c. 9×6×0.8 cm each
Lent by Gesamthochschule Essen
Photo by Andreas Fein, Essen

592, 593
Josep Bernabé, Josep Casal, Maruja Martínez
"Electronic Coins" coins and notes of various denominations, 1987 (prototype)
Made at the Escola Massana (Prof. Santi Giró), Barcelona, for the Italia's Cup
Plastic
592: 5.4×10.8×0.02 cm each
593: Ø c. 3 cm each
Lent by Escola Massana, Centre Municipal d'Art i Disseny, Barcelona

594
Paolo Grasselli
Glove calculator, 1986
Made at the ISIA (Prof. Antonio Rossin), Florence, for the Italia's Cup
Rubber, brass, enamelled or gilt
21×19×0.4 cm
Lent by Paolo Grasselli, Reggio Emilia, Italy

595
Kunstflug
Electronic finger calculator, 1986/87
Implants in skin
Lent by Kunstflug, Düsseldorf
Photo by Walter Vogel, Frankfurt

596 a, b
Marcello Nizzoli
"Divisumma 24" desk calculator, 1956
25×30×40 cm
Olivetti
Lent by Deutsche Olivetti, Frankfurt am Main

596 c
Design Central Team
Desk calculator, 1986/87
With miniaturised thermal printer
Acrylate
10×20 cm
Design Central, Columbus, Ohio

597
Siemens Design Studio (Jürgen Hitzler)
Study for track terminal, 1986
Plastic
5×48×24 cm
Lent by Siemens Design Studio, Munich

597a   Nele Ströbel
PC keyboard with integrated cursor ball-control and neon-coloured programme masks (project study for Siemens), 1985/86 injection-moulded plastic
c. 2 × 60 × 25 cm
Lent by Siemens Design Studio, Munich

598
Anon.
"Quartz Cal 318SE" solar cell calculator
Metal plate with electronic elements, encased in acrylic glass
0.4×5.4×8.5 cm
Lent by Jochen Gros, Offenbach

599
Anon.
Mackintosh software, 1984/85
Pocket calculator, immaterial, operated via cursor
Variable dimensions, depending on size of screen

600
Anon.
Viewdata software for the German Federal Post Office, 1983
Desk calculator as three-dimensional immaterial product
Variable dimensions, depending on size of screen

601
Siemens Design Studio
"Comfo Desk" graphics programme, 1988
Variable dimensions, depending on size of screen
Siemens

602
Kunstflug
Electronic screen, 1987
Collage on paper
c. 56×42 cm
Lent by Kunstflug, Düsseldorf

603 a, b
Wilhelm Anger
"Eyemetrics" system, 1987
Eyemetrics

604
Bellefast (Andreas Brandolini)
"Kalle" hi-fi pre-amplifier, 1986
Brass, chromium-or silver-plated
c. 22×46×42 cm
Burmester

605
Bellefast (Joachim B. Stanitzek)
"Play 846" hi-fi pre-amplifier, 1986
Metal, painted
c. 17×58×23 cm
Burmester

606
Gelb Selectiv (Christian Schneider-Moll)
"Strata ZaZa" hi-fi pre-amplifier, 1986
Sandwich steel plate, cut by laser, silver
c. 5×48×22 cm
Burmester

607
Robert Nakata
Stereo receiver, 1984
Study project at Cranbrook Academy of Arts, Bloomfield Hills, Michigan
Plastic
28×35 cm
Lent by Robert Nakata, Studio Dumbar, The Hague, Netherlands

608
Paul Montgomery
Electronic still-camera, 1987 (project)
First prize in the Frogjunior Competition, 1987, at Cranbrook Academy of Arts
Lent by Cranbrook Academy of Arts, Bloomfield Hills, Michigan

609
Paul Montgomery
"Picture Phone", 1987
28×20 cm
Lent by Cranbrook Academy of Arts, Bloomfield Hills, Michigan

610
Lisa Krohn
Multifunctional telephone answering machine with thermal printer, LCD display and phonebook, 1987
Second prize in the Frogjunior Competition, 1987, at Cranbrook Academy of Arts
Plastic
17×25 cm
Lent by Lisa Krohn, Bloomfield Hills, Michigan

611 a, b
Siemens Design Studio (Hatto Grosse)
Study for compact telephone, 1986
Die-casting
4×20×5 cm
Lent by Siemens Design Studio, Munich

612
Siemens Design Studio (Luitpold Hecht)
"Plasma" study for a telephone, 1986
Plastic
Height 4.5 cm, Ø 24 cm
Lent by Siemens Design Studio, Munich

613
Siemens Design Studio (Jürgen Hitzler and Werner Schuss)
Study for a telephone, 1986
Plastic
15×24×10 cm
Lent by Siemens Design Studio, Munich

614
Siemens Design Studio (Rolf Hering)
"Lobster" study for a telephone, 1986
Plastic
3×17×8 cm
Lent by Siemens Design Studio, Munich

615
Alois Dworschak
Computer workplace, 1986/87 (model)
Wood, PVC
35×35×32 cm
Lent by Alois Dworschak, Lüdenscheid

616 a, b
D. M. Gresham and Martin Thaler
CD video-camera, 1986
Polycarbonate, silicone-coated, soft PVC
c. 15×28×10 cm
Lent by Design Logic, Chicago, Illinois

617
D. M. Gresham and Martin Thaler
Speaking slide-projector, 1985
Plastic
30×20×20 cm
Viewmaster
Lent by Design Logic, Chicago, Illinois

618
VDU workplace
Photo by Hans-Peter Siffert, Zurich

619
D. M. Gresham and Hel Rinkleib
"Book", 1985
Polycarbonate, console silicone-coated
c. 30×30×30 cm
Watertechnics
Lent by Design Logic, Chicago, Illinois

Photo credits for the article by Matteo Thun: Figs. 13 e, 15 –19 Deutsches Archiv für Filmkunde, Frankfurt am Main; all others Matteo Thun, Milan

Photo credits for the article by Jochen Albus: Figs. 7– 9 Reinhart Wolf, Hamburg

Index